Economics
of Poverty,
Discrimination,
and Public Policy

Economics
of Poverty,
Discrimination,
and Public Policy

Mwangi S. Kimenyi
The University of Connecticut

SOUTH-WESTERN College Publishing

An International Thomson Publishing Company

Acquisitions Editor:	Jack Calhoun
Production Editors:	Eric Carlson and Sue Ellen Brown
Marketing Manager:	Denise Carlson
Cover and Internal Designer:	Joseph Devine
Production House:	Montgomery Media, Inc.

I(T)P   ITP International Thomson Publishing

South-Western is an ITP Company. The ITP trademark is used under license.

Printed in the United States of America

1 2 3 4 5 6 MT 9 8 7 6 5 4
Library of Congress Cataloging-in-Publication Data
Kimenyi, Mwangi S.,
        Economics of poverty, discrimination, and public policy / Mwangi S.
    Kimenyi.
                p. cm.
        Includes bibliographical references and indexes
        ISBN 0-538-83191-X
        1. Poverty—United States. 2. Welfare economics. 3. Poor—United
States. 4. Discrimination—United States. I. Title.
        HC110.P6K545   1995
        362.5'0973—dc20   94–15729
                                                                     CIP

For the memory of my father and teacher, Mwalimu F. Kimenyi Kimani, whose extraordinary commitment to his family and distinguished service to the community opened many doors;

and

for my mother, B. Njeri Kimenyi (Nyina wa Wamaitha), for her love, prayers and support through the years.

CONTENTS

PREFACE

The distribution of a society's scarce resources is an enduring topic of economic debate. A market economy produces vast differences in the values of the resources owned by various members of the society. Some individuals have high earnings and accumulated wealth; others have low incomes; and yet others no incomes at all. The economics of poverty focuses its attention on those members of society who have low or no incomes—*the poor*. This book deals with the economics of poverty in the United States.

The United States is a wealthy nation with one of the highest standards of living in the world. Nevertheless, amid the affluence, many persons do not have sufficient resources to consume all of the goods and services that society deems essential. A central focus of the study of poverty is to identify the poor and to analyze the factors that explain their plight.

There is a national concern with the well-being of all members of society from those in the highest economic strata to those in the lowest. Not only is there an interest in understanding why individuals or families come to be poor, there is an interest in identifying public policies that might help alleviate their poverty. Thus, a major area of concentration in the study of the economics of poverty is an evaluation of the purposes and effects of various antipoverty policies.

As our understanding of poverty deepens, poverty in the United States is found to be concentrated among some groups. For example, minorities and females have lower average earnings than whites and males. A conventional explanation for this discrepancy relies on the existence of discrimination both in labor markets and in the provision of education. When poverty is concentrated among some groups of the population, and when it is accepted that the major reason for such an outcome is discrimination, strong arguments are made supporting antipoverty policies designed to target minorities and females. Race and sex considerations introduce a controversial political twist to the design and implementation of antipoverty policies. These controversies have come to dominate politics at the federal, state, and local levels. Because race and gender play such prominent roles in the discussions of poverty, the study of poverty must concentrate to a large extent on issues pertaining to race and sex discrimination. Thus, the subject matter of this book evaluates not only the economics of poverty, but also the economics of discrimination.

In writing and organizing this book, I have taken a number of factors into account. First, many students may not have had sufficient economic principles to analyze some of the issues discussed. I have therefore included a review of microeconomics for the benefit of those who have had only introductory courses in economics. Second, because the subject matter of this book is of interest to students in other disciplines (such as political science, sociology, ethnic studies, women's studies, and so on), I have avoided overly technical economic analysis. Thus, the book should be appealing to a wide cross section of students. Third, I realize that individual faculty members may want to emphasize some topics more than others, and because of time constraints, some of the materials may not be covered. Thus, the book is organized in such a manner that some chapters could be omitted without affecting the flow of the other sections. Finally, issues concerning poverty and poverty policy are controversial and there are extreme positions on both sides. As much as possible, I have attempted to offer a balanced assessment of the issues. Nonetheless, I have not avoided mentioning controversial issues as that would deny students the opportunity to appreciate the intensity of the debate that surrounds antipoverty policies.

This book has several features that make it suitable for use as text in courses dealing with economics of poverty. First, the book provides sufficient economic analysis of the issues rather than merely stating facts. Second, in addition to detailed discussions of the commonly cited causes of poverty (such as labor market problems and discrimination and the public policies that are used to deal with these problems), the book contains topics that are becoming increasingly important in the United States. For example, the text discusses problems of inner cities, transformation of the American family and the feminization of poverty, reforming child support policies, and an analysis of the homelessness problem. The book also contains introductory chapters that focus on theories of optimal distribution and a historical discussion of poverty and poverty policy. Additionally, the book provides a discussion on international comparisons of poverty and poverty policy.

Although the book primarily uses economic principles to analyze the various issues related to poverty and policy, it does not neglect the complex interaction of economic, social, and political forces associated with poverty. A comprehensive analysis of poverty requires a consideration of these forces. The book is written in a manner that considers these other noneconomic aspects of poverty. This text also emphasizes the need to understand antipoverty policy, particularly when evaluating the effects of such policies.

The subject matter of poverty involves real lives that are at stake. As such, the issues should not be treated merely as an academic exercise. It is necessary for students to seriously consider the issues and express their views on contemporary debates. As anyone who has taught this course knows, many students have misconceptions about the problem of poverty;

others have strong opinions about those issues, although they may not have evidence to support their views. Fortunately, most students are genuinely and seriously concerned about poverty. Much is gained by allowing as much class discussion as possible. Study and discussion questions will help start such class discussions. Also, data are included to help support the facts and arguments discussed.

A significant antipoverty policy concerns the issue of health care. This is especially important in dealing with the poverty of low-wage workers. I have not included a chapter on health care because at the time of writing this book the Clinton administration was just beginning to outline major health care reform proposals. Although it is likely that some form of health care reform will become law, it is not clear what reforms will be adopted by Congress.

Some of my students have raised the issue of the appropriate way of referring to some minority groups. In this book, I have used *Black, Hispanic,* and *Native Americans* to refer to the various minority groups. I am aware that the term African-Americans is increasingly being used to refer to Black Americans. However, most publications and all government statistics refer to *Black Americans.* We consulted with a number of authors who suggested that using Black is appropriate especially when referring to government statistics. The terms African Americans and Black Americans could be used interchangeably. I have chosen to use Black Americans throughout the text. Nonetheless, faculty members and students should use either term.

Although I have been interested in issues of poverty in the United States for a number of years, economics of poverty or labor economics were not part of my academic training. As a matter of fact, I did not start research on poverty until 1989 when I was awarded a National Science Foundation research grant to study patterns of welfare dependency in the Deep South. During the course of that project, I became even more interested in various issues concerning the poor. During the fall of 1991, I offered to teach a course on the Economics of Poverty at the University of Connecticut. I was frustrated, however, by the lack of a book that dealt with the issues of poverty in a serious manner and also provided a balanced analysis. Although my students were very interested in learning about poverty and antipoverty policy, they found the book I had recommended grossly inadequate. I am grateful to my students. If it were not for their critical comments about the text I had recommended, I would not have been motivated enough to write this book. I also discussed the project with a number of faculty members who were teaching the course in various other institutions. I am grateful to them for encouraging me to work on this project.

I would like to thank several individuals who have played a vital role in the preparation of this book. My colleagues Stephen Miller (University of Connecticut) and William Shughart II (University of Mississippi) read most of the first draft and made helpful comments and suggestions. The final draft of the book benefitted from detailed critical comments by: Robert Haveman of the University of Wisconsin-Madison, Michael Sattinger of the State University of New York at Albany, Stanley Masters of the State University of New York at Binghamton, Arthur King of Baylor University, McKinley Blackburn of the University of South Carolina, Edward Montgomery of the University of Maryland at College Park, Gerhard Glomm of the University of Virginia, Edgar K. Browning of Texas A & M University, and Peter Gottschalk of Boston College. I have tried to accommodate the comments of the reviewers most of the time. Their comments impressed in me the fact that there is a sensible compromise somewhere in the middle.

The largest burden of writing this book was borne by my wife, Wangui Kimenyi. Her love, patience, and encouragement made it possible for me to complete the project in a timely manner and I am very grateful for her support. Most of the time spent writing this book was at the expense of my children Kimenyi, Kimani, and Mburu. Thank you guys for your patience when I was not able to shoot some hoops or kick the ball with you. Writing this book has made me appreciate my parents even more, and I am proud to dedicate this book to them.

Storrs, Connecticut
April 1994

1

REVIEW OF MICROECONOMICS

Poverty is an important public policy issue. Researchers in various disciplines devote a considerable amount of time and resources analyzing poverty and poverty policy. Each academic discipline approaches the issue of poverty from a perspective that is unique to that discipline. For example, psychologists' and sociologists' unique approaches to analyzing poverty differs in important respects to the economic analysis of poverty. As the title suggests, this book approaches poverty and discrimination from an economics perspective. To appreciate the unique economic approach to analyzing poverty, it is essential that one have a basic understanding of economic principles.

This first chapter reviews the basic tools of analysis used in economics. Specifically, it will focus on microeconomics analysis, which deals with decision-making units such as individuals, households, and firms. We are particularly interested in those decisions that affect behavior, which in turn affects earnings and opportunities. This factor may explain low earnings by some members of society and high earnings by others. These decisions include labor market choices such as the number of hours of work, the level of wages in particular sectors of the economy, or even the decision to work or not to work. Having a good understanding of how the market works will help the student appreciate issues such as the role of human capital in wage determination or the economic theory of discrimination. These issues are dealt with in later chapters. Microeconomic analysis also helps one to understand the effects of government policies on the behavior of individuals and firms.

This chapter is geared primarily to students who have had only basic economics courses. Nevertheless, other students may find the discussion useful before proceeding to Chapter 2. The tools discussed in this chapter are used in the next chapter where theories of optimal distribution and some of the effects of government policies are discussed.

Microeconomics is a broad subject. The review presented herein is not comprehensive; it basically focuses on simple subjects such as demand and supply analysis and the theory of consumer behavior. Although brief, the discussion provides sufficient background for the student to be able to appreciate issues discussed in this book.

THE MARKET: DEMAND AND SUPPLY

The market has both demand and supply sides. The demand side reflects the behavior of consumers. The supply side reflects the behavior of producers. The interaction of demand and supply results in equilibrium price and output of a particular commodity or service. Although demand and supply are simple concepts, they are very useful in the analysis of social issues, including those relating to poverty. The following is a simple analysis of demand and supply. The interaction of both sides of the market are then analyzed.

Demand

The quantity of a commodity that a particular individual desires to consume over a given period of time is determined by several factors. For example, if you wanted to list the factors that determine Irene's demand for chicken, you probably would include factors such as her income, tastes, the price of chicken, and the price of other goods that Irene consumes. Of course, there are numerous other factors that affect Irene's demand for chicken. To simplify analysis, it is necessary to focus on only a few of those factors.

If the price of chicken is allowed to vary while holding all other factors fixed, one can observe Irene's demand schedule for chicken. A demand schedule is a list of prices and corresponding quantities that an individual is willing and able to buy during some time period. Figure 1-1 illustrates a hypothetical demand curve for chicken (*DD*). At a price of $2 per pound of chicken, Irene is willing and able to buy eight pounds of chicken per unit of time. When the price of chicken is $1 per pound, Irene is willing and able to buy 12 pounds of chicken per unit of time.

The demand curve is constructed by studying various prices of a product and the corresponding quantities demanded. Thus, a demand curve reflects the rate at which the individual wishes to consume a certain amount of a good at different prices. As is clear from the figure, the demand curve is downward sloping, reflecting the negative relationship between the price and quantity demanded. This is the law of demand. Note that the change in the price of chicken does not cause the demand curve to move from its original position. The change in quantity demanded is reflected by a movement along the demand curve.

To appreciate the meaning of the law of demand, it helps to note that when Irene purchases one pound of chicken at the prevailing price, she

Figure 1-1   Irene's demand for chicken

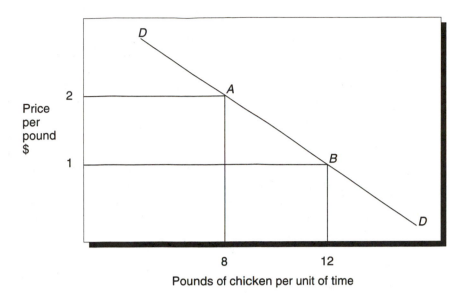

Pounds of chicken per unit of time

essentially gives up purchasing other goods and services. Thus, the cost of consuming one pound of chicken is measured by the value of the consumption of other goods that has to be given up in order to consume that additional pound of chicken. High prices of chicken implies that more alternative consumption has to be given up in order to purchase a unit of chicken. When the price of chicken decreases from $2 per pound to $1 per pound, the relative price of chicken has declined. This implies that less alternative consumption has to be given up in order to consume a pound of chicken. In response, Irene increases her consumption of chicken from eight to 12 pounds. The law of demand can therefore be stated as follows: The lower the relative price of a good, the greater will be the desired rate of consumption.

In deriving the demand curve shown, we assume that all other factors that affect Irene's purchases of chicken are held constant. For example, we assume that Irene's income and the prices of related goods (such as beef and pork) are held constant. When these other factors change, the position of the demand curve also changes. In analysis of demand, we should not ignore the fact that these other factors do change. Such changes provide interesting analysis of consumer behavior. For example, one may be interested in knowing how increasing Irene's income (for example, if her wage increases) would affect her consumption of chicken. Alternatively, one may be interested in knowing how Irene's consumption of chicken is affected by changes in prices of related products such as beef and pork.

When Irene's income increases, her demand for chicken could either increase or decrease.[1] If income increases result in increased purchases of chicken, then such a good is referred to as a *normal good*. The increase is shown by a shift of the entire demand curve to the right so that at every price, the consumer is able and willing to buy more of the commodity. Conversely, income increases could result in a situation where the consumer purchases fall at every price. This is shown by a leftward shift in the demand curve. Goods for which consumers reduce their consumption as income increases are called *inferior goods*. Figure 1-2 shows the shifts in the demand curve resulting from changes in the income. Note that if a good is normal (inferior) and there was a decrease in the income, then the demand curve would shift to the left (right). Thus, D^1D^1 reflects increase in demand and D^2D^2 reflects a decrease in demand.

Demand also is affected by changes in the price of related products. For example, a decrease in the price of beef will result in a decrease in the demand for chicken. That is, when the price of beef decreases, the quantity of beef demanded increases. The result is a decrease in the demand for chicken. This change occurs because there is a shift in consumption from chicken to beef. Such goods that serve the same wants are called *substitutes*. On the other hand, a decrease in the price of sugar is likely to result in

Figure 1-2   Changes in demand

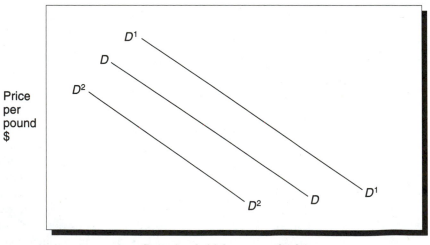

Pounds of chicken per unit of time

---

1. It is possible that increases in Irene's income do not affect her consumption of chicken. In that case, we would not consider income as one of the factors that affect the position of Irene's demand curve for chicken.

increased consumption of coffee. In this case, the price decrease results in an increase in the quantity demanded of sugar. But sugar often is consumed together with coffee and thus the change results in an increase in the demand for coffee. Goods that are consumed jointly are called *complements*.

Demand also is affected by tastes. Although it often is accurate to assume that tastes remain fairly constant, this does not always hold true. For example, new information about products may cause consumers to change their tastes so that they reduce their consumption (decrease in demand) or increase the consumption of those goods (increase in demand).

Market Demand

Thus far, the focus has been on a single individual's demand curve. Most public policy purposes are not interested in just how one person's purchases respond to changes in the various factors. Rather, the interest is in the aggregate demand; for example, the demand for chicken in the United States. In fact, most of the economic analysis focuses on market demand, not on individual demand.

The method to obtain the market demand from individual demand curves is straightforward. Assume that there is a society of four individuals: Irene, Francis, Bedan, and Robert. At a price of $1 per pound of chicken, Irene wishes to consume 8 pounds, Francis wishes to consume 10 pounds, Bedan wishes to consume 11 pounds, and Robert wishes to consume 14 pounds. The individual demand curves are shown in Figure 1-3. In this case, the market demand curve would show the desired rate of consumption by the four members of the society per unit of time when the price of chicken is $1 per pound. Thus, the quantity demanded by all members of society when the price is $1 per pound is equal to 43 pounds (8+10+11+14) of chicken. When all points on the four individual demand curves are totalled, the market demand curve is obtained (*MD*). Thus, the market demand curve is simply the horizontal summation of the individual demand curves.

Supply

While the demand side of the market reflects the behavior of consumers, the supply side reflects the behavior of producers. As in the case of demand, there are a number of factors that determine supply. First, a firm's supply decision is influenced by the price of the product. Producers are concerned primarily in maximizing profits. Therefore, firms base their supply decisions on comparisons of costs and revenues. In most cases, the cost of producing an additional unit of a good increases as the firm attempts to produce at a faster rate. Therefore, one can expect firms to be willing to offer for sale at lower prices those commodities produced at a slower rate than those produced at higher rates.

Figure 1-3   Market demand

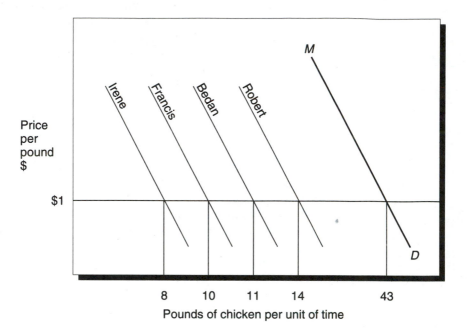

Pounds of chicken per unit of time

A supply schedule is a list of prices and corresponding quantities that a producer is willing and able to offer for sale during some time period. Figure 1-4 shows a firm's supply curve for chicken (*SS*). The horizontal axis shows the quantity of the good (pounds of chicken) the firm supplies per unit of time. The vertical axis measures the price per unit of good (pound of chicken). At a price of $2 per pound the producer is willing and able to offer 15 pounds of chicken (point *D* on the supply curve). At a price of $1 per pound, the producer is willing and able to offer five pounds of chicken for sale (point *C* on the supply curve). The supply curve is constructed by looking at various prices and the corresponding quantities supplied. The supply curve is upward sloping, reflecting the positive relationship between price and the quantity supplied. This is the law of supply. Note that the change in the price of chicken does not cause the supply curve to move. The change in quantity supplied is reflected by a movement along the supply curve, for example *C* to *D*.

As in the case of the demand curve, the supply curve is derived by assuming that all other factors that affect supply decisions are held constant. If these other factors change, then the location of the supply curve also would change. Factors that affect supply include technology, the prices of inputs used to produce the good in question, the prices of related goods in production, and producer expectations about future prices.

Figure 1-4 · Supply of chicken

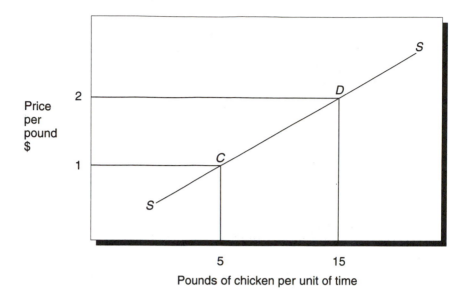

Pounds of chicken per unit of time

In constructing a supply curve such as *SS* shown in Figure 1-5, technology is assumed to be constant and producers just respond to changes in the price. Improvements in technology reduce the cost of production as the production process becomes more efficient. Thus, producers are willing and able to offer more for sale at every price. Improvements in the technology result in an increase in supply which is shown by a rightward shift of the supply curve (from *SS* to S^1S^1). This is called an increase in supply. Although it is rare, it is possible that some changes can result in more inefficient methods of production, which would mean a decrease in supply (supply curve shifts from *SS* to S^2S^2). A good example may be the result of government antipollution regulations that may cause firms to use less efficient methods of production.

If the prices of inputs increase, the cost of production increases. The result of such a change is to shift the supply curve to the right so that at every price, less is offered for sale. The opposite is true for decreases in the prices of inputs.

When a supply curve is constructed, it is assumed that prices of related goods in production are held constant. Goods related in production are those that can be produced using the same resources. A good example is the comparison of corn and wheat, which use the same types of resources. If the price of wheat increases, it would be more profitable for

Figure 1-5   Changes in supply

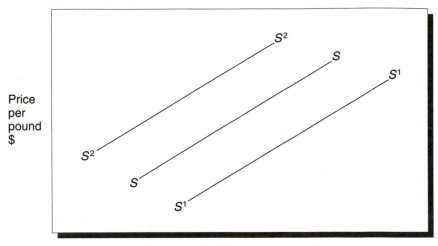

Pounds of chicken per unit of time

the producer to decrease the production of corn and increase the production of wheat. This would result in a leftward shift in the supply curve for corn. The opposite shift would be expected if the price of wheat were to fall.

Finally, producers' expectations about future prices will affect supply. If producers expect the price of their product to be higher in the future than previously expected, they would tend to decrease their supply today, which means a leftward shift in the supply curve. Expectation that prices will be lower in the future would result in a rightward shift in the supply curve (increase in supply) at the present time.

Market Supply

Similar to the example of demand, most economic issues are analyzed in the context of aggregate supply rather than an individual firm's supply. The market supply curve for a particular good shows the total amount of that good that all firms are willing to offer for sale at different prices. It is tempting to sum individual supply curves horizontally to obtain the market supply as when obtaining market demand. Horizontal summation of individual supply curves, however, may lead to an incorrect result.

The supply curves of individual firms show their rate of supply of a particular good in response to prices changes, assuming that all other factors are held constant. In considering the behavior of a single producer, it is reasonable to assume that increases in amount produced does not have much effect on other factors. For example, it is reasonable to assume that in moving along one firm's supply curve for chicken, the price of chicken feed remains constant. Thus, one firm's actions alone are not sufficient to influence the price of chicken feed.

However, when all the firms in the industry attempt to increase the quantity supplied, they are likely to cause the prices of chicken feed and other inputs to rise. This increases the cost of production that each of the firms now face. The increase in cost of production causes the individual supply curves to shift to the left so that at higher prices, each firm produces less than predicted by the individual firm's supply curve. Thus, it would be misleading to horizontally sum the supply curves without considering the shift in supply curves caused by the increase in cost of production.

To clarify the foregoing discussion, refer to Figure 1-6. SS is the supply curve of a single chicken farmer. The supply curve shows the different pounds of chicken that the farmer will offer for sale per unit of time at various chicken prices. All other factors are assumed to be held constant. When the price of chicken is P_1 per pound, the farmer offers Q_1 units for sale per unit of time. If price increases to P_2, the farmer offers Q_2 for sale per unit of time. If all chicken farmers respond to the rise in price (P_1 to P_2) by producing more, the price of factors of production increase. The effect is to shift the supply curves of all farmers to the left. The supply curve of the farmer previously mentioned shifts from SS to S^0S^0. Thus at P_2, the farmer will offer Q_3 units for sale and not Q_2 ($Q_3 < Q_2$). Therefore, the appropriate supply curve for this farmer is S^1S^1. Horizontal summation of supply curves

Figure 1-6   Market supply

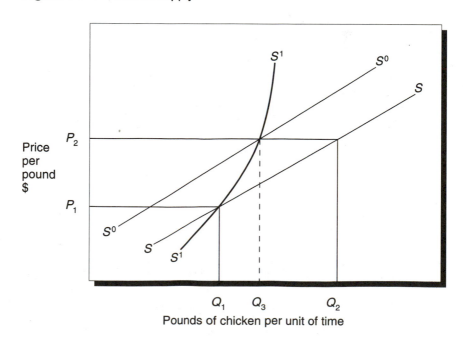

Pounds of chicken per unit of time

(such as S^1S^1) that take into account the change in the cost of production yield the market supply curve.

Market Equilibrium

The market is made up of the supply side and the demand side. The interaction of these two sides of the market result in the prevailing prices. Figure 1-7 combines the market demand (DD) and market supply (SS) curves for the chicken. It is clear from this figure that only one price (P_e) exists for which the quantity demanded is equal to the quantity supplied (Q_e). This is the market clearing price, or the equilibrium price.

It is easy to see why this is called a market clearing price. For a price P_h above P_e, the quantity supplied exceeds the quantity demanded. Thus, at that price, a surplus exists. On the other hand, for a price P_l below P_e, the quantity demanded exceeds the quantity supplied at that price, resulting in a shortage. At a price equal to P_e, no surpluses or shortages exist and therefore P_e clears the market of any shortages or surpluses.

The equilibrium price is not attained instantaneously. The achievement of this price is a result of the market process, which is guided by market signals. If a firm sets a price P_h, it will not be able to sell all of its output.

Figure 1-7   Market for chicken

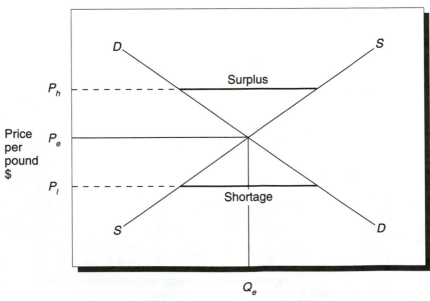

Pounds of chicken per unit of time

The excess supply will act as a signal that the price is too high and that the firm should reduce the price. If, however, the firm sets P_l, it will sell all of its output and leave some willing buyers without any of the product. The shortage is a signal that the price is too low and the firm should raise the price. Of course, the equilibrium price will vary as changes in supply and demand take place.

Thus far supply and demand for commodities has been discussed. Demand and supply concepts have much wider applications in economics. In the economics of poverty, we are especially interested in analyzing labor supply and labor demand decisions by firms and workers, respectively. It is the interaction between labor demand and labor supply that results in the wages earned by workers. By using demand and supply analysis, one can explain labor market outcomes and suggest policies that would influence wages. For example, public policies such as those that seek to increase human capital of workers influence the demand for labor by making workers more productive, thus increasing the demand for their services.

An important consideration is the slope of the demand and the supply curves. The slope of the curves is measured by what is called price elasticity. Elasticity is the absolute value of the percentage change in the quantity supplied or demanded divided by the percentage change in the price. If, for example, the wages increase by 10 percent and the quantity demanded of labor declines by 20 percent, then the price elasticity of demand for labor is 2. This means that a 1 percent increase in wages results in a 2 percent decline in the quantity of labor demanded. Before a government imposes regulation on wages, it is important to determine the possible effects of such policy. Therefore, knowing the elasticities of the demand and supply curves is important in order to provide information of the potential magnitudes of the effects of government interference with markets.

THEORY OF CONSUMER CHOICE

Indifference Curves

A basic assumption about human behavior is that it is consistent with utility maximization. Thus, individuals make choices that maximize their satisfaction subject to some resource constraints. This section outlines the tools used in economics to analyze consumer choice. There is particular interest in the behavior of individuals when the constraints change, which (as will be seen in the next chapter) is relevant to the analysis of the effects of antipoverty policies.

Attempts to demonstrate utility maximization must confront the fact that utility is subjective and not measurable. One cannot measure the real *quantity* of satisfaction as is done in the case of goods or other things that are clearly measurable. To derive the conditions for utility maximization, an approach is used that does not require one to measure the actual utility.

Instead, assume that individuals are able to rank all conceivable bundles of goods in order of preference based on their subjective valuations. For example, for different baskets A and B containing different combinations of two goods X and Y, a consumer is able to state whether A is preferred to B, or B is equally preferred to A, or B is preferred to A. If a consumer states that one bundle is preferred to another, this implies that he or she values that bundle more and expects to enjoy more utility from consuming it. The consumer also is assumed to make choices in a consistent manner. For example, if A is preferred to B, and B is preferred to C, consistency requires that A be preferred to C.

An important tool in the analysis of consumer choice is an *indifference curve*. If a consumer is confronted with various bundles A, B, C, D, E, and F all containing different combinations of X and Y, and the consumer states that A, B, and D are all equally preferred, then it can be said that the individual is indifferent between those bundles, implying that they all yield equal utility. The consumer also could state that he or she prefers both C and E equally, although he or she prefers these bundles more than A, B, or D, and prefers F less than all other bundles. If all combinations of X and Y that yield the same utility to the consumer are plotted, we obtain the indifference curve shown in Figure 1-8. Notice that A, B, and D lie on the same indifference curve (II) and C and E lie on another indifference curve (III) that is farther away from the origin, while F is on an indifference curve (I) that is closer to the origin.

Figure 1-8   Indifference map

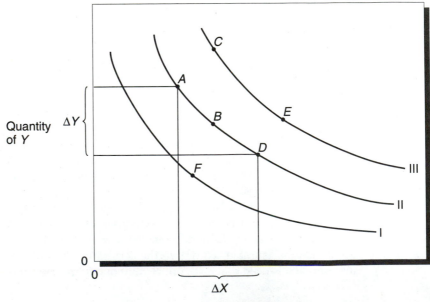

Indifference curves have some important characteristics. First, note from the figure that curves that are farther away from the origin represent higher levels of satisfaction. Secondly, although only three curves are shown in Figure 1-8, there is an indifference curve that passes through each point in the commodity space. Stated another way, each point in the commodity space lies on one, and only one, indifference curve. Another important property of indifference curves is that no two indifference curves can intersect. Intersection of indifference curves would mean that consumers are not making consistent choices in their ranking of the bundles of goods. In fact, it is a logical necessity that indifference curves do not intersect.

An important feature of indifference curves is that they have a negative slope. This outcome is a result of the assumption that consumers prefer a bundle with more goods than one with less. The negative slope implies that amounts of one good must be added to a bundle to offset the reduction in the quantity of the other good if total utility is to remain constant. Finally, an important characteristic of indifference curves is that they are convex to the origin. Convexity implies that the slope of the curve decreases as one moves down the curve. This is the property of decreasing marginal rate of substitution, which is due to diminishing marginal utility.

The slope of an indifference curve is the change in the value of the variable measured on the vertical axis divided by the change in the variable measured on the horizontal axis. Thus, the slope of the indifference curves shown in Figure 1-8 can be calculated as $\Delta Y / \Delta X$. The slope of the indifference, called the *marginal rate of substitution* (MRS), refers to the amount of one good that an individual is willing to give up for an additional unit of another good, and still maintain the same level of satisfaction. Thus, we can express the slope of indifference curves as

(1.1)
$$MRS_{xy} = -\Delta Y / \Delta X.$$

Notice that the negative sign means that some reduction in units of Y must be accompanied by additional units of X if total utility is to remain the same. MRS_{xy} measures the number of units of Y that the consumer is willing to sacrifice to obtain an additional unit of X.

Consider points A and D that are on the same indifference curve. Thus, those two points represent the same level of satisfaction to the consumer. Moving from A to D in Figure 1-8, the consumer gives up ΔY and obtains ΔX. The utility change from A to D (ΔU) is therefore equal to 0. In other words, the loss in utility resulting from giving up ΔY is equal to the gain in utility from obtaining ΔX. The total utility associated with the change in the various quantities of X and Y can be calculated by considering the utility associated with each unit of a good, also called *marginal utility* (MU). Thus the increase in consumption of good X (ΔX) times the marginal utility of X (MU_x) is the total utility gained from consuming ΔX additional units of X. Likewise, the decrease in consumption of good Y (ΔY) times the marginal utility of Y (MU_y), is the total utility lost from reducing the consumption of Y by ΔY. Because the consumer remains at the same level of utility, it must be true that

(1.2)
$$\Delta X\,(MU_x) = -\Delta Y\,(MU_y)$$

and therefore

(1.3)
$$-\Delta Y/\Delta X = MU_x/MU_y = MRS_{xy}.$$

Thus, the slope of the indifference curve (the marginal rate of substitution) is given by the ratio of the marginal utility of the good on the horizontal axis divided by the marginal utility of the good shown on the vertical axis.

As represented in Figure 1-8, the marginal rate of substitution declines as one moves along the indifference curve. This follows from the fact that as one moves down the curve and therefore has less and less of Y, and more and more of X, each remaining unit of Y becomes more valuable and each additional unit of X becomes less valuable. Of course, this is the law of diminishing marginal utility which states that as more units of a good are consumed, the utility associated with each additional unit declines. Therefore, as more units of Y are given up, to remain on the same level of satisfaction, the loss in units of Y must be compensated with increasing units of X.

Budget Constraint

Scarcity of resources implies that individuals are faced by various constraints such as time and income. Indifference curves only represent preferences without showing the budgetary constraints that consumers face. Consumers have limited income and the goods that they consume cost money so that not all bundles of goods are available to the consumer.

Consider the situation of a consumer who has only $100 to spend on goods X and Y. Assume that the price of X (P_x) is $5 per unit and the price of Y (P_y) is $10 per unit. The combinations of X and Y that the consumer buys must meet the budget constraint. That is

(1.4)
$$P_x * X + P_y * Y = \$100.$$

This relationship is this consumer's budget constraint. If the consumer decides to spend all income on X, then he or she can consume 20 units of X and 0 units of Y. On the other hand, if all income is spent on Y, the consumer can buy 10 units of Y and 0 units of X. Figure 1-9 shows the various combination of X and Y that the consumer can purchase by spending all the $100 given the existing prices of X and Y. The line joining all these combinations

Figure 1-9   Budget constraint

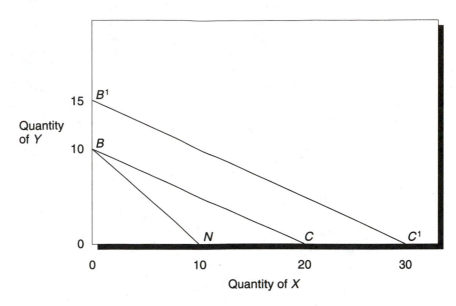

(BC) is called the *budget line* or the *budget constraint.* All points that are on or below BC are within the consumer's reach because they require spending $100 or less. Points above BC are not feasible to the consumer as they require a higher income than the consumer's $100.

The slope of the budget line is important in the application of consumer choice. To generalize the slope of the budget line, let the income = I, and the prices of X and Y be P_x and P_y, respectively. The constraint can then be written as

(1.5)
$$P_x * QX + P_y * QY = I.$$

To obtain the slope, divide the vertical distance (10) (quantity of Y that can be bought if no X is purchased) by the horizontal distance (20) (quantity of X that can be bought if no Y is purchased). Assuming that all income is spent on Y, the vertical distance is equal to I/P_y. Likewise, assuming that all income is spent on X, the horizontal distance is equal to I/P_x. Therefore, the slope of the budget line is

(1.6)
$$10/20 = (I/P_y)/(I/P_x) = -P_x/P_y.$$

The negative sign is added to signify the negative slope. In short, the slope of the budget line is equal to the ratio of the price of X to the price of Y.

The use of the budget constraint is useful in investigating what happens to the behavior of individuals when the constraint changes. The constraint can change if there are changes in the income or the prices of the goods. Both of these changes are very important in the economics of poverty.

Consider the case just presented in which the consumer has $100 and the prices of X and Y are $5 and $10, respectively. If we hold the prices constant and increase the income of this consumer to $150, the new budget line now shifts rightward to B^1C^1. If income decreases, the budget line would shift inward to the left. Note that since in both cases the prices do not change, the slope $-(P_X/P_y)$ remains the same—hence parallel shift. Income transfers have the effect of shifting the entire budget line.

The budget line can also change due to variations in the price of the goods. Returning to our original position of $100 and the same prices of X and Y, if the price of X now increases to $10, and if all $100 is spent on X, only 10 units can be purchased. Thus, the horizontal intercept would change to N, but the vertical intercept remains the same since the price of Y remains the same. A decrease in the price of a good would rotate the budget line outward. Lowering the price of a good is analogous to the effect of a government subsidy.

Consumer Equilibrium

The indifference map shows the choices available to a consumer while the budget constraint shows the choices that are within the reach of a consumer. To find out what the consumer actually does, the indifference map and the budget line must be combined. This is shown in Figure 1-10 which superimposes the indifference map upon the budget line. Our interest is in determining which combination of X and Y actually maximizes the consumer's utility given the budget constraint.

Indifference curve III falls outside the budget line. We have indicated that points above the budget line are not feasible to the consumer. Thus, although the consumer would be on a higher level of utility, bundles of goods that fall on that curve are out of the choice set given the current budget.

Portions of indifference curve I are under, on, or above the budget line. Only one part of the indifference curve II touches the budget line and all other parts of that indifference curve are above the budget line. Those sections that are under or on the budget line are achievable to the consumer. If one assumes that the consumer must exhaust the budget, then there are three possible bundles U, and V on indifference curve I, and point B on indifference curve II. All these points involve the same amount of expenditures. Which of these points maximizes consumer utility?

Points U and V are on a lower indifference curve meaning that although the same amount is spent as is at point B, the consumer obtains lower utility. It is easy to see that only point B is consistent with utility maximization given the budget. This point is where the indifference curve is just tangent to the budget line. This tangency implies that utility maximization

Figure 1-10   Utility maximization subject to budget constraint

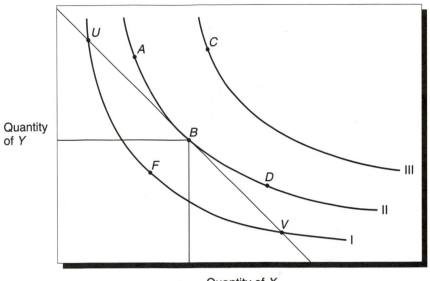

Quantity of X

is achieved at the point where the slope of the indifference curve is equal to the slope of the budget line. This is the same as saying that utility maximization requires the marginal rate of substitution of X for Y (MRS_{xy}) be equal to the price ratio—(P_x/P_y). Thus

(1.7) $$MU_x/MU_y = P_x/P_y.$$

By simple manipulation it can be shown that

(1.8) $$MU_x/P_x = MU_y/P_y.$$

This relationship means that marginal utility per dollar spent on the last unit of X must be equal to the marginal utility per dollar spent on the last unit of Y. If this condition does not hold, the consumer can reallocate the available income by changing the quantities of X and Y consumed and thereby increase the level of satisfaction. Thus, if $MU_x/P_x > MU_y/P_x$, the consumer can increase utility by removing dollars from Y and increasing the consumption of X until the equality is established. This equality occurs because as more of X is consumed, the MU_x falls while as less of Y is consumed MU_y increases. We can generalize this condition for utility maximization for all goods X, Y, and Z as

(1.9) $$MU_x/P_x = MU_y/P_y = MU_z/P_z.$$

Changes in Relative Prices

The equilibrium condition stated suggests that if the price of one product changes, adjustments must be made to restore the equilibrium condition. Here we analyze what happens to consumer equilibrium using the principles discussed previously. We then apply the tool to analyze the important case of labor supply decisions.

Consider Figure 1-11 which shows the budget line and consumer's indifference curves. Originally the consumer equilibrium is at point O on indifference curve I and budget line BN. At this equilibrium, the consumer buys X_0 and Y_0 quantities of X and Y, respectively. If the price of X decreases, resulting in the outward rotation of the budget line to BM, then the consumer would have to make adjustments to achieve a new equilibrium point. In the figure it has been assumed that the new equilibrium is now at point O^1 where both more of X_1 and Y_1 are consumed.

The entire change from O to O^1 is called a *price effect* and is made up of two separate effects. When the price of X falls, X becomes relatively cheaper than Y. This suggests that the consumer should consume more of the relatively cheaper good (X) and less of the relatively more expensive good (Y). This is called the *substitution effect*. The substitution effect suggests that every time the price of one good falls, consumers would buy more of that good and less of the other, now relatively more expensive, good.

Figure 1-11   Changes in consumer equilibrium

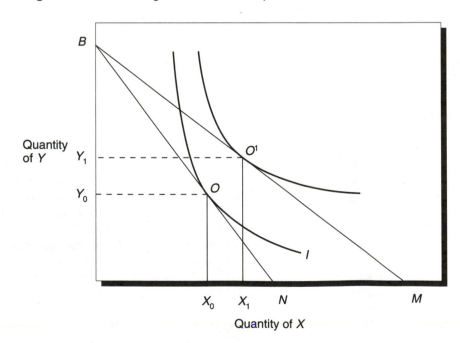

The movement from O to O^1, however, involves an increase in the consumption of both X and Y. This is because there is another effect that influences the consumption of X and Y. When the price of one good falls, the consumer's real income actually increases even though nominal income remains the same. We already have seen that when income increases (decreases), consumers will increase (reduce) their consumption of all normal goods and decrease (increase) their consumption of inferior goods. This is the *income effect*.

The price effect (O to O^1) is made up of both the income effect and the substitution effect. The final equilibrium point depends on whether the goods are normal or inferior to the consumer, and also on the magnitude of the substitution effects relative to the income effect. If the good whose price drops is normal, then the quantity of that good consumed will always increase because the substitution effect and the income effect reinforce each other in the direction of higher consumption of the good. If that good is inferior, then the quantity could fall, remain the same, or decrease depending on the relative magnitudes of the income and substitution effects (which work in opposite directions in this case). If the good whose price does not change is normal, then the effect on the equilibrium quantity will depend on the relative magnitudes of the substitution effects and the income effect. If it is inferior, the final effect will be a reduction in the equilibrium quantity because both the income effect and the substitution effect reinforce each other.

Applications of the Theory of Consumer Behavior: Labor Supply

An important application of the substitution and income effects is in the derivation of the labor supply curve. Assume that a worker has only two choices: earning market incomes or consuming leisure. We assume that the individual can work as many hours as she pleases (maximum of 24 hours in a day). Suppose that the worker is observed to vary the hours of work as the wage changes as follows:

Wage	Hours of work
4	12
6	14
8	10

Of course, this is the worker's labor supply schedule. We can use the tools discussed to explain this behavior. The choice of the number of hours of work reflects the equilibrium outcome of this worker's preferences for leisure and market incomes. One additional assumption that has been used to explain the labor supply decision which is based on empirical observation is that labor is a normal good.

Given this information, one can construct what is called a labor–leisure trade-off. Figure 1-12 shows an individual's indifference map between income and leisure. As the individual works more (less leisure) income increases as shown on the vertical axis. The horizontal axis measures the quantity of leisure in hours per day. The budget lines are determined by the wage rate. When the wage is $4 per hour, then if the worker chooses to work 24 hours, $96 in income would be earned (24 * 4 = 96). If the worker decides not to work at all, then his income would be (24 * 0).

Thus, the different wages yield different budget lines. We know that the choices made by the consumer must reflect utility maximization which implies that for every choice, there is an indifference curve that is tangent to the relevant budget line.

Starting from the initial wage of $4 per hour (point *A*), when the wage increases to $6 per hour, we observe that the worker increases the number of hours worked (point *B*). Further increase of the wage to $8 per hour results in the worker reducing hours of work (point *C*). Increasing the wage rate is the same as changing the price of a good discussed previously. Such price changes have both an income and substitution effect. A wage increase is equivalent to an increase in the price of leisure. For every hour that an individual does not work, he or she must forgo more income. The

Figure 1-12   Labor-leisure choices

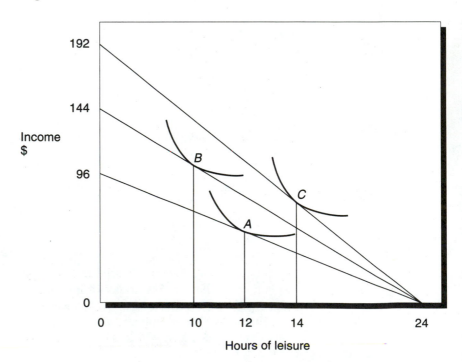

substitution effect would suggest that when the wages go up, the individual should consume less leisure, which is now relatively more expensive. In all cases, when the wage increases, the substitution effect has the effect of increasing the number of hours worked.

Conversely, a wage increase implies that for every hour of work, the individual will have higher income. Thus, there is an income effect associated with wage increases. Since leisure is assumed to be a normal good, we expect that the worker will, according to the income effect, reduce the number of hours worked in order to increase the consumption of the normal good, leisure.

Thus, the effect of a wage increase could work to increase the labor supply (if the substitution effect dominates the income effect), keep the labor supply constant (if the substitution effect is equal to the income effect), or decrease the labor supply (if the income effect dominates the substitution effect). Thus, although we normally draw a labor supply curve as being upward sloping, it is possible that the supply curve could be upward sloping only to a point and then bend backward as shown in Figure 1-13.

An important application of the income and substitution effects discussed is in regard to the effect of transfers on labor supply. In fact, one

Figure 1-13   Labor supply curve

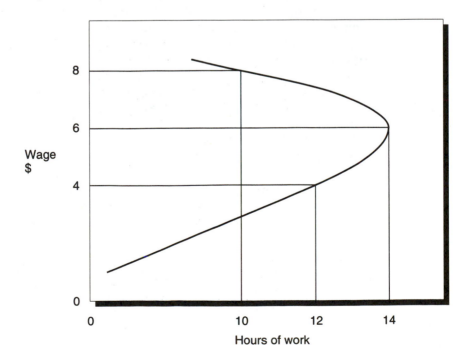

common criticism of welfare programs is that they cause recipients to work less or to totally withdraw from the labor force.

SUMMARY

This chapter developed simple economic concepts of demand and supply as well as some basic principles of consumer behavior. The discussion of the demand and supply concepts emphasized the fact that a given demand or supply curve assumes that all other factors that influence demand and supply are held constant, with the exception to the price of the good in question. Changes in prices result in movement along the demand and supply curves. This is referred to as changes in quantity demanded and quantity supplied. Changes in other factors cause the demand and supply curves to shift from their original position. Such changes are referred to as changes in demand and changes in supply.

Most economic analysis focus on aggregate demand and supply rather than individual consumer demand curves and individual firm supply curves. This chapter demonstrated that the market demand is obtained easily through horizontal summation of individual demand curves. However, in deriving the market supply, it is necessary to take into account the effect of the increase in the cost of production that occurs when all firms expand production. Combining the market demand and market supply, we have demonstrated how the market price is established.

The chapter also has developed a model of human behavior that demonstrates how consumers make utility maximizing choices. Using the basic building blocks of indifference curves and budget constraints, the optimal consumer choices and the conditions that are satisfied at those points of consumer equilibrium were demonstrated. The text also discussed how price and income changes affect consumer equilibrium. The theory of consumer behavior was applied to explain labor supply decisions.

The tools discussed in this chapter will be helpful in analyzing issues of poverty discussed in this book. Chapter 2 uses microeconomic tools to discuss theories of optimal distribution. The basic economic principles are extended in discussing positive analysis as relates to poverty policy. For example, there will be an investigation of how government minimum wages affect the labor market outcomes and the effects of income transfers on labor supply.

STUDY AND DISCUSSION QUESTIONS

1. Using a labelled diagram distinguish between an increase in demand and an increase in quantity demanded.

2. Draw a demand curve for good X. Show and explain what happens when

    (a) the price of Y (a complement) increases.

    (b) income falls and X is an inferior good.

    (c) the price of X (a normal good) falls.

    (d) the price of Z (a substitute) increases.

3. Draw a supply curve for good X. Show and explain what happens when

    (a) the price of fertilizers used to produce X increases.

    (b) the price of Y (a substitute in production) increases.

    (c) the price of X increases.

4. Use the following information to answer the questions that follow. In answering the questions, be sure to explain clearly the sequence that leads to the final prices and quantities.

    (i) Chicken and beef are substitutes.

    (ii) Chicken feed is transported by trucks from the Midwest to chicken farmers in the South.

    (iii) Cattle feed is grown by the farmers using inputs such as fertilizers.

    (iv) Farmers who keep cattle employ immigrants from South America.

    (v) Farmers who keep chickens employ domestic labor.

    (a) Clearly explain how an increase in the price of gasoline affects the equilibrium price of beef.

    (b) Explain what happens to the equilibrium price and quantity of chicken if there is a simultaneous increase in the price of fertilizers and an increase in the wages of domestic labor.

    (c) Suppose the United States government imposes strict regulations that prohibit immigrants from South America from working in the United States. At the same time, suppose that the government increases the tax on gasoline. Explain what happens to the market prices and quantities of beef and chicken.

(d) The government releases a report showing that choles-
terol in beef is far more serious than previously thought.
How would this announcement eventually affect the
price of fertilizers?

5. Clearly discuss the factors that cause changes in demand and
those that cause changes in supply. For each, show how the
change affects the positions of those curves.

6.   (a) What is an indifference curve?

(b) Construct an indifference curve for goods X and Y.
Clearly show how you calculate the slope of the indifference curve (express the slope in terms of utilities).

(c) State at least four properties of an indifference curve.

7. You are provided with the following information:
Budget = M, Price of $X = Px$, Price of $Y = Py$.

(a) Construct the budget line using the above information.

(b) Derive the slope of the budget line in terms of prices of X
and Y.

(c) Show what happens to the budget line and the slope
when the price of X falls.

8. Using indifference curves and budget lines, show what you mean
by consumer equilibrium. What conditions are satisfied at this
equilibrium?

9. Discuss each of the following:

(a) Law of diminishing marginal utility

(b) Marginal rate of substitution of X for Y

(c) Convex shape of indifference curves

(d) Backward bending labor supply curve

10. An individual works six hours when the wage is $5 per hour.
Using a labor–leisure diagram show and explain how a $15 per
day income guarantee could affect labor supply.

11. Using demand and supply analysis, discuss some of the factors
that may have contributed to increased homelessness in the
United States. Focus on demand and supply for housing.

2

NORMATIVE AND POSITIVE ANALYSIS

This book is about poverty; its nature, causes, and the various public policies that are used to deal with it. Chapter 1 noted that this book's approach uses economic theory to analyze poverty and poverty policy which is different from analyzing the same issue from a sociological, psychological, or other perspective.[1] These interdisciplinary differences arise from the fact that each discipline approaches the study of poverty by making some distinct assumptions about human behavior, and contrasts in views about what the organization of society should be like. As would be expected, the varied approaches frequently lead to different policy prescriptions. This is not to say that economists agree on all issues concerning poverty or even what policies should be used to deal with poverty. To the contrary, there is a wide divergence of views among economists as to what the causes of poverty are, and especially on how to deal with it. The differences among economists are, however, basically due to differences in normative views rather than differences in positive analysis.

Normative economics prescribes what ought to be. Thus, normative statements are based on ethical or moral opinions. These opinions are not supported by evidence or scientific fact. Normative analysis is therefore based on value judgments. On the other hand, positive economics is descriptive and value free.[2] In the study of the economics of poverty, both

---

1. Although this text basically follows the economics approach to analyzing poverty, it is not possible to rely exclusively on economic theories. As will become evident, poverty is a complex phenomenon which arises from sociological, cultural, and other factors in addition to economic factors. A good understanding of this problem should incorporate the interaction of all these factors. Inclusion of these other noneconomic aspects of poverty necessarily requires one to borrow ideas and methods of analysis from other disciplines.
2. For detailed discussion of normative approach, see Richard W. Tresch, Public Finance: A Normative Theory (Plano, Tex.: Business Publications, 1981); and for the positive approach, James M. Buchanan, "Positive Economics, Welfare Economics, and Political Economy," Journal of Law and Economics 2 (October 1959): 124–38.

normative and positive analysis play important roles. For example, while positive analysis may suggest that some income redistribution policy will reduce economic efficiency, it does not suggest that such a policy is either good or bad for society. Whether income redistribution is good or bad is a normative question. Usually, antipoverty policy emerges from both normative and positive considerations.

This chapter outlines the basic normative and positive economic tools of analysis. The first step is formulating the principles of welfare economics. Welfare economics is concerned with comparing the social desirability of alternative states. Primary focus is on the desirable state of income distribution, especially theories that justify government intervention to alter the market-determined distribution of income. To distinguish normative economics from positive economics, a brief analysis of positive economics is presented. Emphasis is on the role of positive theory in describing and predicting possible outcomes. As much as possible, both normative and positive analysis are presented in the context of the economics of poverty.

BASIC PRINCIPLES OF WELFARE ECONOMICS

The basic economic problem arises as a result of the fact that society's wants exceed the available resources to satisfy these wants. Land, capital, and entrepreneurial resources are scarce relative to human wants (both individual and collective), which means that choices must be made among competing wants, some of which must go unsatisfied. Economics deals with how society allocates scarce resources to meet unlimited human wants. Because of scarcity, every choice has a cost in terms of the forgone alternatives, that is, the sacrificed consumption. Therefore, the cost of one choice is expressed in terms of its opportunity cost. If a society chooses to build more roads, then it will have to do with less of other things (such as schools). The choices individuals and societies make are not random, but are based on efficiency considerations.

The idea of opportunity cost and efficiency is easily illustrated by a production possibility frontier shown in Figure 2-1. We consider an economy that produces only two goods—corn and honey. We assume that all available resources are used to produce these two goods. The quantity of corn that is produced is shown on the horizontal axis and the quantity of honey, on the vertical axis. If all resources are devoted to producing corn, OP^I bushels of corn will be produced and, of course, no honey will be produced. On the other hand, if all resources are devoted toward the production of honey, then OP units of honey will be produced. PP^I is this economy's production possibilities frontier. The frontier shows the maximum combinations of honey and corn that can be produced given a set of fixed resources and given production technologies. Any combinations of corn and honey

Figure 2-1   Production possibilities frontier

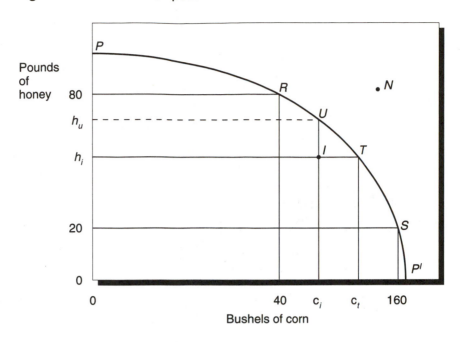

that fall on PP^I (such as on points P, R, U, T, S or P^I) or inside the PP^I curve (such as I) can be produced. Points that are outside to the right of PP^I (such as point N) cannot be produced because such a combination of outputs requires more resources than are available.[3]

Only points on the production possibility frontier satisfy the condition of production efficiency. Efficiency exists if no change can be made that increases the output of one good without reducing the quantity of any other good that is produced. This is called *Pareto efficiency*.[4] For all points along PP^I, an increase in the quantity of one good that is produced must be accompanied by a reduction in the quantity of another good. For example, moving from R (80 units of honey and 40 units of corn) to S (20 units of honey and 160 units of corn) increases the output of corn from 40 to 160 only by sacrificing 60 units of honey. Thus, the opportunity cost of producing 120 units of corn is equal to 60 units of honey. As the reader may have noticed, the opportunity cost is given by the slope of the production possibilities frontier. The slope of the production possibilities frontier shows

---

3. Such points can be attained if there is an improvement in technology or an increase in the resources, both of which cause an outward shift in the production possibilities frontier.
4. Named after Vilfredo Pareto, a nineteenth century Italian economist who formulated the basic conditions of efficiency discussed herein.

how much of one good must be given up in order to produce an additional unit of another good. This slope is called the *marginal rate of transformation (MRT)*. The MRT of corn for honey MRT_{ch} is the number of units of honey that must be sacrificed in order to obtain one more unit of corn.

All points along the production possibility frontier are Pareto efficient while points inside the frontier are inefficient. For example, starting at point I, it is possible to increase the quantity of honey from h_i to h_u (point U on the production possibilities frontier) without any reduction in the amount of corn produced. Likewise, it is possible to increase the amount of corn produced from c_i to c_t (point T on the production possibilities frontier) without any reduction in the amount of honey produced. All points inside the production possibility frontier represent inefficient production and/or some unemployed resources. A movement that results in the increased production of both or one of the goods without the reduction in the quantity of another good that is produced is called a *Pareto efficient move*.

The various points along the production possibilities frontier represent efficient production. At any given time, however, society must choose only one combination of goods. Although all points on the frontier are Pareto efficient, they are not equally desirable to society. Choices must be made that yield the best outcomes in production and consumption. To establish these conditions, start with a brief look at the optimal allocation of goods among consumers given some initial distribution.

To derive some basic results of welfare economics, let's extend the discussion of indifference analysis presented in Chapter 1. We assume a very simple economy where only two goods, corn and honey, are produced. We also assume that there are only two people in this economy: Irene and Beth. We assume that there is a fixed amount of corn and honey and the only problem is to allocate the amounts available between the two individuals. In other words, given a fixed amount of two goods, what is the best way to allocate the goods between the members of society?

Figures 2-2a and 2-2b show indifference curves between two goods (corn and honey) for Irene and Beth, respectively. For each indifference curve, utility is constant. As discussed in Chapter 1, an indifference curve shows combinations of two goods that give the consumer equal satisfaction. Figure 2-2a shows that 12 pounds of honey and 8 pounds of corn provide the same level of satisfaction to Irene as 10 pounds of honey and 14 pounds of corn. Increasing or decreasing the quantities of both goods implies that an individual attains different levels of satisfaction and hence moves to a new indifference curve. A higher indifference curve (one that is farther away from the origin) implies more satisfaction while a lower indifference curve (one that is closer to the origin) implies lower level of satisfaction. Thus, indifference curve I implies a lower level of satisfaction than indifference curve II. Again, as noted in Chapter 1, although we have shown only three curves, it is important to keep in mind that there is an

Figure 2-2   Indifference curves

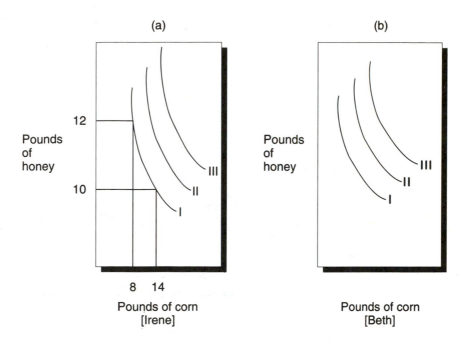

(a)   (b)

Pounds
of
honey   Pounds
                                                       of
                                                       honey

12

10

8   14

Pounds of corn   Pounds of corn
    [Irene]   [Beth]

indifference curve going through each point in the output space. Because of differences in tastes and preferences, indifference curves for one individual will differ from those of other people. It is for this reason that the indifference curves for Irene are different from those of Beth.

We utilize the device known as the *Edgeworth Box* shown in Figure 2-3 to derive distribution results of the allocation of corn and honey between Irene and Beth. The length of the Edgeworth Box shows the total amount of food available to both Irene and Beth. The height of the box shows the amount of honey available to Irene and Beth. In other words, OM (= PN) represents the total amount of corn available and OP (= MN) represents the total amount of honey available. The amounts of honey and corn consumed by Irene are measured from point O. Thus, as one moves away from point O, Irene's consumption of both goods increases which implies that she moves to higher indifference curves. On the other hand, Beth's consumption of both goods increases as she moves away from point N. This means that indifference curves that are farther away from N represent higher levels of satisfaction for Beth.

Now suppose that there is an arbitrary initial distribution of corn and honey at some point X where Irene has an amount of corn equal to OV and OY amount of honey. Conversely, Beth has NU of corn and NW of honey. The question we are interested in answering is whether the welfare of the two individuals could be improved by reallocating the goods. As will be

Figure 2-3   Edgeworth Box

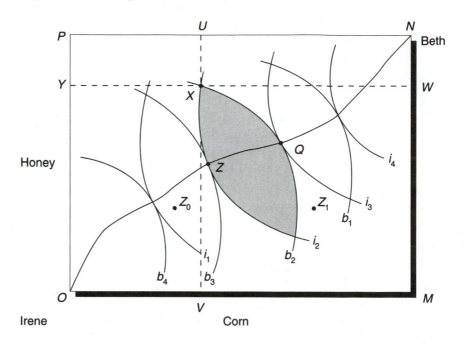

demonstrated, several possible results emerge from reallocation; some make both individuals better off, while others could make one person better off while not affecting the welfare of the other. Other allocations could improve the welfare of one person while making the other person's situation worse.

To illustrate these scenarios, consider an exchange that results in allocation from X to Z. The movement from X to Z occurs along Irene's indifference curve (i_2) so that her utility is not affected by the exchange. However, Z is farther away from N than the original position X, which means that Beth must have attained a higher level of satisfaction (moves from b_2 to b_3). Beth benefits from the exchange. Likewise, if the movement had been from X to Q, then although Beth's utility remains constant (b_2), Irene would have benefitted from the exchange moving from indifference curve i_2 to i_3.

Now consider the effect of reallocating the goods from point Z to Z_0 or Z_1. While Beth would be on a higher level of utility in moving from Z to Z_0, Irene's level of satisfaction would decline. Likewise, moving from Z to Z_1, Irene's level of satisfaction increases while that of Beth decreases. The important fact to note here is that no movement from Z would improve one person's utility without reducing the welfare of another person. Thus, Z represents a Pareto efficient allocation. Point X, however, does not represent an efficient allocation as it is possible to improve the welfare of one person without harming another person. Actually, any reallocation from X that falls within the shaded area (area bounded by the indifference curves passing through X) will improve the welfare of both Irene and Beth. This is the area of mutually beneficial exchange.

In Chapter 1, it was demonstrated that the slope of an indifference curve represents the consumer's marginal rate of substitution between the goods in consideration. Looking at Figure 2-3, we notice that starting from points where Irene's and Beth's indifference curves are tangent to each other (for example, point Z), there is no reallocation that would make one person better off without making someone else's position worse. This means that those points represent Pareto efficiency. Tangency of Irene's and Beth's indifference curves suggests that at that point, the marginal rates of substitution of corn for honey are equal for both individuals. Thus, the condition for Pareto efficiency in consumption is given by

(2.1)

$$MRS_{ch}\text{Irene}= MRS_{ch}\text{Beth},$$

that is, Irene's marginal rate of substitution of corn for honey is equal to Beth's. If all points are joined where Irene's and Beth's indifference curves are tangent (that is, all points where the MRS_{ch} for the two are equal), one obtains a *contract curve*, shown by *ON* in Figure 2-3. The contract curve represents all Pareto efficient allocations. No movement from the contract curve would increase the well-being of one person without making the other person's situation worse.

So far, efficiency in production and consumption have been examined separately. We want to establish the efficiency conditions in both production and consumption. It already has been established that Pareto efficiency in production requires that production take place on the production possibilities frontier. Figure 2-4 shows a production possibilities frontier. An Edgeworth Box has been drawn for the allocation of honey and corn between Irene and Beth. If production is at *V* on the production possibilities frontier, then the MRT_{ch} at this point would be given by the slope of *KK*. For efficiency in both production and consumption, the marginal rates of substitution of food for honey must not only be equal for both Irene and Beth, but also equal to the marginal rate of transformation of corn and honey. This means that not all points on the contract curve satisfy the efficiency condition in both production and consumption.

To demonstrate why equality of *MRS* and *MRT* is necessary for Pareto efficiency, consider an economy where Irene's $MRS_{ch} = 1/4$ and the economy's $MRT_{ch} = 1/2$. At this allocation, Irene could give up four units of corn for one more unit of honey and still remain on the same level of satisfaction. On the production side, one additional unit of honey could be produced by giving up two units of corn. Thus, Irene would be better off by giving up four units of corn and have them transformed into two

Figure 2-4   Efficiency in production and consumption

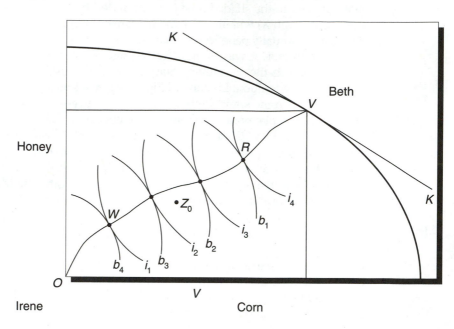

additional units of honey. This change makes Irene better off without making anyone's situation worse. As long as *MRS* does not equal *MRT*, reallocations could be made that make at least one person better off without making anyone's situation worse. Only when *MRS* = *MRT* (slopes of indifference curves equal the slope of the production possibilities frontier) is it impossible to make someone's condition better without making anyone's condition worse. Thus, the necessary conditions for Pareto optimality in consumption and production in our simple economy is

(2.2)
$$MRS_{ch}\text{Irene} = MRS_{ch}\text{Beth} = MRT_{ch}.$$

The fundamental theorem of welfare economics states that for as long as markets are perfectly competitive, the Pareto efficient allocation of resources emerges. Thus, a competitive economy allocates resources efficiently without the direction of government.

Suppose that points *W* and *R* (Figure 2-4) satisfy the efficiency conditions in both production and consumption (MRS_{ch}Irene = MRS_{ch}Beth = MRT_{ch}). Both points are by definition Pareto efficient as they fall on the contract curve. These points, however, reflect different utility levels attained by Irene and Beth. It is possible to illustrate the relationship between the maximum utility that one person can attain given a specific level of the other person's utility. Thus, at point *W*, Irene's utility is i_1 while the maximum utility that Irene can attain given Beth's utility is b_4. On the other hand, at point R, Irene's utility is i_4 and the maximum utility that Beth can attain is b_1. There are several other points that meet the efficiency conditions. If one obtained various points on the contract curve and the associated levels of utility for both Irene and Beth, then the *utility possibilities curve* can be constructed.[5]

In Figure 2-5, we plot Irene's utility on the horizontal axis, and Beth's on the vertical. Curve IB is the utilities possibilities frontier. This curve shows the maximum amount of one person's utility given the utility attained by another person. Points outside the frontier are not attainable while those inside the frontier are attainable. Notice that if Beth's utility increases, such a change must also be accompanied by a reduction in Irene's utility and vice versa. Thus, all points on the utility possibilities frontier are Pareto efficient. From the figure, it is clear that Beth would prefer R to W, while Irene would prefer W to R. Which point on the utility possibilities frontier is most desirable?

This question suggests that issues of redistribution require value judgments. That is, although market-determined outcomes may be efficient from the economic perspective, such outcomes may not be socially optimal.

Figure 2-5   Utilities possibilities frontier

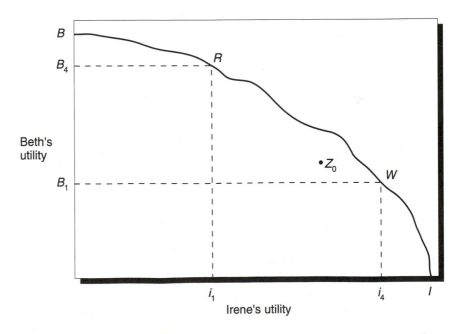

5. See Francis M. Bator, "The Simple Analysis of Welfare Maximization," *American Economic Review* 47 (March 1957): 22–59.

If market-determined distribution (even when it is Pareto efficient) is not socially desirable, what then is the socially desirable state of distribution? The next section discusses various theories of optimal distribution that seek to answer this question.

THEORIES OF OPTIMAL DISTRIBUTION

One of the central concerns in the study of the economics of poverty is the design and implementation of public policies to alleviate poverty. Some policies are geared to reducing market-determined income inequalities. Other programs transfer benefits to the poor so that they can attain a certain level of consumption that society deems necessary or essential. Other policies help the poor obtain education and job skills so that they can become more productive, hence more competitive, in the market. All these government programs change the state of income distribution. This section investigates the basis for government involvement in the distribution of income. Specifically, it seeks to answer why governments should alter the state of income distribution determined by the market.

As previously noted, economists are basically concerned about the efficient use of resources. The allocation of resources in a market economy produces efficient results. This type of efficiency has nothing to do with fairness or just distribution. Although many economists consider government's role in redistributing income as creating inefficiencies, most agree that the market- determined income distribution is not necessarily socially optimal. Consequently, there is a need for the government to change the income distribution. The following examines some of the justifications for government income redistribution.

Utilitarian Viewpoint

In welfare economics, the well-being of the society is defined by the prosperity of the members of that society. Thus, in a society of N members, one can express the social welfare W as a function of all the members of the society, 1 to N:

(2.3)
$$W = f(U_1, U_2, U_3, \ldots U_n)$$

The relationship in Equation 2.3 is called the *social welfare function*. The implication of this relationship is that an increase (decrease) in any individual's utility increases (decreases) the social welfare. Sometimes the social welfare function is written as an additive function:

(2.4)
$$W = f(U_1 + U_2 + U_3 + \ldots U_n)$$

Utilitarians support the idea of redistribution to achieve the greatest level of satisfaction for the entire society, which essentially means attempting to get the highest value of W.

To illustrate the idea of maximizing social welfare, consider the utility possibilities frontier for Irene and Beth shown in Figure 2-6. This is the frontier shown previously. Now, however, we include social indifference curves.[6] Just as an individual's utility function can be represented by the use of indifference curves between two goods, one also can represent a society's indifference curves between the utilities of various members of that society. The curves show that as the utility of one person decreases, the only way to maintain the same level of social welfare is to increase the utility of another person. Generally, society is better off if it is on a higher social indifference curve. According to Figure 2-6, R is on a lower indifference curve than W. Point Z_0, which is not Pareto efficient, is on a higher indifference curve than points W, X, Y, and R that are Pareto efficient. From the society's standpoint, the society is better off if point Z_0 is chosen over W, X, Y, or R, although it is not efficient. That is, the society's welfare

Figure 2-6   Equity *vs.* efficiency

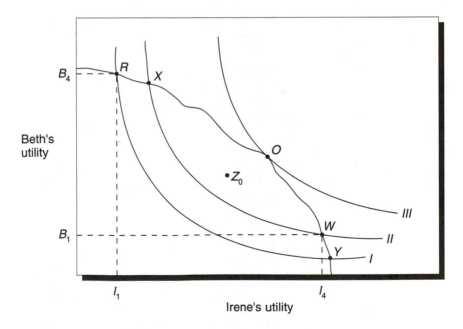

6. See Abram Bergson, "A Reformulation of Certain Aspects of Welfare Economics," *Quarterly Journal of Economics* (1937–1938): 310–34.

is enhanced more by the increased equality as compared to the loss in utility due to loss in efficiency. The most desirable point would be O, which not only meets the condition of efficiency, but also represents higher social welfare.

To apply the social welfare function to explain what the utilitarian distribution principle should be, the following simple assumptions are made.

1. All individuals in society have identical preferences and utility depends only on income.
2. Utility functions are characterized by diminishing marginal utility of income; that is, additions to income yields increasingly smaller units of satisfaction.
3. Total income is fixed.

Given these three assumptions, if a society's goal is to maximize social welfare, then transfers from those with more income to those with less will result in increased welfare. In fact, under the assumption, income transfers should continue until perfect equality is achieved.

To illustrate this result, consider Figure 2-7. The horizontal axis (I–I') measures the income available to Irene and Beth, assumed here to be the only members of a simple society. Irene's income is measured by the distance to the right of I and Beth's income is measured by the distance to the left of I'. As Irene approaches I', her income increases while as Beth approaches I, her income increases. The vertical axis measures the value of marginal utility of income and the linear lines show the marginal utility of income. Notice that Irene's marginal utility of income curve slopes down to the right; as Irene's income increases, the marginal utility of additional income falls. Likewise, as Beth's income increases, the marginal utility of income declines (right to left). Notice that because of the assumption of similar preferences, the marginal utility curves are of same slope (actually mirror images of each other).

Now, assume that Irene's income is IK and Beth's income is I'K (Beth has more income than Irene). Then the question is whether this type of allocation maximizes the social welfare. That is, is this an optimal state of distribution? According to utilitarians, it is not. If LK dollars are taken away from Beth and transferred to Irene (Irene's income increases to IL and Beth's falls to I'L), Beth's situation is obviously made worse by this transfer and Irene's is improved. On the whole, however, Beth's losses are more than compensated by Irene's gains such that total social welfare increases. To appreciate this fact, remember that the amount of income lost by Beth is less valuable to her (due to diminishing marginal utility of income) than it is to Irene who has less income (hence higher marginal utility of income).

The increases in social welfare can be more clearly shown by considering the fact that the area under each person's marginal utility curve measures the change in utility due to a change in income. Thus, distributing LK

Figure 2-7   Utilitarian model of income distribution

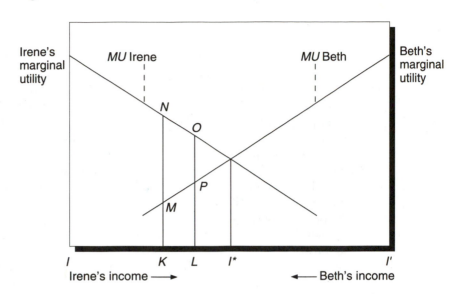

dollars increases Irene's utility by area *NKLO*. At the same time, distributing the same dollars reduces Beth's utility by area *KMPL*. Thus, the social welfare (in this community of two) increases by area *MNOP*. It can be easily shown that maximizing social welfare requires continued transfers from Beth to Irene until both share the fixed income equally at *I**. Any redistribution from this point would lead to a reduction in social welfare.[7]

The Maximin Principle

The maximin principle of redistribution asserts that inequality is only acceptable if it helps raise the position of the person who is in the worst condition. According to this principle, which has been advocated by John Rawls, a person is not entitled to his income just because he is more able than other members of the society.[8] To Rawls, the only just principle of redistribution is one that attempts to maximize the welfare of the most disadvantaged, hence the term maximin.

---

7. Note that if the assumption of identical preferences is relaxed, the optimal distribution under the utilitarian criteria does not imply perfect equality. Maximum welfare would be attained when the loss in utility by those whose income is reduced is equal to the gain in utility by recipients.
8. For a detailed treatment, see John Rawls, *A Theory of Justice* (Cambridge, Mass.: Harvard University Press, 1972).

To illustrate this principle, consider the following social welfare function:

(2.5)
$$W = \delta_1 U_1 + \delta_2 U_2 + \delta_3 U_3 + \ldots \delta_n U_n.$$

where δ's are positive numbers showing how the social welfare increases when the utility of the various members of society changes. For example, if the utility of person 1 increases by one unit, the social welfare increases by δ_1; if the utility of person 2 increases by one unit, the social welfare increases by δ_2, and so forth. If society places more weight on the welfare of persons with low incomes (poor people have higher values of δ than the more wealthy members), then social welfare increases by transferring income to those with the lowest income. According to the maximin criterion, social welfare depends only on the welfare of the person who is in the worst condition, and therefore society's goal should be to maximize the utility of the person with the minimum.

Rawls theory of just distribution keys on the ethical foundation of the maximin principle. He argues that if decision makers are under a veil of ignorance so that they do not know what their position in society is, then people, being impartial and fair, will adopt a maximin principle of redistribution. The maximin principle protects all individuals from the worst possible outcome. People fear to be at the lowest level of income and therefore would choose a situation where the lowest level was as high as possible.

Public Good and Pareto Efficiency

We have already noted that an allocation of resources such that no change can make one person better off without making someone else worse off is said to be Pareto efficient. Pareto efficiency is commonly used to evaluate whether improvements can be made in the allocation of resources. If an allocation is not Pareto efficient, it is possible to change the allocation in a manner that improves the welfare of one person without hurting some other person.

The types of redistribution considered so far result in making one person better off and another person worse off. Thus, such redistributions are not Pareto efficient. It is possible, however, that people with more income gain utility by transferring income to less fortunate persons. In such cases, the donor and recipient actually benefit.[9] In other words, a poor person's consumption enters into the utility function of the wealthy person, a situation that economists characterize as an externality. Under such circumstances, transfers actually increase social welfare and efficiency would

---

9. See H. M. Hochman and J. D. Rodgers, "Pareto Optimal Redistribution," *American Economic Review* (September 1969): 542–57.

imply that such transfers should continue up to the point where no more gains are obtained from the transfers.

Although such voluntary transfers would increase social welfare, it may be difficult for individuals on their own to affect the transfers. It may be costly to make the transfers or even to identify the poor. In this case, it would be desirable for the government to solve the externality problem by taxing the rich and transferring the proceeds to the poor.

If all members of society are made better off if inequality is reduced, then we can consider reducing inequality as a public good. Because no single individual acting alone can affect the state of income distribution, only collective action can affect the desired income distribution. Thus, although some people will make (and do make) voluntary transfers, such transfers are likely to be less than what may be considered socially optimal.

The public good justification for income redistribution can be taken a step further. There are two main characteristics of public goods. First, a public good is one that once produced, there is no additional cost of another person consuming it.[10] Second, once produced, it is impossible (or very expensive) to exclude anyone from consuming the good. The nonexcludability of public goods makes market pricing of the good impossible because of the free rider problem. Knowing that they cannot be excluded from consuming the good, consumers will not be willing to voluntarily pay toward the production of the good. As such, production of public goods requires collective action. If all members of society benefit from reduction in inequality, then when some individual makes a voluntary transfer, all members of society benefit. Therefore, the free-rider problem emerges that can be solved only if government uses its coercive powers to redistribute incomes.

Endowment Criteria

One of the early theories that attempts to define a just distribution of income is referred to as the endowment-based criteria of distribution. The idea of the endowment criteria is consistent with the ideas of the natural-law philosophers such as Locke. The basic idea of the endowment criteria is that individuals are entitled to the earnings that they obtain from participating in the market.[11] Because individuals have the innate right to the fruits of their labor, there is an ethical justification for them to keep what they earn. Since factors of production earn a return which is equal to the value of marginal product, some inputs will command a higher return,

---

10. Public goods are said to be nonrival in consumption.
11. More recent supporters of this view include Robert Nozick, *Anarchy, State, and Utopia* (New York: Basic Books, 1974).

while others will command a lower return depending on the marginal products of those inputs. Just distribution according to the endowment criteria suggests that the rewards to inputs as determined by the market should not be altered. Thus, government should not alter market-determined income distribution.

There are some qualifications to the general endowment criteria that have been suggested. The first of these qualifications is the idea that individuals should only be allowed to keep the earnings that they could get in a competitive market. Thus, earnings that are derived from presence of monopoly power or wage earnings that are above marginal product should not be considered as just. A second qualification has been to allow individuals to keep the earnings from labor, but not from capital. It is commonly suggested that income from capital should not be considered as earned as it does not involve disutility such as is associated with work. A final qualification is that individuals should be allowed to keep what they earn in competitive markets given equal positions at the start. Thus, inequality is acceptable if it originates from differences in innate earning ability, differences in preferences (for example, choice between leisure and income), and motivation. Conversely, differences due to inheritance or different opportunities (such as education) or family status should not be allowed. Thus, the government should be concerned in establishing equality of opportunities rather than equality of outcomes.

POSITIVE ANALYSIS

Positive economics attempts to establish the cause and effect relationships among economic variables. Thus, positive theory is objective and does not seek to define what is good or bad, nor does it attempt to outline what should be done. Thus, unlike normative analysis, positive theory does not require us to make value judgments. Positive theory helps the analyst predict possible outcomes. These theoretical predictions can be confirmed or refuted by comparing them with the actual facts. This section focuses on the theoretical analysis of positive economics. The appendix to this chapter reviews simple procedures that are used to test the predictions of positive theory.

A significant portion of the economic analysis of poverty deals with decision making by individuals and firms. These decisions affect earnings and opportunities and explain low earnings by some members of society and high earnings by others. For example, these may include labor market choices such as the number of hours of work or even the decision to work or not to work, or the level of wages in particular sectors of the economy. In fact, as will be seen, one primary focus of economics of poverty centers on labor market behavior.

The role of positive analysis can be illustrated by studying the simple question of the behavior of workers (for example, in response to changes in the wage rate). Suppose a person who receives $5 per hour works 12 hours. It may be interesting to know what would happen if the wage increased. Would this person work the same number of hours, less hours, or more? Chapter 1 discussed labor supply decisions and demonstrated the various possible outcomes when wages change. Such analysis, which attempts to explain *what is happening* or *what will happen*, falls under the realm of positive economics.

Positive analysis also is important in explaining how government policies affect individual behavior and other market outcomes. The following section discusses the case of a minimum wage law and a minimum guaranteed income, both important policies in the economics of poverty.

Minimum Wage

Consider, for example, the well-known minimum wage law. Figure 2-8 shows labor demand (L_D) and labor supply (L_S) curves. As is clear from elementary economics, labor market equilibrium is that point where the quantity of labor demanded is equal to the quantity supplied. W_0 is the equilibrium wage and L_0 is the equilibrium level of employment in this sector. Use this simple model to demonstrate what happens when government imposes a minimum wage W_m that is above the market clearing wage. Given utility maximization, increases in the wage will cause more workers to enter the labor market so that the quantity of labor supplied increases. On the other hand, increased wages reduces the profits the firm

Figure 2-8   Minimum wage and unemployment

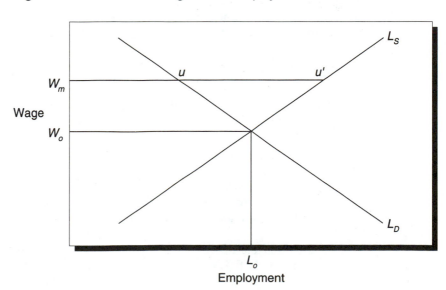

Employment

earns, and given the goal of profit maximization, those firms will reduce the quantity of labor demanded. Governments frequently attempt to help the poor by legislating a higher minimum wage. What results emerge from such legislation? Using positive analysis, one can predict the result. While raising the wages of some workers, this policy also will cause unemployment of workers equal to UU', which is shown by the gap between the quantity supplied and quantity demanded at the set minimum wage. Thus, positive analysis helps one understand the outcomes of such government policies, particularly in relationship to the intended and actual outcomes. These types of issues are important in understanding the economics of poverty.

Minimum Guaranteed Income and Labor Supply

As a final application of the tools of choice discussed here, the effect of income transfers on the labor supply will be discussed. Of course, this is one of our concerns in the analysis of poverty. Suppose as a nation we want to ensure that every citizen in the United States is guaranteed a minimum level of income which is deemed necessary to permit the consumption of some essential goods. What are the likely effects of such a policy?

Figure 2-9 shows the case of an individual who earns $2 an hour and chooses to work 12 hours, thus earning $24 per day (point A). Suppose that the government wants to ensure that every citizen receives at least $30 per day. The person earning $24 would therefore get $6 per day in the form of government transfers such that he would be on point B in Figure 2-9. A person who is not earning market incomes at all would receive a transfer equal to $30 (point C). Obviously, point C is better than point B, and the individual who is working 12 hours will be better off to stop working and receive the entire $30 transfer. This is a good example of some of the problems of the welfare system which will be discussed in the text.

SUMMARY

Normative analysis prescribes what the desirable alternatives should be. Such analysis is useful in providing answers to questions concerning the role of the government in changing the market-determined state of income distribution. We have seen that although we are interested in obtaining efficient outcomes, a society's value judgments may require deviations from efficient conditions. This chapter has presented some of the theories of optimal distribution such as the utilitarian view, maximin principle, the endowment criteria, and the Pareto efficiency-public good justifications for redistribution.

On the other hand, positive analysis focuses on explaining and predicting outcomes. In the area of poverty, positive analysis helps the analyst

Figure 2-9   Minimum guaranteed income and labor supply

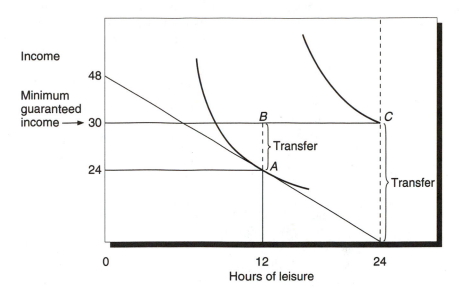

predict the consequences of various public policies. Using examples of minimum wages and guaranteed income, we have shown that although normative analysis may suggest such proposals on fairness grounds, the society also must evaluate the outcomes of those choices. Thus, even though a society may be interested in helping the poor, it is still important for that society to evaluate the actual outcomes and costs of such policies. Such evaluation involves positive analysis. In the study of the economics of poverty, positive and normative analysis play a complementary role.

STUDY AND DISCUSSION QUESTIONS

1. Distinguish between normative and positive analysis using some examples relevant to the economics of poverty.

2. Suppose that in a competitive market economy MRX_{xy} is greater than MRT_{xy}. Explain in detail what you expect to happen. Use a diagram to illustrate your answer.

3. The governor of your state wants to start a policy that provides housing subsidies to the poor in the state. Write a memo to the governor detailing normative and positive arguments both for and against such a policy.

4. John can trade two hamburgers for one six-pack of soda and be equally happy. Sally can trade two of her six-packs of soda for six hamburgers and be equally happy. Is the allocation of soda and hamburgers Pareto efficient? Illustrate this by using an Edgeworth Box.

5. Discuss each of the following theories of optimal distribution. Make sure you present the main arguments as clearly as possible. In your judgment, which theory or theories best fit policy making in the United States? Provide justification for your answer.

    (a) Utilitarian viewpoint

    (b) Pareto criteria

    (c) Maximin principle

    (d) Endowment criteria

6. The United States government is proposing to increase the minimum wage. Provide normative and positive arguments as to whether the government should adopt such a policy.

7. Demonstrate how to construct a utilities possibilities frontier. Explain the relationship between different points on utilities space with points in an Edgeworth Box diagram.

ADDITIONAL READINGS

1. Baumol, William J. *Superfairness: Applications and Theory.* Cambridge, Mass.: MIT Press, 1986.

2. Hyman, David N. *Public Finance.* Chicago: Dryden Press, 1987.

3. Johanson, Per-Olov. *An Introduction to Modern Welfare Economics.* Cambridge, England: Cambridge University Press, 1991.

4. Phelps, E. S., ed. *Economic Justice.* Baltimore: Penguin Books, 1973.

5. Tobin, J. "On Limiting the Domain of Inequality," *Journal of Law and Economics* (October 1970), pp. 263-277.

2 Appendix

STATISTICAL ANALYSIS OF ECONOMIC DATA

In his classic work on the methodology of positive economics, Milton Friedman stated that the "ultimate goal of a positive science is the development of a 'theory' or 'hypothesis' that yields valid and meaningful (i.e., not truistic) predictions about phenomena not yet observed."[1] Since theories and hypotheses explain some possible outcomes or relationships, only factual evidence can show whether those propositions are right or wrong. A hypothesis is either accepted or rejected by comparing the predictions made with the actual outcome. It is important, therefore, that whatever theoretical propositions are made about relationships between variables be supported with some evidence. This appendix discusses some of the methods used in testing theoretical propositions in economics.

The role of statistical testing is illustrated using the determinants of wage rates as an example. We start with the commonly held view that one of the causes of poverty is low or no educational training. People with no or only a few years of education earn lower wages than those with more years of education. This suggests that there is a relationship between the wage rates and the level of education. The goal here is to demonstrate how to investigate whether or not a proposition such as the relationship between education and wages is valid.

UNIVARIATE TEST

Assume there is a linear relationship between two variables: Y and X. The equation of such a linear relationship can be represented by the general equation

(A.1)
$$Y = \alpha_0 + \alpha_1 X$$

---

1. Milton Friedman, "The Methodology of Positive Economics," *Essays in Positive Economics* (Chicago: University of Chicago Press, 1953), p. 7.

where Y is called the dependent variable, implying that values of Y depend on other variables such as X. X is the independent variable which means that X does not depend on the variables shown in the model, that is, it is determined outside the model, and α_0 and α_1 are parameters. α_0 is the intercept, which shows what the value of Y is when X is equal to 0. α_1 is the slope of the straight line. Thus, α_1 shows the magnitude by which Y changes when X changes by one unit. That is, if X changes by one, then Y changes by α_1 units. If α_1 is positive (negative), then an increase in X results in an increase (decrease) in Y. Thus, both the magnitude and sign of the slope parameter are important in interpreting the relationship between the variables.

As an example, suppose that the relationship between Y and X is shown by the following equation:

(A.2)
$$Y = 4 + 2X$$

One can then calculate values of Y for different values of X as shown in Table 2A-1 and plotted in Figure 2A-1. As Figure 2A-1 shows, Y is an exact function of X and therefore the data points generated by the model lie exactly along a straight line.

In specifying models that are appropriate to economic data, it is necessary to allow for randomness. This is because economic relationships in the real world are never exact. Thus, rather than assuming that Y is an exact function of X, we assume that Y is a function of X and a random error, ε. Therefore, the linear model is expressed as

(A.3)
$$Y = \alpha_0 + \alpha_1 X + \varepsilon$$

Data generated by this model would not lie exactly along a straight line as in Figure 2A-1. Instead, the data would lie approximately along the line; some points will lie above the line and some below it as shown in Figure 2A-2. This means that specific values of Y do not coincide with the line, but rather the line shows where average values of Y would fall. Thus the line $\alpha_0 + \alpha_1 X$ shows the expected values of Y. The actual Y differs from expected Y $E(Y)$, by ε. Thus,

(A.4)
$$Y = E(Y) + \varepsilon$$

Suppose one collects data on 20 employees who work in the same firm as shown in Table 2A-2. This table presents the data on wages earned by various employees and some of their characteristics (such as race, gender, work experience, and number of years of education). We focus first only on the relationship between wages and education, assuming that all other determinants of wages are held constant. Figure 2A-3 shows the relationship between the wage rate (vertical axis) and the level of education (horizontal

Table 2A-1   Values of *Y* obtained from the equation *Y* = 4 + 2*X*

X	Y
0	4 + 2(0) = 4
1	4 + 2(1) = 6
2	4 + 2(2) = 8
3	4 + 2(3) = 10
4	4 + 2(4) = 12
5	4 + 2(5) = 14
6	4 + 2(6) = 16

Figure 2A-1   Linear function

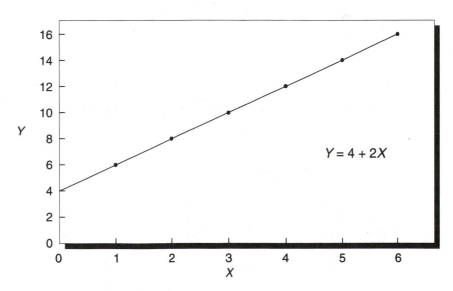

axis). From a casual observation, it appears that those employees with higher levels of education earn higher wages. Although all points do not fall on a straight line, the pattern suggests that there is a general linear relationship between the wage rate and the years of education. In other words, we can fit a straight line (as shown in Figure 2A-3) which, although it does not go through all the points, shows the general direction of the relationship between these two variables.

One can now model the relationship between the wage and the years of education by adding an error term to the general linear model previously shown because one cannot expect the relationship between wage

Figure 2A-2   Linear function

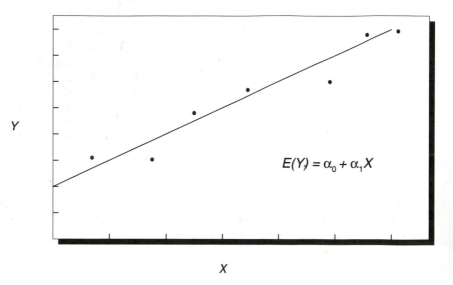

$$E(Y) = \alpha_0 + \alpha_1 X$$

Table 2A-2   Data for the determinants of wage rate

Worker	Wage	Education	Experience	Gender	Race
1	5.0	10.0	1.0	0	0
2	5.0	9.0	1.0	1	0
3	6.0	10.0	1.0	1	0
4	8.0	11.0	2.0	1	1
5	7.5	10.0	2.0	1	1
6	7.0	11.0	2.0	0	1
7	10.0	14.0	2.0	1	1
8	10.0	14.0	4.0	0	1
9	6.0	12.0	0	1	0
10	12.0	18.0	4.0	1	0
11	12.0	18.0	6.0	0	0
12	11.0	16.0	2.0	1	1
13	11.0	18.0	4.0	0	0
14	7.0	8.0	4.0	1	0
15	8.0	10.0	4.0	1	0
16	9.5	13.0	4.0	0	1
17	4.0	8.0	0	0	1
18	4.0	8.0	0	1	0
19	6.0	9.0	2.0	1	0
20	4.5	9.0	0	1	0

Figure 2A-3   Relationship between wage and education

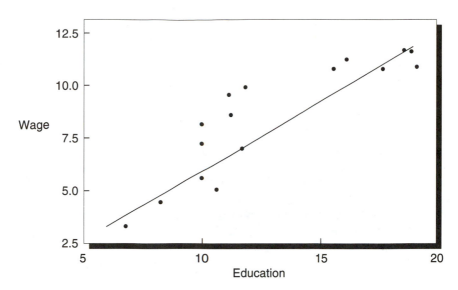

and education to connect all points. Inclusion of the error term allows for some randomness.[2] Thus, we can write the model for the determinant of wage rates as

(A.5) $$WAGE = \alpha_0 + \alpha_1 EDUCATION + \varepsilon,$$

where ε is the random error term. α_0 shows what the wage would be if the years of education were equal to zero. On the other hand, α_1 is the magnitude by which an increase of one year of education increases the wage rate.

The goal of estimating the relationship such as Equation A.5 is to compute values of α_0 and α_1 that best fit the data. The best fit is obtained by obtaining values of parameters that minimize the sum of the squared error terms. Of course, this implies that one achieves a line that comes closest to all points. The specific values of the wage do not coincide with the estimated line, and the line shows where average or typical wage would fall. Such a line is estimated using a method called *least squares regression*. Although one can manually calculate the parameters, many computer packages make this task extremely simple.

---

2. Several assumptions about the error term are made. These include: (1) on average, the value of the error term is zero; (2) all the different error terms have the same variance; (3) the error terms are independent of each other, that is, they are not correlated; (5) the error term has a normal distribution; (6) error terms are independent of the values of the independent variable(s).

Least squares method is used to estimate the relationship between wage rate and education using the data shown in Table 2A-2 to obtain the following results.

(A.6)
$$\text{WAGE} = -0.69 + 0.70 \text{ EDUCATION}$$
$$(0.89) \ (0.072)$$
$$R^2 = 0.84$$

The meaning of R^2 will be discussed later. Note that $\alpha_0 = -0.69$ and $\alpha_1 = 0.70$. Ignoring the number in parentheses for a moment, the results imply that if the number of years of education increases by one, the wage rate would increase by $.70. The intercept term suggests that if years of education were zero, the wage would be $-\$0.69$, that is (WAGE= $-0.69 + 0.70$ (0)). Of course, this figure does not make sense. What it implies is that the straight line has been extended beyond the reasonable limit. Misleading results arise when a linear regression is used to make predictions of values that are far outside the range of the data used in the estimation.

Note that the estimated parameters are only approximations of the true values. Thus, there is some uncertainty associated with each parameter's estimate. In other words, each parameter deviates from its true value by some magnitude. This deviation is measured by what is called the standard error already reported in parentheses. The larger the standard error, the larger the uncertainty about the measured coefficient. Relative to the value of the respective parameters, the standard error for the constant term is much larger than that of the education variable. In other words, we are more uncertain about the estimated parameter for the intercept term.

After estimating the equation, the researcher must conduct tests to investigate the quality of the relationship between the variables. The goal is to test whether there is a systematic relationship between wage and education level. The relationship is tested statistically using a t distribution. To carry out a t test, a researcher first formulates a null hypothesis. For example, if there is no relationship between wage and education, then $\alpha_1 = 0$. This is the null hypothesis. The alternative hypothesis is that $\alpha_1 \neq 0$. In this case, one can test the hypothesis that α_1 is positive (implying that increased years of education result in higher wages) against the null hypothesis that α_1 equals zero; that is, there is no relationship between years of education and wages.

The next stage in testing for significance is to calculate the t-statistics for each of the parameter estimates. The t-statistic is the ratio of the coefficient to its standard error. For the results reported above, the t-statistic for the education coefficient is $0.70/0.072 = 9.76$, while that of the intercept is $-0.69/0.89 = -0.77$.

After calculating the t-statistic, one must choose some probability level that will guide in the selection of the null hypothesis or alternative hypothesis. Based on the hypothesis that $\alpha_1 = 0$, one can compute the t-statistic and determine how likely it would have been to observe the results obtained if $\alpha_1 = 0$. If the likelihood is too small, the hypothesis $\alpha_1 = 0$ is discarded in favor of the alternative, that is, α_1 is not equal to zero. The tests are conducted by comparing the computed values of t to the table vales of t available in most standard statistics and econometric texts. The table t values are reported for different probability levels and degrees of freedom. The degrees of freedom is equal to the number of observations less the number of parameters. In the example, 20 observations and two parameters are used; therefore there are 18 degrees of freedom.

Figure 2A-4 shows a graph of the t distribution. Notice that the distribution is symmetric centered at zero and the area under the curve is equal to 1. For illustration purpose, select a probability level of 5 percent. The table t value for 18 degrees of freedom and 5 percent probability level is 2.101. Thus, 5 percent of the area under the curve shown in Figure 2A-4 lies outside the limits indicated by $t = 2.101$ and $t = -2.101$. Thus, the shaded area is the area where a t value would fall only 5 percent of the time.

The computed t value (9.76) is greater than the table value (2.101). This means that there is less than a 5 percent chance of finding this computed value if the hypothesis $\alpha_1 = 0$ is correct. Thus, one must reject the hypothesis that $\alpha_1 = 0$ and accept the alternative hypothesis, $\alpha_1 \neq 0$. This means that there is statistical evidence of a relationship between the observed wage and level of education.[3] If computed value of t is less than the table value, one can reject $\alpha_1 \neq 0$. Note that this is not the same as saying that $\alpha_1 = 0$.

Figure 2A-4   *t*-distribution

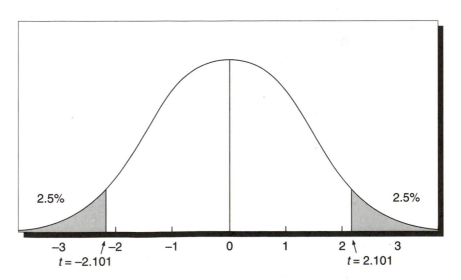

---

3. A simple rule of determining the significance of t-statistic is that if this statistic is greater than 2 (in absolute value), the hypothesis that the value a1 = 0 can be rejected.

Another important statistic for interpreting regression equations is the R-Square, (R^2). The R^2 measures the strength of the association between Y and X.[4] If all the values of Y are exactly on the linear line $Y = \alpha_0 + \alpha_1 X$ as in Figure 2A-1, then R^2 is equal to 1. This means that values of X explain 100 percent of the variations in Y. However, if there is no association between Y and X, then R^2 would be zero. Thus, one can simply express R^2 as the ratio of the explained variation in Y to the total variation in Y. The R^2 for the simple equation herein is 0.84. This means that, for the data used, education explains 84 percent of the variation in the wage rate.

MULTIPLE REGRESSION

So far only one explanatory variable has been discussed, holding all other variables constant. Wages, however, are determined by several other variables such as experience. It is expected that workers who have more experience earn more, other factors being equal. Wages also may vary across racial groups (for example, between Whites and Blacks), and by gender. Inclusion of sex and race controls in a wage model is particularly important in investigating the presence or absence of sex and race discrimination. In this case, multiple variables are used to explain the variations in the dependent variable. This is called *multiple regression.*

Thus, the regression model can be written as

(A.7) $WAGE = \alpha_0 + \alpha_1 EDUCATION + \alpha_2 EXPERIENCE + \alpha_3 GENDER + \alpha_4 RACE + \varepsilon;$

EXPERIENCE as the number of years of work experience. We define GENDER as a binary variable equal to 1 if the worker is a male and equal to 0 if the worker is female. This implies that if the coefficient on GENDER is positive (negative), males earn higher (lower) wages than females, all other things remaining equal. RACE also is defined as a binary variable equal to 1 if the worker is White and equal to zero if the worker is nonwhite. Thus, a positive (negative) coefficient implies that Whites earn higher (lower) wages than nonwhites, all other factors remaining equal.

The results of estimating this model using the data provided in Table 2A-2 are as follows:

(A.8) $WAGE = -1.24 + 0.52\ EDUCATION + 0.69\ EXPERIENCE + 1.13\ GENDER$
            (0.20) (0.017)   (0.03)   (0.10)

$+ 1.16\ RACE$
(0.09)

$$R^2 = .99$$

---

4. Notice that X could be several explanatory variables, as will be discussed below.

The standard errors are in parentheses below the coefficients. The *t*-statistics associated with the parameters follow.

Parameter	Coefficient/standard error	t
Constant	−1.24/0.20	−6.20
Education	0.52/0.017	30.58
Experience	0.69/0.03	23.0
Gender	1.13/0.10	11.3
Race	1.16/0.09	12.8

The calculated *t*-statistics are large, thus one can accept the alternative hypothesis that each of the variables is related to the wage rate in the direction shown.

The results demonstrate that one additional year of education increases the wage rate by $.52 (all other things being equal). On the other hand, one additional year of experience increases the wage rate by $.69. For the data shown (all other things being equal), males earn $1.13 more than females, and Whites earn $1.16 more than nonwhites. The $R^2 = .99$. This means that the variables included in the model explain 99 percent of the variation in the wage rate.

Although regression analysis is useful in testing the validity of predictions of positive economics, it should be used with care. There are several problems that may bias the results. Most common include *multicollinearity*, *autocorrelation*, and *heteroscedasticity*.

Multicollinearity arises when the variables on the right-hand side are highly correlated to each other. Autocorrelation occurs when the errors terms are not independently distributed. Heteroscedasticity arises when the variance of the error terms are not constant. Fortunately, there are simple techniques of detecting and correcting these problems.

Wrong inferences can be made if one starts with a data set that is not "good." If a data set is not representative of the population, the results obtained will be biased. Thus, one of the key issues in statistical testing of economic data is to ensure that the data is as representative as possible. Another serious problem arises when important variables are omitted in the estimation. For example, if experience in the estimation of the wage equation was omitted, the results tend to place more importance on the other variables included in the model. For example, education has a smaller effect on wages when other things are taken into account. The problem of omitted variables is especially critical in making inferences about race and sex discrimination.

Finally, although the above estimation has assumed that the relationship between the dependent and independent variables was linear, this is not always the case. In many cases, a nonlinear relationship exists. Therefore, one should be concerned about not only the variables included, but also the functional relationship.

3

POVERTY POLICY: A HISTORICAL PERSPECTIVE

Public policy courses mainly concentrate on contemporary issues, while historical discussions and evolution of those issues frequently are omitted. As a practical matter, historical discussions are problematic in most courses due to time constraints and the false belief that history is not relevant to today's issues. This is true in the study of poverty. We ignore historical discussions and focus primarily on present-day issues. The main thrust of this book is on contemporary issues concerning poverty and antipoverty policy.

Omitting historical discussions of poverty could be misleading. Students may think that most of the controversial issues concerning poverty policy emerged during the 1930s, when widespread unemployment and poverty paved the way for the enactment of New Deal policies. Or they may think that public policies to alleviate poverty began during the 1960s when President Johnson declared War on Poverty, leading to the policies of the Great Society.

Indeed, most present-day public policies toward poverty in the United States can be traced back to the New Deal and the Great Society. Although those policies marked significant turning points in the way the United States dealt with poverty, they did not mark the beginning of public policies to deal with poverty. As stated by Katz, such accelerated efforts in dealing with needs in society mark a rediscovery of poverty: "Although poor people always are there, only periodically do we rediscover or think about them very much."[1] Societies always have designed policies to deal with poverty. Similarly, criticisms directed at the current welfare system are not new. Most concerns raised about contemporary welfare policies are similar to those raised several hundred years ago.

As a starting point, it helps to review some of the historical developments of poverty policy. To appreciate the evolution of current poverty

---

1. Michael B. Katz, *The Undeserving Poor: From the War on Poverty to the War on Welfare* (New York: Pantheon Books, 1989), p. 3.

policies, the factors that have been attributed to be the causes of poverty, and the policies that have been suggested to deal with this problem are reviewed. Whether past policies have solved the problems of poverty can guide us in evaluating today's issues. This chapter demonstrates that social philosophers have been debating most of today's issues for many years. In fact, the supposed causes of poverty, the suggestions on how to deal with it, and even the probable effects from supporting the poor have changed little over the centuries.

This chapter reviews how societies have dealt with the problem of poverty. It does not evaluate the various policies, nor does it evaluate the correctness of the views of different writers. The goal is to identify suggestions about the causes of poverty and the proposed public policies. The chapter omits discussion regarding the conditions of the poor (such as their standard of living) as measured by the quality of housing, health, nutrition, and so on. The discussion is brief and it does not exhaust all the issues about poverty. Only key issues are presented in order to provide the reader with an appreciation of the past. The discussion begins with policies used to deal with poverty in England and America before the twentieth century. The goal is not to present a comparison between English and American poor laws. Most of the laws adopted in colonial America were derived from English poor laws; therefore a discussion of English poor laws provides a natural background for those enacted in America.

EARLY POOR SUPPORT

Before the seventeenth century, poor support in England was primarily performed by the church. Virtually no government policies to support the poor existed. The church provided services in accordance with the Medieval Poor Law, a part of the canon law. Under the Medieval Poor Law, poverty was not attributed to be a result of a person's shortcomings; it was not a crime to be poor, and the poor were as honorable as other members of society. Thus, the poor had a right to assistance. To be eligible, a demonstration of need was required. Widows and orphans received preference and their support was considered as the sole responsibility of the church. During this period, wealthy people engaged in indiscriminate giving. Such acts were not necessarily altruistic, but rather out of self-interest. The wealthy were concerned about doing good works as a means of salvation, helping the poor was one such good work. This generosity in giving produced a large number of beggars who often were able-bodied.[2] Because of such undesirable outcomes, formal rules were codified into the

---

2. Begging actually became just like any other business. Some schools were started to instruct children in the art of begging.

Medieval Poor Law that made eligibility more difficult. Specifically, some groups of poor were no longer regarded with honor and were considered unworthy—able-bodied beggars, fortune-tellers, and others seeking to avoid work. Still, support of the poor remained fairly liberal.[3]

Events dramatically changed the liberal support policies for the poor. The Black Death (1348–1349) produced severe labor shortages. Because of a fear that the disease would spread and because of labor shortages, laws were enacted that restricted movement of the poor—the Statute of Labourers of 1355 and the Poor Law Act of 1388 being two important laws. All able-bodied men without means of support were required to accept employment offered to them. The mobility of the poor from one region to another was forbidden; the poor were restricted to their parishes.[4] As mentioned, the policies were not primarily designed to help the poor, but rather to serve the interests of employers. In fact, the policies were largely punitive. Other legislative proposals followed. For example, the 1576 Poor Relief Act required beggars to work in return for the relief received. Alms giving and begging by the able-bodied was outlawed. Still, poor support remained largely a function of the church.

Probably the most important early legislative acts that focused on antipoverty policy were the 1601 Poor Law Act and the Poor Law Amendment Act of 1834. The essence of the 1601 Act was the introduction of a compulsory tax-financed poor relief.[5] The act also required that each parish take responsibility of its poor.[6] In addition, the act distinguished between the different categories of the poor and between the types of help that were to be provided. The poor were classified into three categories:

> The "impotent poor" (the old and the sick) were to be accommodated in "almshouses"; the able-bodies were to be given work in a "house of correction" (not at first a residential workhouse); and idlers who refused to work were to be punished in this "house of correction."[7]

The parish and local officials administered the support system and levied taxes dedicated for the purpose of providing relief to the poor.[8] The local officials had discretion as to the generosity of benefits, whether benefits

---

3. For a detailed treatment of early poor relief in England, see Gertrude Himmelfarb, *The Idea of Poverty: England in the Early Industrial Age* (New York: Alfred A. Knopf, 1984).
4. These laws were forerunners to Vagrancy Laws that were to become important in Europe and in the United States.
5. The tax-financed poor relief was first established by an Act of 1597 and then re-enacted and revised in 1601.
6. The 1601 Act was enacted during the reign of the 43rd Elizabeth. The poor laws enacted during this period are commonly referred to as the Elizabethan Poor Laws.
7. See Nicholas Barr, *The Economics of the Welfare State* (Stanford, Calif.: Stanford University Press, 1987), p. 10.
8. The taxes were largely levied on land.

were to be in cash or in-kind (for example, food or housing), and whether payments were made to recipients in their homes (outdoor relief) or in almshouses (indoor relief).

In the early seventeenth century, several changes occurred that necessitated some modification of the poor laws. In particular, commercialization of agriculture and industrialization in the towns forced tenants off the land. These changes precipitated an accelerated migration of poor laborers from the farms to the towns. These changes also increased the number of unemployed, beggars, vagrants, and poor, who wandered in the countryside and frequently posed a threat to law and order. Various interest groups for varying reasons wanted the government to enact support policies to deal with the poor. The owners of large farms wanted local low-cost seasonal workers; industrialists wanted to encourage migration to the cities to provide a pool of low-wage factory labor, but the industrialists also wanted law and order to be maintained so that production would not be interrupted. The towns, however, wanted to minimize the cost of supporting the poor.

The government resolved the various interests with the Act of Settlement of 1662. This act introduced a residency requirement for the receipt of assistance. The decision to make local residency a requirement for recipiency reflected the power of the landed class who benefitted most from restricted migration. Of course, such a policy made it difficult for the poor to leave the farms, hence wages remained low. At the same time, the towns benefitted from reduced cost for the support of the poor; the industrialists benefitted from controlled migration since law and order was more easily maintained. Under provisions of the Settlement Act, people could be forcefully returned to their legal residence.

Another important revision of the poor law was the introduction of workhouses. In 1772, parishes were allowed to build workhouses to house the poor and to deny relief to anyone refusing to enter them. The parishes could then farm their poor to contractors. The contract system was a kind of forced labor and was overly abused. In addition, the conditions in the workhouses were appalling; not only were the residents subjected to long hours of hard labor, but also the food and other amenities provided were quite inadequate, even to the poor. Infant mortality was as high as 93 percent in the workhouses.

In response to the appalling conditions of the workhouse system, a reform movement that advocated more humanitarian policies in treating the poor emerged. The result was the enaction of the Gilbert's Act of 1782. This act outlawed the contract system. Unemployable persons were to be housed in separate poorhouses and provided for by the community. Employable persons who were willing and able to work, were to be provided with work and outdoor relief. It was up to the local officials to create work (for example, by establishing public works programs). Thus, the Gilbert's Act emphasized outdoor relief, better treatment of the poor, and job creation.[9]

The 1601 Poor Law Act operated fairly well for about 200 years, but the system started to show signs of weakness by the end of the eighteenth century. Since enactment, the population had increased dramatically. In addition, the economy experienced major downturns that increased unemployment and poverty. Famines and the Napoleonic wars increased the numbers of people experiencing hardships. Thus, poor support was no longer adequate. Furthermore, laborers experienced a major decrease in wages; their earnings became insufficient to meet the basic necessities such as food. The harvests of 1794 and 1795 were particularly bad and resulted in severe food shortages. The price of bread and other provisions increased rapidly. Rumors spread among the working class that farmers and shopkeepers were exploiting the scarcity by increasing prices even more than was necessary. In some parts of the country, farmers rioted and seized produce, took over shops and fixed what they considered to be fair prices. These events necessitated a review of the method of helping the poor.

In a meeting in Speenhamland in 1795, the Justices of the Peace of Berkshire initiated a new system that extended support to both those working and those not working. Every person whose earnings fell below a given standard would receive a subsidy from the parish that was based on the price of bread.[10] This new method of support, known as the *Speenhamland system*, was imitated by neighboring counties and then adopted by parliament in 1796. The system assured the poor that they could consume the basic necessities.[11] Family size played a role with those who had three or more children receiving more supplements. The system was abused by local administrators who used the system to award political favors. Thus, the cost of relief increased dramatically. For example, between 1803 and 1818, poor rates (taxes to support the poor were derived) doubled and tripled by 1832. At this time, poor relief came under attack by writers such as Robert Thomas Malthus and David Ricardo.[12] These attacks and the economic reality of the time led to the establishment of a Royal Commission in 1832 to study the system of reform. The result was the passage of the Poor Law Amendment Act of 1834.[13]

The Poor Law Amendment Act contained three main principles: the notion of less eligibility, the workhouse test, and administrative centralization. The eligibility test applied to the able-bodied. The provision of relief

---

9. Workhouses were once again to become an important element of the new poor law discussed next.
10. The choice was between establishing a minimum wage and paying subsidies. The minimum wage proposal was rejected.
11. This practice resembles modern proposals for guaranteed incomes.
12. Views of these and others writers are discussed later in this chapter.
13. The act was based on a *Poor Law Report*, written by Nassau Senior and Edwin Chadwick.

discouraged work effort and hence the eligibility test was necessary to ensure that those who were able to work did not become dependent on relief. The workhouse test discouraged able-bodied people from being dependent on relief. To be eligible for relief, the poor had to stay in the workhouse. The workhouse standard of living was lower than the level that the average worker could afford. Other restrictions included the separation of husbands, wives, and children in the workhouse. Residents were not allowed to receive visitors and were subjected to frequent punishments for simple violations. A peculiar feature of workhouses was that often *inmates* were required to do useless tasks so as not to compete with other laborers.[14] The rather harsh policies discouraged those who were considered poor by choice from becoming dependent on public support.[15] Administrative centralization was to ensure uniformity in enforcement of poor support, to increase cost effectiveness, and to reduce corruption and incompetence of local officials.

Although the 1834 Poor Law Amendment Act reduced government support to the poor, future legislative activities in Britain increased it. More social policies emerged, including public support of education, housing, health, old-age pensions, unemployment insurance, laws regulating work hours, child labor laws, and so forth. Thus, by the early 1900s, many programs had been legislated and a large portion of government revenues supported the poor. The welfare system expanded greatly during and after World War I.

National poverty policy in the United States developed more recently. Before 1933, the federal government played only a minor role in supporting the poor. The federal government only provided emergency appropriations following local disasters. Most public relief funds came from state and local governments. Private charities also played an important role in supporting the poor. The only significant federal participation consisted of welfare services to the veterans of the Civil War and their dependents. The federal government also established the Freedman's Bureau in 1865 to help Blacks; the bureau faced numerous problems and was abolished in 1872.

Poor relief policies in colonial America were patterned after English poor laws, particularly the Elizabethan Poor Law of 1601.[16] As early as

---

14. In his criticism of the New Poor Law, Friedrich Engels stated that the quality of life in the workhouses was much worse than in prisons. Therefore, poor persons often committed crimes so that they were put in jail rather than entering workhouses. An analogous argument is made about criminal behavior by ghetto residents. Because of the harsh conditions of ghetto life, residents do not see much difference between the ghetto and jail.

15. The harsh conditions, of course, increase the cost to the individual of relying on poor support, which makes work more attractive compared to being on relief.

16. For details of early poor support in America, see Ralph Segalman and Asoke Basu, *Poverty in America: The Welfare Dilemma* (Westport, Conn.: Greenwood Press, 1981), Chapter 2; *The Almshouse Experience, Collected Reports* (New York: Arno Press and New York Times, 1971); and June Axinn and Herman Levin, *Social Welfare: A History of the American Response to Need* (New York: Dodd and Mead, 1975), Chapters 1–4.

1647, Rhode Island adopted the Elizabethan poor law that stressed public responsibility for the poor. Similar laws were enacted by other colonies. Particular emphasis was on local responsibility, residency requirements, and family responsibility. Basically, local communities cared for the poor within their jurisdictions. Local support varied greatly from one jurisdiction to the next in terms of benefits and eligibility requirements. The eligibility requirements included rules such as disfranchisement (in 14 states); residency requirements; or the condition that recipients live in almshouses and do some work. Where relief was granted to people not living in almshouses, payments were low and frequently only in kind (that is, in the form of goods and services and not cash).[17]

Residency requirements were particularly important in regulating recipiency. The main goal was to prevent local communities from being overburdened by the poor from other areas. Many states established waiting periods before newcomers became eligible for support.[18] The waiting period varied widely: in New York it was 40 weeks, in Massachusetts three months, and in North Carolina one year. Another strategy used by local communities was the screening of strangers. Those who arrived without assets and who were therefore considered potential dependents were escorted out of the local jurisdictions. This practice came to be known as *passing out*.[19]

Poor relief in the United States also placed more responsibility on the poor's family. Persons with resources were expected to support the poor in their families. The authorities could place liens on the resources of those who refused to support dependents. Thus, eligibility for support took into account the resources of the individual and those of close relatives. Those who were poor due to factors beyond their control were treated more generously than those who were considered poor by choice or because of their own actions. The result was the establishment of categorical assistance based on particular circumstances. For example, widows and orphans were treated generously, mothers of illegitimate children were treated less kindly.

Some important methods of poor relief emerged in colonial America. One important method, apprenticeship, was a system of occupational training. Local communities were concerned about families that could not support their children. It was in society's interest to assure that the children

---

17. Nicholas Barr, *The Economics of the Welfare State,* p. 24.
18. Even today, wide regional and state variations exist in the size of welfare benefits. As a result the poor migrate from low to high benefit states. See Robert Moffitt, "Incentive Effects of the U.S. Welfare System," *Journal of Economic Literature,* Vol. 30 (March 1992): 1–61.
19. In the United Kingdom, some parishes bribed their own poor to move to other parishes. In the United States, a contemporary example of such a practice relates to homeless people where small towns give homeless people in their towns bus tickets for destinations to major cities—a practice known as *greyhound therapy* (see Chapter 17).

become productive members of society not dependent on public support. Families that were financially able took responsibility for those children, providing a better education such as in profitable trades and how to read and write. It should be emphasized that while apprenticeship was a system of occupational training, its real thrust was to remove children from their homes and thus was to some degree punitive.[20]

Indenture was a related method for dealing with children in poverty. Children who were unattached, neglected, or dependent could be placed with families that were willing to educate and train them. Those families then recouped their expenses from the child's work. Although the system worked on occasion, it was frequently abused. Masters invested less in children, and obtained more from their services. Voluntary child welfare organizations emerged to serve the interests of these children. Several institutions emerged to take care of children, such as orphanages and houses for children whose parents were poor.

Two methods were used to deal with adults: indenture contracting and farming out. Both methods kept the poor productive. Indenture contracts enforced labor by placing potential poor in some sort of servitude, sometimes to a master of their own choosing or to an assigned master. Other people who were unable to pay for their passage came to the United States under contracts of indenture. Under farming out, the adult poor were given to the bidder willing to contract, at the lowest charge to the local community, to take care of the poor and to put them to work. As a business transaction, the bidder expected to make a profit.

In the American South, Blacks increased rapidly during the seventeenth century. At first Blacks came to the South as indentured workers. By 1661, slavery was institutionalized, and by the turn of the century it was the norm. With forced labor, there were no services provided to Blacks who were still in slavery, but some support services were extended to Whites and free Blacks. For example, in the mid-seventeenth century Virginia adopted some policies to help poor free men (Black and White), orphans, illegitimate children, and mulatto children of White women; no services were available to Blacks in bondage. To some, slavery was merely an extension of the poorhouse, where provision of subsistence was provided in exchange for work.

The Civil War produced many casualties, unemployment, and poverty particularly in the South. Many households were left without a husband, or with a disabled one. Thus, many families existed as widows with dependent children. There also were many orphans whose parents were killed during the war. As a result, federal legislation evolved to support

---

20. Apprenticeship was first put into effect in England by Elizabeth 1 in the Statute of Artificers of 1563, it was later adopted by the American colonies. Benjamin Franklin and Andrew Jackson are examples of famous Americans who underwent apprentice training.

soldiers, veterans, and their dependents. The Pension Act of 1890 was the first federal legislation providing support to veterans, their widows, dependents, and orphans based on need alone. In the South, individual states established orphanages and apprenticeship programs to help children of Confederate soldiers. The South was economically devastated and many people (Black and White) were destitute. Poor Whites received food and clothing from public welfare stations.

Even after the Civil War, there were no serious efforts to deal with Black poverty. The southern Whites still wanted to control Black labor. Several Black codes were established to regulate the economic life of ex-slaves. These included limitations on property ownership and prohibition of Blacks joining some professions such as artisans or mechanics. Some states enforced employment contracts for Blacks who were not working. The economic life and the availability of social welfare services for Blacks did not change in the period immediately after the Civil War.

In 1865, the federal government established the Freedmen's Bureau to deal with the problem of homeless Blacks and with the management of abandoned and confiscated property. The bureau provided several services to both Whites and Blacks, including medical supplies and food rations; it also reunited families separated during the war. In addition, the bureau organized freed Blacks into a labor force, helped in job search, and supervised labor contracts between Blacks and Whites. The bureau set up orphanages for Black children and established institutes of higher learning for Blacks.[21] However, the bureau faced several problems. Northerners were concerned with the redistribution of resources from the North to the South. On the other hand, southern planters were concerned with a program that helped Blacks and argued that it reduced the labor supply, hence causing wages to rise. The bureau was therefore short lived and was dissolved in 1872.

To a large extent, the task of supporting the poor in the United States was performed by the private sector in the form of private charity coordinated by such organizations. During the early 1900s, the private charity movement was very active in promoting the idea that some deserving poor such as the aged, the blind, and female-headed families with children deserved public support. However, up until the Great Depression, public support to the poor remained quite small.

The Great Depression started with the stock market crash in October 1929 and lasted until 1941. Business failures, unemployment, and poverty increased dramatically. Even with increased efforts by the private charity organizations to help the poor, donations dwindled. At the same time local communities could not afford to support their own poor due to decline in

---

21. Some schools started with the help of the Freedman's Bureau include Howard, Atlanta, and Fisk universities, and Hampton and Talladega colleges.

public sector taxes. At the federal level, the Hoover administration resisted appeals for relief and maintained that the responsibility of supporting the poor rested with individuals and localities.

State governments started to increase their support to local governments in order to meet the new challenges of unemployment and poverty. New York state under the leadership of Governor Franklin D. Roosevelt appropriated $20 million to aid relief efforts of the localities. The basic approach was to provide support for work projects. Other states followed the New York state relief efforts.

Supporting the poor and the unemployed became a political imperative. A bill that sought to increase relief to business and included provisions for supporting the unemployed was signed by President Hoover. A new administration took power in 1933, facing the major task of dealing with the unemployment problem. A new agency, the Federal Emergency Administration (FERA) was created to direct federal relief efforts. The main philosophy governing FERA was that employable persons should be put to work. Therefore, several federally funded work projects were started. However, the federal government left the support for the unemployable persons to the states and local governments, and private philanthropy.

Many state and local governments did not have the resources to support unemployable persons. The aged also were becoming more vocal and an important political force. The Townsend Movement, which sought a program to guarantee income to the aged, was becoming increasingly important. As a result of the political and economic conditions, President Roosevelt appointed a commission to draft long-term reform programs that would provide income security to the unemployable persons. The outcome of these efforts was the enaction of the Social Security Act (SSA) of 1935. The SSA included both social insurance and public assistance components.

Thus, the adoption of the SSA marked the first major federal involvement toward fighting poverty. Other significant changes in the system of support to the poor included the adoption of the Great Society policies of the 1960s. As mentioned earlier, most of the contemporary antipoverty policies discussed in this book have their origins in the New Deal or Great Society.

POVERTY IN THE HISTORY OF ECONOMIC THOUGHT

One can broadly classify ideas on poverty and poverty policy into two main schools of thought.[22] The first school of thought, the conservative view, sees poverty as a social ill for which the individual is largely responsible. Thus,

---

22. No accepted classification schema exists for the various schools of thought on poverty. The classification used here merely streamlines the various opinions on poverty.

the problem cannot be eliminated by social policy. This school equates good antipoverty policy with less government intervention. This school argues that attempts to help some groups of the poor, especially those who can participate in labor markets, will generally cause more social ills and magnify the problem of poverty. The second school of thought, the liberal view, believes that poverty can be reduced by the adoption of well-designed programs. This school argues that the adoption of activist social policies represent the most effective way to eradicate poverty. These two divergent views about poverty dominate policy making in the United States today.[23]

These divergent positions on how to deal with poverty are not new. In fact, the positions were historically quite extreme and more clearly defined. One group of social thinkers believed in the natural laws view of how societies and markets were organized. The policies suggested by this group correspond to today's conservative view of limited government. The second group, social reformers, viewed the problems of the poor as a result of institutional imperfections. They advocated active public policies to rectify the problem caused by institutional imperfections, much like today's liberals.

Natural Laws View

Probably the most influential social philosophers in the history of economic thought accepted the concept of natural laws.[24] Natural laws explained the working of markets and the growth of the population. The natural law view relies on self-regulating forces. For example, market prices adjust to a natural price without the direction of government. Likewise, natural forces regulate the population. Those who believed in the natural laws opposed active government policy because such intervention hinders the natural order delaying the best and inevitable outcomes. Adam Smith, the father of modern economics, is probably the most important proponent of the natural laws view of the market. According to Smith, the well-being of all members of society improved by letting the market operate unimpeded.[25] Others in this tradition include Thomas Robert Malthus and David Ricardo, both of whom criticized government aid to the poor.[26]

Smith was nevertheless concerned about the poor. He suggested that society benefitted when the poor are able to get reasonable food, clothing, and shelter. The problem of poverty was best solved by the free functioning

---

23. These positions are extreme; most people will take a position in the middle, albeit one side or the other.
24. The natural laws view was largely inspired by the discovery of the physical laws, such as those elaborated by Isaac Newton.
25. Adam Smith's contribution is contained in his monumental work, *An Inquiry Into the Nature and Causes of the Wealth of Nations*, which was first published in 1776.
26. Malthus' most critical work on this subject is contained in his *An Essay on the Principles of Population*, Vol. 3, which was first published in 1798; Ricardo's views are contained in his *On the Principles of Political Economy and Taxation*, first published in 1819.

of markets. With free markets, the division of labor produced increased output. Consequently, the prices of the goods that the poor consume decline and their welfare improves. Thus, the best outcome for the poor was not government-mandated income transfers, but high wages obtained in free markets. In other words, Smith argued that the well-being of the lowest members of society depends on letting the natural laws of free markets operate without interference.

Smith, however, noted that the well-being of those in the lowest economic strata might deteriorate because the poor have more children than the wealthy. Nonetheless, the increase in wages that the division of labor produces was the best way to eliminate such catastrophes. In fact, Smith believed that the market regulated the size of population to prevent the poor population from growing excessively.

> If the demand [for labor] is continuously increasing, the reward of labour must necessarily encourage in such a manner the marriage and multiplication of labourers, as may enable them to supply that continually increasing demand by a continually increasing population. If the reward should at any time be less than what requisite for this purpose, the deficiency of hands would raise it; and if it should at any time be more, their excessive multiplication would soon lower it to this necessarily level.
>
> The liberal reward of labour, as it encourages the propagation, so it increases the industry of the common people. The wages of labour are the encouragement of industry, which, like every other human quality, improves in proportion to the encouragement it receives. A plentiful subsistence increases the bodily strength of the labourer, and the comfortable hope of bettering his condition, and of ending his days perhaps in ease and plenty, animates him exert that strength to the utmost. Where wages are high, accordingly, we shall always find the workmen more active, diligent and expeditious, than where they are low. . . . [27]

Smith also recognized that the wealthy and poor members of society face different constraints. Thus, the gap between the wealthy and the poor may not narrow without some policy to support the poor. The difference between the wealthy and the poor originated primarily from nurture, according to Smith, not nature. He argued that the habits, customs, and education of different people greatly affect the division of labor by assigning them to different occupations. Thus, although individuals may be born with the same talents, they are provided with different opportunities (such as early schooling), depending on the parent's background. Thus, even though Smith was against most forms of government intervention, he did feel that public education for the poor was essential. He proposed the establishment of publicly funded schools, affordable to even the poorest members of society. Smith also suggested a system of rewards to motivate poor

---

27. *The Wealth of Nations,* pp. 80–81. See recent editions, Oxford University Press, 1976.

children to learn: "The public can encourage the acquisition of those most essential parts of education by giving small premiums, and little badges of distinction to the children of the common people who excel in them."[28]

Adam Smith did not explicitly criticize poor support. He was opposed, however, to some of the conditions placed on the recipients of poor support.[29] In particular, Smith criticized the laws of settlement that restricted the mobility of poor from one region to another. He argued that such restrictions prevented the free movement of wages, hence, the division of labor was hindered which is central to the improvement of the economic well-being of all members of society.

One of the more controversial figures in the natural laws tradition is Thomas Robert Malthus (1766–1834). Malthus advanced the notion that poverty was an inevitable punishment to the poor for overbreeding. He argued that poverty and the associated calamities were necessary to check population growth. Policies to support the poor made poverty worse by prolonging the inevitable. Thus, according to Malthus, the plight of the poor and the death of their children was a natural mechanism for regulating population.

The Malthusian theory of population hinges on a simple theoretical proposition concerning the growth rates of food supply and the population. Food is essential for human existence; the survival and well-being of a population depends on the food supply. Malthus proposed that population follows a geometric growth path, while food production follows an arithmetic growth path. Unless population is checked, it would eventually outstrip the food supply. Thus, if no moral restraint exists to limit the growth of the poor, then misery, pestilence, or other factors will control the population. Malthus suggested, for example, abolishing all support for illegitimate children and punishing those parents who abandoned their children. To him, it did not matter much to society if those children were left to die when young. Another policy suggested by Malthus was to terminate all support to those poor who marry and are not able to provide for their family. For a man to marry knowing that he could not support his family was an immoral act. Such a person "should be taught to know, that the laws of nature, which are the laws of God, had doomed him and his family to suffer for disobeying their repeated admonitions; that he had no claim of right on society for the smallest portions of food, beyond that which labour would fairly purchase. . . ."[30]

---

28. *The Wealth of Nations*, p. 738. Smith's discussion of the importance of education was insightful. One of the more important antipoverty policies today is human capital investment, discussed later.
29. It could be said that Smith tacitly supported poor support.
30. Thomas Robert Malthus, *An Essay on the Principles of Population*, 6th ed., Vol. 11 (London, 1826), p. 339. See also T. R. Malthus, *An Essay on the Principles of Population* with an introduction by Antony Flew (New York: Penguin Books, 1970).

The other important proponent of natural laws was David Ricardo (1772–1823). Ricardo's work focused on the laws of income distribution. His main contribution to the economics of poverty was the "iron law of wages." Increases in population with a fixed supply of land and diminishing returns in agriculture cause the rental share of national income to increase, benefitting the landowners. The owners of capital and laborers lose since they would share the remaining and smaller share of national income.

Those in the laboring classes of society (the poor) were in the worst position because, according to Ricardo, wages adjusted naturally to be equal to the minimum cost of subsistence. If this natural price of labor increases (which increases the well-being of the poor) above the minimum cost of subsistence, then the population also increases and forces wages back to their natural level. If the price of labor falls below the minimum cost of subsistence, the population declines and causes the wage to increase. Essentially, Ricardo's law of wages implies that labor never attains a long-run standard of living above the subsistence level.

The only way to avoid the iron law of wages, which necessarily produced poverty, was if workers had fewer children, or if they acquired better tastes for comforts and therefore raised the subsistence level. Ricardo, however, observed that the poor may not voluntarily regulate their population, and hence were doomed to remain poor.

Ricardo was opposed to government policy that interfered with the natural laws of the market. Thus, he opposed wage regulation. He also argued that the poor laws encouraged procreation, directly increasing poverty, and hence called for their abolition. In addition, he suggested that attempts to help the poor makes society worse off as a whole. Ricardo was convinced that the free market and the total abolition of poor laws was the best antipoverty policy.

> The clear and direct tendency of the poor laws, is in direct opposition to these obvious principles [principles that determine wages]: it is not, as the legislature benevolently intended, to amend the condition of the poor, but to deteriorate the condition of both poor and rich; instead of making the poor rich, they are calculated to make the rich poor; and whilst the present laws are in force, it is quite in the natural order of things that the fund for the maintenance of the poor should progressively increase, till it has absorbed all the net revenue of the country....
>
> No scheme for the amendment of the poor laws merits the least attention, which has not their abolition for its ultimate object; and he is the best friend to the poor, and to the cause of humanity, who can point out how this end can be attained with the most security, and at the same time with the least violence.[31]

---

31. David Ricardo, *On the Principles of Political Economy and Taxation* (Cambridge, England: The University Press of the Royal Economic Society, 1962), pp. 105-107.

Institutional Imperfections View

Although Smith, Malthus, and Ricardo are well known in the history of economic thought, other writers had important and controversial ideas concerning the causes and cures of poverty. These writers had a more sympathetic view about the causes of poverty and they proposed social policies to help the poor. Some of the notable social reformers include Thomas Paine (1737–1809) and Robert Owen (1771–1858).

Thomas Paine advanced his ideas about poverty in the "Rights of Man."[32] Paine attributed the cause of poverty to government that had established a tax system that overburdened the poor and which was biased in favor of the aristocracy. In fact, Paine argued that even the poor were supported not by the most wealthy, but by the working class. At that time, redistribution was primarily a local function (each parish supported its poor). Because the wealthy did not typically live in the areas where the working classes and the poor lived (in the manufacturing towns and laboring villages), the wealthy did not contribute toward the support of the poor. Paine was particularly concerned with the reliance on consumption taxes, which were highly regressive. In fact, some taxes (such as the taxes on brew) did not affect the aristocracy; their own beer was exempted since they made their own. He argued that when taxes paid by the poor were low, the poor were able to maintain themselves. However, under the present system of high taxes, even hard working laborers were likely to end up poor.

Paine was particularly concerned that the people who suffer most from government were the young and old in society. He proposed various policies that were designed to help these two groups and to reduce the burden on laborers. Paine proposed the abolition of the poor rates to be replaced by the remission of taxes to low income earners.[33] He also suggested that because children impose a burden on their parents, the government should make some additional provision for families with children. In turn, the parents must take their children to school to learn reading, writing, and common arithmetic. Other suggestions included making cash transfers available to all new mothers who needed such support and to newly married couples who might be in financial hardship. If a worker died while travelling for work, then Paine proposed that there should be some support to cover the funeral expenses.

One of Paine's central concerns was the welfare of the old. He argued that old people are frequently afflicted with poverty although many had

---

32. Thomas Paine, "Rights of Man," Part 2, in Moncure Daniel Conway, ed., *The Writings of Thomas Paine,* Vol. 2 (New York: G.P. Putnam's Sons, 1894).
33. This is equivalent to cash transfers used by today's governments. In fact, Paine's proposals are very similar to some of the policies that were enacted in the 1930s and 1960s.

paid taxes during their working years. Paine, therefore, proposed policies to transfer incomes to people after they reach the age of 50. Such income transfers, according to Paine, were not some form of charity, but a right. Paine also recognized that many people experienced economic hardships when they migrated to the cities in search of employment. He suggested the erection of public buildings to provide employment for those who came to the cities. Such places would provide some decent shelter and food. The only condition for living in those houses was to do some work and to be compensated with meals and lodging. Work could be provided until employment was found. Paine suggested that a small portion of their wages should be reserved and given to them when they leave the public buildings. Paine's plan of providing help in the public building was not punitive, as in some of the poorhouses suggested by others.

Robert Owen, the other social reformer, was a self-made wealthy person who strongly believed environment shaped human beings. Owen thought that better conditions produced better people. He was convinced that the poor could be changed by education and a good environment. Antipoverty policy can only be effective if it changes the habits and customs of the poor, the primary causes of poverty. Owen was a practical person who went beyond proposing changes. He implemented his ideas by starting model communities in both Britain and the United States. For example, in New Lanark where he owned a factory, Owen built decent homes for workers, established the first preschool nursery in Britain, and provided free schools for children between 5 and 10 years old. In addition, he reduced the work hours (from 17 to 10 hours per day) and increased the wages. He also increased the age below which children could not work. Owen's innovations were not adopted by other employers or by the government, to which he presented his ideas in the House of Commons.[34]

Owen thought that poverty-generating habits would be transmitted to succeeding generations.[35] His suggestions, therefore, included strategies to insulate the children of the poor from absorbing the bad habits of their parents. The most important such strategy established living arrangements whereby the parents would have limited contact with their children. He planned to establish separate living quarters for the parents and children and to provide them with a better environment so that they could acquire good habits.

> Each lodging-room is to accommodate a man, his wife, and two children under three years of age; and to be such as will permit them to have much more comfort than the dwellings of the poor usually afford. It is intended that the children above three years of age should attend the school, eat in the mess-room, and sleep in the dormitories, the parents being of course

---

34. The model community that he established in Indiana did not succeed.
35. Owen's ideas allude to a culture of poverty, discussed in Chapter 11.

permitted to see and converse with them at meals, and all other proper times. That before they leave school they shall be well instructed in all necessary and useful knowledge; that every possible means be adopted to prevent the acquirement of bad habits, from their parents or otherwise; that no pains be spared to impress upon them such habits and disposi- tions as may be most conducive to their happiness through life, as well as render them useful and valuable members of the community to which they belong.[36]

As stated, this book cannot fully exhaust all the views that various people have presented concerning the causes of poverty and what the appropriate policies should be. In fact, the people discussed herein are only a few of the many who had strong opinions about poverty and what to do about it. The point we want to emphasize is that suggestions as to how to deal with poverty depend on what the causes of poverty are believed to be.[37]

CRITICISMS OF POOR SUPPORT

One of the central concerns about helping the poor that has dominated antipoverty policy since the days of the early poor laws is that such help may result in more harm than good. It is frequently suggested that antipoverty policies, if not well designed, may increase poverty. In fact, the severest critics of U.S. welfare policy are not basically opposed to helping the poor; they consider welfare policies to be self defeating. Some researchers actually attribute the increased poverty in the United States to the current welfare system. But this view is not new. No time in history has yet to exist during which supporting the poor has not been criticized. Malthus and Ricardo presented reasons why they thought that poor sup- port should be abolished.

The most important criticism of public support for the poor concerns the effect that support has on work incentives. Researchers estimate the effect of public aid on labor supply. In addition, microeconomic tools demonstrate how individuals may choose to consume more leisure when their available choices include income support. Although these tools of analysis were not available to early writers, the arguments concerning the effects of public support on work incentives mirror present-day argu- ments. Basically, it has been long recognized that without requirement that recipients of public aid supply a certain number of hours of work in return

---

36. Robert Owen, *Report to the Committee of the Association for the Relief of the Manufacturing and Laboring Poor,* laid before the Committee of the House of Commons on Poor Laws (London, 1817).
37. Others who had important views about poverty and antipoverty policy include Edmund Burke, William Pitt, Frederick Eden, Jeremy Bentham, John Stuart Mill, and William Godwin. See Himmelfarb, *The Idea of Poverty: England in the Industrial Age.*

for the aid, many recipients will choose not to work and instead rely exclusively on such support. In addition, because work provides negative satisfaction, some people who are not poor may decide to stop working or to reduce the number of hours that they work in order to receive public support.

Benjamin Franklin strongly opposed colonial poor laws and called for their abolition primarily because of the effect on work effort. Franklin considered poverty to be of one's own making and that attempts to help the poor only encouraged laziness. Like Malthus and others who believed in the natural laws, Franklin considered the suffering of the poor to be inevitable punishment, and therefore, attempts to provide support to the poor were counterproductive because providing assistance was "fighting against the order of God and nature, which has perhaps appointed want and misery as the proper punishments for, and cautious against, as well as necessary consequences of, idleness and extravagance."[38] Franklin suggested that the best way to help the poor was to make them work in exchange for support.[39]

Many other early writers noted the disincentive effects associated with poor support. Thomas Cooper, writing in 1826 after reviewing the effect of aid to the poor in the United States and England, opposed such support on the grounds that it encouraged idleness.[40] Likewise, Willard Phillips, writing in 1828, noted that public support should be kept low so that the poor do not choose to depend entirely on such support. Others, such as John Hill Burton, suggested that because of the disincentive effects associated with poor support, provisions for relief should be subject to humiliation and restrictions particularly when provided to able-bodied poor.[41] The basic idea of providing support in workhouses was to discourage idleness. In the early nineteenth century United States, many poorhouses were associated with a farm where able-bodied poor were required to work. In various studies that were conducted in the early part of the nineteenth century, it was found that supporting the poor by making them work in agriculture was the cheapest and most effective method. On the other hand, supporting the poor in their own homes was expensive and subject to abuse since it encouraged laziness and dependency.

The other common criticism of poor support is its effect on the family. Early thinkers argued that support produced increased population, which propagated poverty. This was the primary criticism presented by Malthus

38. Cited from June Axinn and Hernam Levin, *Social Welfare: A History of the American Response to Need*, p. 20.
39. This is not much different from workfare proposals that are now common in the United States.
40. See Thomas Cooper, *Lectures on the Elements of Political Economy* (New York: Augustus M. Kelly, 1971). Cooper's work was first published in 1826.
41. See John Hill Burton, *Political and Social Economy: Its Practical Applications* (New York: Augustus M. Kelly Publishers, 1970). Burton's work was first published in 1844.

and Ricardo. Poor support distorted the natural increase of laborers by encouraging more births among the poor. In a comprehensive report on poor support in the United States during the early part of the nineteenth century, this fact was well recognized: "It is an axiom abundantly confirmed by experience, that in proportion to the means of support, provided for the poor and improvident, they are found to increase and multiply."[42] Cooper made a similar point, arguing that providing the poor with support increased the number of the poor without reference to the demand; the result was to increase the miseries of the poor as the numbers increase beyond the available food supply.[43]

In addition to the increased numbers, it has long been recognized that because public support relieves parents of the responsibility of rearing children, such support encourages having children out of wedlock. Some early writers attributed increased prostitution to the availability of poor support. To discourage such outcomes, early support policies were designed to discriminate against those who had illegitimate children. Today, increased numbers of out-of-wedlock births in the United States have become a serious problem. Some proposals call for punitive measures to mothers who have more than a certain number of children.

Another criticism of poor support that has been mentioned by many writers is that once programs are established, they continue to expand. This, in turn, means that taxes must be increased regularly to meet the welfare budget. Today, many politicians and economists view the problem of government growth as primarily a consequence of the growth of the welfare state. Public choice theorists criticize the welfare state mainly because of its effects on government growth.

SUMMARY

This chapter has reviewed some of the early ideas about poverty and the various approaches used to help the poor. Although the review is not comprehensive, it does show that societies have always been concerned about their less fortunate members. We also find that the opinions about poor support have always been diverse; antipoverty policy has always been controversial.

This chapter has examined poor support policies in England since the enaction of the 1601 Poor Law. We have discussed some of the changes that necessitated reform and the adoption of the New Poor Law of 1834. It was observed that since the first poor laws, some of the issues that have been important in the design of antipoverty policies have included con-

---

42. *The Almshouse Experience,* "Report of the Committee Appointed by the Board of the Poor, City and District of Philadelphia," p. 25.
43. The tone of these criticisms of poor support suggest Malthusian influence.

cerns on the effects of supporting the poor. For these reasons the poor were classified into categories (such as deserving and nondeserving). Conditions, for eligibility such as residency requirements, the type of support (whether cash or in-kind), or whether support was provided indoors or outdoors were all important features of the support system that was designed to minimize the unintended consequences.

This chapter also reviewed some of the natural laws views of Adam Smith, Thomas Malthus, and David Ricardo in relation to poverty. Natural law philosophers advocated minimum government intervention in supporting poor and in some cases total abolition of poor support. This text also reviewed the position of social reformers Thomas Paine and Robert Owen, who viewed poverty as a result of the institutional setting and not due to the shortcomings of the poor. Proposals suggested by social reformers were for more government intervention.

The discussion in this chapter shows that poor support policies change over time. Economic circumstances, population growth, wars, and changes in the method of production affect the policies used to support the poor. Policies that may be adequate now may not be appropriate later. In addition, because different groups in society have varying interests, poor support depends largely on the political power that the various interest groups command.

As discussed in later chapters, the American welfare system is under attack from various sides. The discussion in this chapter demonstrates that such criticisms of supporting the poor are not new. The criticisms depend on what various analysts believe to be the causes of poverty and the effects of the welfare programs. This suggests that it is necessary not only to investigate the true causes of poverty, but also to seek evidence as to the effects of welfare policies. Such an approach will provide a balanced assessment of the problem and consequently help formulate balanced public policies.

STUDY AND DISCUSSION QUESTIONS

1. Discuss the following as they relate to early poor laws.

   (a) Workhouse

   (b) Speenhamland system

   (c) Passing out

   (d) Indenture and indenture contracting

   (e) Residency requirements

   (f) Apprenticeship

2. The antipoverty policies one proposes largely depend on what one considers to be the causes of poverty. Demonstrate this point by discussing the views of the early philosophers and the policies that they recommended.

3. Compare and contrast the views of Adam Smith, Thomas Malthus, and David Ricardo, and those of Thomas Paine and Robert Owen. Consider the issues of poverty and poverty policy.

4. Throughout history, policies to support the poor have faced opposition for various reasons. Using historical and contemporary examples, explain the reasons provided for opposing poor support. What is your opinion of these criticisms? Are they justified or not?

5. Ask a number of your friends to tell you what they think of the poor. For example, ask them to tell you why they think some people are poor and their opinions about supporting the poor. How different are their views from those of social philosophers discussed in this chapter?

6. There seems to have always been an emphasis on making a distinction between *deserving* and *nondeserving* poor. Do you think that this distinction is necessary? Consider various groups of poor people in the United States. Which group(s) would you consider deserving and which group(s) would you consider nondeserving? Explain how you make the distinction.

7. You have been asked to design policies to deal with the poor in your community. Your task is to suggest several policies that will target the deserving poor and the nondeserving poor. Outline the policies you would suggest for the two groups. Note that you should start by explaining how you made the distinction between the groups.

ADDITIONAL READINGS

1. Blaug, Mark. "The Myth of the Old Poor Law and the Making of the New," *Journal of Economic History* 23 (1963): 151–84.

2. Crowther, M. A. *The Workhouse System 1834–1929: The History of an English Social Institution.* Athens, Ga.: University of Georgia Press, 1982.

3. De Schweinitz, Karl. *England's Road to Social Security.* Philadelphia, Pa.: University of Pennsylvania Press, 1943.

4. Fraser, Derek, ed. *The New Poor Law in the Nineteenth Century.* New York: St. Martin's Press, 1976.

5. Inglis, Brian. *Men of Conscience.* New York: MacMillan Company, 1971.

6. Oxley, Geoffrey W. *Poor Relief in England and Wales 1601–1834.* North Pomfret, Vt.: David and Charles, 1974.

7. Stein, Bruno. *On Relief: The Economics of Poverty and Public Welfare.* New York: Basic Books, 1971.

4

INEQUALITY IN THE
DISTRIBUTION OF INCOME

Thus far, the text has invoked terms such as *income distribution, inequality, poor,* and *poverty* without specifically defining what is meant by those terms. Although the reader may have a fairly good idea of what is meant by inequality and poverty, more precise definitions are essential. It is necessary to use measures that reveal inequality of the distribution of income or the extent of poverty. Because perceptions of what "poor" or "inequality" mean differ from one person to another, some objective measures of inequality and poverty must be used.

Although poverty and inequality have not been explicitly defined, the discussions in the previous chapters implicitly suggest that reduction in poverty and inequality are valued social goals. There are some normative judgments concerning poverty and inequality on which most people in the society agree. For example, most people would agree that more equality in the distribution of income is preferable to less, other things remaining equal. Also, virtually all people agree that existence of very poor people and very rich people in the same society is not socially desirable. Thus, societies would be better off if policies were implemented that reduced the extent of poverty and inequality. These normative judgments influence the type of policies that are adopted.

From a public policy perspective, we are interested in being able to evaluate whether particular policies reduce or increase poverty and inequality. Thus, it is important to understand how poverty and income inequality are defined and measured. This chapter deals with measurement of income inequality. In Chapter 5, issues of poverty definition and measurement are discussed. Note at the outset that defining and measuring poverty and inequality are not simple tasks and the discussion presented in this book is by no means comprehensive. Only the basic issues that are necessary for the student to appreciate discussions of poverty and antipoverty policy are presented.

MEASURES OF INCOME INEQUALITY

To more clearly comprehend the meaning and definition of poverty, it is necessary that one understand the way income is distributed in society. The distribution of income in society changes over time and such changes have implications about poverty levels in society. As a practical matter, it is impossible to separate the problem of poverty from issues of inequality. Statements such as "the rich get richer while the poor get poorer" imply changes in income inequality. As has been evident from recent presidential elections, society is concerned about how different public policies affect the distribution of income in the economy. In virtually all tax and spending proposals, legislatures at all levels of government often dwell on how such policies affect the state of income distribution. One reason why reducing capital gains taxes has generated a heated debate in the United States Congress is precisely that such a tax reduction is perceived as increasing the income of the more affluent members of society, and consequently causing inequality in the distribution of income to increase. A natural starting point for the study of poverty is with a discussion of the state of income distribution. This, in turn, requires an understanding of how inequality in the distribution of income is measured.

Measuring income distribution serves several purposes. First, one central goal of redistributive policies is to affect the state of income distribution by narrowing the gap between the poor and the rich. By comparing income inequality over time, policy makers are able to evaluate the effectiveness of such public policies in improving the well-being of the poor relative to the rich. Measures of income distribution also are used as a basis for designing a relative measure of poverty.

There are several measures of income inequality that have been proposed and some of them are widely used. Some of the measures are easier to compute while others are much more difficult to compute. Also, while no measure is perfect, some measures are better than others, and some measures may be more appropriate for particular tasks than others. In using a particular measure of inequality, it is necessary that one understand what that measure means and what the advantages and shortcomings are of using that measure. In general, each measure of inequality should be evaluated in terms of three basic features that are necessary for a good measure of inequality.

First, a good measure should embody a reasonable notion of *inequality*. Inequality exists whenever one person has more income than some other person in the society. If transfers are made from one person to another, a good measure of income inequality should capture the changes in inequality. Hugh Dalton suggested that measures of inequality should increase whenever income is transferred from a poorer person to a richer person regardless of how poor or how rich or the amount transferred.[1] In general, a transfer from a poor (rich) person to a richer (poorer) person should result in an increase (decrease) in inequality. This is known as the *principle of transfers.*[2]

Second, a good measure of inequality should permit comparisons across countries and over time. This requires the measure to be unit free.[3] Thus, the measure should not be affected by units (such as people, households, income measures) that are used to compute the measure. For example, a good measure should not be affected if income is measured in terms of dollars, yen, or shillings.

Finally, a condition for a good measure of inequality is that it should be bounded. An example of a bounded measure is one that is equal to zero when all individuals have identical incomes and have positive values as inequality increases up to some maximum value, for example, one for perfect inequality.

In interpreting measures of inequality, it is important to be clear what is meant by income and to whom the distribution refers. This text focuses on the distribution of income as opposed to wealth.[4] It follows the definition of income as used by the Bureau of the Census and includes mainly receipts from wages and salaries, net income from self-employment, dividends, interest earnings, income from royalties, and net rental income. The definition of income also includes cash transfers from the government such as social security, Aid to Families with Dependent Children (AFDC), and other public assistance and security income. The measure of income excludes fringe benefits and income-in-kind (such as free meals and housing), and also excludes in-kind transfers (such as food stamps and other government services).

This text discusses measures of income inequality with a focus on families. Many measures of inequality deal with households and families and it is therefore necessary that the reader be familiar with the difference between these two units. A household includes all persons occupying a residential unit. Members of a household could be a single person, a family, or unrelated individuals. A family includes two or more persons related by blood, adoption, or marriage, and who reside together. The key difference in terms of the inequality measures is that in most cases, families

1. Hugh Dalton, "The Measurement of the Inequality of Incomes," Economic Journal 30 (1920): 348–61.
2. The principle of transfers also is referred to as the Pigou–Dalton condition. Although several measures of inequality satisfy this principle, some measures are more sensitive to transfers than others.
3. Another term for unit free is scale invariant.
4. Income is a flow concept and measures current receipts while wealth is a stock concept that measures the total of an individual's access to resources at a particular time.

share consumption, but not all households do. Because families and households include different groups of people, inequality measures differ depending on which unit is used.[5]

For this text's purposes, only a few measures of income inequality are discussed: the coefficient of variation, quintile shares, the Lorenz curve and the Gini coefficient.

Coefficient of Variation

Figure 4-1 shows the distribution of families based on their money incomes in 1989 for the United States. The figure shows that there is a wide dispersion in the distribution of money incomes. A useful concept in the discussion of income distribution, and one that is used in the definition of relative poverty is the median income. In 1989, the median income was $34,213. This means that one-half of all families had incomes below that income level and one-half above.

We can compute a statistical measure of inequality from the data used to construct Figure 4-1. If all families had the same income, then they would be clustered at that level of income. As the distribution in incomes becomes more unequal, there is more dispersion in the frequency distribution, implying more variation. One can therefore use the degree of dispersion to measure inequality. A simple measure of inequality is the Coefficient of Variation (CV) which is the standard deviation (SD) of the frequency distribution divided by the mean (M). The CV is unit free and varies between 0 and infinity. To give the coefficient of variation an upper bound, it is common to express the measure of inequality as $CV/(CV + 1)$.

The coefficient of variation is sensitive to transfers at all income levels. However, it is more sensitive to changes that occur in the upper income ranges.

Quintile Shares

Another method that illustrates the state of income distribution, and one that more clearly shows the changes in the distribution of income over time, divides the population into income groups and examines the share of income received by different segments. The most common method divides families into quintiles as shown in Table 4-1.

---

5. The purpose herein is to present measures of inequality and to investigate the degree of inequality in the United States. Although there are some differences in the degree of inequality depending on whether the unit of measure is households or families, such differences do not alter the basic trends and analysis of inequality in general.

Figure 4-1   Frequency distribution of family income, 1989

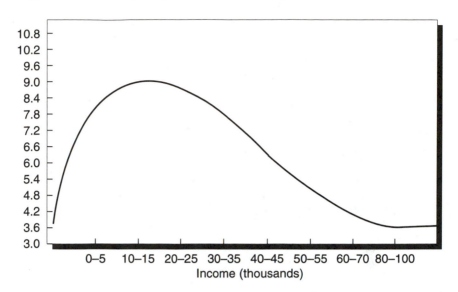

Income (thousands)

Several points can be made about income distribution. First, there is a large inequality in the distribution of income with the lowest group in the economic strata receiving a very small proportion of national income while the richest group receives a large proportion. In 1989, the lowest fifth received only 3.8 percent of national income; the richest fifth, 46.8 percent. Secondly, while the share of national income received by the different groups has changed over time, the changes have been slow. These changes have most affected the richest 5 percent. Thus, while this group received 30 percent of national income in 1929, the group received 18.9 percent in 1989. This change was primarily due to the Great Depression that wiped out a large fraction of wealth and thus reduced the income derived from wealth by the richest group. Since the 1940s, however, the share of national income received by the richest 5 percent has changed very little. The share of income received by the two lowest quintile was 13 percent in 1929, but increased to 17 percent after the Great Depression. In 1989, these two groups received 13.3 percent of national income.[6]

---

6. It also is important to note that income inequalities vary widely across states. The greatest inequalities are in the sourthern states. Nevertheless, there has been a more rapid decrease in income inequality in the South than in other parts of the country in the last few decades.

Table 4-1   Income distribution in the United States, 1929–1989, selected years (in percent)

Family income by Quintiles[a]	1929	1950	1960	1970	1980	1985	1989
Lowest fifth	—	5	5	4.1	4.2	4.0	3.8
Second fifth	13[b]	12	12	10.8	10.2	9.8	9.5
Third fifth	14	17	18	17.4	16.8	16.3	15.8
Fourth fifth	19	23	24	24.5	24.8	24.4	24.0
Highest fifth	54	43	41	43.3	44.1	45.6	46.8
Total all families	100	100	100	100	100	100	100
Top 5 percent	30	17	16	16.6	16.5	17.6	18.9

[a]Family income represents pretax income and includes only cash transfers but not in-kind transfers.

[b]This number includes lowest fifth and second fifth.

Source: U.S. Bureau of the Census, *Statistical Abstract of the United States*, Washington, D.C.: U. S. Government Printing Office, various issues; U.S. Bureau of the Census, *Current Population Reports*, Series O-60, No. 72, "Money Income and Poverty Status of Families and Persons in the United States: 1988 and 1989."

The Lorenz Curve and Gini Coefficient

Inequality in the distribution of income as reflected by the quintile shares also can be shown by the use of a Lorenz curve drawn in Figure 4-2. This curve plots the cumulative percent of total income received against the cumulative percent of the nation's families who receive that income. If income were distributed uniformly across all families, then such a distribution would be represented by the straight line OE. This implies that the poorest 20 percent of the families receive 20 percent of national income; the poorest 40 percent receive 40 percent; and so forth. From the data in Table 4-1, it is evident that income is not distributed equally. The bottom 20 percent of families received only 3.8 percent of national income in 1989. This is shown as point A. The lowest 40 percent (the lowest 20 percent plus the next 20 percent) of families received 13.3 percent (3.8 percent received by the poorest 20 percent plus 9.5 percent received by the next 20 percent) of national income as shown in point B. Points C, D, and E show the income

Figure 4-2   The Lorenz curve, 1989

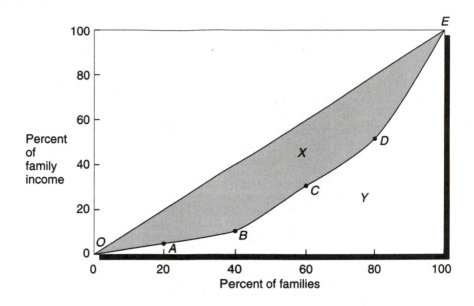

received by 60 percent, 80 percent, and 100 percent of families, respectively. Joining the points of the actual distribution yields what is called a Lorenz curve.

The straight line *OE* is the line of perfect equality. The closer the Lorenz curve is to the line of perfect equality, the more equal is the distribution of income. As income inequality increases, the Lorenz curve moves farther away from the line of perfect equality. Therefore, the more unequal the distribution of income, the larger will be the area between the Lorenz curve and the line of perfect equality. The opposite extreme to perfect equality is perfect inequality—if all income were received by one household. In this case, the Lorenz curve would follow the horizontal baseline and the right-hand side vertical baseline (*OFE*). Perfect equality and perfect inequality are largely hypothetical and only useful for making comparisons with the actual distribution.

The degree of inequality also can be measured numerically by a Gini coefficient. The Gini coefficient (also called the Gini ratio or the Gini Index) is the ratio of the area between the line of perfect equality and the Lorenz curve (shown as shaded areas *X* in Figure 4-2) to the total area under the line of perfect equality (sum of area *X* and *Y*).[7] Remember that

---

7. The idea that the extent of inequality in a society can be measured by the ratio of the area between the Lorenz curve and the line of perfect equality was first proposed by Corrado Gini in 1912, hence the name Gini Index.

as inequality increases, the Lorenz curve bows outward. In the extreme case of perfect inequality, the Gini coefficient equals one. The Gini coefficient equals zero in the case of perfect equality. As mentioned, these two cases are extremes and the Gini coefficient always will fall somewhere between these two extremes.[8] The Gini Index is sensitive to transfers, but is more sensitive to changes that occur within the middle ranges of the income distribution than those that occur among the very poor or the very rich groups.

The Gini coefficient is a useful tool for comparing changes in the distribution of income over time or for comparing the state of income distribution in different countries or regions. When one talks about inequality as having increased over a given period of time, we are implying that the Gini coefficient has increased. Likewise, countries that have more equal distribution of income (planned economies) have lower values of the Gini coefficient than those countries where income distribution is more unequal (such as in market-oriented economies). Figure 4-3 plots the Gini coefficients for the United States for families incomes for the period 1947 to 1989. Notice that the Gini coefficient increased for most of the years since 1967, implying increased inequality.

Although useful for some purposes, the Gini coefficient should be interpreted with caution when making judgments as to whether the state of income distribution is good or bad. For example, is lower inequality in the distribution of income in the former Soviet Union or China better than the relatively high inequality in the United States? Are individuals in different countries with similar distributions of income equally well off? What is a good or a bad state of income distribution? Because there is no "right" standard or "ideal" income distribution, judgments based on such comparisons are meaningless. Similarly, although we can state that the income inequality has decreased or increased in the United States, such statements are positive statements and do not necessary entail normative implications unless one has defined a certain degree of inequality as the one which is socially optimal. Deviations from this optimal could then be a basis for making judgments about good or bad states of income distribution.[9]

----

8. For a more detailed discussion of the measurement of income inequality, see Michael Taussig, *Alternative Measure of the Distribution of Economic Welfare* (Princeton, N. J.: Princeton University Press, 1973); and Martin Brofenbrenner, *Income Distribution Theory* (Chicago: Aldine-Atherton, 1971).

9. Two other important measures of inequality which we do not discuss here and which the student who wants to do more research in the area of inequality should review are Theil's Index of Inequality and Atkinson's measure of inequality. Both of these measures are more widely used in the Economic Development literature. See A. B. Atkinson, "On the Measurement of Equality," *Journal of Economic Theory* 2 (1970): 244–63; A. B. Atkinson, *Wealth and Inequality* (Harmondsworth, England: Penguin Books, 1973); A. B. Atkinson, *The Economics of Inequality* (Oxford: The Clarendon Press, 1975); and H. Theil, *Economics and Information Theory* (Amsterdam: North-Holland Publishing Company, 1867).

Figure 4-3   Gini coefficient of family income: 1947–1989

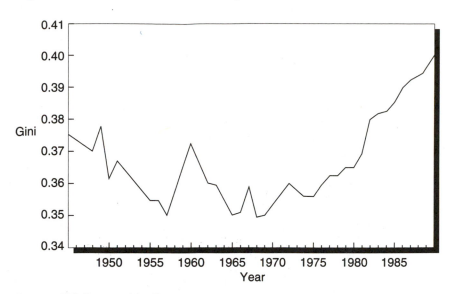

Source: U.S. Bureau of the Census.

ADDITIONAL ISSUES IN THE MEASUREMENT OF INEQUALITY

There also are several factors that affect income distribution and that are not captured by the data used previously. These factors make some adjustments necessary. Among the more important considerations include: life cycle income inequality, number of income earners in a household, the role of noncash transfers, and the use of wealth vs. income in the calculation of inequality. Each of these issues will be discussed.

Life Cycle Income Inequality–A large part of the dispersion in income among primary earners originates from differences in age. Young adults may only work part time and spend most of the other time investing in human capital. Conversely, individuals between the ages of 40 and 55 earn high incomes because of accumulated experience and because they work full time. After the peak earning years, individuals experience reduced earnings upon retirement. When income inequality is calculated using earnings for only one particular year, inequality is higher than if based on lifetime or age-adjusted earnings.

Morton Paglin has suggested a measure of income inequality that considers an individual's earnings over his or her life cycle.[10] Paglin's coefficient,

---

10. Morton Paglin, "The Measurement and Trend of Inequality: A Basic Revision," *American Economic Review,* Vol. 65 (4) (September 1975): 598–609.

like the Gini coefficient, takes on values from zero to 1, with a coefficient of zero indicating perfect equality of lifetime earnings, while a coefficient equal to 1 implies perfect inequality of lifetime earnings. While the Gini coefficient was 0.378 in 1947, the Paglin coefficient was .303 in the same year. More noticeable, while both coefficients declined from 1947 to 1972, the Gini coefficient declined by only 5 percent to .359 and the Paglin coefficient declined by 21 percent to .239.

The Gini coefficient may have failed to capture the decrease in income inequality because of the increase in educational levels attained by income earners over time, which has produced steeper earning profiles. Such an increase in education attainment increases the Gini coefficient, although no apparent increase in inequality of lifetime earnings may have taken place. Thus, it may be much better to use the Paglin Index.

Number of Earners–Income inequality responds to the average number of income earners in a household. Households with two primary income earners have (other things remaining constant) a higher median income than households with only one income earner. Over the past few decades, there has been a marked increase in the labor force participation rates of females, resulting in more households having two income earners. As expected, the labor force participation rates of women from low-income households has been much higher than that of women from high-income households. Such trends reduce the inequality of family income.[11] To some extent, this effect is neutralized by the phenomenon of *assortative mating*— high-income females tend to marry high-income males.[12] In addition, there has been an increase in single-female-headed households, which results in more inequality.

Noncash Transfers–The use of earned income and other cash transfers in the calculation of income inequality seriously underestimates the resources that individuals, particularly those in low-income quintiles, receive in the form of noncash transfers. As noted, measures of income inequality use a definition of income that excludes noncash transfers such as food stamps, medicaid, and public housing. Edgar Browning provides evidence suggesting that the inclusion of in-kind transfers increases the share of income received by the poorest 20 percent of the population significantly.[13] Therefore, the inclusion of in-kind transfers reduces the degree of income inequality. Thus, a good measure of inequality should include noncash benefits.

---

11. See David Betson and Jacques von der Gaag, "Working Married Women and the Distribution of Income," *Journal of Human Resources* 19 (4) (Fall 1984): 532–43.

12. See Gary S. Becker, *A Treatise on the Family* (Cambridge, Mass.: Harvard University Press, 1981).

13. Edgar Browning, "The Trend Toward Equality in the Distribution of Net Income," *Southern Economic Journal*, Vol. 43 (1), (July 1976): 912–23.

Wealth vs. Income–If the concern in measuring inequality was to measure the ability of individuals, families, and households to consume goods and services, then wealth or net worth should be used rather than income. Although the distribution of wealth has become more equal over recent decades,[14] the distribution of wealth is far more unequal than the distribution of income. Table 4-2 shows the distribution of wealth in the United States from 1922 through 1972, the last year for which data of this type are available. In 1922, the top 1 percent of wealth holders owned 31.6 percent of all personal wealth in the United States. Although this share has declined, this group still owned 20.7 percent of all personal wealth in 1972. A more recent study found that the concentration of wealth has actually increased.[15] This study found that in 1983, the top 1 percent of wealth holders owned 34 percent of all wealth in the United States. Estimates suggest that one-fifth of all assets and one-third of financial assets are owned by families in the top one-half percent of the income distribution, and half of all wealth is owned by families in the top 10 percent of the income distribution.

Table 4-2   Share of personal wealth owned by top 1 percent of wealth holders, 1922–1972, selected years

Year	*Percent Owned by Top 1 Percent*
1922	31.6
1929	36.3
1933	28.3
1939	30.6
1945	23.2
1949	20.8
1953	24.3
1956	26.0
1958	23.8
1962	22.0
1965	23.4
1969	20.1
1972	20.7

Source: U.S. Bureau of the Census, *Statistical Abstract of the United States* (Washington, D.C.: U. S. Government Printing Office, 1979).

---

14. See, for example, Lee Soltow, *Distribution of Wealth and Income in the United States in 1798* (Pittsburgh, Pa.: Pittsburgh University Press, 1989).
15. U.S. Congress, Joint Economic Committee, "The Concentration of Wealth in the United States" (July 1986), Table 4.

The factors just discussed should be considered when one evaluates the meaning of Gini coefficient or the other measures of income distribution. Failure to take into account those factors will result either in overstating or understating the true magnitude of inequalities.

INEQUALITY AND POVERTY

Increasing inequality in the distribution of income (as has been the case in the United States over the last two decades) is of concern. However, it is important not to confuse increasing inequality as implying increasing poverty. Likewise, decreasing inequality does not necessarily imply decreasing poverty. Understanding how inequality relates to poverty is important.

Figure 4-4 plots the income distribution in a country for two years: year 1 and year 2. The horizontal axis measures money income in constant dollars and the vertical axis measures the number of families receiving a certain level of income. The main difference is that in year 2 the country has experienced economic growth as compared to year 1. Also, there is more dispersion in the distribution of income in year 2 than in year 1. Thus, there is more inequality in the distribution of income in year 2 than in year 1. An additional assumption is made that the political process has established a certain level of income P as the poverty threshold. That is, families with incomes below P are considered poor and those with incomes above P are nonpoor.

As noted, there is more inequality in year 2. However, the population that has income less than P is lower in year 2 than in year 1. In this case, economic growth and increased inequality are accompanied by a reduction in poverty.

The foregoing result critically depends on the definition of poverty. It has been assumed that the poverty threshold income is fixed and therefore does not change when a country experiences economic growth. Suppose another approach is adopted whereby the poverty income is set at 50 percent of the median income. Panels (a) and (b) of Figure 4-5 show the distributions shown in Figure 4-4. M_1 is the median income in year 1 and M_2 is the median income in year 2. Thus, P_1 and P_2 are the poverty threshold incomes in year 1 and year 2, respectively. Note that both P_1 and P_2 are set at 50 percent of the median income. Based on the assumed distributions, the population of poor is much lower in year 1 than in year 2. In this case, economic inequality also is accompanied with an increase in the poor population. Notice that a large number of poor in year 2 are much better off than some of those classified as nonpoor in year 1.

Thus, although inequality and poverty are related, care should be taken in making inferences about poverty from the degree of inequality.

Figure 4-4   Inequality and poverty

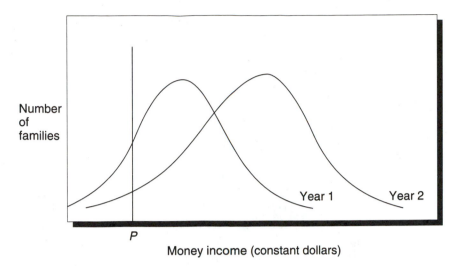

Money income (constant dollars)

However, the discussion shows that the poverty level depends on how one defines poverty, an issue discussed in Chapter 5.

SUMMARY

How income is distributed in a society has important implications on poverty and poverty policy. Increasing inequality means that those with lower incomes are relatively worse off as compared to those who have higher incomes. Thus, the degree of inequality can be used to illustrate the well-being of the poor relative to that of the well-off. If more equality and less poverty are valued social goals, then understanding how income is distributed in society is an important guide for formulating public policy.

This chapter has discussed the meaning and measurement of income inequality. It has outlined some of the main characteristics of a good measure of inequality. Measures should be sensitive to transfers, bounded, and unit free. In measuring inequality, it also is important to make a distinction between income and wealth and between households and families. Measures of inequality discussed in the chapter include the coefficient of variation, quintile shares, the Lorenz curve, and the Gini coefficient. Some data are presented showing the trend in the inequality in the United States using the Gini Index. The evidence suggests that income inequality has been increasing since the late 1960s.

The chapter also discussed some additional issues that should be taken

Figure 4-5   Inequality and poverty

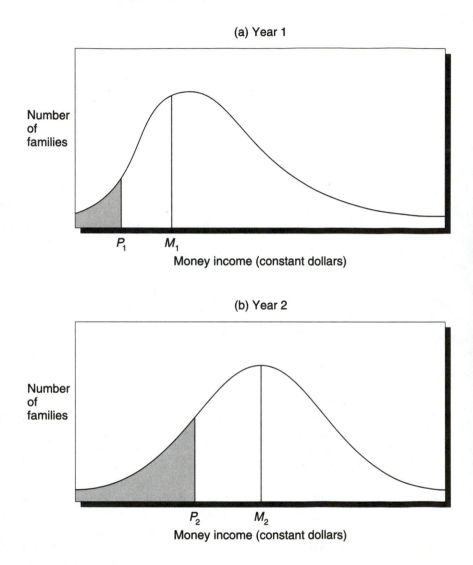

(a) Year 1

Number
of
families

P_1 M_1
Money income (constant dollars)

(b) Year 2

Number
of
families

P_2 M_2
Money income (constant dollars)

into account in measuring and interpreting measures of inequality. In this connection, we have discussed the role of earning over the life cycle, number of earners, and noncash transfers. The chapter also discussed the difference between inequality in the distribution of income and inequality in the distribution of wealth.

The last section of the chapter attempted to show the relationship between poverty and inequality. It was demonstrated that increasing inequality may be accompanied by increasing or decreasing inequality.

The main point of the discussion made is that the incidence of poverty depends on how one defines poverty. Defining and measuring poverty is the main focus of the next chapter.

STUDY AND DISCUSSION QUESTIONS

1. Discuss and explain three characteristics of a good measure of inequality.

2. (a) Using the appropriate diagram, show how a Lorenz curve is constructed. Label the axis.

   (b) Income inequality has increased in the United States. Using the Lorenz curve in 2(a), show how you can demonstrate such an increase in inequality.

   (c) Using the diagram in 2(a), explain how you calculate the Gini Index. What happens to this index when inequality increases?

3. Discuss the various measures of income inequality.

4. Write a paragraph on each of the following in relation to measurement of inequality:
   (a) Paglin Index
   (b) Wealth vs. income
   (c) Inclusion of noncash benefits
   (d) Number of income earners

5. Distinguish between increase in inequality and increase in poverty.

6. Income is more equally distributed in Sweden than in the United States. List several factors that could explain this outcome.

7. Is the increasing inequality in the United States bad? Qualify your answer.

8. There are wide differences in inequality across states. For example, inequality in the state of Mississippi is much higher than in Wisconsin. Discuss why you could expect inequality to vary across states.

9. Economists often talk about inequality as a necessary and beneficial outcome in a market economy. What do they mean? Why do you think they are or are not correct?

10. What is the difference between equality of outcomes and equality of opportunities? Is it possible to have one without the other? Explain.

ADDITIONAL READINGS

1. Dovring, Folke. *Inequality: The Political Economy of Income Distribution*. New York: Praeger Publishers, 1991.

2. Maxwell, Nan L. *Income Inequality in the United States, 1947–1985*. New York: Greenwood Press, 1990.

3. Osberg, Lars. *Economic Inequality in the United States*. Armonk, N.Y.: M. E. Sharpe, 1984.

4. Osberg, Lars, ed. *Economic Inequality and Poverty: International Perspective*. Armonk, N.Y.: M. E. Sharpe, 1991.

5. Williamson, Jeffrey G. and Peter H. Lindert. *American Inequality: A Macroeconomic History*. New York: Academic Press, 1980.

5

EXTENT, COMPOSITION, AND CAUSES OF POVERTY IN THE UNITED STATES

Most people readily admit that poverty exists in the United States, one of the wealthiest countries in the world. Disagreements arise as to what proportion of the population actually is poor. Wider differences of opinions emerge concerning the causes of poverty. Differences in perceptions concerning how many people are poor and what causes poverty entangle discussions about poverty policy in politics. The rather wide variations in the types of antipoverty policies enacted by different administrations in the United States largely reflect differences in how politicians view the problem of poverty.

Poverty means different things to different people. Researchers across disciplines have different perspectives on what poverty is. Even in the same discipline, however, differences exist as to how poverty should be defined. Mollie Orshansky, who has done some of the significant work on definition and measurement of poverty, states that "poverty, like beauty, lies in the eye of the beholder."[1] Martin Brofenbrenner states that poverty is like an ugly person, "easier to recognize than to define."[2] From the economic perspective, poverty commonly implies a lack of resources—money or material possessions that are necessary for individuals or households to consume goods and services above a certain subsistence level. Generally, the minimum level of goods and services that comprise the subsistence level is subjective. Although many people would agree that the subsistence level should include items such as food with a certain daily caloric and nutritional value, housing that meets some minimal standards, some level of health care, clothing, and such basic goods and services, no agreement exists as to what quantities and qualities of these items comprise the subsistence level of living. Thus, while one may define poverty as a lack of

1. Mollie Orshansky, "How Poverty Is Measured," Perspectives on Poverty Symposium, *Monthly Labor Review* 92 (2) (February 1969): 37–41.
2. Martin Brofenbrenner, *Income Distribution Theory* (Chicago: Aldine-Atherton, 1971), p. 38.

resources, determining the amount of resources below which one is considered poor is not a simple matter.

The concept of poverty also includes what society perceives as acceptable. Harry Johnson, for example, defines poverty as existing when the resources of families or individuals are inadequate to provide a socially acceptable standard of living.[3] Such a view of poverty could be based on comparisons between individuals in society. A relative definition raises the question as to how low the income received by those in the lowest economic strata should the society consider to be acceptable. This level may have little to do with the amount required to meet certain needs, but rather it is more dependent on the degree of disparities in society. Thus, while the concept of poverty does include a certain level of income or spending power, it also has a relative as well as an absolute meaning.[4]

Defining poverty is not an easy task and measuring it is even more difficult. In this chapter, the definitions and the measurement of poverty are discussed followed by a brief look at the extent of poverty in the United States as officially defined. A brief discussion of alternative measures of poverty also is presented. The last section of the chapter studies the composition and causes of poverty. Subsequent chapters investigate the causes of poverty in more detail.

POVERTY: DEFINITION, MEASUREMENT, AND EXTENT

Good measures of poverty serve several purposes. First, such a measure provides information on the extent of deprivation in the society. Before policy makers can propose policies to deal with poverty, it is necessary to have a good idea as to the extent of that problem. Second, measuring poverty accurately also is important because we need to evaluate the effectiveness of antipoverty policies by observing what happens to the level of poverty after particular programs are implemented. Third, poverty measures are useful

---

3. Harry G. Johnson, "Unemployment and Poverty," in Leo Fishman, ed., *Poverty Amid Affluence* (New Haven, Conn.: Yale University Press, 1966), pp. 182–99.
4. In addition to these concepts of poverty which key on a subsistence level of living and on inequality in society, some researchers have suggested a concept where poverty is viewed as an externality because of its consequences to other members of the society. Smolensky suggests that the poverty line should serve "as an index of the disutility to the community of the persistence of poverty." See Eugene Smolensky, "Investment in the Education of the Poor: A Pessimistic Report," *American Economic Review* 56 (2) (May 1966): 370–78. The sociological view of poverty not only considers poverty in terms of resources necessary to enable an individual to consume a certain level of goods and services, but also considers the social aspects associated with being poor. Jackson, for example, defines poverty as inadequate social functioning which not only includes not having gainful employment, but also the inability to maintain a household and inability to get involved in satisfying personal and social relationships. See Dudley Jackson, Poverty (New York: MacMillan Company,

for making comparisons across groups. Such comparisons are important when designing antipoverty policies that target particular groups of people or regions.

Although there is agreement that good measures of poverty are critical to the design of public policy, there is no clear agreement as to how poverty should be measured. Although most discussions of poverty refer to the official poverty rate, there is no reason to believe that this is the best measure of poverty. In fact, the correct poverty measure may depend on the particular purpose that we have for the measure.

What Is Poverty?

There are two main ways of defining poverty. The first definition considers poverty as the lack of resources to consume a certain bundle of goods and services. Such a bundle of goods may contain what could be considered an objective minimum, which includes basic necessities. A definition of poverty that sets a certain minimum level of consumption or resources yields what is called *absolute poverty*. The second definition places more weight on relative comparisons of various groups in society. Such a definition results in what is called *relative poverty*. A third, more recent, and less widely used way of defining poverty asks individuals to evaluate their own sense of well-being. Poverty measures derived from such an approach yields what is called *subjective poverty*.

Absolute poverty–The absolute poverty definition starts by establishing a certain minimum level of goods and services. Families and individuals who do not have resources to purchase this minimum bundle of goods and services are then considered poor. In its simplest form, the minimum level of consumption could include items such as food of a certain caloric value, and some form of shelter. After establishing what should be included in the minimum level of consumption, then the income necessary to purchase the goods and services can be established using the prevailing market prices. Thus, when one considers poverty in the absolute sense, the discussion centers on those people who lack resources to obtain some objective minimum level of consumption.

Although an absolute poverty measure is appealing, particularly when policy makers are interested in ensuring that all citizens consume basic goods and services, the concept of an objective minimum is itself arbitrary. What exactly should be included as part of this objective minimum? Years ago, electricity would not have been considered part of the objective minimum, while today it would. Should we also include a microwave, telephone, television, or a car? In sum, such a minimum is arbitrary and largely subjective.

Even if we could agree on a certain minimum bundle of goods and services, such a minimum may not be relevant over time, even when we adjust for changes in prices. Changes in consumption patterns cause the absolute minimum to change. Failure to consider the changing consumption patterns may lead to an exaggeration of the well-being of the poor. Another problem is that an objective minimum may differ across different groups in society. The elderly's minimum bundle of goods and services may be quite different from that for young children.

Absolute poverty also has been defined by the *appropriate maximum*, which refers to the maximum proportion of income that a family spends on certain subsistence goods.[5] For example, if families spend more than one-third of their income on food, then they might be considered poor. Other maximum definitions consider the amount of income that should be spent on certain basic needs such as housing, food, health care, and so forth. Families that spend more than the specified maximum share of their income on those goods and services are then considered poor.[6]

Relative Poverty–Relative definitions of poverty consider not only the ability to consume a certain minimum, but also compare the welfare of those with the lowest amount of resources with others in the society. The simplest such definitions consider the bottom 10, 15, or 20 percent of the income distribution as poor. Other researchers define poverty as below a certain percentage of the median income. The 50 percent of median income threshold discussed in Chapter 4 is an example of a relative measure of poverty.

Relative measures of poverty have some advantages in comparing the well-being of those with the fewest resources with other members of society because a relative measure takes into consideration changes in living standards. On the other hand, a relative definition of poverty poses serious problems, particularly in policy implementation. Consider a median income of $12,000 in one year and a median income of $20,000 in some later year. If relative poverty is below 50 percent of the median income, all those earning less than $6,000 in the first year and less than $10,000 in the later year would be considered poor. This implies that, even though the well-being of the low-income population may have increased, the number of those considered poor actually could increase. Thus, relative measures of poverty have been criticized for being too much of a moving target. Not only is it difficult to reduce relative poverty, it also is almost impossible to assess the effectiveness of transfer programs. In addition, establishing the cutoff (whether it is the lowest 10 or 20 percent in the income distribution, or 50 or 30 percent of the median) income is itself quite arbitrary.

Subjective Poverty–The previous definitions of poverty assume that experts are able to establish the appropriate cutoffs. A subjective definition

---

5. See Harold W. Watts, "The Iso-Prop Index: An Approach to the Determination of Differential Poverty Income Thresholds," *Journal of Human Resources* 2 (1) (Winter 1967): 3-18.

6. For more discussion of this and other issues concerning poverty measurement, see Patricia Ruggles, *Drawing the Line: Alternative Poverty Measures and Their Implications for Public Policy* (Washington, D.C.: The Urban Institute, 1990).

of poverty approaches the issue from the perspective of the individual and asks the poor to define what they consider to be a decent or minimally adequate standard of living. Such definitions are complex to apply because of the divergence in responses given the differences in individual utility functions and prevailing circumstances. Thus, while such definitions may be appealing because they rely on information from the poor themselves, they may be of little value in the design and implementation of policy.[7]

Official Measure and Extent of Poverty

All measures of poverty start by establishing a certain threshold income. One of the earliest attempts to establish such a threshold was made by Charles Booth, who in 1890 compiled a list of goods and services, which he called a "state of chronic want," for a family living in England. Booth used prevailing prices and established that 24 shillings per week were needed to purchase those goods and services. In essence, Booth had set a poverty line which could be used to distinguish poor from nonpoor. Current measures of poverty still rely on establishing some level of income to construct the line separating the poor from the nonpoor. In a study of poverty in York, England, B. S. Rowntree defined poverty as a level of income needed to obtain necessities for the maintenance of physical efficiency.[8] Such cutoffs imply a minimum level of resources below which persons are considered as poor.

Efforts to count and classify the poor in the United States have been more recent. A 1947 study by the staff of the Subcommittee on Low Income Families established $2000 as a poverty threshold for a typical family in 1948. Another serious attempt to measure the number of people living in poverty was made by Robert J. Lampman, who conducted the study for the Joint Economic Committee.

Lampman's cutoff basically updated the one established by the Subcommittee on Low Income Families by considering price changes.[9] Lampman suggested a threshold of $2500 for a family of four in 1957. The president's Council of Economic Advisers (CEA) established a cutoff of $3000 per year for families and $1500 for individuals in 1962. In 1964, Walter Heller of the CEA suggested a modification to allow $1500 for single individuals and an additional $500 for each additional family member of the family up to seven members. Thus, for a family of four, Heller's cutoff would have been $3000 and $4500 for a family of seven. Although adjustments for family

---

7. For a discussion of subjective poverty definition, see Aldi Hagenaars and Klaas de Vos, "The Definition and Measurement of Poverty," *Journal of Human Resources* 23 (2) (1988): 211–21.
8. B. S. Rowntree, *Poverty: A Study of Town Life* (London: MacMillan, 1901).
9. Robert J. Lampman, "The Low Income Population and Economic Growth," Study Paper No. 12 (Washington, D.C.: U.S. Congress Joint Economic Committee, 1959).

size are important, Heller did not take into account any differences in economies of scale based on family size.

Official Measure of Poverty

The current official measure of poverty primarily relies on a methodology of setting the threshold established by Mollie Orshansky of the Social Security Administration (SSA).[10] The Orshansky threshold relies on a simple approach of using food budgets. Surveys established that food represented about one-third of all expenditures of a typical family in 1955. Orshansky started by classifying different families based on family size, adjusting for characteristics such as whether the family is headed by a male or a female, number of children, and whether or not the family lived on a farm. Using these primary variables, Orshansky classified all families into 124 family types. She then established the minimally adequate food budgets for the various types of families using data that were previously calculated by the Department of Agriculture. Orshansky then simply multiplied the food budgets by a factor of three to establish the income threshold. Note that by multiplying the food budget by a factor of three (called the multiplier) the income threshold should then meet not only the food requirements, but also other goods and services. Given that each of the family types had different food requirements, the Orshansky thresholds varied by family type.

The poverty measure based on Orshansky's approach was widely adopted by government agencies and by 1969 the Bureau of Budget mandated the measure as the basis for the official government measure of poverty. Today the official measure of poverty follows Orshansky's approach. The threshold level of income is obtained by adjusting for changes in prices over time using the consumer price index (CPI). Thus, while in 1963, a family of four required a minimum of $3,130, the same family would have required $12,684 in 1989 based on CPI of 1963.

Extent of Poverty

As mentioned, a measure of poverty helps one know how many people are poor at any given time. Also, by looking at trends in the poverty rates over time, one can determine what is happening to the numbers of the poor population. The following presents some of the statistics on the extent of poverty in the United States based on the official measure discussed.

Data for official poverty rates in the United States are shown in Table 5-1 and plotted in Figure 5-1. In 1959, the poverty rate was 22.4 percent and

---

10. Mollie Orshansky, "Children of the Poor," *Social Security Bulletin* (July 1963): 3-13; and "Counting the Poor: Another Look at the Poverty Profile," *Social Security Bulletin*, 51 (10) (October 1988): 25–51.

Table 5-1   Poverty status of persons in the United States, 1959–1990

Year	Below Poverty Level Numbers	Below Poverty Level Percent
1990	33,585,000	13.5
1989	31,528,000	12.8
1988	31,745,000	13.0
1987	32,221,000	13.4
1986	32,370,000	13.6
1985	33,064,000	14.0
1984	33,700,000	14.4
1983	35,303,000	15.2
1982	34,398,000	15.0
1981	31,822,000	14.0
1980	29,272,000	13.0
1979	26,072,000	11.7
1978	24,497,000	11.4
1977	24,720,000	11.6
1976	24,975,000	11.8
1975	25,877,000	12.3
1974	23,370,000	11.2
1973	22,973,000	11.1
1972	24,460,000	11.9
1971	25,559,000	12.5
1970	25,420,000	12.6
1969	24,147,000	12.1
1968	25,389,000	12.8
1967	27,769,000	14.2
1966	28,510,000	14.7
1965	33,185,000	17.3
1964	36,055,000	19.0
1963	36,436,000	19.5
1962	38,625,000	21.0
1961	39,628,000	21.9
1960	39,851,000	22.2
1959	39,490,000	22.4

Source: U.S. Bureau of the Census, *Current Population Reports*, Series P–60, No. 175, 1991.

about 39 million Americans were considered poor. Poverty rates fell for several years, reaching a low of 11.1 percent in 1973. Since then, the poverty rate has increased, reaching a high of 15.2 percent in 1983. Even though the poverty rate has declined since 1959, the number of poor remains high because of population increases. In 1990, there were 33.5 million Americans who were classified as poor compared with 36.4 million in 1963.

Figure 5-1   Trends in poverty in the United States, 1959–1990

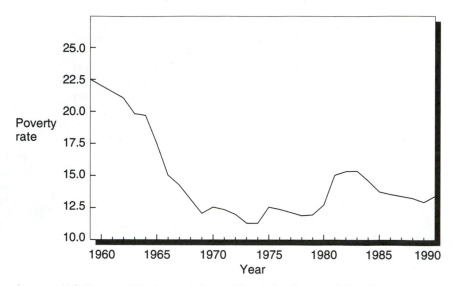

Source: U.S. Bureau of the Census, *Current Population Reports*, Series P–60.

Some interesting questions emerge from the trends in poverty rates. Why, for example, did poverty rates decline during the 1960s, but increase during the 1970s and 1980s? Why has poverty persisted even though billions of dollars have gone toward fighting poverty? These questions will be dealt with in later chapters.

As noted previously, one important use of a poverty measure is that it allows comparisons of poverty among different groups of the population or even across regions. Figure 5-2 plots data on poverty by race and female headship for 1970 through 1990. The figure reveals that there are significant differences between Whites, Blacks and Hispanics. The figure also shows that female-headed families have the highest poverty rates of all the groups shown. This information is important as it can be used to target particular polices on the high poverty groups.

Just as there are variations in the poverty rate over time, across racial groups, and by sex of the family head, there also are significant regional variations in the poverty rate even in the same year. In 1990, the poverty rate was 23.6 percent in Louisiana and 25.7 percent in Mississippi. In the same year, the poverty rate in Connecticut was only 6 percent. Once again, such variations prompt us to ask why these differences exist and persist for long periods of time. Table 5-2 provides data of poverty rates across states for 1980, 1985, and 1990.

The observed variations in the poverty rate across states conceal much information, because, even within the same state, there often are wide variations in the poverty rate. This is especially the case when one compares

Figure 5-2   Family poverty rates, by race and female headship

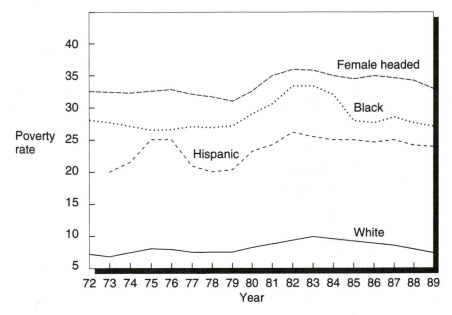

Source: U.S. Bureau of the Census, *Current Population Reports*, Series P–60, No. 168, and the *Economic Report of the President*, 1991.

the poverty rate in urban areas with that in smaller towns and rural communities. For, example, in 1980, the poverty rate in the city of Hartford, Connecticut, was 25.2 percent and the poverty rate in the city of Milford, Connecticut was only 4 percent. The tendency of the poor to be concentrated in some geographical areas has important implications concerning how we deal with poverty.[11] Knowledge of where poverty is concentrated is useful in the formulation and targeting of public policy.

ALTERNATIVE POVERTY MEASURES

Although the Orshansky approach continues to be the official way of establishing the poverty line, several criticisms have been directed at this approach. Some researchers have even suggested completely different approaches to establishing a poverty threshold. The following discusses some of the suggested modifications.

---

11. As discussed in a later chapter, the high concentration of poverty in inner cities and the isolation of the poor from the nonpoor is associated with negative forces that make the eradication of poverty difficult.

Table 5-2   Poverty rates by states and the District of Columbia, 1980, 1985, and 1990

State	Poverty Rates		
	1990	*1985*	*1980*
Alabama	19.2	20.6	21.2
Alaska	11.4	8.7	9.6
Arizona	13.7	10.7	12.8
Arkansas	19.6	22.9	21.5
California	13.9	13.6	11.0
Colorado	13.7	10.2	8.6
Connecticut	6.0	7.6	8.3
Delaware	6.9	11.4	11.8
Washington, D.C.	21.1	20.4	20.9
Florida	14.4	13.4	16.7
Georgia	15.8	17.7	13.9
Hawaii	11.0	10.7	8.5
Idaho	14.9	16.0	14.7
Illinois	13.7	15.6	12.3
Indiana	13.0	12.0	11.8
Iowa	10.4	17.9	10.8
Kansas	10.3	13.8	9.4
Kentucky	17.3	19.4	19.3
Louisiana	23.6	18.1	20.3
Maine	13.1	11.9	14.6
Maryland	9.9	8.7	9.5
Massachusetts	10.7	9.2	9.5
Michigan	14.3	14.5	12.9
Minnesota	12.0	12.6	8.7
Mississippi	25.7	25.1	24.3
Missouri	13.4	13.7	13.0

Using an Updated Multiplier–The share of the household budget spent on food plays a central role in the establishment of the official poverty threshold. Some of the earliest criticisms of the Orshansky measure focused on the use of a multiplier of three. Friedman argued that the use of a multiplier of three for the poor was inaccurate because the poor spent about 60 percent of their budget on food while the typical family spent about 33 percent of their budget on food.[12] Consequently, Friedman suggested using a

---

12. Rose D. Friedman, *Poverty: Definition and Perspective* (Washington D.C.: American Enterprise Institute, 1965).

Table 5-2   (Continued)

State	Poverty Rates		
	1990	1985	1980
Montana	16.3	16.0	13.2
Nebraska	10.3	14.8	13.0
Nevada	9.8	14.4	8.3
New Hampshire	6.3	6.0	7.0
New Jersey	9.2	8.3	9.0
New Mexico	20.9	18.5	20.6
New York	14.3	15.8	13.8
North Carolina	13.0	14.2	15.0
North Dakota	13.7	15.9	15.5
Ohio	11.5	12.8	9.8
Oklahoma	15.6	16.0	13.9
Oregon	9.2	11.9	11.5
Pennsylvania	11.0	10.5	9.8
Rhode Island	7.5	9.0	10.7
South Carolina	16.2	15.2	16.8
South Dakota	13.3	17.3	18.8
Tennessee	16.9	18.1	19.6
Texas	15.9	15.9	15.7
Utah	8.2	10.9	10.0
Vermont	10.9	9.2	12.0
Virginia	11.1	10.0	12.4
Washington	8.9	12.0	12.7
West Virginia	18.1	22.3	15.2
Wisconsin	9.3	11.6	8.5
Wyoming	11.0	12.0	10.4

Source: U.S. Bureau of the Census, *Current Population Reports*, Series P–60, No. 175.

far smaller multiplier to obtain the threshold. Using the lower multiplier, Friedman calculated a 1963 threshold of $2200 for a family of four rather than Orshansky's threshold of $3100. Using Friedman's multiplier, the calculated poverty rates were about 10 percent lower than those obtained by Orshansky.

Other critics of the Orshansky measure argued that the multiplier was too low. In fact, since she had used 1955 data to establish the multiplier in 1963, she had ignored changes in spending patterns between 1955 and 1963. As established in the 1960–1961 Consumer Expenditure Survey (CES), the typical family was at that time spending one-quarter of their budget on food as compared to the one-third share for 1955. Hence, the appropriate multiplier should have been closer to four and not three. Today, the share of budget spent on food by the typical family has declined dramatically to about one-fifth and some estimates place this at one-sixth of total budget. This suggests that a more accurate measure of poverty should use an updated multiplier that takes into account changes in the share of food budget to total expenditures. Continued use of the multiplier of three grossly underestimates the number of the poor.

Adjusting for Changes in Prices–We have already indicated that the official poverty rate takes into account changes in prices by using the consumer price index (CPI). The CPI is based on a weighted average of prices of a fixed market basket of goods in a number of cities in the United States. Some of the items included in the CPI are the prices of new housing and other items that are not part of the poor's consumption bundle. Thus, although the price of new houses may have increased significantly during the 1980s, such does not reflect changes in the prices of the goods that the poor consume. By using the consumer price index, the tendency is to estimate a poverty threshold that is artificially high. Many analysts now accept that a more appropriate price index for the purposes of adjusting the threshold should reflect more of those goods that the poor consume. A new index called CPI-X1 which takes into account rental prices and the rental equivalent of owned housing rather than new housing prices has been reported by the Census Bureau since 1981.

Adjusting for Changes in Relative Incomes–The official poverty rate is based on an absolute definition. Suggestions have been made to establish the poverty threshold at a certain percent of the median income.[13] This implies that the threshold would shift with changes in the median income.

We already have mentioned that such a measure is a moving target and it may be quite difficult to assess the effectiveness of public policy and even to know the truly needy members of the population. If we wanted to make comparisons between different groups, however, then such a measure could be useful. Some researchers have argued that the 50 percent of median income cutoff comes close to the original threshold established by Orshansky.

Changes in the Consumption of Necessary Goods–Consumption patterns change over time. Thus, even the bundle of necessary goods will change over time. A few decades ago, child care may not have been considered as part of the necessary bundle of services because most mothers did not seek work outside the home. Today, with the high labor force participation rates of females, child care is considered part of the minimum necessary services. The official measure of poverty does not take into account such

---

13. Fuchs defines a poor family as one whose income is less than one-half the median income. See Victor R. Fuchs, "Redefining Poverty and Redistributing Income," *The Public Interest* (Summer 1967): 88–95.

changes in the consumption patterns. It is quite difficult to establish an objective set of necessary goods at any particular time. Some researchers suggest that the best way to update a set of necessary goods is to have experts establish some normative standards of consumption.[14] However, others have argued that expert opinion on such matters will be arbitrary and subjective.[15]

A "housing consumption" standard which is based on the "Fair Market Rent" for rental units of varying sizes has much appeal for a threshold measure. One such standard has been set under Section 8 of the subsidized housing program. Using guidelines of the Housing and Urban Development (HUD) on the number of people who can live in a house of specific size without crowding, an estimate of minimum housing needs for various families can be estimated. Then the minimum standard for total housing consumption for a family of a given size can be derived using the housing share established by HUD. In 1987, for example, HUD set 30 percent of income as the maximum that can be spent on rent. Such a housing share can then be used to set the income threshold based on the housing consumption standard.

Table 5-3 shows poverty rates of persons based on the various alternative thresholds discussed previously.[16] As can be seen, the poverty rates differ depending on the threshold used. For example, using the CPI-X1 yields a poverty rate that is lower than the official rate, while using the housing consumption standard and the updated multiplier yields much higher poverty rates. The poverty rate based on median income approaches the official rate in some years, but is much different in others. A poverty measure based on median income will fluctuate widely depending on the state of the economy.

Adjusting for the Resources Used to Set the Threshold–One of the serious shortcomings of the official poverty measure is the classification of what is and is not counted in setting the threshold. First, the official poverty measure uses before-tax cash income, which excludes the value of noncash income such as food stamps, medicare, housing subsidies, and so on. Because noncash transfers are a significant portion of the poor's resources, omitting them overstates the true degree of deprivation. Thus, a better measure of poverty should include the monetary value of the noncash benefits.

To include the noncash benefits, one must measure their value. The simplest approach values noncash benefits at their market value. That is, a

---

14. See Ruggles, *Drawing the Line,* 1990.
15. See Martin Rein, "Problem in the Definition and Measurement of Poverty," in *Poverty in America,* Revised edition, ed. Louis A. Ferman, Joyce L. Kornbluh, and Alan Haber (Ann Arbor: University of Michigan Press, 1969); and Harold W. Watts, "Special Panel Suggests Changes in BLS Family Budget Program," *Monthly Labor Review* (December 1980): 3–10.
16. Notice that measure of poverty looks at persons, not families.

Table 5-3   Poverty rates of all persons under alternative thresholds, 1972–1987, selected years

Year	Official Poverty	Indexed by CPI-X1	Indexed by Median Income	Housing Consumption	Updated Multiplier
1972	11.9	11.3	14.3	N/A	17.3
1977	11.6	10.7	13.8	20.7	18.0
1982	15.0	13.2	15.3	25.1	25.5
1987	13.5	12.0	16.1	23.4	25.9

Source: Patricia Ruggles, *Drawing the Line: Alternative Poverty Measures and Their Implications for Public Policy* (Washington, D.C.: Urban Institute, 1990), p. 55.

food stamp coupon with face value $20 is counted as worth $20 to the recipient. Nevertheless, a $20 food stamp coupon may not be worth $20 to the recipient because the coupon cannot be used to buy other goods and services. Thus, a recipient may be forced to overconsume some goods and services and underconsume others.[17] Therefore, the recipient's valuation of noncash benefits is lower than the market value. The calculated poverty rate with noncash transfers included will therefore depend on how the benefits are valued. As would be expected, a large difference exists in the poverty rates when cash only resources are used and when both cash and noncash resources are used. Moreover, the method of valuing benefits (market value or recipient value) results in different poverty rates.

Another shortcoming of the income measure used to calculate official poverty rates is that it does not incorporate the effect of taxes and the value of assets such as homeowners' equity. Since the objective in measuring poverty is to indicate well-being, the relevant income concept should be a more comprehensive measure of income. Because tax codes affect families with different incomes differently, the relevant income concept should incorporate taxes paid and include offsetting tax credits received. Table 5-4 presents data on poverty rates when we include various taxes and benefits by age groups. The official poverty rate is p1 while p11 is a comprehensive measure that excludes all taxes and includes benefits and equity on homes. The comprehensive measure produces poverty rates considerably lower than the official rates. Disaggregating the population

---

17. Consumers attain a higher level of utility when they receive cash transfers as opposed to in-kind transfers of equal market value.

Table 5-4   Taxes and poverty data

	All	under 18	18–24	25–44	45–64	65–74	>74
	Poverty Rates of All Persons (1986)						
p1	13.6	20.5	15.6	10.2	9.1	10.3	15.8
p2	20.8	23.4	18.6	12.7	15.2	42.9	57.6
p3	20.4	23.0	18.2	12.4	14.8	41.4	56.2
p4	19.9	22.2	17.7	11.9	14.5	41.3	56.0
p5	21.2	24.0	19.5	13.2	15.4	41.8	56.6
p6	14.9	21.9	17.3	11.3	10.2	11.5	18.0
p7	14.4	21.7	17.1	11.1	9.7	9.5	15.0
p8	13.5	20.8	16.2	10.5	9.0	8.3	13.0
p9	12.0	18.2	14.9	9.4	8.3	7.4	11.9
p10	11.6	17.1	14.3	9.0	8.1	7.3	11.8
p11	10.3	16.0	13.7	8.4	6.4	4.7	7.4

Definitions

p1 = Poverty rate before taxes and excluding capital gains (current official mea
sure of poverty)
p2 = p1 less government transfers
p3 = p2 plus capital gains
p4 = p3 plus health insurance supplements to wage or salary income
p5 = p4 after income and payroll taxes
p6 = p5 plus nonmeans tested government cash transfers
p7 = p6 plus the fungible value of medicare
p8 = p7 plus means-tested government cash transfers
p9 = p8 plus food and housing benefits
p10 = p9 plus the fungible value of medicaid
p11 = p10 plus the net imputed return on equity in own home

Source: U.S. Bureau of the Census, *Current Population Reports*, Series P–60.

by age groups, we find that official poverty rates greatly exaggerate the poverty of the older groups. Table 5-5 shows poverty rates when different measures of income are used for 1987, 1988, and 1989. In all cases, poverty rates based on the comprehensive measures are significantly lower than official poverty rates.

The various measures of poverty suggest that various ways exist to measure poverty, and that no measure is free from errors. Some measures

Table 5-5   Measures of income and poverty

Poverty Rates—1987, 1988, and 1989 by definition of income			
	1989	*1988*	*1987*
y1	12.8	13.0	13.4
y2	20.0	20.2	20.4
y3	19.9	20.2	20.2
y4	19.4	19.7	19.7
y5	20.3	20.6	20.5
y6	20.1	20.3	20.4
y7	20.3	20.5	20.6
y8	13.9	14.1	14.3
y9	13.4	13.6	13.8
y10	13.4	13.6	13.8
y11	12.5	12.7	13.0
y12	11.7	12.1	12.4
y13	10.4	10.8	11.0
y14	8.9	9.2	9.4

Definitions

y1 = money income before taxes and excluding capital gains (current official mea
       sure)
y2 = y1 less government transfers
y3 = y2 plus capital gains
y4 = y3 plus health insurance supplements to wage or salary income
y5 = y4 less social security payroll taxes
y6 = y5 less federal income taxes
y7 = y6 less state income taxes
y8 = y7 plus nonmeans-tested government cash transfers
y9 = y8 plus medicare
y10 = y9 plus regular-price school lunches
y11 = y10 plus means-tested government cash transfers
y12 = y11 plus medicaid
y13 = y12 plus other means-tested government noncash transfers
y14 = y13 plus net imputed return to equity in own home

Source: U.S. Bureau of the Census, *Current Population Reports*, Series P–60.

will underestimate poverty while others will overestimate it. There actually is no basis for saying that one poverty measure is the best. A poverty measure that may be good for a particular purpose may not be suitable for another. Thus, the best poverty measure may largely depend on the purpose we have for measuring the poverty.

COMPOSITION AND CAUSES OF POVERTY

Profile of the Poor

Although poverty cuts across all categories of people, some groups are disproportionately represented among the poor. Table 5-6 shows the percentages of persons and families below poverty by selected characteristics of age, race, marital status, family size, education, and labor force status. As can be seen, the prevalence of poverty varies considerably among the different groups. Next, we provide a brief summary of the groups with a high incidence of poverty.

Age–Poverty rates are the highest among those under 16 years of age, those between 16 and 21 years of age, and the elderly (over 65). Those under 21 are more likely not to be in the labor force, to work part time, and to have no work experience and hence to command lower wages. One of the reasons for poverty rates among the younger populations is that many children are now growing up in low-income, female-headed families. A large number of those over 65 years old are not in the labor force and thus rely mainly on social security, private pensions, or other savings.

Race–Racial minorities, such as Blacks and Hispanics, have higher poverty rates than other groups.[18] In 1989, about one-third of all Blacks in the United States were poor.

Female-Headed Families–Families headed by females have a higher incidence of poverty than families that are headed by males. For example, while 10.3 percent of all families in 1989 were poor, the poverty rate was 32.2 percent for female-headed families and 46.5 percent for families headed by Black females as compared to a poverty rate of 27.8 percent for all Black families. As already mentioned, most of the poor children live in households headed by females.

Education–Most of the poor have less than a high school education. The probability of falling into poverty decreases significantly for those who hold a college degree.

Labor Force Status–There is a high correlation between the incidence of poverty and labor force status. Most of the poor are either not in the labor force, work part time, or are unemployed.

Knowing which categories of people have a high incidence of poverty is important in the formulation of public policy, since particular policies target groups facing specific circumstances. However, before we can suggest policies, it is necessary that we first seek answers as to why some groups are overrepresented among the poor. As will be seen, composition of poverty largely reflects the causes of poverty.

---

18. The other groups include Native Americans. In addition, Hispanics of Cuban origin have very low poverty rates while Hispanics of Puerto Rican origin have higher poverty rates than Black Americans.

Table 5-6   Characteristics of families and persons below poverty, 1989

Characteristic	All	Percent Below Poverty White	Black	Hispanic
Age				
Under 16 years old	20.1	15.2	44.7	36.6
16 to 21 years old	15.3	12.0	31.7	28.5
22 to 44 years old	10.3	8.4	22.7	20.9
45 to 54 years old	7.4	6.1	17.4	17.0
55 to 59 years old	9.7	7.6	28.6	18.6
60 to 64 years old	9.5	7.5	27.0	18.8
65 years old and over	11.4	9.6	30.8	20.6
Family Size (Persons)				
Two	8.2	6.6	22.7	18.6
Three	9.8	7.1	27.3	21.5
Four	10.1	8.0	25.8	24.5
Five	13.5	10.3	33.2	23.6
Six	21.1	15.6	44.3	30.3
Seven or more	32.3	25.5	51.2	38.0
Education of Family Head				
Elementary				
Less than 8 years	25.5	22.7	34.8	32.5
8 years	15.9	14.0	33.4	29.2
High school				
1 to 3 years	19.2	14.0	41.9	28.4
4 years	8.9	7.0	23.4	16.2
College				
1 year or more	3.6	2.6	12.3	8.1
Labor Force Status (1989)				
Worked				
50 to 52 weeks	3.5	2.9	8.9	10.0
49 weeks or less	19.0	15.4	39.7	34.1
Did not work	23.4	17.1	54.3	47.8
Family poverty				
All families	10.3	7.8	27.8	—
Female-headed families	32.2	20.8	46.5	—

Source: U.S. Bureau of the Census, *Current Population Reports,* Series P–60, No. 168, and *Economic Report of the President,* 1991.

Causes of Poverty

To formulate relevant public policy to deal with the problems of poverty, policy makers must first have a clear understanding of the causes of poverty. Since different groups of poor will be poor for various reasons, specific public policies may be necessary for different groups of people. In addition, because there is no single cause of poverty, the plight of some poor could be due to several factors, each contributing to some degree to observed poverty. It is important to establish the extent to which each of the causes contributes to observed poverty. Failure to isolate the real causes of poverty may result in public policies that not only do not alleviate poverty, but could actually cause it to increase. As will be seen, understanding the causes of poverty also helps provide a clearer picture of the composition of poverty as discussed previously.

Most of the controversies concerning poverty and poverty policy originate from differences in what are perceived to be the causes of poverty. As observed in Chapter 3, there generally are two opposing views about the causes of poverty. The first view blames poverty entirely on society while the second view places the blame on the individual. These extreme positions will lead us to recommend solutions in which either society must play the dominant role in solving the poverty problem or the individual poor must solve their own problems. As will be seen, the causes of poverty cannot be viewed in such simple terms because poverty may result from the interaction of various factors involving the individual and society. Some people may be poor because they make bad choices while others are poor because of circumstances beyond their control. This suggests that both society and the individual may have to play a role in the alleviation of poverty. What then are the causes of poverty?

Of course, poverty is associated with either low or no earnings. Consequently, some of the most important causes of poverty relate to problems experienced in the labor market.[19] These problems involve either the lack of sufficient jobs or the availability of too much low wage employment. It also is true that some individuals do not participate in the labor market because of poor health, lack of child care services, and so forth. However, poverty also could be a result of individuals' attitude toward work. A discussion of some of the more important causes of poverty follows.

Unemployment–Probably the most important cause of poverty is the lack of employment opportunities. As will be shown in Chapter 6, although the unemployment rate is not the only cause of poverty, there is clear evidence of a high correlation between the two variables. The years

---

19. To some extent, the study of the economics of poverty is an extension of labor economics.

that unemployment rates have experienced the largest declines have also been the years of the largest declines in poverty, and vice versa. Clearly, to reduce poverty requires an understanding of the nature and causes of unemployment and the types of public policies that can influence the level of employment. As will be seen, some other questions regarding why some groups tend to have very high unemployment rates are important in the formulation of poverty policy.

Low-Wage Employment–To a large extent, many poor people actually work—the working poor. The main cause of poverty for this group is low wages. Economic theory suggests that wages are determined primarily by individuals' productivity. Hence, one of the main causes of poverty is low productivity, which translates into low wages. Individual productivity depends on human capital; most people who are poor usually have low levels of education. To the extent that the lack of human capital explains poverty, public policies designed to increase human capital represent an important strategy for eliminating poverty.

Although human capital probably is the most important factor in wage determination, other factors matter, too. Structuralists argue that low wages result from the structure of labor markets. For example, people with the same level of human capital may earn quite different incomes depending on the industry in which they work. The structuralist view explains low wages by two theories: the dual labor market and labor market stratification theories.[20]

Discrimination–We have already noted that minorities and women tend to have higher poverty rates than other groups. One of the common explanations for the high poverty rates among these groups is the existence of barriers in the labor market that either result in a concentration of members of those groups in low-wage employment, or reduce the available opportunities to them. The most important barrier is race and sex discrimination. Other types of discrimination (for example, age) are becoming increasingly important.

Such discrimination is called *market discrimination*, which is discrimination in the hiring stage. As already mentioned, human capital is important in increasing productivity and hence eliminating poverty. If there is discrimination in the provision of education, then even if there is no market discrimination, some groups of individuals will still command lower wages because of lower productivity associated with lower levels of human capital. Thus, another explanation for high unemployment rates and low wages among minorities is the existence of premarket discrimination.

Female Headship and Family Size–The data presented in Table 5-6 show that female-headed families have a considerably higher incidence of

---

20. These views are discussed in Chapter 7.

poverty than male-headed families. Single female family heads earn less than males, and when females take the role of primary providers in households with children, the probability of falling into poverty increases dramatically. As mentioned before, there has been a consistent increase in female-headed households in the United States, and given the relationship between poverty and female headship, we can expect this trend to have been important in explaining the high poverty rate. To deal with the family structure and public policies, it is necessary to determine what factors explain increased female headship and what policies might reverse those trends.

Poor families tend to have more children than higher income families. Here we have two-way causation. First, more children in the family directly increase the probability of those in the household being poor as available resources have to be divided among more members. In addition, large family size is likely to result in reduced labor force participation rates of the householders because of the time required to take care of the young family members. Household size, therefore, directly increases poverty. Second, poor families tend to have more children. Thus, those who start off poor are likely to be even poorer since they have larger families. Either way, the size of a household is an important factor in explaining poverty.

Culture–Some people are born into an environment of poverty and have a lifestyle that perpetuates poverty. These individuals may have poor attitudes toward work, a weak work ethic, a low aspiration for independence, and a lack of motivation to achieve. Children are not encouraged to perform well in school and end up performing poorly, often dropping out of school at an early age. These attitudes and values are not conducive to success and lead the individual to be largely dependent on public support. Explanations of this behavioral pattern is called the *culture of poverty*.[21]

The culture of poverty hypothesis argues that individuals brought up in poverty tend to acquire behavioral traits that lead to failure, and these traits are transmitted across generations. One important outcome of the culture of poverty is a high incidence of teenage pregnancies out of wedlock. Thus, for those communities with a culture of poverty, a large number of families are headed by females. Of course, childbearing at an early age inhibits further human capital investment by the mothers, who frequently do not participate in the labor market, but rather rely entirely on public support. The result is a heavy dependence on welfare which is passed on from one generation to the next.

---

21. See Oscar Lewis, *Five Families: Mexican Case Studies in the Culture of Poverty* (New York: Basic Books, 1959); "The Culture of Poverty," *Scientific American* (October 1966): 19–25; *La Vida: A Puerto Rican Family in the Culture of Poverty—San Juan and New York* (New York: Random House, 1966); and Michael Harrington, *The Other America* (Baltimore, Md.: Penguin Books, 1962).

Divorce rates also tend to be high among those with the culture of poverty. Several studies suggest that the poverty of some minority groups can be explained partly by the existence of a culture of poverty. Thus, culture affects poverty by affecting behavior in the labor markets and also influencing family structure.

Old Age and Poor Health—Most people now live longer, which has resulted in a large increase in the number of retired persons. Because they do not participate in the labor market, retired individuals must rely on their savings which may not last through their retirement period, especially if savings are partly wiped out by inflation. Coupled with longevity, health problems emerge as a serious issue among older people. Consequently, a significant portion of their resources may have to be devoted to medical costs. Even younger families can become poor if a family member is afflicted with long-term health problems.

SUMMARY

This chapter has examined the main issues concerning the definition and measurement of poverty, and the extent, composition, and causes of poverty in the United States.

Whether poverty is defined as relative, absolute, or a subjective measure has implications on the level of poverty and policy. This chapter has described the basic elements of the official poverty measure as first formulated by Mollie Orshansky and the adjustments, such as prices and family size that are used to obtain the poverty threshold. The chapter also has presented some data on poverty rates and poverty counts obtained using the official measure. We have noted that poverty rates change from one year to another, and that there are wide differences in the poverty rates among different demographic groups.

Although the official poverty measure is widely used in research and policy formulation, we have presented some of the criticisms that are directed at this measure. These criticisms key on the use of the multiplier, the use of the consumer price index in computation of the cost of living, and the use of an appropriate consumption standard. Other criticisms focus on the type of resources that are used to calculate the threshold income level. Some data are provided that show how poverty rates differ depending on which approach and what adjustments are used. Thus, although the official measure often is referred to, it is important to understand what it measures and does not measure.

This chapter also has presented a brief profile of the poor and the causes of poverty. This last section sets the tone for the discussion in the following chapters, which concentrate on the various causes of poverty and the policies used to deal with them.

STUDY AND DISCUSSION QUESTIONS

1. Distinguish between absolute, relative, and subjective poverty.

2. What is the purpose of measuring poverty?

3. In your opinion, should the official measure of poverty be an absolute, relative, or subjective measure? Explain your choice.

4. You have been asked to design a needs-based measure of poverty. Outline how you would go about establishing the poverty line. You should explain the various factors that you take into account such as family size, location, and so on. What would you consider to be the main problems of your measure of poverty?

5. Carefully discuss the various causes of poverty and relate these causes to the composition of poverty (who is poor). You should briefly outline how each cause of poverty actually affects earnings.

6. Clearly outline how the official poverty rate is established in the United States.

7. Discuss the various shortcomings of the official poverty measure and the suggestions that have been made as to how the measure could be improved.

8. In your opinion, should the goal of the government be to reduce poverty, inequality, both, or should the government not be involved in the redistribution of income? Provide normative and positive arguments.

9. Using the sources cited in this chapter, compile the poverty rates (total, by race, gender, age, state) for the recent years. Write a paragraph on the recent trends in poverty rates.

10. People often talk about eradicating poverty. What exactly do they mean by this statement? Is it possible to eradicate poverty?

ADDITIONAL READINGS

1. Atkinson, A. B. "On the Measurement of Poverty," *Econometrica* 55 (4) (1987): 749–64.

2. Perlman, Richard. *The Economics of Poverty*. New York: McGraw-Hill, 1976.

3. Sen, A. K. "Issues in the Measurement of Poverty," *Scandinavian Journal of Economics* 81 (February 1979): 285–307.

4. Thon, D. "On Measuring Poverty," *Review of Income and Wealth* 25 (December 1979): 429–40.

5. Wilber, George L., ed. *Poverty: A New Perspective.* Lexington, Ky.: University of Kentucky, 1975.

6

LABOR MARKETS AND POVERTY: UNEMPLOYMENT

An important factor that explains the economic status of a majority of persons in the United States, and in other countries, is their labor force status: whether working or not; whether they have a high- or a low-paying job; and whether they work full-time or part-time. A large number of poor persons either do not work, work only part-time, or work at low-paying jobs. Nonparticipation in labor markets and the lack of jobs translates to no incomes while those who are in low-paying jobs (although they may work full-time) earn low incomes that are not sufficient to lift them above the poverty level. Some persons are only able to work part-time so that even if they earn reasonable wages, their aggregate earnings may not be sufficient to bring them out of poverty. Thus, the lack of jobs, poor jobs (low-wage), and nonparticipation in the labor market, play a central role in the analysis of economics of poverty. We should note, however, that people with no labor market earnings are not necessarily poor (for example, children and retired persons). The people we are concerned with in this discussion exclude the children and others, such as the severely handicapped and very old who are not expected to participate in labor markets.

This chapter deals with the problems of unemployment and nonparticipation in the labor market. There is no doubt that unemployment and nonparticipation are some of the more pressing economic problems and also are important causes of poverty. The first section of this chapter examines the meaning and measurement of unemployment. Next, the chapter provides some data and a brief discussion of the relationship between labor force status and poverty focusing on unemployment and nonparticipation. There also is discussion of theories and causes of unemployment. Finally, there is a brief discussion of some of the factors that explain high unemployment rates among some groups and also the increased unemployment rates over time. Although the main goal of this chapter is to show the link between labor market status and poverty, it also lays the foundation for public policies discussed in Chapters 8. To appreciate the problem of unemployment and how to deal with it, it helps to discuss in detail the economics of labor markets.

The discussion of the labor market and poverty would not be complete without considering low-wage employment and public policies to deal with labor market problems. The discussion of low-wage employment will be presented in the next chapter. Public policies designed to deal with labor market problems are discussed in Chapter 8.

UNEMPLOYMENT: DEFINITION AND MEASUREMENT

Before demonstrating the connection between the importance of labor market status and poverty, it is necessary to understand what is meant by unemployment and how it is measured. An individual is unemployed if he or she wants to work, but is not able to get a job. Although this concept is straightforward, several problems arise in the definition and measurement of unemployment.

Prior to the Great Depression, the United States government did not collect data on unemployment on a regular basis. Without such labor market statistics, it was not possible to accurately evaluate trends in the economy or the extent of economic hardship experienced by most of the population. These problems prompted the U.S. Congress to authorize the Census Bureau and the Bureau of Labor Statistics (BLS) to collect and analyze labor force statistics. Currently the unemployment rate is reported by the BLS. The source of the data is the Current Population Survey (CPS), also called the household survey. The survey is conducted each month and contains data on various aspects of the labor market. The surveys are conducted by trained interviewers who sample approximately 60,000 households across the United States.[1] The data collected from the survey are reasonably accurate and closely approximate the trends in the national economy.[2]

Figure 6-1 illustrates how the unemployment rate emerges. Persons under the age of 16 are excluded from the labor force. People in institutions (such as prisons and mental hospitals) also are excluded. Thus, only the noninstitutional population over 16 years of age is considered in the calculation of the labor market activity. In 1992, the noninstitutional population that was 16 years and older was just over 193 million people. Not all of the noninstitutional category are considered as part of the labor

---

1. For a discussion of the CPS, see National Commission on Employment and Unemployment Statistics, *Counting the Labor Force* (Washington, D.C.: U.S. Government Printing Office, 1979).
2. The sample size, however, is too small, so that it is not accurate for measuring local changes in the labor force status. For a detailed discussion on this issue, see Terry F. Buss, "Assessing the Accuracy of BLS Local Unemployment Rates: A Case Study," *Industrial and Labor Relation Review* 39 (2) (January 1986): 241–50.

Figure 6-1   Measuring the unemployment rate (numbers shown are in thousands and are for 1992)

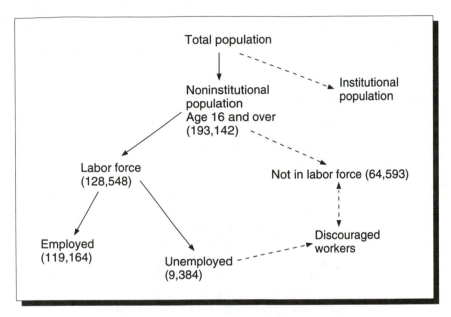

Source: The labor-force data from the U.S. Department of Labor, Bureau of Labor Statistics, *Employment and Earnings*, July 1993, Table A–1.

force. Some choose not to work—enroll in schools, remain at home, or retire.

The remaining part of the population is called the labor force. In 1992, the population in the labor force was 128.5 million. A person is in the labor force if that person is either working or actively looking for a job. One important labor market statistic is the labor force participation rate that measures the number of people in the labor force as a percentage of the noninstitutional population.[3] If individuals are not actively searching for work or would not accept a job if offered, then they are not included in the labor force.

The labor force contains two groups: the employed (civilian or armed forces) and the unemployed. Individuals are employed if they worked for pay for at least one hour per week. Persons who work 15 hours or more a week without pay in a family business, or those who have a job, but are

---

3. Thus the labor force participation rate, LFPR = (noninstitutional population 16 years or over in the labor force/noninstitutional population 16 years or over) * 100. In 1992, the labor force participation rate was 66.6 percent.

not working for health, weather, strike, or personal reasons also are counted as employed. The unemployed are those who do not have a job, but are seeking one. The most important labor statistic is the unemployment rate, which is the number of unemployed as a percentage of the total labor force.[4] In 1992, just over 119 million people were employed and slightly over 9 million were unemployed. Thus, the unemployment rate in 1992 was 7.3 percent.

An important aspect in the calculation of the unemployment rate is the definition of who is unemployed. A person is considered unemployed if he or she meets the following conditions: out of work; looking for work; and able to accept a job if offered one. A person is looking for work if over the past four weeks that person has made some effort in the search process such as answering a help wanted advertisement, going for an interview, and so forth. If the person doesn't have a job, and has not been actively searching for work in the last four weeks, then that person is not considered unemployed but is counted as not in the labor force. These people are referred to as discouraged workers; workers who have given up looking for work because of poor job prospects.

The official unemployment measure has been criticized for various reasons.[5] The most common reason is that it excludes discouraged workers. The exclusion of these workers artificially understates the hardships experienced by the population, especially the most disadvantaged members of society.[6]

Another valid criticism of the official unemployment measure concerns the issue of underemployment. Underemployment occurs when a person wants to work more hours, but is only able to obtain a few hours of work. Although such people work less than they want, they are counted as employed. Underemployment also arises when workers do not get work that fully utilizes their skills and talent. For example, during bad economic times, a computer programmer may only be able to get employment as a typist. To the extent that the official measure does not take into account

---

4. The unemployment rate therefore = (unemployed population/labor force) * 100.
5. For an excellent review of various issues concerning measuring unemployment, see National Commission on Employment and Unemployment Statistics, *Counting the Labor Force: Readings in Labor Force Statistics* (Washington, D.C.: U.S. Government Printing Office, 1979).
6. However, the National Commission on Employment and Unemployment Statistics which was established by Congress in 1976 to examine methods of data collection and measurement of the various labor force concepts recommended that discouraged workers should not be included in the labor force statistics. The reason for this was that most discouraged workers are not strongly attached to the labor market. See Robert L. Stein, "National Commission Recommends Changes in Labor Force Statistics," *Monthly Labor Review* 103 (4) (April 1980): 11–21. A recent study found that over 50 percent of those classified as discouraged workers had not actively searched for work in over one year. See Paul O. Flaim, "Discouraged Workers: How Strong Are Their Links to Job Market?" *Monthly Labor Review* 107 (8) (August 1984): 8–11.

underemployment, official unemployment statistics understate the hardship experienced by workers.

On the other hand, several factors exist that counter those that understate the unemployment rate. In some sense, the official unemployment rate overstates the hardships experienced by the population. Among the more important of these factors concerns unemployment insurance and welfare transfers. These government transfers reduce the hardships of those not working, thus, they can afford to remain unemployed for a longer period. Recipients of transfer programs such as Aid to Families with Dependent Children (AFDC) are required to register for work as a condition for receiving benefits. Thus, although they may not be actively searching for work, they artificially cause the measured unemployment rate to rise by registering to work.

The changing composition of the American workforce also has tended to overstate the true unemployment rate. These days, more teenagers and women participate in the labor force than was the case before 1960. These groups also have higher turnover rates and often are counted as unemployed.[7] Likewise, the growth of two-earner families has reduced the financial burden on individual family members, reducing the pressure to take the first job offered, hence, a longer job search translates into a higher unemployment rate. Despite these shortcomings, the official unemployment rate is important in the analysis of poverty and poverty policy.[8]

LABOR FORCE STATUS AND POVERTY

Begin by looking at some data that reveal the relationship between labor force status and poverty. Table 6-1 presents data of the poverty rate of various categories of people based on their labor force status.[9] Column A shows the percentage of all persons who worked (year-round or part of year) during the previous year who were poor in 1990. Thus, in 1990, of all persons who worked in the previous year, 6.5 percent were below poverty. Column B shows the percentage of all persons who worked full-time all year-round who were below poverty. Column C shows the percentage of all persons who worked full-time but did not work all year-round who were poor. Column D shows the percentage of those who did not work any time during the year who were below poverty.

---

7. As discussed later in this chapter, the change in the composition of the labor force has been one of the causes of increased aggregate unemployment rates over time.
8. For more discussion on the measurement of unemployment, see Julius Shiskin, "Employment and Unemployment: The Doughnut or the Hole?" *Monthly Labor Review 99* (2) (February 1976): 3–10.
9. The previous chapter discussed some of the inadequacies of the official measure of poverty. This and the following chapters use only the official measure because this is the statistic used in policy discussions. Also poverty measures based on other thresholds are not available for many years.

Table 6-1   Work experience during year, by selected characteristic and poverty status in 1990 of civilians 16 years old and over

Population Below Poverty as a Percent of Total in Each Category

Characteristic	All Workers A	Worked Year-round Full-time B	Not Year-round Full-time C	Did Not Work During Year D
All Persons				
Both sexes				
Total	6.5	2.5	12.6	22.1
16 to 17 years	9.8	*	9.8	22.7
18 to 64 years	6.6	2.6	13.4	29.4
18 to 24 years	11.2	4.5	14.8	36.5
25 to 34 years	7.8	3.2	16.6	39.5
35 to 54 years	4.7	2.0	11.6	28.4
55 to 64 years	3.9	1.8	7.6	19.1
65 years and over	3.5	1.5	4.4	13.8
Male				
Total	5.7	2.5	12.5	19.6
16 to 17 years	8.7	*	8.6	20.5
18 to 64 years	5.8	2.5	13.7	32.8
18 to 24 years	9.3	4.5	12.3	29.1
25 to 34 years	6.7	3.0	17.0	48.4
35 to 54 years	4.5	2.1	14.9	40.6
55 to 64 years	3.3	1.8	7.1	22.0
65 years and over	2.6	1.4	3.2	9.1

We note that, for all categories of workers (by age, sex, and race), persons who worked full-time and all year-round have the lowest poverty levels. There are considerable differences in poverty rates between the proportion of full-time workers who worked all year-round and those who only worked part of the year. For example, while only 2.5 percent of year-round workers were poor, the poverty rate was 12.6 among those who did not work all year-round. Those who did not work any time during the year have the highest proportion below poverty. For example, of all those who did not work during the previous year, 22.1 percent were below poverty in 1990.

The data reported in Table 6-1 also reveals some interesting differences across age groups, gender, and race. Those persons who are 65 years

Table 6-1   (Continued)

Characteristic	All Workers A	Worked Year-round Full-time B	Not Year-round Full-time C	Did Not Work During Year D
Female				
Total	7.5	2.6	12.7	23.4
16 to 17 years	11.2	*	11.1	24.9
18 to 64 years	7.5	2.6	13.3	28.2
18 to 24 years	13.2	4.5	17.1	41.1
25 to 34 years	9.0	3.4	16.4	37.2
35 to 54 years	5.0	1.9	9.8	25.0
55 to 64 years	4.7	1.7	7.9	17.8
65 years and over	4.8	1.8	5.7	16.9
Race total				
Black	14.4	5.5	26.9	47.9
Hispanic	15.0	7.2	25.7	40.1
White	5.6	2.2	10.8	17.7

*Negligible. Very few in this age group worked full-time all year-round.

Source: U.S. Department of Commerce, *Current Population Reports: Poverty in the United States: 1990,* Series P–60, No. 175 (Washington, D.C: U.S. Government Printing Office, 1991), Table 14.

and over and work full-time all year-round have the lowest incidence of poverty. Conversely, those between 18 and 24 years have the highest proportion below poverty regardless of the labor force status. Blacks and Hispanics have much higher poverty rates as compared to Whites in each labor status category. The most striking difference between males and females relates to the poverty rate of the population that is 65 years and over that did not work. Although only 9.1 percent of males in this labor market status category were poor, 16.9 percent of females in the same category were poor. One reason could be differences in the social security payments and age differences. There are more older females (over 80 years) than there are males. At those advanced ages, health problems are a major cause of poverty.

One of the central concerns in terms of poverty policy is the well-being of children. Since society does not expect children to participate in labor markets, their well-being largely depends on the labor force status of their parents. Tables 6-2 and 6-3 present data on the sources of income for families with children for 1989 and 1990. We consider families with a male present (Table 6-2) and those headed by a female (Table 6-3). The data reported shows the importance of the labor market as the main source of income for poor and nonpoor families with a male present. For example, in 1990, of all poor families with a male present, 82.2 percent had some labor market income, accounting for 65.3 percent of those families' incomes. For nonpoor families with a male present, 99.4 percent had some labor market income, accounting for 92.7 percent of these families incomes. Although there is a major difference in the incomes between the poor and nonpoor male-present families as reflected by the mean income per family member, the differences are primarily due to the fact that male heads of poor families do not work enough (work only part-time), earn low wages, or both.

A different story emerges when one considers the sources of income of families headed by females. In particular, the percent of poor families receiving market income is considerably lower. In 1990, only 50.6 percent of the poor families headed by females had labor market incomes, accounting for only 27.8 percent of the income of those families. For the nonpoor families headed by females, 95.6 percent had labor market incomes, which is considerably closer to that of families with a male present. Earnings, however, only accounted for 79.2 percent of incomes of nonpoor female-headed families. For poor families headed by females, the primary cause of low income is nonparticipation in the labor market. Also, the relatively small share of earnings for both the poor and nonpoor families headed by females may be low wages, or it may be that many female heads work only part-time.[10]

Figure 6-2 illustrates the importance of unemployment in explaining poverty. It plots annual changes in civilian unemployment rates and changes in poverty rates in the United States for the period 1960 to 1990. The figure shows that increases in the unemployment rates are associated with increases in the poverty rate. This unemployment-poverty relationship has been confirmed in several empirical studies. For example, Blank and Blinder (1986) found that a one point increase in the prime-age male unemployment rate increases the poverty rate by 0.7 percent in the same year.[11] Although the relationship between the unemployment rate and the poverty rate is strong, it is much weaker for some groups. Poverty rates for single

---

10. The lower share of earnings to the total earnings of female-headed families also is a result of the fact that alimony and child support payments are more important sources for female-headed families than for male-headed households. It is important to note that child support and alimony to families headed by females are higher for the nonpoor families. Nonetheless, child support and alimony payments comprise only a small fraction of the total income of female-headed families. Low or no child support payments by absent parents is one of the causes of poverty among female-headed families. The issue of child support is discussed in Chapter 13.

11. Rebecca Blank and Alan Blinder, "Macroeconomics, Income Distribution, and Poverty," in *Fighting Poverty: What Works and What Doesn't*, Sheldon Danziger and D. H. Weinberg, eds. (Cambridge, Mass.: Harvard University Press, 1986).

Table 6-2   Income composition of male-present families with children
(1989 and 1990)

	Poor[a]		Nonpoor[a]	
	1989	1990	1989	1990
Male-Present				
Percent of Families Receiving Income From				
Earnings	83.7	82.2	99.1	99.4
OASDI, railroad retirement pensions	8.7	10.6	5.6	5.2
Pensions	1.7	2.5	4.7	5.1
UC and other compensation	15.7	13.7	12.9	14.8
AFDC, SSI, general assistance	25.0	26.6	2.7	3.1
Child support, alimony	12.0	12.0	15.3	16.7
Interest, dividends	20.4	21.0	73.3	72.9
Food stamps	42.2	45.0	2.5	2.8
Housing assistance	10.2	9.7	0.8	1.0
Percent of Total Income From				
Earnings	66.8	65.3	93.2	92.7
OASDI, railroad retirement pensions	5.3	5.4	1.0	0.9
Pensions	0.6	1.1	0.9	1.0
UC and other compensation	4.4	3.5	1.0	0.9
AFDC, SSI, general assistance	10.8	11.2	0.2	0.3
Child support, alimony	2.2	2.0	0.9	1.1
Interest, dividends	1.3	1.3	3.5	3.3
Food stamps	7.7	8.0	0.1	0.1
Housing assistance	1.8	1.8	0.0	0.0
Mean income per family member in 1990 dollars	2,254	2,259	12,279	11,930
Percent with 50 percent or more of income from public assistance	16.5	16.5	0.2	0.2

[a]Poverty definition based on the official (Orshansky) levels.
Details may not sum to totals due to rounding.

Source: Committee on Ways and Means, U.S. House of Representatives, *Background Material on Programs Within the Jurisdiction of the Committee on Ways and Means* (Washington, D.C.: U.S. Government Printing Office, 1990).

Table 6-3   Income composition of female-headed families with children (1989 and 1990)

	Poor[a]		Nonpoor[a]	
	1989	1990	1989	1990
Percent of Families Receiving Income From				
Earnings	49.0	50.6	96.2	95.6
OASDI, railroad retirement pensions	10.8	9.2	16.3	14.3
Pensions	1.7	1.5	5.8	5.6
UC and other compensation	4.7	5.4	11.3	12.2
AFDC, SSI, general assistance	60.9	63.8	11.0	12.0
Child support, alimony	26.9	27.9	45.5	46.3
Interest, dividends	11.2	12.1	53.5	52.4
Food stamps	66.5	70.7	10.4	10.5
Housing assistance	29.9	34.1	6.0	6.3
Percent of Total Income From				
Earnings	27.8	27.8	79.1	79.2
OASDI, railroad retirement pensions	5.9	4.8	4.6	4.0
Pensions	0.6	0.5	1.5	1.6
UC and other compensation	1.0	1.2	1.5	1.6
AFDC, SSI, general assistance	32.9	31.7	1.5	2.0
Child support, alimony	5.8	5.9	8.1	7.9
Interest, dividends	0.3	0.4	3.4	3.1
Food stamps	16.5	17.3	0.4	0.5
Housing assistance	9.2	10.4	0.2	0.3
Mean income per family member in 1990 dollars	2,334	2,403	9.166	8,776
Percent with 50 percent or more of income from public assistance	55.2	57.0	1.6	2.3

[a]Poverty definition based on the official (Orshansky) levels.
Details may not sum to totals due to rounding.

Source: Committee on Ways and Means, U.S. House of Representatives, *Background Material on Programs Within the Jurisdiction of the Committee on Ways and Means* (Washington, D.C.: U.S. Government Printing Office, 1990).

Figure 6-2   Unemployment and poverty

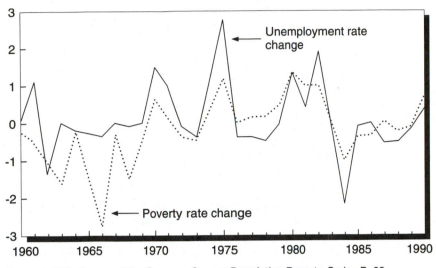

Source: U.S. Bureau of the Census, *Current Population Reports*, Series P–60, *Economic Report of the President*, 1992.

mothers, for example, respond much less to changes in the unemployment rate. Recent evidence by Blank and others suggests that the relationship between unemployment and poverty was weaker during the 1980s. Thus, although the unemployment rate declined from 9.7 to 5.3 percent in 1989, the poverty rates did not show significant declines. A primary reason for this weaker relationship is that a large proportion of the jobs created during the 1980s were low-wage. Thus, many people had jobs yet remained below the poverty level.

Although unemployment is important in explaining poverty, it is necessary to review briefly the trends in labor force participation rates and to evaluate the role of participation in contributing to poverty. Labor force participation rates tell us the percentage of the total noninstitutional population over 16 years of age who are in the labor force. As has been mentioned in the discussion of the measurement of unemployment, only those people who are actively searching for work are included in the unemployment statistics. The unemployment rate ignores many other people who are not actively searching for work, implying that they are not part of the labor force. As expected, groups that have low participation rates are likely to have high poverty rates.

Several reasons exist as to why some people do not participate in labor markets. A large number of nonparticipants are either sick or disabled. The other large group are the discouraged workers who have given up hope of ever finding work. The problem of discouraged workers is particularly important among residents of inner cities where limited employment opportunities exist. After searching for jobs for prolonged durations without success, these individuals stop searching. Some of the discouraged workers resort to underground activities: dealing with drugs, crime, and so forth.

Nonparticipation is more important among women. Although the female labor force participation rates have increased over time and the participation rates of males have declined, the female labor force participation rates remain much lower than those of men. For example, in 1950 the labor force participation rate for males was 88 percent and that of females was 34 percent. In 1992, the labor force participation rate for males was 75.9 percent and the participation rate for females was 57.8 percent. Thus, although the unemployment rates for females and males are almost the same (7.6 for men and 6.9 for women in 1992), there is a significant gap in the participation rates, which translates into differences in the poverty rates.

Several reasons have been attributed to the changes in the labor force participation rates. The decline in the participation rates for males is largely attributed to increased availability of social security and private pensions, and the growth in disability benefits. Social security and private pensions tend to induce early retirement.[12] The growth in disability benefits has affected the participation of prime-age men. This effect has been more pronounced in reducing the participation rates of black adults who otherwise earn low wages.[13] As expected, the more generous the disability benefits, the higher the probability of nonparticipation.[14] It should be noted that, measured in real terms, the generosity of most public assistance and social insurance programs has been declining or stagnant since the late 1970s.

Increased labor force participation rate of females is attributed to a number of factors. These include the increased employment and education opportunities for women, the enactment of laws that prevent discrimination, and the changes in societal attitudes concerning females working outside the home. Another important factor is declining fertility.[15] There is a negative relationship between the number of children and the participation rates. Although it is clear that lower fertility is associated with increased

12. See Gary Burtless and Robert Moffitt, "The Effects of Social Security Benefits on the Labor Supply of the Aged," in Henry J. Aaron and Gary Burtless, eds., *Retirement and Economic Behavior* (Washington, D.C.: Brookings Institute, 1984); Roger Gordon and Alan Blinder, "Market Wages, Reservation Wages and Retirement Decisions," *Journal of Public Economics* 14 (2) (October 1980): 277–308; and Gary S. Fields and Olivia S. Mitchell, *Retirement, Pensions, and Social Security* (Cambridge, Mass.: MIT Press, 1984).
13. See Donald O. Parsons, "Racial Trends in Male Labor Force Participation," *American Economic Review* 70 (5) (December 1980): 911–20.
14. See Robert Haveman, Barbara Wolfe, and Jennifer Warlick, "Disability Transfers, Early Retirement, and Retirement," in Henry J. Aaron and Gary Burtless, eds., *Retirement and Economic Behavior* (Washington, D.C: Brookings Institute, 1984): 65–93.
15. The decline in fertility is due primarily to the availability of contraceptives and increased number of abortions. It also is the case that females now postpone having children because they spend more years in school.

labor force participation rates of females, the direction of causality is not very clear. It also is possible that fertility has declined as a result of increased female labor force participation rates due to increased employment opportunities. Increased labor force participation rates also have been due to a desire for families to increase their standard of living which has been eroded by inflation and declining wages.

Rising divorce rates have been accompanied by increased female labor force participation rates. Married females, realizing there is a significant probability that they may get divorced, may protect themselves by entering the labor market. Those who divorce and were not working previously are likely to enter the labor market.[16]

In attempting to understand the causes of poverty, we also are interested in explaining the low participation rates particularly of the heads of poor households. This is especially important for female heads of households. Usually, the primary reason for nonparticipation by female heads is to take care of children.[17] In absence of low-cost child care, it often is not feasible for single mothers to work. However, it is possible that transfer benefits are much more attractive than what women would earn in the market so that it is rational for them to withdraw from the labor market.[18]

TYPES OF UNEMPLOYMENT

In order to appreciate some of the labor market policies discussed in Chapter 8, it helps to discuss the types and causes of unemployment. In this section, the types of unemployment are discussed. Causes of unemployment are discussed in the next section.

Economists generally classify unemployment into three types: frictional, structural, and cyclical or demand-deficient.[19] As will be seen, different types of unemployment often require different types of public policies. For example, some policies are better suited to deal with structural unemployment, while others deal with frictional or cyclical unemployment.

Frictional Unemployment

Consider a labor market in equilibrium such that the quantity of labor demanded equals the quantity of labor supplied. At the equilibrium wage, no shortages or surpluses exist and the level of employment represents full

---

16. It is possible that as females have become self-supporting by participating in the labor market, they have chosen to establish their own households. This would mean that participation leads to divorce. Issues about female headship are discussed more fully in Chapter 12 which focuses on the changing family structure.
17. See Mark S. Littman, "Reasons for Not Working: Poor and Nonpoor Householders," *Monthly Labor Review* (August 1989): 16–21.
18. The discussion of the effects of transfers appears in Chapter 13.
19. Seasonal unemployment is sometimes identified as another type of unemployment.

employment. At the prevailing wage, those workers who want to work have jobs. Nevertheless, this full employment equilibrium also involves some unemployment, because at any given time workers are caught between jobs. This is called *frictional unemployment*.

Workers frequently move from one job to another, into and out of the labor force. Because of imperfect information, job searchers and employers may not be well matched and some unemployment arises. Thus, even when job openings exist which could be suitably filled by the job searchers, frictional unemployment emerges because no instant matches can be made. If information were perfect and resource mobility costless, then this unemployment would not arise. In a sense then, frictional unemployment is unavoidable.

Frictional unemployment affects a relatively large number of people across demographic groups, locations, and industries. Turnover rates are higher in some industries than in others. Consequently, these industries will experience higher levels of frictional unemployment. Likewise, some demographic groups have higher turnover rates than others. For example, teenagers experience higher levels of frictional unemployment than older workers because young workers move in and out of the labor force more frequently.

The duration of frictional unemployment depends on economic conditions. Factors that affect the duration of job search generally will affect the duration of frictional unemployment. However, factors that reduce the duration of search, while they may be expected to reduce the duration of frictional unemployment, may also motivate some currently employed to quit, since they expect to be searching for only short durations. Thus, factors that reduce job search costs may not necessarily reduce frictional unemployment. Although frictional unemployment entails costs, it also has some benefits. For some workers, a spell of unemployment provides an opportunity to search for better job offers, making it an investment.

Structural Unemployment

Structural unemployment arises due to a mismatch between job skills demanded and those supplied. To illustrate how structural unemployment arises, consider a two-sector labor market model. Sector A is the market for computer programmers; Sector B, the market for teachers. Initially, both labor markets are in equilibrium so that no unemployment exists. If the demand for computer specialists increases, the wage for programmers will rise. If, at the same time, the demand for teachers declines, assuming that wages are not downwardly flexible, then unemployment occurs in sector B. If occupational mobility were costless, then labor would move from sector B to sector A and the unemployment problem would be resolved. The fact that occupational mobility is not costless and that wages are not always downwardly flexible implies that some people will be unemployed even though demand exists for their services in other sectors. Likewise, even when individuals have the necessary skills that are in demand, they may be living in one geographical location while jobs are available in another. Because it is costly to move (due to actual moving costs and social ties), mismatches are likely to persist. Thus, structural unemployment arises when labor demand changes in the face of rigid wages and costly regional and occupational mobility.

Structural unemployment continues to be pervasive, particularly among the poorest groups. For example, although many inner city teenagers seek jobs, their skills do not allow them to secure jobs in sectors of the economy that have job openings. Likewise, the unemployment rate in the Midwest has remained relatively high when compared to rates in the South.[20] Although migration has gone to the employment centers in the South, adjustment times allow structural unemployment to persist.[21]

A problem faced by residents of inner cities is that there has been a trend of outward migration of low-skill jobs to the suburbs. Although there are many residents of inner cities who would be willing to take those jobs, and although there may be openings for those jobs in the suburbs, inner-city residents are frequently not able to fill those openings either because they do not have information about the jobs or because it is too costly to travel to job centers. This is the idea of spatial mismatch and is discussed more fully in Chapter 11.[22]

Structural unemployment differs from frictional unemployment. The most important feature of structural unemployment is its concentration in particular groups of workers and industry types. Structural unemployment also tends to be of longer duration than frictional unemployment.

Cyclical Unemployment

Cyclical unemployment results from insufficient aggregate demand under conditions of downward rigidity of wages. As the name suggests, cyclical unemployment is closely linked to the business cycle. During periods of

---

20. See for example, "A Maddening Labor Mismatch," *Time* (April 26, 1986): 48–49; and "The Great Jobs Mismatch," *U.S. News and World Report* (September 7, 1987): 42.
21. For a discussion of the extent of structural (and frictional) unemployment and its causes, see Katharine Abraham, "Structural/Frictional vs. Deficient Demand Unemployment: Some New Evidence," *American Economic Review* 73 (4) (September 1983): 708–24; David Lilien, "Sectoral Shifts and Cyclical Unemployment," *Journal of Political Economy* 90 (August 1982): 777–93; and Katharine Abraham and Lawrence Katz, "Cyclical Unemployment: Sectoral Shifts or Aggregate Disturbances?" *Journal of Political Economy* 94 (June 1986): 507–22; and Jonathan S. Leonard, "In the Wrong Place at the Wrong Time: The Extent of Frictional and Structural Unemployment," in Kevin Lang and Jonathan S. Leonard, eds., *Unemployment and the Structure of Labor Markets* (New York: Basil Blackwell, 1987), pp. 141–63.
22. See George E. Peterson and Wayne Vroman, *Urban Labor Markets and Job Opportunity* (Washington, D.C.: Urban Institute Press, 1992).

economic expansion, the demand for goods and services causes an increase in the demand for labor such that unemployed persons are able to secure employment. On the other hand, the demand for goods and services declines during periods of economic downturns, and so does the demand for labor. If wages are not flexible downward, then unemployment emerges (as illustrated earlier in the case of teachers).

Unlike frictional and structural unemployment, cyclical unemployment varies widely, depending on the state of the economy. Although cyclical unemployment affects many workers, it affects those workers in durable goods industries more than those in nondurable goods industries. Cyclical unemployment spells generally are longer than those of frictional unemployment, but shorter than those of structural unemployment.

CAUSES OF UNEMPLOYMENT

The previous discussion has identified some of the causes of unemployment. To more fully understand the problem of unemployment, we briefly discuss some of the theories of unemployment: wage rigidity, search models, and efficiency wages.

Wage Rigidity

Figure 6-3 depicts the labor demand market D_L and L_S the labor supply. The quantity of labor demanded varies inversely with the wage rate. At higher wages, employers willingly hire a smaller workforce than at lower wages. The quantity of labor supplied is positively related to the wage rate. At higher wages, workers willingly offer more hours of work. When wages fall, workers supply fewer hours. The labor market is in equilibrium when labor supplied equals labor demanded (L_0). The wage when labor demand equals labor supply (W_0) is the equilibrium wage. At this wage rate, the labor market clears and no shortages or surpluses exist, except for frictional unemployment.

Suppose labor demand falls as shown by curve D^1, possibly due to a decrease in consumer demand for goods and services. If wages are freely flexible, then a new equilibrium wage is established at W^1, and the labor market clears. This occurs as businesses hire more people at lower wages and as some workers withdraw from the labor force because of the low wages, seeking instead to go back to school, or even to work at home. But, wages do not adjust as easily and a tendency will be for wages to be downwardly rigid. Thus, although labor demand decreases to D^1, the wage rate remains at W_0. In this case, a disequilibrium emerges, resulting in an excess supply of labor (unemployment). Consequently, wage rigidity causes unemployment.

Figure 6-3   Wage rigidity and unemployment

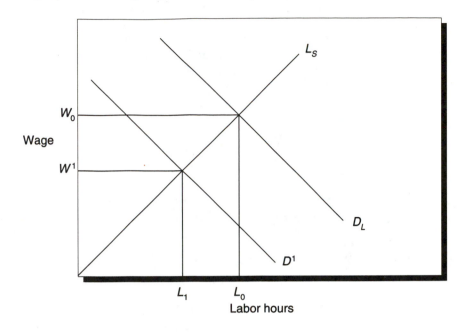

For public policy purposes, it is important to understand the factors that cause wage rigidity and, consequently, unemployment. Why don't wages decline with declining consumer demand and high unemployment?

Government-mandated minimum wages are among the more important factors that may explain wage rigidity. If the market clearing wage is below the minimum wage, then even though market conditions may require wages to fall, such adjustment will not take place and the wage will remain above the market clearing levels.

Another source of wage rigidity comes from labor union contracts. Labor union contracts are of a certain duration (frequently three years) and often specify minimal wages during this period. If economic conditions change during the contract period, it often is difficult to make any adjustments in the wages. Although labor unions may sometimes agree to wage cuts, such concessions are rare and often come too late after several workers have already been laid off.[23]

23. See James Medoff, "Layoffs and Alternatives Under Trade Unions in United States Manufacturing," *American Economic Review* 69 (3) (June 1979): 380–95; and Robert J. Flanagan, "Wage Concessions and Long-Term Union Wage Flexibility," *Brookings Papers on Economic Activity*, 1984 (15) (1): 183–216.

The growth of government transfer programs may also have contributed to wage rigidity. Programs such as unemployment compensation, food stamps, AFDC, social security, and so forth, reduce the pressure to accept jobs at lower wages. Being unemployed is not as costly today as it used to be when transfer programs were less available. Thus, workers have less incentive to lower their reservation wage.[24]

Flexible wages implies that when slack labor demand occurs, employers will lower wages. Even if unemployed workers may accept jobs at lower wages, employers may be unwilling to replace current workers because of turnover and training costs. Costs are incurred when experienced workers quit and are replaced with less-experienced ones. These costs include hiring expenses such as advertising, interviewing, and testing. In addition, new hires are probably less productive. That is, labor productivity falls when less experienced workers replace experienced ones. Lower wages also increase quit rates of workers at all levels. By adopting a strategy of selective layoffs, however, employers can keep the experienced and more productive workers while releasing the inexperienced and less productive workers. With this approach, the employers keep those workers with more firm specific human capital. Employers will, therefore, reduce employment rather than money wages.

Employees also may resist a reduction in the money wage because such reductions are viewed as affecting their relative position in the income distribution. Employees are more likely to accept a decline in their real wage due to prices rising, rather than a fall in real wages resulting from a decline in money wages. An increase in prices affects all people such that the relative position in the income distribution is not affected. Consequently, a tendency exists for workers to resist reductions in wages.[25]

Another source of wage rigidity may be implicit contracts. During economic downturns, employers can adjust by reducing the workforce or reducing the wages of all workers. Most employees, however, prefer that the employer reduce the number of employees. As it turns out, those fired are the least experienced.[26] In unionized industries, those with the least seniority are laid off and, because union leaders are elected by majority rule, laying off a minority of the most recent hires is the politically most acceptable situation. Although the layoff policy is not explicitly stated in

---

24. See Martin Feldstein, "Temporary Layoffs in the Theory of Unemployment," *Journal of Political Economy* 84 (5) (October 1976): 937–58; Robert Topel, "On Layoffs and Unemployment Insurance," *American Economic Review* 73(4) (September 1983): 541–59. We again note that the generosity of benefits stagnated through the 1980s.
25. This is the Keynesian argument for rigid wages; see John Maynard Keynes, *The General Theory of Employment, Interest and Money* (New York: Harcourt, 1936).
26. See Costas Azariadis, "Implicit Contracts and Underemployment Equilibria," *Journal of Political Economy* 83 (6), (December 1975): 1103–1202; and Martin Bailey, "Wages and Employment Under Uncertain Demand," *Review of Economic Studies* 41 (1) (January 1974): 37–50.

nonunion industries, implicit contracts probably exist between employers and employees. Here again, the most preferred line of action is to reduce employees without affecting wages.[27]

Job Search Explanations

Most workers experience an unemployment spell during which they engage in job search. Even workers who are already employed and who only want to search for a better job are likely to experience a spell of unemployment. Such spells of unemployment are likely to be fairly short. For those who have lost jobs, the search process may take much longer. Job search models of unemployment attempt to explain the factors that determine the length of time that persons remain unemployed as they search for jobs. The two main theories of job search are the cost-benefit model by George Stigler, and the reservation wage model by John McCall. Both models will be briefly discussed.

George Stigler was the first to formalize a model of job search.[28] According to Stigler, the duration of job search depends on the expected costs and benefits. Job search costs arise from both direct and indirect sources. Direct costs are directly incurred in the search and include such items as applications, visits to employers and employment agencies, and so forth. Indirect costs arise from the forgone earnings when an offer is turned down. As a person turns down offers, the forgone income is an opportunity cost. Continued job search incurs increasing marginal cost. The benefits of search exist because better offers are likely to come from more prolonged search. Because individuals try to interview with the more promising offers first, the marginal benefit of search declines with additional searches. Thus, the marginal benefit of search is subject to diminishing returns.

According to Stigler, search continues until the marginal cost of search equals the marginal benefit. If the marginal benefit exceeds the marginal cost, then the individual will not accept the job offers and will continue to search. Job search ends when $MC = MB$ as shown in Figure 6-4.

Stigler's model suggests that increasing government transfers to the unemployed makes it less costly to be unemployed. The marginal cost shifts to the right as shown in Figure 6-4 and the optimal duration of search increases from S^* to S^1.

---

27. Another theory, the "insider-outsider" hypothesis, suggests that union members are insiders and do not care much about former members who have been laid off. Consequently, the insiders will negotiate wage increases that benefit them and not wage cuts that would result in a recall of previous members. See Assar Lindbeck and Dennis J. Snower, *The Insider-Outsider Theory of Employment and Unemployment* (Cambridge, Mass.: The MIT Press, 1988). See also Robert M. Solow, "Insiders and Outsiders in Wage Determination," *Scandinavian Journal of Economics* 87 (1985): 411–28.
28. See George Stigler, "Information in the Labor Market," *Journal of Political Economy* 70 (Supplement), (October 1962): s94–s105.

Figure 6-4   Stigler's model of job search

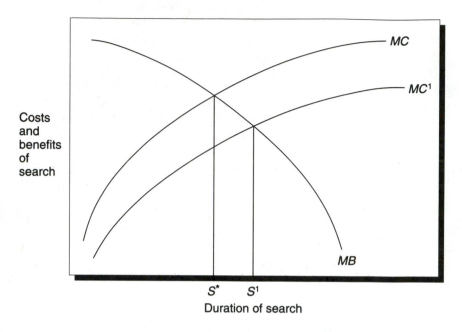

The model by John McCall keys on the minimum acceptance wage.[29] Unlike the Stigler model where workers base their decision to accept an offer based on the costs and benefits, the McCall model assumes that workers will continue looking for offers until they get one that exceeds their minimum acceptance wage. The minimum acceptance wage is the lowest wage that an unemployed person will consider accepting. Because different individuals have different minimum acceptance wages, the length of job search will vary from one individual to another.

The minimum reservation wage depends on individual characteristics such as age, experience, education, previous pay, and so forth. A person who has a relatively low minimum acceptance wage will accept a job offer sooner than a person who has set a higher minimum wage. The minimum acceptance wage, however, is not fixed. After an individual searches for a job and does not secure the offers at the desired wage, that individual can

---

29. John J. McCall, "Economics of Information and Job Search," *Quarterly Journal of Economics* 84 (1) (February 1970): 113–26. See also Dale T. Mortensen, "Job Search and the Duration of Unemployment, and the Phillips Curve," *American Economic Review* 60 (5) (December 1970): 847–62.

reevaluate and lower the minimum acceptance wage. As the acceptable wage falls, more jobs become available to the individual.[30]

Efficiency Wages

The efficiency wage theory of unemployment postulates that work effort and efficiency are positively related to the wage rate.[31] At a higher wage, workers work harder and are easier to monitor. This suggests that a firm can increase profits by paying wages that are higher than those determined by the market. Employers therefore have an incentive to pay employees above the market wage. The higher wage results in more work effort as workers value their jobs more and also raises the employees' cost of being fired. Simply put, losing a job at a higher wage rate entails a higher opportunity cost than losing a job at a lower wage. As firms compete by offering higher wages, prevailing wages rise above those that would clear the labor market. Thus, a type of voluntary unemployment emerges because some of the workers who are not employed would have been willing to work at a lower wage.

EXPLAINING THE COMPOSITION OF UNEMPLOYMENT AND CHANGES IN UNEMPLOYMENT RATE

Table 6-4 presents data that show the distribution of unemployment by various demographic groups and race. The data illustrate that some groups experience higher unemployment rates than other groups. For example, Whites have the lowest unemployment rate, Blacks have the highest. Of all demographic groups, teenagers have the highest unemployment rates. For antipoverty policy, it is important to understand why these groups experience such high unemployment rates, which translate to poverty. Another concern is that the aggregate unemployment rates have increased over time. Such a change would be expected to have contributed to increasing poverty. This section briefly reviews the underlying causes of these outcomes.

---

30. See William Barnes, "Job Search Models, the Duration of Unemployment and the Asking Wage: Some Empirical Evidence," *Journal of Human Resources* 10 (2) (Spring 1975): 230–40; and Nicholas M. Kieffer and George R. Neumann, "An Empirical Job Search Model, with a Test of the Constant Reservation-Wage Hypothesis," *Journal of Political Economy* 87 (February 1979): 89–107.
31. See Janet Yellen, "Efficiency Wage Models of Unemployment," *American Economic Review* 74 (May 1984): 200–05; and George A. Akerlof and Janet L. Yellen, eds., *Efficiency Wage Models of the Labor Market* (Cambridge, England: Cambridge University Press, 1986); George A. Akerlof and Janet L. Yellen, "The Fair Wage-Effort Hypothesis and Unemployment," *Quarterly Journal of Economics* 105 (2) (May 1990): 255–84.

Table 6-4   Unemployment rate by race and demographic groups (1988)

Age	White Male	White Female	Black Male	Black Female	Hispanic Male	Hispanic Female
16–17	16.1	14.4	34.4	35.9	29.5	24.5
18–19	12.4	10.8	31.7	29.6	19.5	18.9
20–24	7.4	6.7	19.4	19.8	9.2	10.7
25–54	3.8	3.9	8.9	9.4	6.5	6.6
55+	3.0	2.5	5.4	4.5	6.8	4.3
Total	4.7	4.7	11.7	11.7	8.1	8.3

Source: U.S. Department of Labor, Bureau of Labor Statistics, *Employment and Earnings*, various issues.

Composition of Unemployment

Probably the most important explanation for high unemployment rates among minorities is lack of skills. People with low skills are likely to have a more difficult time getting a job and are the ones who are the first to be let go by employers during times of declining demand. It also is the case that those with low skills are less likely to be self employed. It follows, therefore, that skill development is crucial to solving the unemployment problem of minorities and teen workers who do not join college.

For teenagers, the primary cause of high unemployment rate is that they frequently leave employment and move in and out of the labor force. Although they also are more vulnerable to layoffs, teenagers frequently quit jobs voluntarily. It also has been suggested that a major cause of teenage unemployment is the minimum wage regulation. As was demonstrated in Chapter 2, minimum wages have the effect of generating unemployment. It is clear that an employer who is under the minimum wage constraint is likely to lay off those employees with lowest productivities.

The unemployment problem of minorities also is attributed to the fact that there are just no jobs in most of the areas in which a large number of Blacks and Hispanics live—the inner cities. The exodus of employment centers from the inner cities to the suburbs have left many minorities with very limited employment opportunities. As would be expected, the lack of jobs in the inner cities is highly correlated with poverty rates in those areas. The problem of unemployment by inner-city minorities is compounded by the fact that they rarely have any connections outside the ghetto that would provide them with better information about job availability.

It has been observed that minorities have higher unemployment rates than Whites even when they reside in the same area. One explanation for this result is that of labor market discrimination discussed in Chapter 9. Another explanation keys on the reservation wage job search model. It has been observed that Blacks tend to set a fairly high reservation wage compared to what they are actually able to get in the market. For example, a 1979 survey found that the average reservation wage for Black youths was $4.22 per hour while the wages they actually received averaged $3.90 per hour. For White youths, the reservation wage was $4.30 and the average wage actually received was $4.63 per hour. This implies that Black youths are likely to remain unemployed for much longer durations than White youths.[32]

Increasing Unemployment Over Time

We now turn to the issue of changing unemployment rates over time. The causes of unemployment discussed previously produce the various types of unemployment, the sum of which is the unemployment rate reported by the Bureau of Labor Statistics. To a large extent, major fluctuations in the unemployment rate are cyclical. Nevertheless, both structural and frictional unemployment have increased over time. Even after unemployment declines following a recession, the unemployment rate has settled at a higher level than before the recession. This result is more clearly shown by examining the average unemployment rates for different periods. The unemployment rate averaged 4.5 percent during the 1950s, 4.7 percent during the 1960s, and 6.2 percent during the 1970s. The average unemployment rate during the 1980s was above 7.4 percent. Given the relationship between unemployment rate and poverty, we can expect such increases in unemployment to also have contributed to increases in the poverty rates over time.

Some of the causes for increased frictional unemployment has been the change in the composition of the labor force. This has involved the increased participation rates of females and teenagers. Both of these groups have much higher turnover rates, which would be expected to result in higher frictional unemployment. Another factor is the increase in government transfers, such as the unemployment insurance benefits. As discussed, availability of benefits during the nonwork spells, lowers the cost of being unemployed.

The increase in structural unemployment has been attributed primarily to the technology changes and the decline in blue collar employment, such as in manufacturing. Another important factor has been the increased number of baby boomers in the labor market who have tended to crowd the teenage market after failing to secure employment in higher paying jobs. Finally,

---

32. See Harry J. Holzer, "Reservation Wages and Their Labor Market Effects for Black and White Male Youth," *Journal of Human Resources* 21 (Spring 1986): 157–77.

there has been a rapid growth in the Black underclass which experiences high structural unemployment rates. The main reasons for the growth in the Black underclass are discussed in Chapter 11.

SUMMARY

This chapter has concentrated on the relationship between unemployment and poverty, and the various aspects of unemployment including measurement, its causes, trends over time, and its composition. The primary goal of the chapter is to demonstrate the link between unemployment, nonparticipation, and poverty.

The first issue discussed in this chapter relates to the definition and measurement of unemployment. It was shown that while unemployment rate is an important statistic, one must note its shortcomings, especially the fact that it mismeasures hardships experienced by some members of the population. Specifically, the unemployment rate does not take into account discouraged workers, underemployed workers, and low-wage workers.

Nonetheless, the unemployment rate and other measures of labor force status are important in explaining the incidence of poverty. This chapter presented data that illustrate that labor market status is a very important determinant of poverty status. For example, families whose heads work full-time and all year-round have the lowest poverty rates. On the other hand, families with heads who do not work have the highest poverty rates.

This chapter also discussed frictional, structural, and cyclical unemployment and how these different types of unemployment emerge. Various theories of unemployment were discussed including wage rigidity, job search explanations, and efficiency wage explanations. There also was discussion of how the causes of unemployment relate to the composition of unemployment, and why unemployment has increased over time.

Understanding a problem such as unemployment and nonparticipation in the labor market is the first stage in designing appropriate policy. This has been this chapter's main goal. Before focusing on labor market policies, Chapter 7 will focus on the other labor market problem—low-wage employment.

STUDY AND DISCUSSION QUESTIONS

1. Explain how the unemployment rate is measured in the United States.

2. Discuss some of the shortcomings of the official measure of unemployment.

3. One of the reasons that some people are poor is that they do not participate in labor markets. Explain several factors that affect labor force participation.

4. Outline the various factors that may explain the trends in labor force participation rates in the United States.

5. Write an essay on the three types of unemployment. You should discuss how each arises, the composition (who is affected by such unemployment and which industries), and the duration.

6. Carefully discuss four factors that have been responsible for increased structural and frictional unemployment in the United States.

7. Write a paragraph on each of the following:

   (a) Factors that cause wage rigidity

   (b) Job search explanation for why the unemployment rate for Black teens is much higher than that for White teens

   (c) Discouraged workers

   (d) Underemployment

8. Think about some people whom you personally know who are not working at present. Your task is to classify them into different labor market categories: not in labor force, in the labor force, or unemployed. For those not in labor force, provide some explanation why they are not participating in the labor market. For those who are unemployed, explain what type of unemployment they are facing. Are the people you discussed poor? To what extent do you think their economic status is due to their labor market status? Are any of them discouraged workers? Explain why you think they are discouraged workers.

9. Using sources of data cited in this chapter, look at the recent trends in unemployment rates and poverty rates. Write a short paragraph on the relationship between the two variables.

10. One often hears statements such as "They are poor because they do not want to work," and "The poor want to work but there are simply no jobs." Which of these statements do you think is correct? Do you have any evidence? Do you know any persons who are poor because they do not want to work? You should provide

evidence that shows that the people you mentioned simply do not want to work.

ADDITIONAL READINGS

1. Anderson, Bernard E. and Isabel V. Sawhill, eds. *Youth Employment and Public Policy.* Englewood Cliffs, N.J.: Prentice-Hall, 1980.

2. Beckerman, Wilfred, ed. *Wage Rigidity and Unemployment.* Baltimore: Johns Hopkins University Press, 1986.

3. Bergmann, Barbara R. *The Economic Emergence of Women.* New York: Basic Books, 1986.

4. Berkowitz, Monroe and M. Anne Hill, eds. *Disability and the Labor Market: Economic Problems, Policies and Programs.* Ithaca, N.Y.: ILR Press, 1986.

5. Ehrenberg, Ronald G. and Robert S. Smith. *Modern Labor Economics: Theory and Policy.* New York: Harper Collins, 1990.

6. Kaufman, Bruce E. *The Economics of Labor Markets.* Chicago: Dryden Press, 1989.

7. McConnell, Campbell R. and Stanley L. Brue. *Contemporary Labor Economics.* New York: McGraw-Hill, 1989.

8. Rees, Albert. "An Essay on Youth Joblessness," *Journal of Economic Literature* 24 (June 1986): 613–28.

7

LABOR MARKETS AND POVERTY: LOW-WAGE EMPLOYMENT

As shown in Chapter 6, many poor families have a head of household who is employed. In particular, a large fraction of poor households with a male present rely primarily on labor market incomes. Table 7-1 presents data that shows the prevalence of working poor. The data shows the characteristics of poor and nonpoor workers in 1987. Of all persons who spent at least 27 weeks in the labor force, 6.4 million were poor. Thus, having an employed person in the household does not guarantee that a family necessarily escapes poverty. A major cause of poverty among the working poor is the fact that they do not work enough.[1] Thus, although they may be employed for most of the year, this group experiences spells of unemployment, or only works part-time. Many other people work full-time all year round and still have incomes below the poverty standard. Low-wage employment causes poverty for this latter group of working poor.[2]

The data reported in Table 7-1 reveal some important characteristics of the working poor. Column A shows the number of poor workers in various categories and column B is the percent of poor workers in each category. Column C shows the number of nonpoor workers in various categories and column D is the percentage of nonpoor workers in each category. Column E is the poverty rate among the working population; it measures the number of poor workers as a percentage of all workers who spent 27 weeks or more in the labor force in 1987. Although other factors such as age and sex are important, the data suggests that poverty among the working population is mainly linked to family relationships, race, and education of the worker.

---

1. This is the underemployment problem discussed in Chapter 6.
2. In 1984, there were three million full-time working poor in the United States, comprising one-fifth of the able-bodied poverty population of working age. For data on the working poor for various years, see the U.S. Bureau of the Census, *Statistical Abstract of the United States* (Washington, D.C.: U.S. Government Printing Office, various issues); and the U.S. Bureau of the Census, *Money, Income, and Poverty Status of Families in the United States*, Series P-60 (Washington, D.C.: U.S. Government Printing Office, various issues).

Table 7-1   Characteristics of poor and nonpoor workers (1987) (numbers in thousands)

| Characteristic | Poor Workers | | Nonpoor Workers | | Poverty rate[a] |
	Number A	Percent B	Number C	Percent D	E
Age					
Total, 16 years +	6,400	100.0	107,089	100.0	5.6
16 to 19 years	494	7.7	4,275	4.0	10.4
20 to 24 years	1,175	18.4	11,837	11.1	9.0
25 to 54 years	4,163	65.0	76,490	71.4	5.2
55 years +	568	8.9	14,487	13.5	3.8
Sex					
Men	3,346	52.3	60,022	56.0	5.3
Women	3,054	47.7	47,067	44.0	6.1
Race					
White	4,647	72.6	93,649	87.4	4.7
Black	1,567	24.5	10,269	9.6	13.2
Family Relationship					
Husbands	1,669	26.1	38,088	35.6	4.2
Wives	685	10.7	27,114	25.3	2.5
Women who maintain families	1,091	17.0	5,074	4.7	17.7
Men who maintain families	158	2.5	1,857	1.7	7.8
Others in families	860	13.4	17,071	15.9	4.8
Unrelated individuals	1,937	30.3	17,886	16.7	9.8
Education					
Fewer than 4 years of high school	2,466	38.5	16,051	15.0	13.3
4 years of high school	2,620	40.9	43,355	40.5	5.7
1 to 3 years of college	867	13.5	22,215	20.7	3.8
4 years of college or more	447	7.0	25,468	23.8	1.7

Notes:
Because of rounding, sums of individual items may not equal totals.

[a]The number of poor workers as a percent of all workers who spent 27 weeks or more in the labor force in 1987.

Source: Bruce W. Klein and Philip L. Rones, "A Profile of the Working Poor," *Monthly Labor Review* 112 (October 1989): 5.

Working women with families experience higher poverty rates than working men with families. Even though males probably earn higher wages than females on average, the data show that families with a working husband have a higher probability of being poor than families with a working wife. This is because husbands are more likely than wives to be the sole income earner in the family. Unrelated individuals living together have higher poverty rates than those who live with relatives.[3]

Poverty rates differ significantly between Black and White workers. One reason for this is that Black workers have family types that perpetuate poverty.[4] In particular, Black men are disproportionately represented among the group of poor households comprised of unrelated individuals. Moreover the poverty of Black workers is exacerbated by their relatively low levels of education.[5] As the data shows, while the poverty rate of those with four years of college education or more was 1.7 percent, in 1987 the poverty rate was 13.3 percent among those with fewer than four years of high school.

Clearly, low-wage employment is an important cause of poverty. Two approaches can help explain why some people earn low wages. The first approach uses the concept of human capital while the second uses imperfections in the labor market. One important labor market imperfection is race and sex discrimination, which may cause minorities and females to command low wages relative to their human capital. Other labor market imperfections emerge from the structure of labor markets. The structuralist approach relies on dual labor market theory. This chapter considers human capital and structuralist explanations of low wages and defers discussion of discrimination to a later chapter.

HUMAN CAPITAL INVESTMENT, EARNINGS, AND POVERTY

Human capital refers to factors that increase the quality of labor.[6] Thus, human capital investment includes not only expenditures on formal education and specific job training, but also expenditures on health, migration, job search, and preschool nurturing of children. These investments affect

---

3. Unrelated individuals are those who live with others to whom they are not related.
4. See, for example, Bruce W. Klein and Philip L. Rones, "A Profile of the Working Poor," *Monthly Labor Review* 112 (10) (October 1989): 3–13.
5. Black workers also are more likely to face labor market discrimination that translates to lower earnings.
6. See Lester Thurow, *Investment in Human Capital* (Belmont, Calif.: Wadsworth Publishing Co., 1970); and Gary S. Becker, *Human Capital*, 2nd ed. (New York: Columbia University Press, 1975).

the qualitative aspects of labor that essentially implies increased productivity of labor. Just as investment in physical capital increases productivity, human capital investment refers to expenditures that increase individual productivity.

To the extent that wages reflect the productivity of individuals, human capital investment should affect the level of wages. Those with more human capital should earn higher wages, and vice versa. Figures 7-1A, B, and C map the age-earning profiles of various categories of the population. Figure 7-1A shows that annual earnings increase as the level of human capital increases. This trend also is evident in Figures 7-1B and 7-1C. These figures demonstrate that, at any level of human capital, Blacks earn less than Whites, and females earn less than males. Increased human capital is nevertheless associated with higher earnings for all groups.

The importance of education in the determination of earnings has been supported by various empirical studies. John Akin and Irwin Garfinkel estimated the returns to schooling using regression analysis. Their results document that, on average, earnings rise by about 13 percent for each additional year of schooling.[7] Gary Becker calculated the internal rate of return on human capital investment to be 14.5, 13.0, and 14.8 percent in 1939, 1949, and

Figure 7-1A   Mean income of males in the U.S., by age and education, 1990

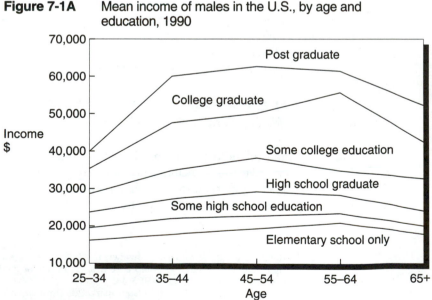

Source: U.S. Statistical Abstract, 1992.

———————
7. John Akin and Irwin Garfinkel, "School Expenditures and the Returns to Schooling," *Journal of Human Resources* 12 (4) (Fall 1977): 460–81.

Figure 7-1B   Median income of males in the U.S., by education and race, 1990

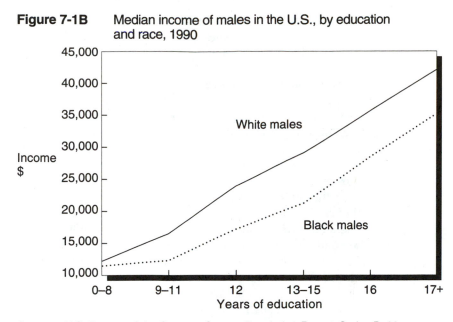

Source: U.S. Bureau of the Census, *Current Population Report,* Series P–60, No. 174, Table 29.

Figure 7-1C   Median income by education and sex, 1990

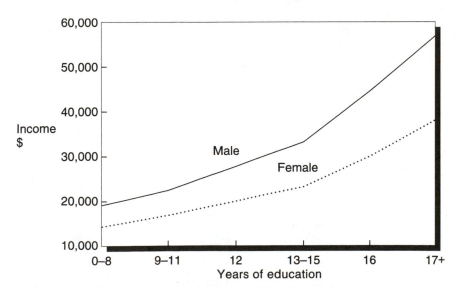

Source: U.S. Statistical Abstract, 1992.

1958, respectively.[8] Peter Mattila found that the rates of return on human capital investment for males was between 10 to 13 percent for the 1956 to 1979 period.[9] Richard Freeman deduced the returns to college for men to be in the range of 8 to 10 percent.[10]

The available evidence on the relationship between education and earnings clearly suggests that many people are poor because they do not invest enough in human capital. Before proposing antipoverty policies that focus on human capital formation, it is necessary to explore why some people seem to underinvest in human capital. This discussion requires a model of the human capital investment decision. We ask why the optimal investment in human capital is difficult for some individuals to achieve.

Although this discussion primarily focuses on the role of human capital in raising productivity, it is important that we also mention nonmarket benefits of human capital investments. Such benefits are relevant because they affect the well-being of the population in ways that reduce poverty. There is evidence for example that the level of parents' schooling increases child quality through home activities. Also, schooling positively and significantly affects health status and thus reduces mortality. Education also is positively associated with reduced criminal activity. Children of better-educated parents receive better care, guidance, and so forth. This implies that investment in education has valuable intergenerational effects. Thus, although the text focuses only on the market benefits, it is important to keep in mind these other nonmarket benefits from education.[11]

MODEL OF HUMAN CAPITAL INVESTMENT BY THE INDIVIDUAL

This section considers a model of the decision to invest in human capital by the individual. This decision could be thought of as the decision to acquire a college education after graduating from high school. Like all other economic choices, the decision to invest in human capital is the outcome of a rational optimizing process. Such a process involves a comparison of the costs and benefits associated with acquiring human capital.

---

8. Gary Becker, *Human Capital.* We define the rates of return as used in connection with human capital investment later in this chapter.

9. Peter Mattila, "Determinants of Male School Enrollments: A Time Series Analysis," *Review of Economics and Statistics* 64 (2) (May 1982): 244–51.

10. Richard B. Freeman, "Overinvestment in College Training?" *Journal of Human Resources* 10 (3) (Summer 1975): 287–311. See also Giora Hanoch, "An Economic Analysis of Earnings and Schooling," *Journal of Human Resources* 2 (3) (Summer 1967). A review of empirical literature on returns to higher education is presented in Howard Bowen, *Investment in Learning* (San Francisco: Jossey-Bass Publishers, 1977), Chapter 12.

11. For an excellent discussion of nonmarket benefits from education, see Robert H. Haveman and Barbara W. Wolfe, "Schooling and Economic Well-Being: The Role of Nonmarket Effects," *Journal of Human Resources* (Summer 1984): 377–406.

Two types of costs are incurred to acquire a college education. The first are direct or explicit out-of-pocket costs. Direct costs include tuition and other fees, books, and supplies. (Food and housing costs incurred at college are not included because the student would have incurred these costs even if he or she chose not to attend college). The other costs are indirect, implicit, or opportunity costs, representing the forgone benefits, typically earnings, that would have been earned in the labor market. If a student could earn $20,000 per year with a high school diploma, then this is the opportunity cost of attending college.

The benefits associated with a college education are not realized immediately; they accrue in the future in the form of increased earnings. Thus, the benefits of attending college are measured by the increased flow of earnings above those that would have been earned with only a high school diploma. Figure 7-2 portrays the costs and benefits associated with a college education.

The earnings profile *HS* represents those who decide not to attend college. We assume that individuals begin to work at 18 years of age. If a person goes to college, his or her earnings profile is *FKL*. During the four years at college, students incur indirect costs (*A*), that is, forgone earnings, and direct costs (*B*) reflected in the figure as negative earnings. When the student graduates from college, he or she earns more than the high school graduate. The benefits of a college education emerge as the incremental earnings in area (*C*).

Figure 7-2   Benefits and costs of human capital investment

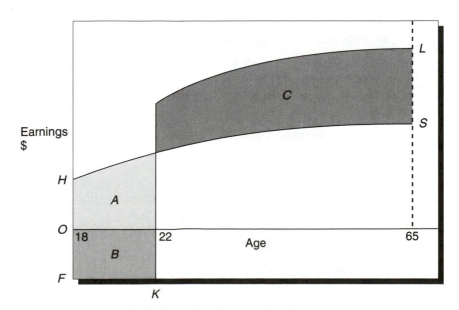

At first glance, the choice to acquire a college education may appear simple and direct; we just compare the costs and benefits. If C is greater than $(A + B)$, then the person should invest in a college education. However, this simple calculation is misleading. The benefits and costs of a college education accrue at different points in time. Money that is spent or received in the current time period is not directly comparable to money spent and received in the future. A proper comparison requires that the costs and benefits be evaluated in terms of a common time, for example the current period. That is, we want to know the present value of costs and benefits of a college education.

To illustrate the present value concept, we use a simple example. Suppose you have $\$R_0$ today that you save for one year. If the rate of interest is i, then after one year, the original $\$R_0$ will be worth $\$R_1$ the principal plus interest payments. That is,

(7.1)
$$R_0 (1 + i) = R_1$$

If R_1 is reinvested for another year, it will again earn interest such that after the second year the amount will be equal to R_1 plus interest payments. Thus,

(7.2)
$$R_1 (1 + i) = R_2$$

But $R_1 = R_0 (1 + i)$. Therefore,

(7.3)
$$R_2 = R_0 (1 + i) (1 + i), \text{ or}$$
$$R_2 = R_0 (1 + i)^2$$

In general, the future value of $\$R_0$ invested for t years at the interest rate i is given by

(7.4)
$$R_t = R_0 (1 + i)^t$$

To more clearly show how the future value of an investment is calculated, assume that we start with $5000 in year one. If the rate of interest is 10 percent, then at the end of 10 years, the initial $5000 will be equal to R_{10}, where,

(7.5)
$$R_{10} = \$5000 (1 + .10)^{10} = \$12,968.71$$

To obtain the present value, we reverse the problem. If you receive R_t t years in the future, then what is R_t worth today? This is the same as calculating R_0 given R_t and i;

(7.6)
$$R_t = R_0 (1 + i)^t, \text{ and therefore,}$$
$$R_0 = R_t/(1 + i)^t$$

If an income stream is received over n years, then the present value can be generated as follows:

(7.7)
$$R_0 = \sum_{t=1}^{n} R_t/(1+i)^t$$

To illustrate this, assume that $1000 is received for three years at the rate of interest of 5 percent. The present value in this case is equal to the amount in the first year plus the discounted value in the second year and the discounted value in the third year. Thus,

(7.8)
$$R_0 = \$1000 + \$1000/(1+0.5) + \$1000/(1+0.5)^2$$
$$= \$1000 + \quad \$952.38 + \qquad \$907.44 \qquad = \$2859.82$$

Note that the present value is less than the amounts actually received ($2859.82 as compared to $3000).[12]

Use the formula for the present value to calculate the incremental benefits of a college education over a high school education. The idea is to maximize the present value of the amount invested in human capital.

Finally, we need to consider both the direct and indirect costs associated with a college education. Because the costs are incurred over several periods, it is necessary to calculate the present value of costs. As above, the future value of $\$C_0$ cost incurred in the current period can be expressed as

(7.9)
$$C_t = c_0 (1+i)^t$$

and the present value of cost is

(7.10)
$$C_0 = C_t/(1+i)^t$$

The decision as to whether to attend college is based on the net present value (NPV), which is obtained by subtracting the present value of costs from the present value of benefits. Thus,

(7.11)
$$NPV = \sum_{t=0}^{n} R_t/(1+i)^t - \sum_{t=0}^{n} C_t/(1+i)^t$$

The individual should make the investment if the net present value is greater than zero. Such a positive value implies that the present discounted value of benefits exceed the present discounted value of costs.

---

12. This arises because of the idea of time preference. Given a choice, most people prefer to consume goods and services today rather than in the future.

An alternative approach of making investment decisions on human capital is to calculate the internal rate of return (IRR) on the investment and compare it with the market rate of interest. The internal rate of return of an investment is the rate of discount at which the net present value of that investment will be zero. In other words, if the internal rate of return of an investment is greater than the market rate of interest, then such an investment is profitable. In using the internal rate of return, one determines the rate of discount that equates the present value of future costs and benefits so that the net present value is zero. Thus, one calculates the IRR by setting the present value of benefits equal to the present value of costs and solving for the discount rate r. The internal rate of return is then compared with the rate of return on other investments. If internal rate of return on human capital investment is greater than the discount rate, then one should invest in human capital.

The Equilibrium Level of Human Capital Investment

The model just presented helps answer several questions concerning human capital investment. We are, for example, interested in understanding why there are differences in the level of human capital investment between various individuals. Some people drop out of high school, others attend college, while still others go on to graduate school. These outcomes can be understood by studying a simple model of the equilibrium level of human capital investment.

Although investing in human capital leads to increased earnings, the rate of increase diminishes. The marginal benefit or demand for human capital investment declines with increased investment. That is, the rate of return decreases with increased human capital investment. Human capital investment results in increased labor market skills and knowledge that ultimately translate into higher earnings. Years of schooling are a variable input that is combined with a fixed set of individual endowments. Such endowments include a person's physical and mental abilities and other innate characteristics such as motivation. Increased human capital investment leads to increased knowledge and skills, but the rate of increase eventually starts to decline. The benefits of human capital also decrease because a person has a limited amount of time for which to earn market income. Thus, investing more in human capital reduces the amount of time left to earn market incomes.

A second factor that enters the demand for human capital investment is cost. With more years of schooling, the costs increase and benefits decrease. First, the opportunity cost of schooling rises as one invests more and more in human capital, since the wage that one would earn in the market increases with the level of human capital. This means that area A in Figure 7-2 increases implying increasing opportunity cost. In addition, the private cost of education increases with additional investment. For example, the cost of acquiring an elementary school education is lower than the cost of acquiring a high school education. Likewise, a college education is more expensive than a high school education. Thus, because of diminishing returns and increasing costs of additional education, the rate of return to human capital investment declines with more investment. This implies that the demand for human capital investment is downward sloping.

Previously, we determined that a person should invest in human capital if the internal rate of return r_h is greater than the interest rate i. Figure 7-3 plots the interest rate and the internal rate of return along the vertical axis. The horizontal axis measures years of education. As described above, we expect the demand for human capital investment (D_h) to be downward sloping. Suppose that the interest rate is equal to i_h. We assume that a person can borrow funds to invest in human capital regardless of the level of investment. Thus, i_h is the supply of investment funds for human capital.

Human capital investment is worthwhile if the internal rate of return is at least equal to the interest rate. For levels of human capital investment less than e^*, the internal rate of return is higher than the interest rate. In this case, the individual will benefit from investing more in human capital. For levels of human capital investment greater than e^*, the internal rate of return is less than the rate of interest. It is consequently not beneficial for the individual to invest beyond e^*. From another viewpoint, the problem is that the demand curve measures the marginal benefit while the supply curve measures the

Figure 7-3   Equilibrium level of human capital

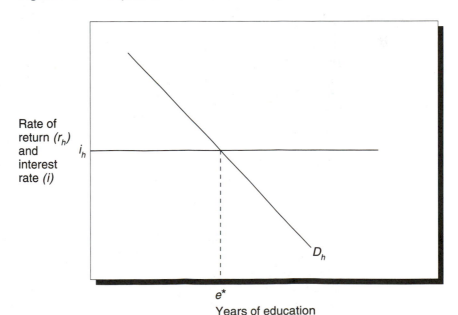

Years of education

marginal cost. The optimal choice is to invest up to the point where the marginal benefit is equal to the marginal cost, in this case e^*.

The use of a perfectly elastic supply of loanable funds in Figure 7-3 assumes that the student can borrow all funds for human capital investment at the same cost. Often this simplification is incorrect. For most students, the cost of funds increases as they move from elementary to high school, and then to college. At the elementary school level, the interest cost for most students is zero because the costs are met by the parents. As the students attend higher levels of education, they may have to rely on their own source of funds, starting with those funds that have the lowest interest cost. At first, they may use low-interest education loans. After exhausting this facility, they may have to rely on their own funds, the cost of which is the forgone interest earnings. Eventually, students may have to rely on higher interest bank loans. This implies that the supply of investment funds is upward sloping as shown in Figure 7-4. The upward sloping supply curve of investment funds, however, does not alter the optimal decision making rule already discussed.

HUMAN CAPITAL INVESTMENT BY THE FIRM

Firms also invest in human capital. This is done through on-the-job training and a variety of other formal training programs. Firms invest in human capital because such investment increases the productivity of labor. In addition, the firm's physical capital becomes more productive because of the complementality between the human and physical capital. The benefits of advanced technology are not realized by the firm unless there are workers who are well trained to use such technology.

The investments that firms undertake can be specific or general. Specific training is peculiar to the firm. For example, a computer manufacturer could train its workers to install a computer chip used only in computers made by that firm. General training, on the other hand, involves broader general skills development. For example, training a worker to use a particular word processing software that is used by many other employers could be considered general training. Just like individuals, firms follow the rational choice model in their decisions to invest in human capital.

Unlike investing in physical capital where returns are owned by the firm, investment in human capital is not legally owned by the firm. A person can benefit from the training in one firm and then leave to work for another firm. Thus, human capital investment by the firm is associated with free-rider problems. This is the outcome whereby other firms bid away workers from the employer who undertook the human capital investment. That is, although Firm A incurs the training costs that make a particular worker more productive, Firm B hires the now more productive

Figure 7-4   Equilibrium level of human capital (with increasing costs of funds)

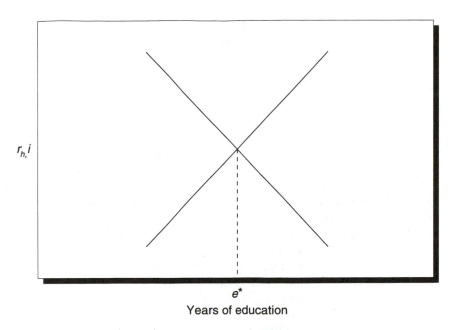

e^*

Years of education

worker and thus gets the benefits without incurring the costs of training. The free-rider problem motivates firms to underinvest in general human capital choosing instead to invest primarily on specific human capital.

PROBLEMS ASSOCIATED WITH HUMAN CAPITAL INVESTMENT

The investment decision rules just discussed are straightforward. We expect individuals and firms to make optimal investment choices given the necessary information. There are a number of problems, however, that cause nonoptimal results and that may have implications for poverty. These issues will be discussed briefly.

Risk and Uncertainty–Because the returns to human capital investments are realized over an extended period of time, risk and uncertainty affects the benefits. Such factors cause individuals to underinvest in education.

Switching Costs–Unlike other types of investment, human capital investment has high switching costs. If a person makes a mistake and realizes the mistake several years later, there may be little that he or she can do. This all-or-nothing nature of human capital investment translates to lower levels of human capital investment.

Consumption Aspects of Human Capital–Investment in human capital has some consumption aspects. It is difficult to separate the consumption from the investment aspects.

Ability Differences–There are wide variations in ability. It is therefore difficult to use the experience of others as a guide in deciding on the optimal level of investment. Ability differences translate into different levels of human capital investment across individuals.

Discrimination–Some people may encounter discrimination in the process of acquiring human capital. Even after attaining the education, some people may encounter discrimination in the labor market. The existence of discrimination therefore reduces the net present value of an investment that in turn leads to a reduction in the level of human capital investment.

Access to Funds–Like all investment, one needs to have access to funds. Although the net present value of human capital investment may be high, this may not be realized if funds are not available to invest in education.

To illustrate how ability, discrimination, and differences in access to funds affect the level of human capital investment, consider two individuals, A and B. If B has greater mental and physical talents than A, then at any level of schooling, B will be more productive than A. Thus, the rate of return to B is higher than to A, and hence B's demand curve for human capital is to the right of A's demand curve. As shown in Figure 7-5, A's optimal level of human capital investment is lower than B's.

If, on the other hand, both A and B have equal abilities but A is likely to encounter labor market discrimination, then A's expected earnings are lower than B's. That is, A's rate of return from human capital investment is lower than B's as shown in Figure 7-5. The result is that A invests less than B.

Now consider the case where A and B have equal abilities but different access to investment funds. Thus, although the two have similar demand curves for human capital, the supply of investment funds differs. Suppose B is from a wealthy family such that he or she is able to obtain funds at lower interest rates while A is from a poor family and is only able to borrow at higher interest rates.[13] This situation is shown in Figure 7-6. The optimal level of human capital investment by A (e_a) will be lower than for B (e_b).

For the poor and minorities, the process of human capital investment can be an even more serious problem. Minorities are much more likely to encounter discrimination in both the labor market and in the provision of education. Both of these will result in lower levels of human capital investment as already illustrated. Conversely, most of the poor do not have access to funds to invest in education. For this reason, many end up not investing or only investing in limited amounts of human capital.

---

13. A person from a wealthy family is able to post certain assets as collateral against a loan; such a person can borrow at a low rate of interest. Those from poor families are risky borrowers and have no assets to place as collateral. Thus, they are able to borrow funds only at an interest rate that includes a risk premium.

Figure 7-5   Ability, discrimination, and human capital investment

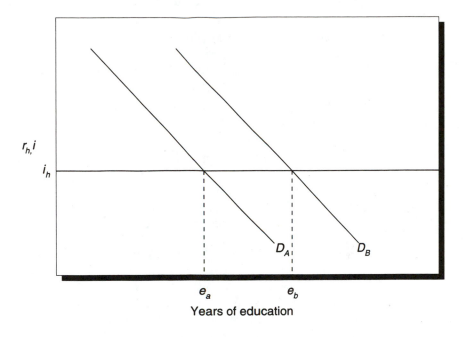

Years of education

Figure 7-6   Access to funds and human capital investment

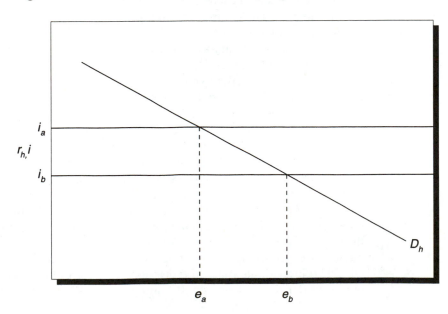

Although all individuals face uncertainty in investment in human capital, this is a more serious problem among the poor. In addition, the poor have lower early education opportunities that affects their expected return from a college education. Finally, the poor have a greater need to earn current income than those from more wealthy households. The existence of these factors increases poverty and income inequality. Thus, while human capital investment can increase the income of the poor and can reduce inequality, in the absence of policies to aid the poor, human capital investment magnifies poverty and inequality.

PUBLIC INVESTMENT IN HUMAN CAPITAL

The largest proportion of human capital investment is undertaken by the government. This occurs through grants to institutions or to individuals. Public investment in human capital development covers a wide array of education and training programs starting from preschool to colleges and vocational training schools. Human capital investment is probably one of the most important functions that governments perform.

The problems associated with human capital investment discussed previously justify the involvement of the government. Because of risk and uncertainty about future returns, many people are likely to underinvest in human capital. The government can reduce the risk and uncertainty by contributing some of the human capital investment funds. Likewise, lack of funds, particularly by those from poor families, leads to underinvestment in human capital. Many students are not able to borrow money from the private markets because they do not have collateral to borrow against. Government is then required to support those with limited funds or to act as a guarantor of their loans.

Finally, although we focus on the return to human capital investment that accrues to individuals, human capital investment has some social benefits, too. Society benefits from educated persons. For example, educated persons are less likely to be unemployed and, as such, less likely to receive benefits such as unemployment compensation or to be on welfare. Educated persons are also less likely to be involved in socially costly activities such as crime. Furthermore, an educated population is much more likely to make better political choices that may benefit society at large. In other words, human capital investment entails positive externalities in the form of benefits that spill over to others in society.

Figure 7-7 shows the private and social benefits of education. MB_i is the marginal benefit of an additional year of schooling to an individual. MB_S is the marginal benefit to society when the individual in question attends one more year of school. MC is the supply of investment funds for human capital. When individuals make the decision to invest in human capital, they only consider the private benefits and costs. Thus, the individual would

Figure 7-7   Private and social benefits of education

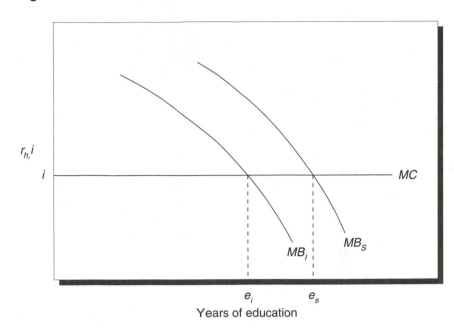

Years of education

select e_i. However, at this level of education, the marginal benefit to society exceeds the marginal cost. The best point for society is where MB_S equals the MC, shown by e_S. Failing to incorporate the social benefits implies that the resulting level of human capital, although optimal from the individual's perspective, is not socially optimal. Government participation is necessary to help achieve the socially optimal levels of investment.

DUAL LABOR MARKET THEORY

The human capital model links low wages to low human capital investment that translates into lower marketable skills. The human capital theory is consistent with the orthodox model of wage determination. This model assumes that the market wage is determined entirely by the interaction of labor demand and labor supply. Any factor that increases the marginal product of labor shifts the demand for labor outward, thereby resulting in a higher equilibrium wage. Persons with lower human capital are less productive and, hence, command a lower market wage. This model does not take into account institutional factors such as job assignments and barriers in the labor market. In other words, the orthodox model assumes that all that matters is the labor market conditions: the position and slope of the demand and supply curves. Thus, the level of wages is entirely the result of the market process.

The dual labor market theory challenges the orthodox theory of wage determination by considering institutional factors. Specifically, the theory states that the labor market is divided into primary and secondary sectors. These two segments of the labor market have different characteristics and strong institutional barriers separate the two so that mobility from one sector to the other is virtually nonexistent. The wages in the two markets also are markedly different. The primary sector is characterized by employment and job stability; high and consistently increasing wages; lucrative benefits (including health insurance and life insurance); and opportunities for upward mobility. The secondary sector, on the other hand, is characterized by bad, low-paying jobs. Employment in this sector often is unstable; has high turnover rates; receives wages that are not only low but stagnant for prolonged periods; has no opportunities for upward mobility, offers dead-end jobs; and involves production that is mainly labor intensive. While in the primary sector job security often is assured by the presence of labor unions, workers in the secondary sector are not unionized and therefore those workers' job security is at the mercy of management. Another important difference between the two sectors is the provision of on-the-job training. Workers in the primary sector have opportunities to invest in human capital through a variety of on-the-job training programs. Such opportunities do not exist in the secondary sector. As expected, those in the secondary market end up primarily as working poor.[14]

The characteristics in each of the sectors are self-reinforcing and thereby keep the two sectors distinct. In the primary sector, rising wages compel management to adopt strategies to increase productivity so as to offset the increased cost of production. Such strategies involve investment in advanced technology. The use of modern sophisticated technology necessarily requires the firm to continually invest in on-the-job training for their workers. Because of the investment cost incurred in training workers, employment stability is essential for the firm to realize the returns from such investment. Employment stability, in turn, provides a climate conducive to unionization, which assures job security. In the secondary sector, management faces no pressure to raise productivity by introducing new technology because of the low wages. Thus, wages remain lower and stagnant in this sector. Likewise, management has no incentive to provide on-the-job training for workers in the secondary sector. As expected, no strong

---

14. Some important literature on dual labor market theory includes Michael J. Piore, "Jobs and Training," in *The State and the Poor,* S. Beer and R. Barringer, eds. (Cambridge, Mass.: Winthrop Press, 1970); Peter B. Doeringer and Michael J. Piore, *Internal Labor Markets and Manpower Analysis* (Lexington, Mass.: D.C. Heath & Co., 1971); Michael Reich, David M. Gordon, and Richard C. Edwards, "A Theory of Labor-Market Segmentation," *American Economic Review* 63 (2) (May 1973): 359–65; David M. Gordon, *Theories of Poverty and Underemployment* (Lexington, Mass.: Lexington Books, 1972); Richard C. Edwards, Michael Reich, and David M. Gordon, eds., *Labor Market Segmentation* (Lexington, Mass.: D.C. Heath & Co., 1975); and David M. Gordon, Richard Edwards, and Michael Reich, *Segmented Work, Divided Workers* (Cambridge, England: Cambridge University Press, 1982).

relationship exists between workers and employers such that turnover is high. High turnover rates are not conducive to unionization that would otherwise help attain job security.

The distinctiveness of the two sectors is further magnified by the worker attitudes that evolve. In the primary market, with stable employment and rising wages, workers become reliable and develop good work habits; that is, they report to work on a regular basis and on time. Workers in the secondary sector have no opportunity for upward mobility and hence develop poor work habits; high absenteeism and tardiness are common in the secondary sector. Those who end up in this sector become trapped. Thus, even if a worker has good work habits, but is assigned to the secondary sector, these good habits eventually disappear. As expected, those in the secondary sector are likely to be the working poor and to remain so throughout most or all of their working lives.

How does labor market segmentation arise? The answer relates to *internal labor markets*. An internal labor market is an administrative unit where wage determination and the allocation of job assignments are determined primarily by administrative procedures rather than market forces. In this setting, there exists a clearly stipulated hierarchy of jobs. A worker starts at one job and climbs the career ladder to jobs with more responsibility and privileges. The initial point where an employee gains access to the job ladder, called the port of entry, is where management can assign some employees to the primary sector and others to the secondary sector. According to dualists, one's earnings and productivity does not necessarily depend on the amount of human capital investment, but rather on the success at the port of entry. Those who gain access to a good job ladder in the primary market end up with high incomes. Those on a job ladder in the secondary market end up earning lower wages and hence have a high probability of being poor.

Dualists argue that while human capital investment may be important in determining the sector to which workers are assigned, other factors are more important. One explanation for dual labor markets is the desire of management to create divisions among workers. Having some workers in privileged well-paying jobs and others in bad low-paying jobs reduces the probability of unity between the two groups. A unified labor force, according to structuralists, has the potential of threatening the stability of the capitalist system by raising class consciousness. Dualists argue that employers exploit existing race, ethnic, and gender antagonisms such that class conflicts are deflected into race, ethnic, and gender conflicts.[15]

Of critical importance in the assignment of workers to particular sectors is discrimination. How an employer assigns jobs to a worker is based primarily on subjective evaluation of how a worker will perform in the internal labor market. This causes statistical discrimination whereby some groups of

---

15. Some evidence that supports this view is the fact that Black workers have historically been used as strikebreakers when blue collar, White workers strike.

workers are assigned to job ladders in the secondary sector while other groups are assigned to job ladders in the primary sector.[16] The empirical evidence suggests that statistical discrimination assigns minorities and females to the secondary sector where they earn low wages and develop poor work skills. Dualists see the large number of working poor minorities and females as a result of statistical discrimination exercised at the port of entry.

STRUCTURALISTS' VIEWS ON POVERTY

In order to appreciate the policies suggested by structuralists to deal with the problem of the working poor, it is necessary to review briefly how structuralists view the problem of poverty in society. Unlike human capital theorists who view poverty as a result of underinvestment in human capital, structuralists consider poverty as having clear and useful functions in a capitalist system.[17] Specifically, structuralists see the existence of poor as essential for the maintenance of capitalist institutions. The following discussion mentions a few of the important functions of poverty as presented by structuralists.

First, the existence of poverty ensures that undesirable jobs are performed. Poverty serves to provide a pool of lower-wage workers who are willing to do "bad" jobs at a low cost. Secondly, low wages translate to lower prices for goods and services that the affluent consume. Thus, the wealthy are better able to save most of their incomes and accumulate wealth because of the low cost of goods that they buy. Structuralists contend that the presence of a large army of unemployed workers serves the system by ensuring that wages remain low for those with jobs. This process also weakens the bargaining position of the workers as they can be easily replaced by the unemployed.

Thirdly, the poor purchase goods and services that others do not want, such as old automobiles and houses. The poor, therefore, provide a ready market for products that the more affluent want to discard because the poor are not able to buy new products. Finally, structuralists argue that the presence of the poor acts as a warning to the nonpoor that if they do not comply with the rules set by the employers, their fate can be worse. Such strategies create divisions among the workers which helps the employers.

Although the empirical relevance of the structuralist view is difficult to ascertain, this view is important as it helps one to understand some of the

---

16. Statistical discrimination is discussed more fully in Chapter 9.
17. For a detailed analysis of the structuralist view, see Herbert J. Gans, "The Functions of Poverty," in David M. Gordon, ed., *Problems in Political Economy: An Urban Perspective*, 2nd ed. (Lexington, Mass.: D.C. Heath & Co., 1977), pp. 312–16; and Howard M. Wachtel, "Capitalism and Poverty in America: Paradox or Contradiction?" *American Economic Review* 62 (2) (May 1972): 187–94.

public policies suggested. Specifically, the structuralists view suggests that while policies to increase human capital of the poor are important, such policies may not be sufficient to deal with the labor market problems of minorities and women. Interventionist policies may be called for to monitor the hiring and job assignment procedures used by employers.

SUMMARY

There is a widely held perception that the poor are generally lazy people who do not work and who do not want to work if jobs are available. This chapter demonstrated that many poor people work. They earn wage incomes that are too low to pull them above the poverty standard. This text has presented two diametrically opposed explanations for the existence of lower wages: the human capital theory and the structuralist perspective. The human capital view considers low wages to be the result of low investment in human capital. Some problems that limit human capital investment by the poor were identified. For example, we have looked at how access to funds and discrimination could result in low levels of human capital investment.

The structuralist view, however, places the blame for the existence of lower wages on the structure of labor markets. The dual labor market theory, which is used by structuralists to explain the emergence of lower wage employment, was presented. The differences between the two approaches were emphasized by a brief look at the structuralist view of poverty.

Naturally, the different views of the causes of lower-wage employment lead to different policy prescriptions. Chapter 8 focuses on labor market policies to deal with both unemployment and lower-wage employment.

STUDY AND DISCUSSION QUESTIONS

1. Consider a person whom you know who works full-time but has low earnings. Based on what you know about that person, list the various reasons you think he or she earns low wages.

2. Discuss the various explanations for the causes of low-wage employment as outlined in this chapter. In your opinion, what is the more credible explanation for low-wage employment?

3. Discuss the issues involved in making human capital investment by the individual. (You should present a human capital investment model.)

4. Outline problems that result in underinvestment in human capital.

5. Why should the government be involved in human capital investment?

6. Clearly explain what you understand about the dual labor market theory. Discuss the differences between the primary and secondary sectors.

7. Critically evaluate the structuralists' views on poverty.

8. Classify various jobs in your institution into primary and secondary sector jobs. List the race and gender of the people in the different jobs. Discuss the pattern that you observe and provide an explanation. Based on your analysis, do you think that the dual labor market theory is credible? Why or why not?

9. Some studies show that the relationship between unemployment and poverty was weaker during the 1980s than it was in the 1960s. Explain what the reason might be for this weaker relationship.

10. Consider some of the people who attended high school with you and who did not enter college. Based on the human capital model, provide explanations as to why you think they ended up with only a few years of schooling.

ADDITIONAL READINGS

1. Cain, Glen G. "The Challenge of Segmented Labor Market Theories to Orthodox Theory: A Survey," *Journal of Economic Literature* 14 (4) (December 1976): 1215–57.

2. Schwarz, John E. and Thomas J. Volgy. *The Forgotten Americans.* New York: W.W. Norton and Co., 1992.

3. Wachtel, Howard M. and Charles Betsey. "Employment at Low Wages," *Review of Economics and Statistics* 54 (2) (May 1972): 121–23.

4. Willis, Robert J. "Wage Determinants: A Survey and Reinterpretation of Human Capital Earnings Functions," in Orley Ashenfelter and Richard Layard, eds., *Handbook of Labor Economics*, Vol. 1. Amsterdam: Elsevier Science Publishing Co., 1986.

8

LABOR MARKET POLICIES

Chapters 6 and 7 examined three causes of poverty: unemployment, non-participation in labor markets, and low-wage employment. A shortage of jobs means that some people cannot find work and do not earn labor market incomes. Others may find only part-time work that does not fully utilize their skills and may not provide sufficient income to keep them out of poverty. Still other people work full-time, but earn wages that are so low that they fall below the poverty level. Low-wage employment results primarily from low investment in human capital, or from the existence of imperfections in the labor market, such as race and sex discrimination. As noted in Chapter 7, the dual labor market theory suggests that minorities and females are concentrated in low-paying jobs in the secondary sector not because of their low productivity, but because of discriminatory hiring practices. This chapter concentrates on antipoverty policies that address the problems of unemployment and low wages. The problems of discrimination in labor markets and in the provision of human capital, as well as the public policies designed to deal with such imperfections, are discussed in Chapters 9 and 10.

Policies that deal with unemployment and with low-wage employment involve job creation and employability improvement. Other policies that deal with low-wage employment focus on better pay for work. As discussed in Chapter 6, there are various reasons for unemployment. For example, frictional unemployment emerges because of insufficient information necessary to match jobs and skills. In this case, appropriate policies increase job information. Structural unemployment occurs because of mismatch between skills and jobs. The solution to this source of unemployment centers on improving human capital, for example, by providing education and training for the unemployed. Cyclical unemployment results from a deficiency in aggregate demand. Policies that deal with cyclical unemployment focus on influencing aggregate demand for labor directly or by providing incentives to increase production, which, in turn, increases the demand for labor. Policies that deal with the problem of low-wage employment key primarily on increasing productivity, such as providing opportunities for training and job experience (that is, so-called manpower policies). Policies that focus on better pay for work influence the wage directly (for example, mandating minimum wages for work), or increase benefits to workers (for example, medical and child care benefits).

Since the early 1930s, a large array of government programs have been used to deal with the labor market problems. Not all of these programs are discussed here. However, to simplify the discussion that follows, Table 8-1 lists some of the more important federal programs that have been used to deal with labor market problems since 1932. The list includes job creation programs and employability improvement programs. To give the reader the basic goals of the programs and the population they were meant to serve, the program description and target group are included. The table reveals that the government has been actively involved in dealing with labor market problems, particularly of the most disadvantaged populations: long-term unemployed, low-wage earners, those with limited human capital, and so forth. In the section that follows, some of the job creation programs and policies are introduced, followed by a discussion of some manpower policies.[1]

JOB CREATION

Direct job creation policies involve more public service jobs. Indirect job creation policies influence the equilibrium level of output that, in turn, affects the equilibrium level of employment. Indirect job creation policies involve two broad categories: demand side and supply side. Demand side policies affect the equilibrium level of output by increasing aggregate demand. Supply side policies affect the equilibrium level of output by providing incentives for increasing production. The increase in the equilibrium level of aggregate output leads to an increase in the demand for labor, thus reducing unemployment.

(A) Public Service Employment–The U.S. government deals with unemployment with more government jobs. This policy is equivalent to increasing the demand for labor so that the equilibrium level of employment rises. This strategy has been used during times of chronic unemployment including the Great Depression, when the country experienced high and persistent unemployment. In 1929 the unemployment rate was 3.2 percent; by 1933, it was 24.9 percent. Between 1931 and 1940, joblessness never fell below 14 percent and remained above 20 percent between 1932 and 1935. These high unemployment rates, and the resulting poverty, led to the

---

1. For a more detailed explanation of the labor market policies in the United States that will be discussed in this chapter, see Thomas Janoski, *The Political Economy of Employment* (Berkeley: University of California Press, 1990).

Table 8-1   Federal labor market programs, 1932–1993

Program	Years	Description	Target Group
Relief and Construction Act	1932–1933	Public construction projects	Unemployed
Civilian Conservation Corps	1937–1943	Temporary jobs in national parks and forests	Unemployed youth
Civil Works Administration	1933–1934	Temporary jobs on small-scale public works projects	Unemployed
Public Works Administration	1933–1943	Temporary jobs on large-scale public works projects, such as roads and dams	Unemployed and Veterans
Works Progress Administration	1935–1942	Temporary jobs on small-scale projects for community betterment	Unemployed
Social Security Act (Unemployment Insurance)	1935–Present	Partial and temporary income support	Unemployed, laid-off from regular jobs
Area Development Act	1961–1965	Grants and loans to help attract industry and to retrain workers	Unemployed residents of economically depressed areas
Public Works Acceleration Act	1962–1963	Temporary jobs on federal public works projects	Employed and unemployed job applicants in areas of high unemployment

Table 8-1   (Continued)

Program	Years	Description	Target Group
Manpower Development and Training Act	1962–1974	Vocational training	Initially, unemployed workers displaced by automation; later low-income youth and adults
Economic Opportunity Act	1964–1974	Vocational training, part-time jobs, remedial education	Principally low-income youth
Emergency Employment Act	1971–1974	Temporary jobs in state and local government services	Unemployed
Comprehensive Employment and Training Act (CETA)	1973–1983	Training, part-time and full-time jobs, employment services	Long- and short-term unemployed and low income
CETA Title I (changed to Title II in 1978)	1973–1983	Comprehensive employment and training services, including vocational training, and part-time work experience	Initially the unemployed and low-income; after 1978, only long-term unemployed and low-income
CETA Title II (changed to Title IID in 1978)	1973–1983	Temporary jobs in state and local government and the private sector	Initially, the unemployed and low-income; after 1978, only long-term unemployed and low-income

Table 8-1   (Continued)

Program	Years	Description	Target Group
CETA Title III	1973–1983	Training and part-time work experience	Long-term unemployed Native Americans, migrants, and youth
CETA Title IV (Job Corps revised from the Economic Opportunity Act)	1970–1983	Residential training and remedial education programs	Low-income, unemployed youth
CETA Title VI (Emergency Jobs and Unemployment Act of 1974 and Emergency Jobs Programs Extension Act of 1976)	1974–1983	Temporary jobs in state and local government and the private sector	Initially, the unemployed and low-income; after 1978, only long-term unemployed and low-income
CETA Title VII (Private Sector Initiative Program)	1978–1983	Established private industry councils to carry out employment training program	Long-term unemployed and low-income
CETA Youth Employment Demonstration Program	1977–1982	Several experimental training and part-time jobs programs	Low-income youth, high school students or dropouts
Trade Adjustment Act	1975–Present	Temporary income support and retraining programs	People unemployed because of import competition
Local Public Works program	1976–1977	Temporary jobs on small-scale public works	Employed and unemployed construction workers

Table 8-1   (Continued)

Program	Years	Description	Target Group
New Jobs Credit	1977–1978	Tax credits to businesses hiring new employees	Businesses hiring new workers and unemployed
Targeted Jobs Tax Credit	1977–Present	Tax credits to businesses hiring workers from targeted groups of unemployed	Low-income youth, Vietnam-era veterans, ex-convicts, welfare recipients, participants from vocational rehabilitation programs
Job Training Partnership Act	1983–Present	Replaced CETA's vocational training programs; increases involvement of private sector in program planning and operation	Long-term unemployed and low income

Source: *Employment and Training Report of the President*, various issues.

enactment of New Deal policies. Some of the more important public service employment programs included the Civil Works Administration (CWA), the Works Progress Administration (WPA), the Civil Conservation Corps (CCC), and the National Youth Administration (NYA).[2]

CWA was established in November 1933 by President Franklin D. Roosevelt. This program's purpose was to create four million jobs by December 1933. By January 1934, more than four million Americans were put to work at prevailing wages by the federal government. Individuals who were hired built and improved roads, schools, airports, playgrounds, and a variety of other projects. CWA was terminated in April 1934.

WPA was established under the Emergency Relief Appropriation Act of 1935. The goal of WPA, as stated by President Roosevelt, was to provide jobs to all able-bodied unemployed persons in the United States. Unlike CWA, WPA paid wages that were below the prevailing wages. At its peak, WPA employed more than three million people who worked on various public projects such as roads, bridges, and public buildings.

CCC and NYA focused on young people. CCC provided employment to a total of 2.5 million young men. This program emphasized conservation projects: planting trees, stocking fish, and building roads and trails in forests and parks. NYA served more than 1.5 million high school students, over 600,000 young people in colleges, and an additional 2.6 million out-of-school jobless youths.

Public service employment was resurrected during the 1970s. The Emergency Employment Act of 1971 established the Public Employment Program (PEP) in an attempt to alleviate the unemployment problem.[3] Under this program, the federal government provided funds to state and local governments to hire the unemployed and to subsidize their wages in transitional public sector jobs. Also, the Comprehensive Employment and Training Act of 1973 (CETA) provided public service jobs.[4] In response to the recession of 1974 to 1975, a new Title VI of CETA was included that provided approximately 300,000 public service jobs for the cyclically unemployed. Eligibility required only that a person be unemployed for seven days. During the late 1970s, the public service employment program under CETA was expanded. In May 1977, Congress appropriated more than $8 billion for temporary job measures through October 1978. By

---

2. See, for example, Arthur M. Schlesinger, Jr., *The Coming of the New Deal: The Age of Roosevelt* (Boston: Houghton Mifflin, 1959), and Harold L. Sheppard, Bennett Harrison, and William J. Spring, *The Political Economy of Public Service Employment* (Lexington, Mass.: Lexington Books, 1972).
3. Public Service Careers (PSCs) discussed later in this category could also be included but the main purpose of this program was training. The program, however, focused on helping disadvantaged workers obtain jobs in the public sector.
4. Other aspects of CETA are discussed later in this chapter.

March 1978, approximately 739,000 people were provided with CETA public service jobs.[5]

(B) *Demand Side Policies*–The most important demand side interventions are fiscal and monetary policies. Expansionary fiscal policy involves discretionary actions that adjust taxes and expenditures to promote full employment, price stability, and economic growth. Conversely, monetary policy involves discretionary actions by the Federal Reserve to adjust the nation's money supply and interest rates. When there is a decline in the demand for national output, there is a concomitant decline in the demand for labor, and hence an increase in unemployment. The intended effect of expansionary fiscal and monetary policy is to increase the demand for national output to increase the demand for labor.

To illustrate how fiscal and monetary polices affect employment, consider the goods and labor markets shown in Figures 8-1A and 8-1B. Initially, aggregate demand and supply of national output are shown by curves D_0 and S_0, respectively. The equilibrium level of national output is equal to Q_0 and the equilibrium price level is P_0. This level of output corresponds to the demand for labor shown by LD_0 in Figure 8-1B. If the labor supply curve is LS_0, then E_0 represents the equilibrium level of employment and W_0 the equilibrium wage. Q_0 is the full employment level of output, and E_0 is the natural rate of employment.[6] If there is a decrease in the demand for national output from D_0 to D_1, the level of national output declines to Q_1. The corresponding effect in the labor market is a reduction in the demand for labor from LD_0 to LD_1. The decline in the demand for labor, under conditions of downwardly rigid wages, results in a reduction in the level of employment to E_1. Thus, $(E_1 - E_0)$ is the unemployment that results from the decline in aggregate demand for labor from LD_0 to LD_1. The goal of expansionary fiscal and monetary policy is to increase the demand for national output from D_1 to D_0 so that the demand for labor shifts from LD_1 to LD_0.

Some policies that could accomplish this task include the following three plans.

1. *Tax cuts for individuals.* Tax cuts increase the disposable income available for consumption. Increased consumer income causes an increase in the aggregate demand for goods and services that, in turn, leads to an increase in the demand for labor by firms. Some tax cuts intended to increase consumer demand were enacted in 1964, 1970, and 1974.

---

5. See MDC, Inc., *The Planning and Implementation of CETA Title VI PSE Expansion Projects Under the Economic Stimulus Program of 1977,* Report to the Employment and Training Administration (Washington, D.C.: U.S. Department of Labor, June 1978).
6. This is the level of unemployment that is compatible with price stability. Deviations from this natural rate imply disequilibrium in the labor market caused by real wages departing from their market clearing levels.

Figure 8-1   Demand side policies

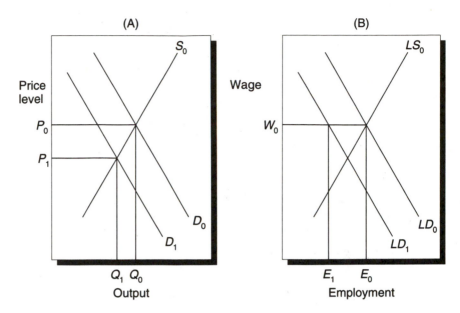

2. *Increasing government expenditures.* The government can increase its purchases of goods and services from the private sector that, in turn, leads to an increase in the demand for labor by private sector employers. Good examples of government spending programs to create employment were the New Deal programs. Rather than directly providing public service employment, the government contracted out projects to the private sector. The Public Works Administration (PWA) was established in 1933 to over-see the construction of such projects. For example, between 1933 and 1939, PWA was responsible for the construction of about 70 percent of the nation's new schools, and 65 percent of the courts, city halls, tunnels, bridges, libraries, and highways.[7]

Although the use of public works as an antipoverty tool has been abandoned in recent years, it may be resurrected by the Clinton adminis-tration. Clinton has proposed investing in the nation's infrastructure as a way of creating jobs. Whether such a program will be enacted by Congress remains to be seen.

7. For a detailed discussion of public work projects created under the New Deal, see John K. Galbraith, *The Economic Effects of the Federal Public Works Expenditures,* 1933–38 (Washington, D.C.: U. S. Government Printing Office, 1940), and William J. Tobin, *Public Works and Unemployment: A History of Federally Funded Programs* (Washington, D.C.: Economic Development Administration, Department of Labor, 1975).

3. *Monetary expansion.* Increasing the money supply reduces the cost of funds by lowering interest rates, which promotes investment. Increased investment by firms necessarily translates into an increase in the demand for labor.

Although the use of fiscal or monetary policy instruments to change aggregate demand may appear easy, in practice some complications arise. For example, even if policies are effective, the policy-making process takes time. Thus, the effects of policy always occur with a time lag. One needs to forecast to implement macro policy.

A more serious problem with the use of demand management policies to increase employment is inflation. The previous analysis assumed that the government was able to use various instruments to shift demand back to its original level, D_0, consistent with the natural level of output and employment, thereby maintaining price and wage stability. However, governments are likely to overshoot this target, resulting in wage and price inflation.

Figures 8-2A and 8-2B demonstrate what happens when the government overshoots its target. Instead of shifting demand to D_0, demand shifts to D_2 and the price level increases to P_2 that is higher than the expected price P_0. The increase in aggregate demand increases the demand for labor to LD_2 and the level of output to Q_2, above the natural level of output. The level of employment increases to E_2 and the new money wage rises to W_2. Once suppliers of labor realize that the actual inflation rate exceeds the expected rate, however, labor supply decisions adjust, reducing the quantity of labor supplied at every wage.[8] As shown in Figure 8-2B, labor supply shifts to LS_1. Workers are unwilling to supply as much labor at each money wage at the higher price level. The leftward shift in labor supply produces a higher equilibrium nominal wage, W_h. At this higher nominal wage, the level of output and employment return to their natural levels, Q_0 and E_0, respectively. However, both the price level (P_h) and the new money wage (W_h) are now higher than before.

(C) *Supply Side Policies*–Supply side policies shift the supply curve causing a higher equilibrium output.[9] In Figure 8-3A, D_0 and S_0 are the original aggregate demand and supply curves and LD_0 and LS_0 in Figure 8-3B are the corresponding labor demand and supply curves. The equilibrium level of output and employment are Q_0 and E_0, respectively. The goal of supply side policies is to shift the supply from S_0 to S_1, which results in a higher equilibrium level of output, Q_1. For firms to increase the supply of output,

8. The real wage is lower due to the increase in the price level.
9. The term "trickle down" often refers to supply side policies. Benefits provided to businesses eventually trickle down to workers.

Figure 8-2   Demand side policies—inflation

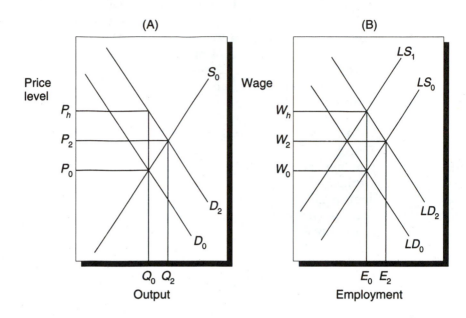

(A)

Price level

P_h
P_2
P_0

S_0

D_2

D_0

Q_0 Q_2
Output

(B)

Wage

W_h
W_2
W_0

LS_1

LS_0

LD_2

LD_0

E_0 E_2
Employment

Figure 8-3   Supply side policies

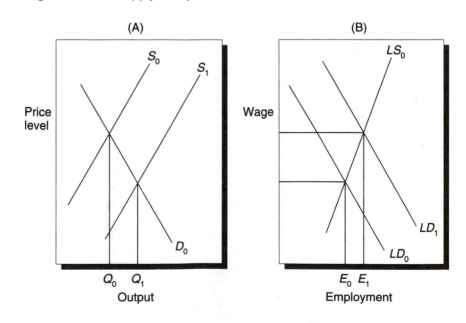

(A)

Price level

S_0 S_1

D_0

Q_0 Q_1
Output

(B)

Wage

LS_0

LD_1

LD_0

E_0 E_1
Employment

they must hire more inputs, including labor, which shifts the demand to LD_1, and which causes a higher level of employment.[10]

Supply side policies operate by lowering the cost of production. A firm's supply curve measures its marginal cost of production.[11] Therefore, to increase supply, costs of production must necessarily decline. Some policies that reduce the cost of production include wage subsidies and employment tax credits, business tax cuts, and the elimination of costly regulations.

1. *Wage subsidies or employment tax credits.* Governments can encourage firms to hire unemployed workers by paying direct wage subsidies or by granting tax credits. Frequently these policies are targeted to low-wage workers who face structural unemployment. General wage subsidies apply to all unemployed workers and are mainly used to deal with cyclical unemployment that affects a large cross-section of workers.[12]

Figure 8-4 illustrates the employment and wage effects of a wage subsidy. The labor demand and supply are shown by D_0 and S_0 respectively. The resulting equilibrium level of employment is E_0 and the equilibrium hourly wage is $4. If the government grants $1 to employers for every hour of employment provided, then the firm's demand for labor increases to D_1. The difference between D_0 and D_1 reflects the subsidy. At the previous wage, W_0, an excess demand for labor exists that can be cleared only if the wage increases to W_1 resulting in employment equal to E_1. Note that the employment effect of a wage subsidy largely depends on the elasticity of the supply and demand curves, with more elastic curves resulting in larger employment effects. Employment tax credits work like wage subsidies. Firms that hire particular groups of unemployed are given a tax credit that increases after tax revenue. In other words, an employment tax credit reduces the after-tax cost of labor.[13]

---

10. To ensure that firms increase labor rather than capital, benefits to firms often are conditioned on the number of workers hired.
11. This is strictly true for a perfectly competitive firm.
12. For a discussion of the economics of wage subsidies, see James R. Knickman, "Wage Subsidies and Employment," in Frank C. Pierson, ed., *The Minimum Level of Unemployment and Public Policy* (Kalamazoo, Mich.: W. E. Upjohn Institute for Employment Research, 1980), pp. 171–88; Daniel S. Hamermesh, "Subsidies for Jobs in the Private Sector," in John L. Palmer, ed., *Creating Jobs: Public Employment Programs and Wage Subsidies* (Washington, D.C.: The Brookings Institute, 1978), pp. 87–122; and John Bishop and Robert Haveman, "Selective Employment Subsidies: Can Okun's Law Be Repealed?" *American Economic Review* 69 (2) (May 1979): 124–30.
13. For a discussion of the effects of employment tax credits, see Orley Ashenfelter, "Evaluating the Effects of the Employment Tax Credit," in U.S. Department of Labor, *Conference Report on Evaluating the 1977 Economic Stimulus Package* (Washington, D.C.: U.S. Government Printing Office, 1979); Jeffrey Perloff and Michael Wachter, "The New Jobs Tax Credit: An Evaluation of the 1977–78 Wage Subsidy Program," *American Economic Review* 69 (May 1979): 73–79; and John Bishop, *Subsidizing Hiring and Training of the Disadvantaged* (Kalamazoo, Mich.: Upjohn Institute for Employment Research, 1989).

Examples of wage subsidies and tax credit policies include the Targeted Jobs Tax Credit plan that was implemented in 1979 and the Work Incentive Program (WIN). The Targeted Jobs Tax Credit plan provides subsidies to firms that hire unemployed youth, handicapped persons, and other disadvantaged workers. WIN provides tax credits to firms that hire persons who are enrolled in the Aid to Families with Dependent Children (AFDC) program.[14]

2. *Business tax cuts and deregulation.* Business tax cuts increase business investment spending and this translates into a higher demand for labor and a lower level of unemployment. Regulations add various direct and indirect costs to business as resources have to be devoted to the preparation of compliance reports for government agencies. During the 1980s, the Reagan administration relied on deregulation and business tax cuts to increase production and employment.

IMPROVING EMPLOYABILITY: MANPOWER POLICIES

Serious efforts to deal with the problem of poverty in the United States through improving employability can be traced to the 1960s. Previously, few programs focused on improving employability. For example, the GI Bill of Rights enabled World War II veterans to attend college or to receive other kinds of training. The first programs designed specifically to deal with unemployed workers, however, were established in the 1960s. The continuation of serious unemployment and poverty motivated the design of labor market policies to reduce unemployment and to stimulate the economy. President Kennedy had campaigned on an agenda to revive the economy that had been sluggish. For example, in 1961 the unemployment rate was above 7 percent, considered to be high at that time.

One of the first public policies that dealt with unemployment in the 1960s involved a national manpower policy. Manpower policies are designed to help those with low skills to become more competitive in labor markets by providing opportunities to upgrade their skills, and by removing barriers to employment. Employment barriers include the absence of job information and other social and psychological handicaps, including lack of support services such as child care and transportation.

The first major national manpower policy was the Manpower Development and Training Act (MDTA) of 1962. The initial aim of MDTA was to retrain mature, experienced workers who had lost jobs because of technological change. However, as the unemployment rate declined during

---

14. The primary goal of WIN is to train AFDC recipients so that they can be more competitive in the labor market. We discuss this program under Manpower programs.

the early 1960s and as those who had lost jobs regained them, the emphasis of MDTA shifted to those who lacked skills and work experience. The establishment of MDTA was followed by the enactment of the Economic Opportunity Act (EOA) of 1964 and the declaration of the War on Poverty. Both EOA and the War on Poverty produced various new programs that specifically targeted the poor and minorities. Several other manpower development programs were established.[15] This chapter highlights just a few of the more important programs.

Manpower policies can be classified into four primary categories according to the specific roles they play: (1) *skill training programs;* (2) *job development programs;* (3) *employability development programs;* and (4) *work experience programs.* Nonetheless much overlap exists and there is no clear-cut classification of the manpower programs by purpose.

1. *Skill training programs.* The more important skill training programs of the unemployed and low-wage earners are the Manpower Development and Training Act (MDTA) of 1962, the Comprehensive Employment and Training Act (CETA) of 1973, and the Job Training and Partnership Act (JTPA) of 1982. MDTA authorized the U.S. Departments of Labor and Health, Education, and Welfare to promote and support training programs that upgrade job skills. MDTA primarily assisted hard-to-employ persons and youth in gaining work experience and institutional or on-the-job training. The goal was to provide skills to help the participants more easily get and hold jobs. MDTA had two components: programs with institutional training and those with on-the-job training.

Initially, MDTA was exclusively an institutional training effort. This involved classroom instruction in remedial and skill training, focusing mainly on job training for available jobs. Course work extended for about four to five months. Some programs such as practical nursing and automotive and electrical repair programs took up to one year. Classroom instruction was provided through local skill centers some of which operated in cooperation with public school systems.

The on-the-job (OJT) training component of the MDTA was incorporated later. The OJT program helped the jobless secure employment in the private sector. Such employees received training at employers' work sites.

---

15. See, for example, Edward B. Jakubauskas and Neil A. Palomba, *Manpower Economics* (Reading, Mass.: Addison-Wesley Publishing Company, 1973); Sar A. Levitan and Joyce K. Zickler, *The Quest for a Federal Manpower Partnership* (Cambridge, Mass.: Harvard University Press, 1974); Charles R. Perry, Bernard E. Anderson, Richard L. Rowan, and Herbert R. Northrup, *The Impact of Government Manpower Programs* (Philadelphia: University of Pennsylvania, 1976); Janet Wegner Johnston, "An Overview of U.S. Federal Employment and Training Programmes," in Jeremy Richardson and Roger Henning, eds., *Unemployment: Policy Responses of Western Democracies* (London, England: Sage Publications, Inc., 1984), 57–115; and Donald C. Baumer and Carl E. Van Horn, *The Politics of Unemployment* (Washington, D.C.: Congressional Quarterly, Inc., 1985).

Figure 8-4   Wage subsidy

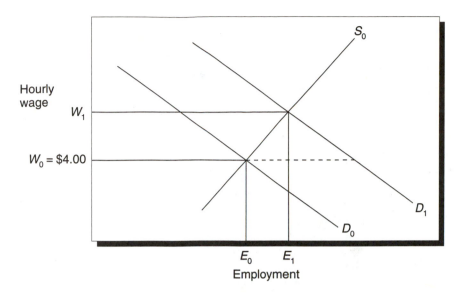

OJT programs also intended that employers would upgrade the skills of the underemployed while still on the job. The employer paid wages while the training costs were paid with public funds.

MDTA was superseded by the Comprehensive Employment and Training Act (CETA) of 1973, the most significant employment and training legislation of the post-World War II era.[16] Between 1973 and 1983, CETA was the centerpiece of United States policy for the unemployed. During its life span, over $60 billion were spent to train millions of unemployed and to create millions of jobs.

Under CETA, state and local jurisdictions gained authority and responsibility to design employment and training plans for their communities. Thus, a primary goal of CETA was to decentralize the programs. State and local governments were designated as the primary sponsors and had a great deal of discretion in the use of funds. Programs under CETA were similar to those that existed before its establishment except CETA had more decentralization. There was a mixture of institutional teaching (classroom), remedial education, and counseling and other supportive services. On-the-job training was less important under CETA.

One important aspect of CETA was its concentration on targeting particular disadvantaged groups. For example, the 1978 CETA reauthoriza-

---

16. See Grace A. Franklin and Randall B. Ripley, *C.E.T.A: Politics and Policy, 1973–1982* (Knoxville: University of Tennessee Press, 1984).

Table 8-2   Job training programs for the disadvantaged: new enrollees
and federal outlays, fiscal years 1975–1992

Fiscal Year	New Enrollees	Outlays (Millions)	Outlays in Constant 1990 Dollars (Millions)
1975	1,126,000	$1,304	$3,099
1976	1,250,000	1,697	3,775
1977	1,119,000	1,756	3,636
1978	965,000	2,378	4,627
1979	1,253,000	2,547	4,550
1980	1,208,000	3,236	5,203
1981	1,011,000	3,395	4,958
1982	NA	2,277	3,107
1983	NA	2,291	2,990
1984	716,200	1,333	1,669
1985	803,900	1,710	2,066
1986	1,003,900	1,911	2,252
1987	960,700	1,880	2,154
1988	873,600	1,902	2,092
1989	823,200	1,868	1,961
1990	630,000	1,803	1,803
1991	603,900[a]	1,761	1,676
1992	602,300[a]	1,769	1,632

Figures shown in years 1975 through 1983 are for training activities under the Comprehensive
Employment and Training Act (CETA); public service employment under CETA is not included.
Figures shown in years 1984 through 1992 are for activities under Title-IIA of the Job Training
and Partnership Act.

NA—Comparable figures not available.

[a]Estimate.

Source: Committee on Ways and Means, U.S. House of Representatives, Overview of
Entitlement Programs, *1992 Green Book,* Table 36.

tion targeted the economically disadvantaged and low-income persons—
minorities, youth, the unemployed and underemployed. Program autho-
rization under CETA required targeted groups. Thus, by the late 1970s,
nearly all CETA participants were economically disadvantaged; those participating in public assistance programs, or those who though not participating, could qualify for public assistance.[17]

CETA was superseded by the Job Training Partnership Act (JTPA) of
1982, the main manpower policy since its enactment. Under JTPA, local

---

17. As discussed earlier, CETA also involved direct creation of public service jobs.

communities are more involved with program administration. JTPA places primary administrative responsibility in the hands of state governments; the federal government has only minimal administrative responsibility. JTPA differs from CETA in various ways. First, overall funding has been cut and the public service employment program has been eliminated. JTPA emphasizes the role of the private sector in job creation. Still, JTPA targets the disadvantaged. Title IIA of JTPA provides training for chronically disadvantaged youth and adults, and Title III serves dislocated workers who lose jobs because of plant closings or major layoffs.

Although federal job training programs continue to be important in helping the disadvantaged population, this role has declined substantially since 1981 when the Reagan administration came to office. Table 8-2 shows the number of enrollees in job training programs and federal outlays for fiscal years 1975 through 1992. While total federal outlays in 1975 totalled $3099 million (1990 constant dollars), this figure was $1632 million in 1992. Likewise, the number of enrollees declined from 1,126,000 in 1975 to just over 600,000 in 1992.[18]

2. Job development programs. Several programs have enhanced job skills development. The first such program was the Job Opportunities in the Business Sector (JOBS) of 1968. JOBS was created as a federal-private partnership. The program focused primarily on poor, urban youth. Private employers were to relax their hiring standards to accommodate poorly trained long-term unemployed persons. While employed, they received job related training. The programs were implemented with cooperation of the business community together with representatives of the U.S. employment service. Under JOBS, the employer paid the participant a market wage and the training costs were reimbursed under contract with the government. Clients were referred to this program by employment and poverty agencies.

Another program that provided work experience was the Public Service Careers (PSC) of 1970. This program was confined to public sector employment since the public sector was a major employer and since many of the public sector jobs are easily accessible to the poor. The purpose of PSC was to provide work experience for disadvantaged persons in local, state, and federal agencies. The program focused on unemployed and underemployed persons and discouraged workers. The PSC program offered on-the-job training, support services to new employees, and upgraded the skills of those at lower employment levels. Those enrolled were able to secure permanent employment in public service agencies

Another job development program was the Apprenticeship Outreach Program (AOP). AOP was funded under MDTA and targeted minority

---

18. The changes demonstrate some of the policy shifts in dealing with poverty that were part of the Reagan revolution.

recruits for apprenticeships mainly in the construction industry. AOP was primarily a job service program that served to recruit and to disseminate information, so that minorities could access the apprenticeship programs administered by trade unions. In some cases, AOP representatives made arrangements with members of a craft union to allow some qualified minorities to obtain journeymen status after a short trial period following completion of the apprentice program. AOP was operated by various community organizations and civil-rights groups, with trade unions under contract from the U.S. Department of Labor.

3. *Employability development programs.* Several programs have been created over time to improve the employment prospects of low-skilled workers. One such program was the Opportunities Industrialization Centers (OIC). OIC prepared enrollees for entry level jobs. OIC served various tasks, including outreach, counseling, prevocational training, and job placement. The duration of OIC skill-training programs depended on the availability of jobs in the local market. OIC was primarily located in urban areas.

A similar program was the Concentrated Employment Program (CEP) of 1967. CEP was part of the MDTA and the Economic Opportunity Act of 1964. CEP provided a one-stop service in manpower and related programs for disadvantaged persons living in areas with high unemployment and poverty, mainly in urban centers. CEP responded to the fact that even during times of tight labor markets, pockets of poverty remain. CEP did not focus on skill training but on remedial services. Like JOBS, the goal of CEP was to increase the labor force participation of the disadvantaged.

A major concern of manpower policies is the effect of transfer payments on the labor force participation of recipients. One major problem is that recipients become long term dependents. A program that has been enacted to deal with this issue is the Work Incentive Program (WIN) of 1967, an amendment to Title IV of the Social Security Act. The goal of WIN was to provide training and support services for employable AFDC recipients so that they can become economically independent. The program responded to the increase in the number of welfare recipients in the 1960s. To encourage the hiring of AFDC recipients, employers receive a tax credit of up to 20 percent of the first year's wages of WIN hires. The federal government also pays up to 90 percent of the training costs. To encourage participation, enrollees were allowed to keep some of their earnings without losing welfare benefits.

Another employment development program is Job Corps. Job Corps, established by the Economic Opportunity Act of 1964, provides intensive basic education and skill training for severely disadvantaged, out-of-school youth aged 16 to 21 years. Almost 75 percent of Job Corps participants are members of minority groups and about 80 percent have not graduated from high school. The program usually is conducted in residential neighborhoods away from the participants' home environment. The goal is to remove the disadvantaged from their home environment in order to break negative reinforcements. The main role of Job Corps is to give the poor job skills, not job creation. Job Corps currently is funded under JTPA. In 1992, the outlays for this program were $649 million and 108 residential training centers were in operation around the country. In 1992, 565,500 persons participated in the Job Corps programs. The data for the 1990 program year reported 64 percent of the enrollees were male, 52 percent Black, 31 percent White, and 12 percent Hispanic. Eighty-two percent of all enrollees were high school dropouts and 73 percent had never worked full-time. In 1990, 40 percent of Job Corps enrollees came from families on public assistance.

4. *Work experience programs.* Two programs that provided work experience were the Neighborhood Youth Corps (NYC) and Operation Mainstream (OM). NYC was created in 1964 under the Economic Opportunity Act. The purpose of NYC was to keep young people in school, or increase their employability if they were school dropouts. The in-school program emphasized job market orientation and work experience. Skill training was the focus for all out-of-school youth. The goal of Operation Mainstream was to provide work experience to chronically unemployed older persons. Most OM activities centered on local beautification projects.

BETTER PAY FOR WORK

The government can use wage and tax policies that increase the earnings of low-wage workers as a way of protecting such workers from falling into poverty. Two policies in this area are the minimum wage and earned income tax credits. A particular problem faced by low-wage workers is the lack of affordable medical and child care services. The government can help such low-wage workers escape poverty by designing affordable health and child care programs. Such policies, together with wage and tax policies, increase the earnings retained by low-wage earners, making work worthwhile.[19]

Minimum wages–Minimum wage legislation in the United States was first enacted in 1938 as part of the Fair Labor Standards Act. The act set a wage rate below which hourly wages could not fall. The goal of a minimum wage is to guarantee reasonable compensation for work effort and to reduce the incidence of poverty. The initial minimum wage was set at $.25 per hour

---

19. See the discussion in Sar A. Levitan and Isaac Shapiro, *Working But Poor: America's Contradiction* (Baltimore, Md.: Johns Hopkins University Press, 1987).

in 1938. Since then, the wage has been adjusted periodically. In April 1991, the federal minimum wage reached $4.25 per hour. The minimum wage affects many workers; in 1986, there were over 3.5 million minimum wage workers.

Although the nominal minimum wage has increased, the real minimum wage has decreased during the 1980s and early 1990s. In 1986, for example, the real minimum wage was 20 percent less than its average in the 1970s, and 33 percent lower than its peak in 1968. In fact, minimum wages that are supposed to protect families from falling into poverty do not appear to be serving this purpose. For example, in 1986, a full-time employee receiving the minimum wage earned an annual income of $6968, nearly $1800 less than the poverty line for a family of three, and about $4200 less than the poverty line for a family of four. During the 1960s and 1970s, the minimum wage was sufficient to bring a family of three out of poverty. This has not been the case since 1980. As a result, suggestions have been made to increase the minimum wage. The most common proposal is to restore the minimum wage to its initial level of 50 percent of the average nonsupervisory private hourly wage. During the late 1980s and early 1990s, this policy would have required an increase in the minimum wage of about between 30 and 35 percent.

As was demonstrated in Chapter 1, while the minimum wage benefits some workers, it also creates unemployment. Proponents of the minimum wage argue that legislating a minimum wage has many benefits such as keeping people out of poverty and improving the work ethic among the poor. In addition, by encouraging work, the minimum wage has the salutary effect of getting people off welfare, hence increasing the benefits to society. Although these effects are appealing, an evaluation of the minimum wage should account for both the expected benefits and costs.

Evidence suggests that the job losses from increases in the minimum wage are small. However, the minimum wage has the largest negative effect on young workers. The Minimum Wage Study Commission found that a 10 percent increase in the minimum wage results in a 1 percent decrease in the employment opportunities available for teenagers.[20] This effect was greater for youth who earn close to the minimum wage. For this reason, a subminimum wage—a wage below the established minimum wage—has been proposed for youth. Such a subminimum wage was put into effect by the Reagan administration, called the Youth Opportunity Wage, and was set equal to 75 percent of the minimum wage. The administration estimated that the subminimum wage would open up a maximum of 400,000 jobs as a result of the lower cost of hiring youth. However, youth unemployment rates continued to rise during the late 1980s, casting

---

20. *Report of the Minimum Wage Study Commission* (Washington, D.C.: U.S. Government Printing Office, 1981).

doubts on whether such a wage could solve the youth unemployment problem.[21]

Taxes–Some analysts argue that the Social Security tax places an undue burden on low-wage earners because the tax rate is the same for all workers from the first dollar of earned income through an income of about $54,000.[22] The government can use its taxing powers to increase the earnings retained by low-wage workers and reduce this tax burden. This can be accomplished by increasing the amount of earned income that is exempt from taxation (in other words, the standard deduction) and by increasing the amount of the personal exemption allowed for each individual covered by a tax return. The 1986 Tax Law increased the standard deduction from $1080 in 1986 to $2000 in 1989.

Since 1975, the government has used the Earned Income Tax Credit (EITC) to reduce the tax burden on low-wage workers. EITC is a tax credit on a percentage of initial earnings and is phased out as earnings increase. If the credit is greater than the tax liability, the taxpayer receives a federal tax refund. EITC has been changed periodically to benefit low-income families. In 1986, EITC was 11 percent of the first $5000 and was phased out as income rose from $6500 to $11,000. The 1986 tax change increased the EITC to 14 percent of the first $5,714 and was phased out as income increased from $9000, falling to zero when income reached $17,000. In 1990, the EITC granted a 14 percent credit to workers for each dollar of earnings up to $6,810, thus providing a $953 credit to a family. The $953 credit was maintained until earnings reached $10,730, after which it declined at a rate of 10 percent for each additional dollar earned. The credit was zero when family earnings reached $20,264. The current tax law provides for the expansion of EITC through 1994.

Suggestions that deal with the low-wage workers have been to increase the standard deduction, personal exemption, and expand the EITC. For example, the EITC could be designed so that it bridges the gap between a fully employed family's income working at the minimum wage, and a self-sufficiency income.[23] Targeting these tax policies on low-wage earners could be better than raising the minimum wage.

---

21. Whether increasing the minimum wage is an effective antipoverty policy remains unresolved. In a 1990 study, Ronald Mincy demonstrated that increasing the minimum wage would reduce poverty more than previously thought. On the other hand, in a 1993 study, Burkhauser and Finegan find that increasing minimum wages would not help the poor. See Ronald B. Mincy, "Raising the Minimum Wage: Effects on Family Poverty," *Monthly Labor Review* (July 1990): 18–25; and Richard V. Burkhauser and T. Aldrich Finegan, "The Minimum Wage and the Poor: The End of A Relationship," *Journal of Policy Analysis and Management* 8 (1) (1989): 53–71.
22. This figure was $53,400 in 1991. See Committee on Ways and Means, U.S. House of Representatives, *Overview of the Federal Tax System, 1991* (Washington, D.C.: U.S. Government Printing Office, 1991).
23. See, for example, the proposal by John E. Schwarz and Thomas J. Volgy, *The Forgotten Americans: Thirty Million Working Poor in the Land of Opportunity* (New York: W.W. Norton and Co., 1992).

Medical protection–A consensus is emerging that low-wage workers should be provided with medical protection. The poorest in the United States are covered by medicaid that normally extends benefits to those on public assistance such as AFDC and SSI recipients. Generally, single parents with low incomes, the aged, and the disabled receive some form of government medical protection. Low-wage workers, however, have the least medical protection. On the one hand, they are in jobs that do have employer provided benefits; on the other hand, their earnings may be above the eligibility levels established for medicaid.

Some analysts suggest that medical protection be provided to the working poor. In fact, with the election of Bill Clinton, some form of national medical program to cover the uninsured workers probably will be put in place, or, at least, seriously debated. Two approaches dominate the discussion of how to provide health protection to low-wage workers. The first is a national health insurance program. There is fear, however, that this program will be extremely costly and will add to the already huge government debt. The alternative is an employer-provided health coverage that is mandated by the government. This program would increase the costs to firms that may react by reducing wages or the level of employment—both undesirable and counterproductive results. Furthermore, a mandated health insurance program may give firms the incentive to hire those workers who are not likely to use medical insurance—youth and single individuals. Although there are no easy choices, there is need to reform the U.S. health care system.

Child care–The provision of affordable child care is crucial to the well-being of low-wage workers and nonparticipants. This is especially important to single heads of households with children. More than 50 percent of female heads of households with a child under six years old currently work. Thus, the availability of affordable child care makes work far more attractive for these workers.

A modest child care credit currently is available. However, the credit does not help the poorest families and only about 1 percent of child care credit benefits go to families with incomes under $10,000. The credit is applied only to reduce taxes that are owed. Thus, because most poor owe little, if any, taxes, the child care credit is not a benefit to them even though they may have incurred child care expenses. One proposal is to make child care credit refundable. If so, then even the poorest workers who incur child care expenses benefit, similar to the earned income credit.

Other suggestions that deal with child care focus on the provision of child allowance payments to all families with young children; the establishment of a national child care program; expansion of the Head Start program; encouraging employer provided child care facilities; and stricter enforcement of child support policies to relieve the burden placed on single parents. With the continued increase in the number of single-parent households, provision of child care continues to be an important policy goal for improving the welfare of the working poor. The subject of child care will be covered in more detail in Chapter 13.

COSTS AND BENEFITS OF LABOR MARKET POLICIES

Labor market policies, including job creation, manpower programs, and those policies that provide better pay for work, present difficult choices for policy makers. Even the most successful policies often involve large expenditures of public funds. Furthermore, all policies involve interference with the market mechanism, thereby introducing inefficiencies in the allocation of resources. Thus, the conflicting goals associated with income redistribution come into play. In evaluating the costs and benefits of the various policies, one must not only focus on the positive aspects, but also on normative aspects.

We already have mentioned that employment policies can be inflationary. Most programs (such as direct job creation, or those that improve pay) involve large public expenditures. Such programs increase the government debt and the tax burden on individuals and businesses. These effects have costs that lead to a reduction in employment opportunities, especially for the disadvantaged. Likewise, increasing the minimum wage places costs on some groups. On the other hand, although they may be effective in creating jobs, supply-side policies create jobs (according to existing evidence) that are low-wage variety. The beneficiaries of the trickle-down policies generally have been businesses, not workers. The increased inequality in the distribution of income that occurred during the 1980s has been partly attributed to the supply-side policies that dominated policy making in that decade.

Education and training programs are more politically acceptable.[24] Several studies also suggest that the benefits of training programs exceed the costs. For example, some evidence from the National Research Council suggest that the Job Corps has been successful given the difficulty experienced in placing disadvantaged youth. The results show that participation in the Job Corps significantly increased employment, earnings, and education of the participants, moreover, the benefits generally exceed the costs that accrue to the public

Likewise, studies show that placement rates for JTPA participants are quite high. In 1986, for example, about 75 percent of JTPA participants obtained employment or some other activity after training. Among JTPA titles, disad-

---

24. For an evaluation of manpower programs, see Grace A. Franklin and Randall B. Ripley, *C.E.T.A Politics and Policy, 1973–1982;* Donald C. Baumer and Carl E. Van Horn, *The Politics of Unemployment;* and Alan L. Sorkin, *Education, Unemployment, and Economic Growth* (Lexington, Mass.: Lexington Books, 1974).

vantaged participants and dislocated workers experienced an average placement rate of two in three. In 1990, of all Title II-A participants who terminated training, 55 percent entered employed at an average hourly wage of $5.54, which is fairly good given the economic conditions of the time.[25] Evidence also shows that programs such as WIN, which are supposed to help those on welfare become self-supporting, have been fairly successful. Some states show savings on AFDC as a result of WIN participants securing employment and getting off welfare. Usually, most evaluation studies find that participants of manpower programs have had increased earnings after training.

Although such evidence favors the continuation of manpower programs, this evidence should be interpreted with caution. First, the success rates vary widely across various demographic groups, across the level of expenditures, and across program administration. For example, some of the success attributable to JTPA is due to the selection of program participants. Under JTPA, local authorities are required to set and meet performance standards. This leads officials to select those whose chances of employability are better—what is called creaming.[26] In addition, most programs have multifaceted goals, many immeasurable. Finally, the success of manpower programs reported in many studies may be faulty. Michael Borus has suggested that the reported gains in earnings can be expected even if no training is received. Since most programs focus on those with low or no earnings, often these participants are at low points in their careers. Thus, they are unlikely to have earnings below what they had before training. The reported gains may just reflect regression toward the mean.[27]

SUMMARY

Labor market policies are central to fighting poverty. This chapter has focused on policies that deal with unemployment and low-wage employment. As noted, these policies involve difficult choices, both because of the cost involved and the undesirable side effects that result from the use of such policies.

---

25. See Committee on Ways and Means, U.S. House of Representatives, Overview of Entitlement Programs, *1992 Green Book,* May 15, 1992 (Washington, D.C.: U.S. Government Printing Office), p. 1690.
26. Some recent evidence shows that creaming may not be so extensive. In a 1993 study, Kathryn Anderson and her colleagues found that while the placement rate of JTPA participants in the state of Tennessee was high (71 percent) partly because of creaming, the placement rate would only fall to about 62 percent if participants were randomly selected from among the economically disadvantaged population. See Kathryn H. Anderson, Richard V. Burkhauser, and Jennie E. Raymond, "The Effect of Creaming on Placement Rates Under the Job Training and Partnership Act," *Industrial and Labor Relations Review* 46 (4) (July 1993): 613–24.
27. See Michael E. Borus, "Assessing the Impact of Training Programs," in Eli Ginzberg, ed., *Employing the Unemployed* (New York: Basic Books, 1980), pp. 25–40.

Although government job creation programs may solve short-run unemployment problems, long-term solutions require the design of manpower programs that increase the employability of disadvantaged workers. Given that training and education policies receive more support across the political spectrum, the approach should be to concentrate on those programs that yield the highest benefits. This requires careful evaluation of the benefits and costs of various programs.

This book has suggested that the provision of medical protection and child care should be given priority as antipoverty policy tools. In addition, the tax structure, especially increasing the earned income credit, will go a long way in helping the working poor.

STUDY AND DISCUSSION QUESTIONS

1. List and discuss some of the policies that are used to deal with unemployment.

2. For public policy purposes, it is important to distinguish between the three types of unemployment. Outline policies that are appropriate for structural, cyclical, and frictional unemployment.

3. List and discuss some of the policies that are used to deal with low-wage employment.

4. Critically evaluate the various policies that are used to deal with labor market problems. That is, consider the benefits and shortcomings of those policies.

5. The government can influence employment and wages by using policies that affect the labor market either on the demand side or the supply side. Discuss these policies using clearly labeled diagrams where possible.

6. Demonstrate how a wage subsidy or an employment tax credit influences employment and wages. Demonstrate that the effectiveness of those types of policies largely depends on the elasticity of demand and supply.

7. Consider why some people do not participate in labor markets and then outline the type of policies that could be used to deal with nonparticipation. Identify some of the programs mentioned in the text that seek to increase labor force participation.

8. Suppose we know that minorities and women are concentrated in low-wage jobs. Consider the following two policies: (1) The government adopts a policy that benefits low-wage workers; (2) the government adopts a policy that benefits low-wage workers who are minorities or women. Are these policies equivalent? Is there

anything wrong with targeting policies to specific disadvantaged groups? For example, is it wrong to target specific policies such as the Targeted Jobs Tax Credit on Vietnam-era veterans?

9. Compare and contrast direct and indirect job creation policies. Which of these approaches do you consider to be more effective in fighting poverty in the short and long run?

10. One reason why minorities and women may invest less in human capital is because the expected future earnings are lower due to labor market discrimination. Suggest some policies that would cause the minorities and women to increase their investment in human capital.

ADDITIONAL READINGS

1. Ashenfelter, Orley. "Estimating the Effect of Training Programs on Earnings," *The Review of Economics and Statistics,* Vol. LX, No. 1 (1978): 47–57.

2. Barnow, Burt, S. "Impact of CETA on Earnings," *Journal of Human Resources* 22 (2) (Spring 1987): 157-193.

3. Bishop, John H. "Toward More Valid Evaluations of Training Programs Serving the Disadvantaged," *Journal of Policy Analysis and Management* 8 (2) (1989): 209–28.

4. Cook, Robert F., Charles F. Adams, Jr., V. Lane Rawlins, and Associates. *Public Service Employment: The Experience of a Decade* (Kalamazoo, Mich.: Upjohn Institute for Employment and Research, 1985).

5. Ketron, Inc. *The Long-Term Impact of WIN II: A Longitudinal Evaluation of the Employment Experiences of Participants in the Work Incentive Program,* report prepared for the Employment and Training Administration, U.S. Department of Labor (Wayne, Pa., 1979).

6. Wise, Recascino L. *Labor Market Policies and Employment Patterns in the United States* (Boulder, Colo.: Westview Press, 1989).

9

GENDER, RACE, AND POVERTY: DISCRIMINATION

The discussion in Chapter 4 revealed that wide inequalities exist in the distribution of income in the United States. A small proportion of the population receives a large share of the national income while the poorest groups receive only a very small share. Inequality also is evident in other areas: some people invest less in education while others invest much more. Some people live in safe neighborhoods while others live in crime-ridden neighborhoods.

Indicators such as differences in income and levels of education attained only identify inequality of outcomes. Although society may be concerned about outcomes, it is necessary to consider the sources of inequality. In formulating public policies to deal with inequalities, it is important to understand sources of inequalities especially in regard to how they relate to inequality of opportunities. This inequality suggests that there may be some role for public policy.

In a market economy, equality of outcomes is not expected, nor would it be desirable. Talents, intelligence, and capabilities are unequally distributed among members of society. Likewise, motivation and personal appearance vary widely across members of society. All these factors are important in determining wages and earnings. Because the market places higher value on some qualities over others, inequality of outcomes are expected. In some cases, inequality in earnings reflect differences in preferences for occupations and jobs. Thus, even with equal opportunity for all, inequalities in outcomes would persist. Public policy is not geared to eliminating unequal outcomes if equality of opportunities exist at the start.

Given the differences in abilities and initial endowments (such as appearance, strength, and so forth), incomes will vary across families. This implies that children will be raised in families that differ considerably in terms of the income and other amenities available to them. Some will enjoy high incomes and wealth, while others will live in poverty because of their parents' low-earning capacity. Additionally, children will experience differences in terms of the attitudes, aspirations, and perceptions of self-esteem that they acquire from their parents. To the extent that these factors influence future career choices and earnings, they represent inequality of opportunities.[1]

As demonstrated in Chapter 7, the quantity of schooling is an important determinant of earnings. Equally important is the quality of schooling. Ten years of schooling in an inner-city public school may be quite different from the same years of schooling in a high-cost private school in the suburbs. There is ample evidence that there is maldistribution of quantity and quality of schooling available to different persons and groups in the country. The inequality in the distribution of education resources contributes to wide inequalities in earnings gaps. Children of poor families often attend poorer schools and because of various problems do not invest as much in education as children from higher income families. Thus, differences in the levels of education attained by different people is partially due to inequality of opportunity.

The career and other choices that young people make also are influenced by communities in which they live and by their peers. For example, ghetto and suburb environments influence choices of young people in significantly different ways. Children raised in inner cities face various negative forces that are not conducive to success. Peer pressure to drop out from school and to engage in underground activities are more pronounced in poor inner cities than in more wealthy suburbs. To the extent that community environmental factors differ widely and affect choices that young people make, they represent inequality of opportunities. Such inequality eventually translates to differences in earnings.

The inequality of opportunities just discussed affects a wide cross section of the population: males and females; Whites, Blacks, Hispanics, Native Americans, and other racial groups; and young and old people. Because such inequality of opportunities results in undesirable outcomes (such as poverty), there is a justified role for the government to reduce inequality of opportunities responsible for those outcomes. Such a role may involve income transfer programs and other policies that target the general population facing inequality of opportunities. An example of such policies would be a government subsidy on education that is available to all Americans with low incomes.

Conventional wisdom asserts, however, that some of the observed inequalities in outcomes emerge from unequal opportunities that are specific to racial minorities and women. The lower economic status of racial minorities and women has been attributed to the lack of equal opportunities. For example, poverty statistics (see Chapter 5) reveal a higher incidence of poverty among racial minorities than among Whites. In 1989, for

---

1. For a good discussion of inequality of outcomes and opportunities, see Robert Haveman, *Starting Even: An Equal Opportunity Program to Combat the Nation's New Poverty* (New York: Simon and Schuster, 1988).

example, 27.8 percent of all Black families and 23.4 percent of Hispanic families were poor as compared to only 7.8 percent of White families. Also, because females earn less than males, families that have a female head experience much higher incidence of poverty than those with a male head. Thus, in 1989, poverty in all female-headed families was 32.2 percent as compared to 10.3 percent for all families.[2] Other indicators of well-being also document clear and systematic inequalities between racial groups, and between males and females. Moreover, these race and sex inequalities have persisted for many years.

A particular source of inequality of opportunities that is of special concern in the study of economics of poverty is racial and sexual discrimination. Thus, in addition to the general inequality of opportunities that affect other persons, minorities and women face an additional inequity of opportunity due to discriminatory practices.

Discrimination implies that different groups face differing opportunities to develop their talents and to apply those talents fully. In other words, discrimination prevents some individuals from reaching their full potential such as market incomes. Thus, discrimination is one of the causes of the lower earnings of racial minorities and females.

Discriminatory practices occur in a wide variety of settings. The most commonly analyzed, and one that bears directly to poverty, is labor market discrimination, where workers of equal productivity face different employment opportunities and earn different wages.[3] Another important form of discrimination is in education, which can take dimensions such as the quality of teachers and facilities (for example, libraries and playgrounds). Discrimination in education also occurs in the workplace if some groups are denied equal opportunities for on-the-job training. The housing market is another area in which discrimination has produced long-term inequalities between racial groups in the United States. As Chapter 11 will demonstrate, the isolation of Blacks and other minorities in the inner cities relates partly to discriminatory practices in the housing market. These discriminatory practices directly or indirectly affect the economic status of one group relative to another by introducing inequality of opportunities.

Women also have been subjected to discriminatory laws during most of American history. Up until the 1960s, laws in the United States assumed the patriarchal nuclear family to be the basic unit of society and the fact that men had control over women was emphasized. For example, in a

---

2. The higher poverty rates in female-headed households as compared to the poverty levels in male-headed households is much more complex than just due to lower earnings of females as compared to the earnings of males. We discuss the poverty of female-headed households in Chapter 12.

3. Arrow defines labor market discrimination as "the valuation in the labor market of personal characteristics of the worker that are unrelated to productivity." Kenneth J. Arrow, "The Theory of Discrimination," in Orley Ashenfelter and Albert Rees, eds. *Discrimination in Labor Markets* (Princeton, N. J.: Princeton University Press, 1973).

famous 1908 case, *Muller v. Oregon,* the U.S. Supreme Court justified pro-
tectionist legislation that prevented women from working as many hours
as men on the grounds that "a woman's physical structure and the performance of maternal functions place her at a disadvantage in the struggle for
subsistence.... History discloses the fact that woman has always been
dependent upon man."[4] Even as recently as 1961, the U.S. Supreme Court
denied the right for women to participate in jury duty because a "woman
is still regarded as the center of the home and family life."[5] This view that
women's place was at home and not in the labor market obviously has
denied women full participation in labor markets. Even when they do participate, women have been relegated to jobs that pay less and that command lower responsibility. Thus, women, like minorities, have not enjoyed
equality of opportunities.

The desire to eliminate racial and sexual differences in opportunities
has led to public policies that seek to eliminate current discrimination.
Other policies reduce inequalities created by past discrimination. Such
race- and gender-based policies have been, and still remain, controversial.
To appreciate these antipoverty policies (discussed in Chapter 10), it is necessary to review the various explanations of discrimination and their
effects on observed race and sex differences in outcomes.

This chapter considers two types of discrimination: labor market discrimination and premarket discrimination. Various theories of discrimination are examined to see how they may explain observed race and sex disparities. To begin, a brief examination of some indicators of race and sex
inequalities is useful. Next, the extent to which these inequalities could be
due to discrimination is investigated. Theories of discrimination in the labor
market are discussed followed by a brief look at discrimination in education. Public policies that address discrimination are discussed in Chapter 10.

RACE AND SEX INEQUALITIES

The economic status of minorities and women is related to poor labor market prospects. Minorities have much higher unemployment rates and
lower average earnings than Whites. Although female unemployment
rates do not differ from those of males, the earnings of females are much
lower than those of males. As a group, minorities and women are over represented in low-wage occupations (secondary sector jobs) while White
males are concentrated in occupations with high wages that offer opportunities for upward mobility (primary sector jobs).

A primary factor that explains the poor labor market prospects of
minorities and women is relatively low levels of human capital. Chapter 7

---

4. *Muller v. Oregon,* 208 U.S. 412 (1908).
5. *Hoyt v. Florida,* 368 U.S. 57, 61-2 (1961).

notes that one of the causes of low-wage employment is low human capital. A number of factors could explain low investment in human capital such as lack of funds or the existence of race and sex discrimination. Even without labor market discrimination, discrimination in education can produce differences in labor market opportunities. Minorities and women face discrimination in the labor market. The combination of discrimination in education and employment helps explain the relatively higher incidence of poverty among minorities and families headed by women.

Figure 9-1 plots the unemployment rates for Whites and Blacks for the period between 1952 and 1991. Even during periods of low unemployment rates (before 1970), unemployment rates for Blacks averaged about two times those for Whites. In most years during the 1970s and 1980s, Black unemployment rates were more than double those of Whites. Between 1984 and 1990, Black unemployment rates were 2.4 or 2.5 times those of Whites.

In discussing the economic conditions of minorities, it is common to discuss Hispanics as one homogeneous group. It is important to note that Hispanics are a very heterogenous group and their economic status varies widely. Hispanics include Cuban Americans, Mexicans, various groups from Central and South America, and Puerto Ricans. Although Cuban Americans have incomes above the national median income, Puerto Ricans have much lower incomes and experience poverty rates that compare to

Figure 9-1   Unemployment rates of Blacks and Whites, 1952-1991

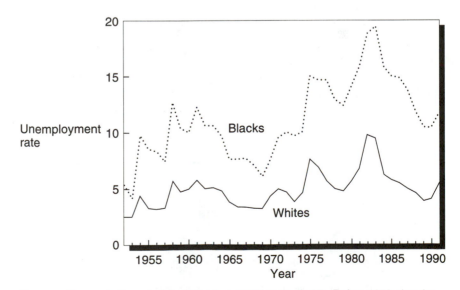

Source: Economic Report of the President, 1992, Table B–37. Before 1972, data for Blacks includes for Blacks and other groups.

those of Blacks. The differences among Hispanic groups are highlighted in Figure 9-2 that shows the unemployment rates of persons of Spanish origin and of Whites. As Figure 9-2 shows, Puerto Ricans face much more unfavorable labor market prospects as compared to Cuban Americans. Still, the economic status of most Hispanics (Mexicans and Puerto Ricans) is much lower as compared to that of Whites.

Although Hispanics and Blacks experience much higher unemployment rates than Whites, the problem is much worse among Native Americans. Because of their small numbers and concentration in various regions of the country, national unemployment rates of Native Americans are not recorded by the Bureau of Labor Statistics on a regular basis. The data available, however, reveal that the labor market prospects of Native Americans are dismal. For example, in 1979, unemployment rates of Native Americans in Colorado, Alaska, Michigan, and Minnesota exceeded 50 percent.[6] In most other states with a significant Native American population, the unemployment rates exceed 30 percent.[7] Recent indications

Figure 9-2   Unemployment rates of persons of Spanish origin and for Whites, 1976–1991

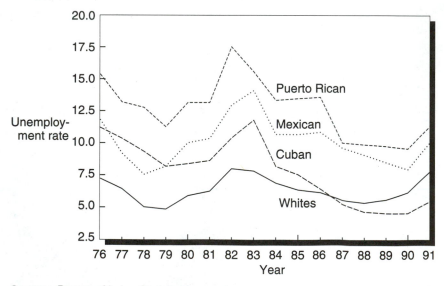

Source: Bureau of Labor Statistics.

6. See Fact on File Publications, *The New Book of American Rankings* (New York: Facts on File Inc., 1984), Table 102.
7. I admit rather apologetically that much more information about Native Americans should be included in discussions about the economics of poverty. For example, we need to discuss conditions on reservations and other barriers that Native Americans face in pursuit of a better life in America. Clearly this is an area to which researchers have not devoted suffi-

are that unemployment conditions for Native Americans worsened during the 1980s and early 1990s.

Figure 9-3 plots unemployment rates for women and men for the period 1962 to 1992. Unlike the unemployment rates by race (for which wide differences are evident), few or no differences exist in unemployment rates by gender. This, however, does not imply that men and women face similar labor market prospects. First, remember that many women do not participate in labor markets because of child rearing responsibilities. Second, as already noted, women are concentrated in jobs that pay much lower wages than those earned by men. Thus, the fact that unemployment rates do not differ should not be interpreted as implying equality of opportunities.

Racial and sexual inequalities emerge more clearly in income differences. Figure 9-4 plots the median incomes by race from 1970 to 1990. Data for years before 1970 shows that, between 1950 and 1960, Black family incomes remained fairly constant at about 55 percent of White family incomes. During the 1960s, the gap between Black and White family incomes narrowed so that by 1975 the median Black family income was 65 percent that of Whites. Since then, however, the gap between Black and White family incomes has increased. In 1991, the median Black family income was 57 percent that of Whites. Since 1973, the income of Hispanic families has remained at about 65 percent that of White families. Nevertheless, the gap between the Hispanic and White family incomes has increased slightly. In 1973, Hispanic family income was 69 percent that of

Figure 9-3   Unemployment rates by sex, 1962–1992

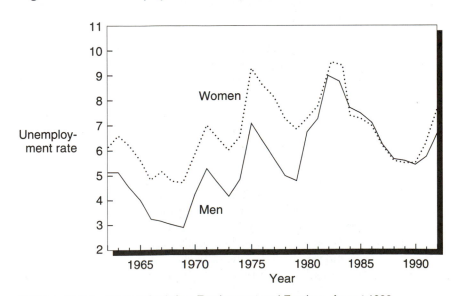

Source: Bureau of Labor Statistics, Employment and Earnings, August 1993.

Figure 9-4   Money income of families, median income in current dollars, by race, 1970–1990

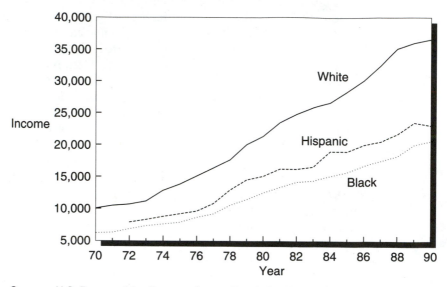

Source: U.S. Bureau of the Census, *Current Population Report*, Series P–60, No. 151 and No. 174.

White families. In 1991, the median income of Hispanic families was 63 percent that of White families.

Table 9-1 reports the data for the median income of male and female full-time workers by age and race for 1985 and 1990. Although clear differences exist in income inequalities between men and women, these differences vary by age group. Male and female incomes are more equal for those under 25. A number of suggestions have been advanced to explain the varying income difference between males and females by age, including the effect of interruptions of women's labor force attachment due to child rearing responsibilities and discrimination in career advancement. Although the data shows that the gap between the earnings of males and females narrowed between 1985 and 1990 for most age groups, significant earning discrepancies still remain. Although White women earn more than Black women, White women's earnings are relatively lower than White men when compared to the earnings of Black females relative to the earnings of Black males. This does not mean that Black females face less discrimination for being female, but the outcome is due to the disadvantages faced by Black men in labor markets.

Table 9-2 presents data on the number of years of school completed by sex and race in 1991. The data show that differences exist in the number of years of school completed by Blacks, Hispanics, and Whites, and between

Table 9-1   Incomes of male and female full-time workers by age and race, 1985 and 1990

| | Annual Median Income (Dollars) | | | | Ratio of Median Income, Females to Males | |
| | Females | | Males | | | |
Age	1985	1990	1985	1990	1985	1990
15-19	8,372	13,955	9,050	15,580	0.93	0.90
20-24	11,757	NA	13,827	NA	0.85	NA
25-34	16,740	20,178	22,321	25,502	0.75	0.79
35-44	18,032	22,483	28,966	32,611	0.62	0.69
45-54	17,009	21,937	29,880	35,731	0.57	0.61
55-64	16,761	20,765	28,387	33,180	0.59	0.63
65+	18,336	22,866	26,146	35,520	0.70	0.64
Race						
White	16,482	20,840	29,846	30,186	0.55	0.69
Black	14,590	18,518	20,706	21,540	0.70	0.85
Hispanic	13,522	16,186	18,570	19,314	0.72	0.83

Source: U.S. Bureau of the Census, *Statistical Abstract of the United States,* 1992.

Table 9-2   Years of school completed by selected characteristics, 1991

| | Percent of Population with | | |
Characteristic	4 years of high school or more	1 or more years of college	4 or more years of college
Sex			
Male	78.5	42.5	24.3
Female	78.3	37.4	18.8
Race			
White	79.9	40.8	22.2
Black	66.7	29.0	11.5
Hispanic	51.3	22.0	9.7

Source: U.S. Bureau of the Census, *Statistical Abstract of the United States,* 1992.

males and females. Furthermore, the differences increase at higher levels of education. For example, 79.9 percent of Whites, 66.7 percent of Blacks, and 51.3 percent of Hispanics completed four or more years of high school. In contrast, while 22.2 percent of Whites had four or more years of college, only 11.5 percent of Blacks, and 9.7 percent of Hispanics completed that level of education. Likewise, virtually the same proportions of females (78.3 percent) and males (78.5 percent) had four or more years of high school. Although 24.3 percent of males had four or more years of college, only 18.8 percent of females attained that level of education.

A final factor that is offered as evidence of current labor market discrimination is occupational segregation, which is much more pronounced between men and women than between minorities and Whites. Generally, men are concentrated in higher-paying occupations, women in lower-paying occupations. Table 9-3 reports data on the percentage of women in various higher- and lower-paying occupations in 1980. The data show that few women are employed in higher-paying occupations. Generally, women are overrepresented in lower-paying occupations. Note, however, that such occupational segregation does not necessarily imply existence of sex discrimination as it could be due to differences in preferences between men and women.

MEASURING DISCRIMINATION

Although the data presented herein clearly show racial and sex disparities, the cause of the disparities cannot be inferred from the data. Racial income inequalities could be a result of current labor market discrimination and premarket factors, or to various other factors. For example, to measure that portion of earning disparity that is due to racial discrimination, it is necessary to isolate that portion of the disparity that is due to racial discrimination in the labor market. Similarly, the observed disparity in earnings between males and females should not be attributed entirely to the existence of sex discrimination. In particular, lower earnings by women could reflect the fact that females have a much shorter market life. As such, it may be rational for women to invest less in school and on-the-job training since they expect a smaller return from such productivity enhancing investments.

The lower level of human capital investment by women implies lower earnings than men. Also, because of child rearing responsibilities, women may choose occupations requiring shorter hours and lower wages. That is, women may choose lower-paying occupations that allow more time for child rearing. Thus, an accurate measure of sex discrimination should control for all these potential sources of disparities.

In summary, to measure the magnitude of earnings disparity due to market discrimination, it is necessary to hold constant all other things that affect earnings. One must ask what the Black-to-White or female-to-male earnings

Table 9-3   Occupational segregation, 1980

Occupation	Percent Female	Mean Earnings (Dollars)
High-paying		
Physicians	11	57,166
Dentists	5	46,369
Lawyers	10	39,132
Podiatrists	5	38,402
Medical science teachers	17	37,958
Law teachers	13	36,411
Securities and financial sales occupation	17	35,448
Airline pilots and navigators	1	34,448
Optometrists	6	34,211
Medical scientists	35	33,909
Low-paying		
Child care workers, private households	98	4,473
Household cleaners and servants	92	5,530
Housekeepers and butlers	95	5,612
Child care workers, except private household	89	6,617
Cooks, private household	83	7,082
Waiters and waitresses	83	7,095
Miscellaneous food preparation	56	7,548
Waiters' and waitresses' assistants	46	7,623
Teachers' aides	88	7,628
Textile sewing machine operators	93	7,726

Source: U.S. Bureau of the Census, *1980 Census of Population, Vol. 2, Subject Reports, Earnings by Occupation and Education*, 1984.

ratios would be if these groups had the same productivity characteristics. Failure to account for differences in productivity characteristics will attribute more of the differentials to discrimination even when such differences arise from other factors.

A number of studies have attempted to explain Black-to-White and male-to-female earning differentials by carefully controlling for various factors such as age, on-the-job training, education, experience, region of residence, labor union membership, and so forth. The common procedure is *residual analysis,* in which a regression for the determinants of wages is estimated. The idea is to obtain estimates of the magnitude of the wage gap that is explained by the various productivity characteristics and also hold the occupational type constant. The remaining portion of the wage gap that is not explained by the explanatory variables (the residual) is then attributed to discrimination.[8] The existing studies suggest that the magnitude of earnings disparity explained by labor market discrimination is substantial though other factors also are important. Flanagan (1973) and Blinder (1973) found that without measurable differences in productivity characteristics, Black males in the late 1960s would have earned between 85 and 90 percent of what White males earned.[9] That is, although Black males earned between 55 and 60 percent of what White males did, a portion of the earnings gap was due to differences in productivity characteristics and the other portion was due to labor market discrimination. Corcoran and Duncan (1979), using data for the mid-1970s, found that in absence of premarket differences, earnings of Black males would have been about 88 percent of the earnings of White males.[10] Studies using more recent data show that when premarket factors are accounted for, Black males would earn between 83 and 94 percent of the incomes earned by White males.[11] Thus, over half of the 30 percent difference between the earnings of Blacks and Whites is due to premarket factors while the other portion could be attributed to labor market discrimination.

Empirical studies on the female-to-male earnings disparity show that when all other factors are taken into account, personal and job attributes account for between one-third to two-thirds of the earnings gap between men and women. When occupation type is included with other productivity characteristics, only about 10 percent of the earnings gap between females and males remains unexplained. This 10 percent gap can be considered as the portion of the earnings gap due to labor market discrimination.[12]

---

8. See Chapter 2 Appendix for details of the estimation procedure. As noted in that appendix, the problem of omitted variables can seriously bias the estimates. It is therefore critical that most important variables that determine wages be included in the regression, or the residual attributed to discrimination may appear to be much larger than it is.

9. Robert J. Flanagan, "Labor Force Experience, Job Turnover, and Racial Wage Differentials," *Review of Economics and Statistics* 56 (4) (November 1974): 521–29; and A. S. Blinder, "Wage Discrimination-Reduced Form and Structural Estimates," *Journal of Human Resources* 8 (4) (Fall 1973): 436–55. See also James D. Gwartney and James E. Long, "The Relative Earnings of Blacks and Other Minorities," *Industrial and Labor Relations Review* 31 (3) (April 1978): 36–46.

10. Mary Corcoran and Greg Duncan, "Work History, Labor Force Attachment, and Earnings Differences Between the Races and Sexes," *Journal of Human Resources* 14 (1) (Winter 1979): 3–20.

11. See Saul Hoffman and Charles Link, "Selectivity Bias in Male Wage Equations: Black - White Comparisons," *Review of Economics and Statistics* 66 (2) (May 1984): 320–24; and Leonard A. Carlson and Caroline Swartz, "The Earnings of Women and Ethnic Minorities, 1959–79," *Industrial and Labor Relations Review* 41 (4) (July 1988): 530–46.

12. See Corcoran and Duncan, "Work History, Labor Force Attachment, and Earnings Differences Between the Races and Sexes," and Ronald Oaxaca, "Male-Female Wage Differentials in Urban Labor Markets," *International Economic Review* 14 (3) (October 1973): 693–709; Andrea H. Beller, "Occupational Segregation by Sex: Determinants and Changes," *Journal of Human Resources* 17 (3) (Summer 1982): 371–92. For a review of the various studies on gender earnings differentials, see Morley Gunderson, "Male-Female Wage Differentials and Policy Responses," *Journal of Economic Literature* 27 (1) (March 1989): 46–72.

Although the effect of labor market discrimination may be a relatively small part of observed disparities, discrimination in the labor market could influence the premarket factors. As observed in Chapter 7, the optimal level of human capital investment depends on expected returns. Labor market discrimination reduces the expected return to human capital investment. As such, some of the observed differences in premarket factors between Whites and minorities, and between males and females arise from the expectation that labor market discrimination will occur. Thus, the role of discrimination in explaining racial and sex disparities could be much larger than the empirical evidence discussed herein seems to suggest.

As will be seen in Chapter 12, a common argument for the cause of poverty is family structure. Specifically, the increased proportion of households headed by females is closely related to increased poverty. A sizable number of female heads are those who become pregnant while teenagers. McCrate (1991) has argued that teenage childbearing by Black women is a rational response to discrimination. Because Black women receive lower-quality education and because they expect to experience labor market discrimination, they also expect lower returns to education. As such, Black women have a lower incentive to avoid teenage births.[13]

Conversely, the estimated magnitudes of racial discrepancies in earnings also could be an overestimate. Specifically, earnings do not depend on years of schooling alone, but also on quality of schooling. Other factors (such as differences in work attitudes) also matter. Empirical estimates of discrimination do not control for these factors. Because many racial minorities attend relatively poor schools, it is likely that a portion of the earnings gap is due to differences in quality of schooling and not discrimination.[14]

As noted earlier, sex differences in occupational choice (thus differences in earnings) also could reflect preferences and not necessarily discrimination. Men and women have different trade-offs between wages and nonpecuniary aspects of jobs. A large number of women expect to interrupt their careers sometime in the future due to child-rearing responsibilities. Such interruptions are penalized in terms of wage loss due to depreciation of human capital. The penalty for intermittency or "atrophy" varies across occupations. Solomon Polachek has shown that women may choose jobs or occupations that involve lower skill atrophy if they plan to be out of

---

13. Elaine McCrate, "Discrimination, Returns to Education, and Teenage Childbearing," in Richard R. Cornwall and Phanindra V. Wunnava, eds., *New Approaches to Economic and Social Analysis of Discrimination* (New York: Preager, 1991), pp. 281–93.
14. See June O'Neill, "The Role of Human Capital in Earnings Differences Between Black and White Men," *Journal of Economics Perspectives*, 4 (4) (Fall 1990): 25–45. Nevertheless, just because quality of schooling explains part of the gap does not necessarily imply that there is less discrimination. One must also consider the role discrimination has played in causing the low quality of schooling that minorities receive.

the labor force for some period of time in the future.[15] Such occupations and jobs have a flat earnings profile and pay less than occupations with higher skill atrophy.

Although the choice aspect is important, it also is crucial to note that women may be denied access to certain higher-paying jobs because of discrimination. If employers expect women to interrupt their careers sometime in the future, the jobs that involve costly training to the employer will be less accessible to women.

Although there are several problems in measuring the magnitude of earnings that is due to discrimination, the foregoing discussion suggests that race and sex discrimination play an important role in explaining racial and sexual disparities in earnings, and therefore poverty rates. There are serious disagreements as to the magnitude of observed disparities caused by discrimination, but it is well accepted that discrimination is, and has been, important in the American society. This text's concern is to explain why discriminatory practices occur. Researchers in various disciplines—including economics, psychology, sociology, history, and anthropology—have formulated theories that seek to explain discrimination. Discrimination is a complex phenomenon that may require explanations from various disciplines, but this text's focus is only on economic theories of discrimination as they relate to labor markets. It also considers how discrimination is manifested in the provision of human capital.

THEORIES OF LABOR MARKET DISCRIMINATION

Discrimination in labor markets occurs when equally productive workers are paid different wages or do not have equal access to some jobs solely because of their race, sex, age, or any other characteristic not directly related to productivity. Several economic theories have been offered to explain the phenomenon of discrimination. These explanations include the neoclassical, statistical, and monopoly power theories of discrimination.

Neoclassical Theory of Discrimination

Gary Becker (1957) was the first to formulate a systematic theory of discrimination that maintained the primary assumption about human behavior used in economics, namely the rational utility maximization axiom.[16]

---

15. Solomon William Polachek, "Occupational Self-Selection: A Human Capital Approach to Sex Differences in Occupational Structure," *Review of Economics and Statistics* 63 (February 1981): 60-69.
16. Gary S. Becker, *The Economics of Discrimination* (Chicago: University of Chicago Press, 1957, 1971).

Becker's model hinges on the idea that those with a taste for discrimination experience disutility from associating with members of another, nonpreferred group. The model assumes that such individuals are both able and willing to pay for the positive evaluation of members of the preferred group and/or to avoid the negative evaluation of members of the nonpreferred group. Thus, discriminating employers, workers, or consumers are willing to sacrifice profits, accept lower wages, or pay higher prices to satisfy their preference to avoid associating with members of a nonpreferred group. For those discriminatory employers, workers, or consumers, utility maximization implies that differences will exist in the way they treat members of their own group. In essence, discriminatory behavior represents this negative utility experienced by an individual or group as a result of associating with members of another group. The magnitude of the negative utility that arises from associating with members of the nonpreferred group depends on the extent of personal prejudice against that group and is proxied by what Becker calls the discrimination coefficient, d. The more intense the degree of prejudice, the larger the discrimination coefficient, and the larger the difference in treatment between members of preferred and nonpreferred groups.

Consider two groups of workers, Black and White who are otherwise equally productive.[17] To a nondiscriminating employer, Blacks and Whites are perfect substitutes in production. If wages of Blacks and Whites are equal, the employer will hire at random without regard to race. Suppose, however, that a White employer is prejudiced against Black employees. This means that to this employer, there is an added disutility of employing Black workers. In other words, employing Black workers imposes some psychic costs on the employer because of disutility experienced by the prejudiced employer. As such, Blacks are more expensive inputs to this employer because of these psychic costs. The monetary value of the psychic cost can be measured by the discrimination coefficient, d. The more prejudiced the employer, the higher the psychic costs.

To illustrate Becker's model of discrimination, assume a competitive market in which several firms produce a homogeneous product using the same technology. Firms employ equally productive Black and White workers (in other words, equal marginal products, MP) and thus they are perfect substitutes for one another. Absent discrimination, market equilibrium emerges when the wage paid to White (W_w) and Black (B_w) workers equal the marginal product, that is, $MP = W_w = W_b$. In other words, the relative wage of Blacks to Whites (W_b/W_w) = 1.

Suppose that employers are prejudiced against Black workers but not against Whites. To the prejudiced employer, the cost of hiring Blacks at

---

17. This analysis applies when considering female and male workers in situations where the female workers face discrimination by male employers.

wage W_b is $(W_b + d_b)$ while the cost of hiring White workers is W_w. In equilibrium, the cost should equal the marginal product. Thus, for Black workers, $MP = W_b + d_b$ and for White workers, $MP = W_w$. Since Black and White workers are equally productive, then W_b must be less than W_w. That is,

(9.1)
$$W_w = W_b + d_b$$

therefore

(9.2)
$$W_b = W_w - d_b$$

This implies that, since the marginal product of Blacks is devalued by prejudiced employers, Blacks will be employed only if they offer their services at a lower wage than Whites. Specifically, in order for the prejudiced employer to hire Blacks, their wage must be less than the wages of Whites by the amount of the discrimination coefficient, d_b.

For example, suppose that the market wage is $6 per hour. If the psychic cost that an employer experiences from hiring Blacks is $1 ($d_b$ = $1), then Blacks will be hired only at a wage of $5 per hour. To the employer, hiring a Black worker at $5 and a White worker at $6 is equivalent. This means that the employer is willing to pay a premium of $1 to White workers in order to satisfy his or her taste for discrimination. More prejudiced employers will have larger values of the discrimination coefficient. These employers will hire Black employees only if their wages are much lower as determined by the values of d_b.

Becker's model can be illustrated with demand and supply. Figure 9-5 assumes a competitive labor market. Rather than plotting the wage on the vertical axis, it plots the ratio of Black to White wages, W_b/W_w. The horizontal axis shows the number of Black workers. Notice that the demand for Black workers D_b has a kink at A. Between O and A, wages of Black and White employees are the same such that $W_b/W_w = 1$. This horizontal portion of the demand curve reflects nondiscriminating employers, that is those employers whose discrimination coefficients equal zero. As long as wages of Black and White employees are equal, these employers do not discriminate between the two groups of workers. The downward sloping portion of the demand curve reflects discriminating employers. As one moves down the demand curve, the employers' discrimination coefficients increase; that is, employers to the right are more prejudiced and hire Blacks only at increasingly lower relative wages. S_b shows the supply of Black workers; the quantity of Black labor supplied increases as the relative wage of Blacks increases. The intersection between the demand curve (D_b) and supply curve (S_b), establishes the quantity of Blacks employed and their relative wages. In Figure 9-5, the relative wage (W_b/W_w) is 0.8 and the level of Black employment is equal to B_1. Thus, the wages of Blacks are 80 percent of the wages of Whites.

Figure 9-5   Neoclassical model of discrimination, wage differentials caused by employer prejudice

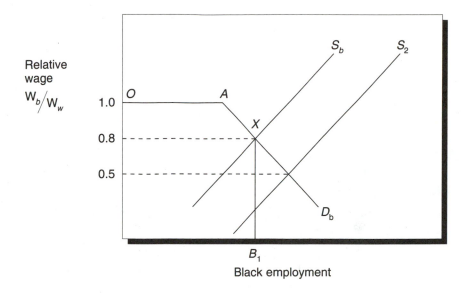

Two main factors determine the size of the wage differential between Black and White workers: the extent of prejudice and the supply of Black workers. If more nondiscriminating employers exist, then the horizontal portion of the demand curve will be larger and many of the Black workers will be hired at the same wages as Whites. In Figure 9-6, for example, the intersection of the demand and supply curves occurs where the wages of Blacks and Whites are equal. Thus, all Black workers are absorbed by nondiscriminating employers. On the other hand, if more prejudiced employers exist, then the demand curve will slope downward to the right and more Blacks will be hired at lower wages. The steeper the demand curve, the lower the ratio of Black to White wages.

The supply of Black workers also affects relative wages. More Black workers cause the supply curve to be much more to the right, say S_2 in Figure 9-5. This implies that wages of Blacks must decline more than when the supply is S_1 to induce prejudiced employers to hire them. Thus, one can expect to find larger wage differences between Whites and minorities in those areas where there are more minority workers.

A prediction of Becker's model is that discrimination by employers should result in segregated workplaces. If the supply of Black workers is S_b as shown in Figure 9-5, then employers to the left of X would hire only Black workers while those to the right of X would hire only White workers. To the left of X, the lower relative wages of Blacks is more than sufficient to compensate for the employers' prejudice. Thus, those employers

Figure 9-6   Neoclassical model of discrimination, wage equality due to low supply of Black workers

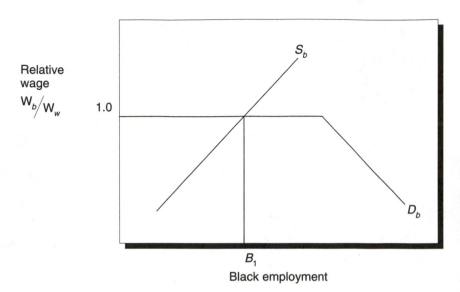

will choose Black workers at relatively lower wages than equally productive White workers at higher wages. Employers to the right of X would hire only White workers because the lower relative wage of Blacks is not sufficient to compensate for their prejudice.

Becker's model also can be used to explain customer and employee discrimination. Customer discrimination arises when customers prefer to be served by members of a particular group of workers. For example, customers may prefer White males in jobs that require more responsibility such as stock brokers, accountants, and pilots, while they prefer minorities and women in jobs that require less responsibility such as janitors and receptionists. These consumer preferences result in occupational segregation such that minorities and females are concentrated in lower-paying jobs. For minorities and females to be hired in those occupations for which customers prefer White males, they must either accept lower wages and/or be more qualified than the average White male employee.

For example, employee discrimination arises if White males avoid interacting with minorities or females in the workplace. White males may want to boss Black and women workers rather than be subordinates to members of either group. As such, prejudiced White males quit or avoid firms that employ minorities and females. Therefore, if employers hire and retain these prejudiced White males, they must pay them more in order to induce them to work with minorities and females. Thus, again the neoclassical model predicts that employee discrimination would result in segregated workplaces.

The neoclassical model of discrimination has been criticized on various grounds. As observed, the model predicts segregated workplaces. However, there has not been dramatic segregation by firms as predicted by the model. In addition, the neoclassical model implies that discrimination would disappear under conditions of competitive markets. For example, in the previously discussed model showing the wages paid to Black and White workers, prejudiced employers hire White workers at a wage that is higher than they would have paid equally productive Blacks. As such, firms that do not discriminate have a cost advantage over those that do discriminate. Although discrimination is consistent with utility maximization, it is not consistent with profit maximization. In a competitive economy, discriminating firms will be driven out of business by those who do not discriminate. As such, market forces would be expected to eradicate discrimination. However, evidence shows that discrimination has persisted throughout history.[18] This has promoted several other explanations of discrimination.

Statistical Discrimination

Unlike the neoclassical theory of discrimination that views the activities of those who discriminate as due to personal prejudice, the theory of statistical discrimination suggests that discrimination arises due to the lack of perfect information about individual characteristics.[19] For example, when making hiring decisions, employers use the information available that they think is correlated with productivity such as education, experience, age, and test scores. Nevertheless, these measures are not perfect indicators of productivity and employers may need to supplement those measures with their own subjective evaluation of the candidate's probability of success. Such subjective evaluation may be based on the average characteristics of the group to which an individual belongs rather than his or her own true characteristics. If the employer must pay the same wage to all workers, then the profit-maximizing employer will prefer to hire workers from the group that he or she considers most productive. This is referred to as statistical discrimination. If, on average, the employer's perceptions are accurate, then competitive pressures will not reduce statistical discrimination. As a result, statistical discrimination can occur in a long-run competitive equilibrium.

To illustrate statistical discrimination, consider the productivity distribution for two groups of workers, females and males, shown in Figure 9-7. The average productivity of females is 20 units per day while the average

---

18. See Kenneth J. Arrow, "The Theory of Discrimination."
19. See Kenneth J. Arrow, "Some Mathematical Models of Race Discrimination in the Labor Market," in Antony Pascal, ed., *Racial Discrimination in Economic Life* (Lexington, Mass.: D.C. Heath & Co., 1972), and Dennis J. Aigner and Glen G. Cain, "Statistical Theories of Discrimination in Labor Markets," *Industrial and Labor Relations Review* 30 (2) (January 1977): 175-87.

Figure 9-7   Frequency distribution of worker productivity among males and females

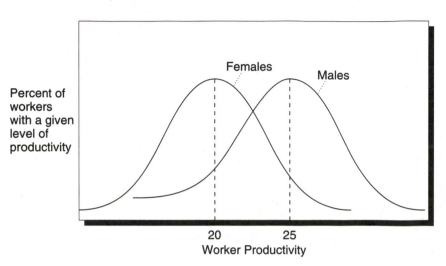

productivity of males is 25 units per day. Although females as a group have lower productivity, some females are more productive. If two applicants, a male and a female who otherwise have similar productivity characteristics such as education and experience, apply for the same job, the employer probably hires the male applicant. Such decisions screen potential hires and the employer minimizes the hiring cost. If the female applicant has a productivity of 30 units per day and the male 20 units per day, the use of group averages suggests that the male applicant should be hired although the female actually is more productive. Thus, the use of group averages results in discrimination.

It is important to emphasize the fact that the statistical discrimination model, unlike the neoclassical model, adequately explains persistence of sex and race discrimination even under conditions of competitive markets. Even if employers are not prejudiced, employment discrimination persists because those employers continue to use stereotyped beliefs such as minorities and women having lower productivity. Therefore, these groups are ranked lower in the queue of job applicants.

Monopoly Power and Discrimination

As in the case of statistical discrimination, monopoly power models of discrimination suggest that discrimination persists because it is profitable to those who discriminate. Specifically, these models suggest that race and gender are used to divide labor into noncompeting groups, thereby separating these workers. Three versions of the monopoly power models exist—the dual labor market model (discussed in Chapter 7), the crowding or occupational segregation model, and the political economy model.[20]

Crowding Model–Blacks and females are concentrated in lower-paying occupations. The crowding model of discrimination suggests that minorities and women earn lower wages because they are crowded into relatively few occupations.[21]

The crowding model can be easily explained by the use of demand and supply as shown in Figure 9-8. This figure depicts demand and supply of labor for two occupations. If no employment barriers exist in the two occupations, free mobility of labor will occur so that wages in the two occupations will equal W_0. If women and Blacks are prevented from working in occupation 1, then the supply of workers in this occupation shifts to S_1 and a new and higher wage is established at W_h (panel A). If women and Blacks work only in occupation 2, then the supply of workers in this

Figure 9-8   Crowding model of discrimination

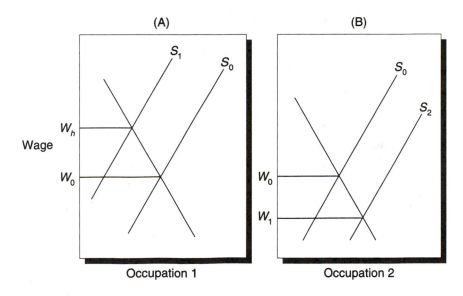

20. See Glen G. Cain, "The Challenge of Segmented Labor Market Theories to Orthodox Theory: A Survey," *Journal of Economic Literature* 14 (4) (December 1976): 1215-57.
21. See Barbara R. Bergmann, "The Effects on White Incomes of Discrimination in Employment," *Journal of Political Economy* 79 (2) (March-April 1975): 294-313; Barbara R. Bergmann, "Does the Market for Women's Labor Need Fixing?" *Journal of Economic Perspectives* 3 (1), (Winter 1989): 43-60; Robert P. Strauss and Francis W. Horvath, "Wage Rate Differences by Race and Sex in the U.S. Labor Market: 1960–1970: *Economica* 43 (171), (August 1976): 287-98; and Andrea H. Beller, "Occupational Segregation by Sex: Determinants and Changes."

occupation increases to S_2 (panel B). Wages for workers in this occupation fall to W_1. Thus, occupational segregation results in higher wages for Whites and males, while females and Blacks earn lower wages in crowded labor markets.

Occupational segregation can occur if worker productivity depends largely on team effort. If workers do not interact well socially, team effort is affected, resulting in lower productivity. If males (Whites) are uncomfortable working with women (Blacks), then employers may segregate workers by race and sex. Other explanations suggest that some jobs have been designated as "male" and others "female" through social custom.[22] Whatever the cause, the crowding model suggests that some groups (males and Whites) benefit from discrimination, while others (females and minorities) lose.

Political-economic model of discrimination—Both the neoclassical and statistical models of discrimination have been criticized by radical economists on the basis that they do not reflect real conditions in the labor market. Criticism of the neoclassical model states that it assumes that the tastes of discriminators are independent of economic interests. In addition, the neoclassical model fails to explain the persistence of discrimination even under competitive conditions. Conversely, the statistical model is criticized on the basis that it exaggerates the costs of screening job applicants. A lot of information that employers could use about job applicants is available. For example, information is readily available about applicants' education, performance in job-related tests, and so forth. Also, employers can hire workers on a probationary basis and thus observe individual productivity. Thus, less-prejudiced employers can be expected to use these relatively inexpensive sources of information in making hiring decisions.

Radical economists have suggested an alternative model of discrimination called the *political-economic model of discrimination*. This model suggests that discrimination benefits employers while Black and White employees lose.[23] By segregating Black and White employees, and by treating them differently, employers are able to exploit racial divisions such that worker unity is minimized. Thus, divisions created by employers reduce worker unity, and thereby reduce labor's bargaining power. Worker disunity lowers the probability of unionization. Thus, discrimination is a divide-and-conquer strategy used by employers to increase their profits. This model proposed that Whites see themselves as better than Blacks and are therefore not interested in working together to demand better conditions. Unfortunately, although the political-economic model is

---

22. See Millicent Fawcett, "Equal Pay for Equal Work," *Economic Journal* 28 (March 1918): 1-6.
23. See Lester Thurow, *Poverty and Discrimination* (Washington, D.C.: The Brookings Institute, 1969); and Michael Reich, *Racial Inequality: A Political Economic Analysis* (Princeton, N. J.: Princeton University Press, 1981).

appealing, there is little contemporary empirical evidence that supports the validity of this theory.[24]

These monopoly theories of discrimination suggest that discrimination introduces imperfections in labor markets such that wages do not necessarily reflect labor productivity. These theories demonstrate that discrimination creates inequality of outcomes. Statistical discrimination theory and the monopoly power theories suggest that government intervention is necessary to equalize opportunities. However, the neoclassical model suggests that discrimination will be eliminated by the market and probably the most the government can do is to create conditions that are conducive for competitive markets. As noted, however, the neoclassical model performs poorly in explaining observed facts. This then suggests that it would be unrealistic to expect the market to eliminate discriminatory practices.

DISCRIMINATION IN EDUCATION

We have observed that a large portion of earnings disparities between minorities and Whites, and between females and males are due to premarket factors. In particular, there are significant racial and gender differences in the levels of human capital accumulation. Although differences in human capital investment could be due to several factors (including ability and preferences), a major source of observed differences is the inequality of educational opportunities. Inequalities may result from differences in family incomes; children of wealthy families generally receive superior educations. Inequality in educational opportunities also arise from racial and sexual discrimination.

For a long time, Blacks in the United States were denied the opportunity to acquire an education. Discrimination in the provision of education was extensive and explicit. For example, until the late nineteenth century, teaching slaves was prohibited in most Southern states. During the era of slavery, about 95 percent of all adult Blacks were illiterate. Even when teaching of Blacks was permitted, such access was provided in segregated and inferior facilities. The practice of segregation was condoned by the U.S. Supreme Court in 1896 when it declared in *Plessy v. Ferguson* that "separate

---

24. In the past, two pieces of evidence have been used to support the validity of the political-economic model of discrimination. First, Black workers have historically been used as strikebreakers. Creating a situation in which Black and White workers are in conflict assures employers that Blacks will be ready to take jobs from Whites when called upon to do so. Whites, knowing that a pool of Black workers is ready to take their jobs, are therefore less likely to go on strike or to demand large wage increases.

Second, areas of the country that have less discrimination have higher labor shares of national income. That is, when there is no discrimination, the labor movement is stronger and receiving a higher share of national income. When labor is united, it receives a larger share of national income relative to capital. In areas with more discrimination, the labor movement is weaker and labor's share of national income is lower. See Michael Reich, *Racial Inequality: A Political Economic Analysis.*

but equal" public services was constitutional. Rarely was the quality of Black schools equal to that of White schools. It was not until the 1954 *Brown v. Board of Education* that the Supreme Court declared that separate educational facilities were inherently unequal.[25]

Probably the clearest indication of the continued inequality of educational opportunities is the persistent racial segregation in schools. Racial segregation by law, de jure segregation, is now illegal. But de facto segregation, which is the segregation that arises from circumstances, still exists in many parts of the country. In fact, a large number of Black, Hispanic, and Native American students attend schools that are composed predominantly of minorities. Furthermore, most of the schools attended by minorities have poorer facilities, are poorly funded, and have less qualified teachers than those attended by White students. Thus, racial isolation and inequality in education still exist. Today, minorities lag behind in the number of years of schooling attained and in the quality of education acquired. Even when non-Whites and Whites have the same number of years of education, non-Whites face poorer labor market prospects as the quality of their education is much lower. The next discussion includes some factors that lead to de facto segregation that have, in turn, resulted in racial isolation and inequality in education.[26]

Housing patterns–A major factor that explains the isolation of minorities in education is the segregated housing patterns that have emerged in many areas, particularly metropolitan areas. As Chapter 9 documents, poor minorities locate in the inner cities while more affluent Whites reside in the suburbs. Since public schools are funded primarily by local property taxes, poor inner cities provide limited resources for education while more wealthy suburbs spend much more. Thus, residential segregation by economic status and race results in a situation where minorities are in schools that are poorly funded.

Nonpublic Schools–Even in those places where Blacks and Whites live together, and as such would be expected to attend the same schools, various mechanisms have emerged to reduce racial integration in schools. A common method has been the establishment of private or church schools.

Before 1960, most Whites and Blacks in the South attended segregated schools. After federal integration efforts began, many Whites chose to avoid integration by enrolling their children in nonpublic schools. The result of this *white flight* was that many Black schools remained that way, and some of the previously White schools became predominantly Black with only a few, mainly poor, Whites.

---

25. See Wallace Mendelson, *Discrimination* (Englewood Cliffs, N. J.: Prentice Hall, 1962).
26. See, for example, U.S. Office of Education, *Equality of Education Opportunities* (The Coleman Report), (Washington, D.C.: U.S. Government Printing Office, 1966), and Congressional Budget Office, *Inequalities in the Educational Experiences of Black and White Americans* (Washington, D.C.: U.S. Government Printing Office, 1977).

Educational policies and practices–Communities have adopted several policies and practices that reduce the chances of racial integration. One method that has resulted in segregated schools is called *gerrymandering*—the purposeful design of school attendance zones to avoid integration. In areas where racial communities live in adjacent areas and would in some cases attend the same schools, communities have avoided integration by creating smaller attendance zones. In some cases, school districts are drawn to ensure that integration is minimized.

Another practice, closely related to gerrymandering, is the establishment of optional attendance zones. These are small geographical areas in which students are allowed to choose the schools they want to attend. Although optional zones can be used to promote more integration, they have been used to increase segregation. Almost always, optional zones were designed to help White students avoid predominantly Black schools that may be located close to their neighborhoods.

Another method involves the selection of sites where new schools are constructed. For example, if Black and White communities are adjacent to each other, schools can be located in areas distant from the boundary separating the two communities. One school draws students primarily or wholly from the Black community while the other from the White community. Thus, the school site can be an effective way of avoiding integration.

Another way to avoid integration is to alter the grade structure of schools. Increasing the number of grades a school serves reduces the attendance zones that the school serves. Schools that have only a few grades draw students from a wider area. Thus, to avoid integration, some communities have established schools that have many grades and that draw students from relatively small, often racially homogeneous, areas.

The main point to emphasize in regard to racial discrimination in education is that extensive racial segregation in schools also is accompanied by large fiscal disparities. Schools with predominantly minority student bodies often have relatively low funding so that those students continue to receive inferior educations.

Sex discrimination in education is much less extensive, but does take place. One way that sex discrimination in education is manifested is by encouraging girls at early ages to take particular courses that are considered more appropriate for women (such as typing and home economics). On the other hand, they are discouraged from taking courses in science and business. The effect is that women are discouraged from taking courses that may help them obtain high-paying jobs later in life. Females also have faced discrimination in admissions to professional schools.

Although racial inequalities in educational opportunities have persisted (there are some indications that racial inequalities in opportunities have widened in recent years), sex inequalities in education have diminished.

SUMMARY

Race and sex discrimination restrict opportunities of minorities and women such that they are not able to achieve their full potential. Inequality in opportunities due to discrimination leads to disparate outcomes in earnings. Thus, discrimination is one plausible reason that poverty is more prevalent among minorities and women.

This chapter has examined discrimination in both labor markets and education. Theories of labor market discrimination discussed offer credible explanations for some of the racial and sex differences in labor market outcomes. The discussion of discrimination in education also illustrates the continued inequality in opportunities that explains some of the premarket differences across racial groups. Although observed racial and sexual differences in earnings, unemployment, and education are not entirely due to discrimination, discrimination is an important contributory factor to these disparities. To the extent that discrimination creates inequalities in opportunities, public policies must establish equality of opportunities by preventing discrimination.

STUDY AND DISCUSSION QUESTIONS

1. Discuss the difference between "equality of outcomes" and "equality of opportunities."

2. Outline the various sources of inequity of opportunities in the United States.

4. Write an essay on theories of discrimination. Critically evaluate the theories. Which theory do you think best explains the observed patterns of inequalities?

5. Explain how you would go about investigating the proportion of a racial wage gap that is due to discrimination. What are some of the problems from which your estimates are likely to suffer?

6. Compare the various schools with which you are familiar. What is the approximate racial composition of those schools? Is there any relationship between racial composition and the quality of those schools? If so, what do you think are the sources of those inequalities?

7. Distinguish between de jure segregation and de facto segregation. Suppose that there is evidence that segregation by itself constitutes inequality of opportunity. For public policy purposes, do you think that it matters whether observed segregation is de facto or de jure?

8. Outline various factors that have been responsible for continued racial segregation in education.

ADDITIONAL READINGS

1. Amsden, Alice, H., ed. *The Economics of Women and Work.* New York: St. Martin's Press, 1980.

2. Bergmann, Barbara R. *The Economic Emergence of Women.* New York: Basic Books, 1987.

3. Hamermesh, Daniel S. and Albert Rees. *The Economics of Work and Pay,* 5th ed. New York: Harper and Row, 1988.

4. Kaufman, Bruce, E. *The Economics of Labor Markets,* 3rd ed. Chicago: Dryden Press, 1991.

5. Lundahl, Mats and Eskil Wadensj. *Unequal Treatment: A Study in the Neo-Classical Theory of Discrimination.* New York: New York University Press, 1984.

6. Mosteller, Frederick and Daniel Patrick Moynihan, eds., *On Equality of Education Opportunity.* New York: Vintage Books, 1972.

7. Polachek, S. W. and W. S. Siebert. *The Economics of Earnings.* Cambridge, England: Cambridge University Press, 1993.

8. Shulman, Steven and William Darity, Jr., eds. *The Question of Discrimination: Racial Inequality in the U.S. Labor Market,* Middletown, Conn.: Wesleyan University Press, 1989.

9. Wachtel, Howard. *Labor and the Economy.* San Diego, Calif.: Harcourt Brace Jovanvich, 1988.

10

RACE, GENDER, AND POVERTY: EQUAL OPPORTUNITY POLICIES

Chapter 9 discussed the sources of disparities between males and females, and between Whites and minorities. The disparities manifest themselves in various ways—minorities are more often unemployed, and those employed are frequently concentrated in low status, low-paying jobs. As a result, members of those groups have disproportionately low earnings and have relatively higher incidence of poverty than Whites. Similarly, although there are no significant differences in unemployment rates between men and women, women are concentrated in low-paying jobs. The disadvantaged positions of these groups suggest that public policies should target those groups.

While the observed racial and sexual disparities result from the interaction of many factors, a primary factor is unequal opportunities. Inequality in opportunities may exist because of initial differences in income or because of discrimination in labor markets and education. This suggests that one way to deal with the low earnings of minorities and females should be to equalize opportunities by adopting antidiscrimination policies. At the same time, however, because preventing current discrimination may not solve existing disparities, public policies could be directed to correct the effects of past discrimination.

This chapter discusses equal opportunity policies in the United States. It begins with those policies that provide equal opportunities in labor markets. Next, the focus is on policies that provide equal education opportunities. The chapter concludes with an evaluation of equal opportunity policies.

EQUAL EMPLOYMENT OPPORTUNITY

The discussion in Chapter 9 suggested that inequalities between minorities and Whites, and between males and females are partly due to discriminatory practices in hiring, promotion, and pay. In response, various policies have been adopted by states and by the federal government to

combat discrimination. Since the 1930s, states have adopted fair employment practice laws that prohibit discrimination on the basis of race.
Nevertheless, these state laws have not been effective in eliminating discrimination. Since the 1960s, the federal government has taken an active
role in providing equal opportunity by outlawing discriminatory practices in the workplace and by establishing appropriate enforcement mechanisms. Some of the more important federal antidiscrimination efforts
were expressed in the Equal Pay Act of 1963, Title VII of the Civil Rights
Act of 1964, and Executive Orders of 1965 and 1968 that called for the
establishment of affirmative action programs.

Recently, a heated debate concerning the male–female wage earnings
inequality has revolved around what is called *comparable worth*. Although
no federal legislation currently mandates a comparable worth policy, there
is a strong movement in favor of such a policy. By the early 1990s, over
two-thirds of the states had introduced or were attempting to introduce
comparable worth legislation, and six states had already implemented
explicit forms of comparable worth programs for their public employees.
The following discusses this policy and various federal antidiscrimination
policies already mentioned.

Equal Pay Act of 1963

As noted previously, women generally earn less than men. The Equal Pay
Act (EPA) of 1963, which was an amendment to the Fair Labor Standards
Act, was the first federal legislation that sought to eliminate sex discrimination in the workplace. The main thrust of the act was to ensure equal pay
for equal work. The act made it illegal for employers to pay men and
women different wage rates if they perform equal work in jobs, the performance of which requires equal skill, effort, and responsibility. Thus, the
main goal of the act was to eliminate overt sex discrimination in the workplace. Courts have enforced the Equal Pay Act by imposing compensatory
damages on employers who pay women less than men for equal work.
EPA is universally observed across all states and, by and large, women
receive the same pay as men for performing the same work.

One of the commonly cited shortcomings of EPA is that it did not
focus on providing equal opportunity in hiring and promotion. Thus,
equal pay may not necessarily translate into equal opportunity. In fact, it
has been argued that EPA may have reduced employment opportunities
for women. If there is prejudice against women, employers treat women as
less productive and thus devalue their marginal product. The result is for
women's wages to be lower than those of males. By eliminating disparity
in wages, but with no requirement for equal opportunity in hiring and promotion, EPA could have reduced the employment opportunities available
for women as prejudiced employers reacted by employing fewer women

or by crowding women into low-paying jobs such as secretaries, clerks, and so forth.[1]

Title VII of the Civil Rights Act of 1964

The most important federal antidiscrimination legislation to date is Title VII of the Civil Rights Act of 1964. Title VII made it unlawful for an employer "to refuse to hire or to discharge any individual, or otherwise to discriminate against any individual with respect to compensation, terms, conditions, or privileges of employment because of such individual's race, color, religion, sex or national origin." The act required equal treatment for all in hiring, firing, promotion and compensation. As amended in 1972, the act applies to all employers involved in interstate commerce with fifteen or more workers, members of employment agencies, and to workers employed by educational institutions, federal, state, and local governments. An important aspect of the act was its addressing of labor unions practices. Before the act, racial minorities were denied opportunities to join some craft unions, which denied them access to training provided through union apprenticeship programs and also employment opportunities.

To enforce the act, Congress established the Equal Employment Opportunity Commission (EEOC). EEOC is an independent, five-member agency appointed by the president, but requiring the consent of the Senate. EEOC has the mandate to hear complaints, encourage lawsuits by individuals or the U.S. attorney general, and to recommend resolutions of disputes. Since 1972, EEOC has been empowered to bring suits against employers on behalf of complainants. To widen the impact of lawsuits, courts permit individuals to expand their suits against employers into class action suits.[2]

Although Title VII prohibited discrimination, it did not clearly stipulate how evidence of economic discrimination would be established, but left that task to the courts. Over the years federal courts have used two standards in determining alleged employment discrimination: *disparate treatment* and *disparate impact*. The most direct approach to determining the existence of discrimination is disparate treatment, which involves investigating whether persons are treated differently because of their sex, race, color, religion, or national origin, with the intent to discriminate. Most of the time, however, the courts have not relied solely on this approach

---

1. Note that an employer with an all-male labor force would not be in violation of EPA. Inclusion of women in the Equal Pay Act was done by Representative Howard Smith of Virginia at the last moment in an attempt to defeat the act. This could explain the lack of progress for women in reducing earnings inequality until the 1980s, as enforcement of the act was weak.
2. A class action is a suit that is filed by a group of individuals on their own behalf and that of all others with the same complaint.

because discrimination could still take place although there is no apparent disparate treatment in the workplace. Practices that may appear neutral in regard to race, gender, and so forth, may perpetuate the effects of past discrimination. For example, information about job vacancies in a predominantly White male workplace may be passed by word of mouth only to White males. The result is that applicants for positions will not include minorities and females.

Because of this problem with the use of a disparate treatment standard to demonstrate discrimination, courts frequently rely on disparate impact to establish discrimination. This standard seeks to evaluate outcomes, not the employer's motivation. For example, if a firm's employment profile by race differed radically from the racial profile of the labor force in the local labor market or in the industry or in the occupation, then an inference of discrimination could be drawn. In the past, when such disparate outcomes were shown to exist, the burden of proof was on the employer to show that employment practices are not discriminatory. However, recent Supreme Court decisions (for example, *Grove City*) are moving rapidly away from disparate impact and shifting the burden of proof toward workers. Such changes that occurred during the 1980s have greatly weakened the enforcement of antidiscrimination laws.

Of course, Title VII does not ignore the importance of using various productivity characteristics (such as education and training) as screening devices in hiring decisions. However, it does prohibit employment policies that, although they appear to be neutral in regard to race, sex, and so forth, result in disparate outcomes unless it can be shown that those practices are related to job performance. In a landmark case (*Willie S. Griggs v. Duke Power Company*) the Supreme Court ruled that Duke Power Company was guilty of discrimination because the requirement it had set disproportionately affected Blacks adversely and the company could not show that the requirements were necessary for successful job performance. The specific requirements were that all new employees should have a high school diploma and satisfactory aptitude test scores. Only 6 percent of Blacks were able to pass the aptitude tests as compared to 58 percent of Whites.[3] The court did not outlaw the use of screening devices, but required that such devices be related to job performance in a way that could be demonstrated. Similarly, marital status cannot be used as a screening device unless such is uniformly applied to both men and women and can be demonstrated that it is job related. It is important to note that the hiring requirements established by Duke Power took effect on the same day as Title VII. Previously, the company had excluded Blacks from most jobs and

---

3. Thus, in *Griggs*, the court used disparate impact as the standard and not disparate treatment in establishing discrimination. See Arthur B. Smith, Jr., "The Law and Equal Employment Opportunity: What's Past Should Not Be Prologue," *Industrial and Labor Relations Review* 33 (4) (July 1980): 493–505.

did not have educational requirements. Moreover, Whites who did not meet these requirements had been hired and had performed satisfactorily.[4]

Affirmative Action Programs

Title VII provides a mechanism for dealing with discrimination if it is proven to have occurred. The federal government also has adopted procedures to prevent discrimination from occurring at the present time. Executive orders issued in 1965 and 1968 sought to eliminate discrimination by businesses and other institutions that receive government contracts. Specifically, the executive orders require that contractors with $50,000 or more business with the federal government evaluate their underutilization of minorities and women and design plans to remedy such underutilization. Such a plan, referred to as an *affirmative action plan*, requires a firm to include a statistical profile of those employed and of the available pool of qualified women and members of minority groups from which the firm could hire. If there is a wide discrepancy between those hired and those in the available work pool, then the particular firm is required to set numerical goals and a timetable for increasing the employment of minorities and women. To administer affirmative action programs, the Office of Federal Contract Compliance Programs (OFCCP) was established within the Department of Labor in 1965.

Before 1971, compliance with Title VII was voluntary and most businesses had not established programs to increase the employment and promotion of minorities and women. In 1971, President Nixon instructed the Assistant Secretary of Labor Art Fletcher to formulate a way to enforce the hiring provisions stipulated in Title VII. Fletcher recommended the so-called Philadelphia plan. According to this plan, federal contractors in Philadelphia were required to meet specific numeric goals in hiring minorities. The long-term goal of the plan was to increase the number of minorities to the level that was equal to the percentage of minorities in the labor force.

President Nixon accepted recommendations to adopt the Philadelphia plan for federal contractors and issued Federal Contract Compliance (OFCC) Revised Order No. 4. Under the revised order, federal contractors were to adopt affirmative action plans that stipulated numeric goals for increasing the employment of minorities and women. Federal judges throughout the country immediately started using the revised order to compel public employers to integrate the workforce.

Federal contract recipients that fail to comply with affirmative action requirements risk losing those contracts. Soon after the revised order was

---

4. In a more recent case, *Wards Cove v. Atonia*, the court held that an employer that uses employment procedures that result in disparate impact must provide a plausible explanation of how those procedures relate to job performance.

issued, virtually all businesses affected initiated affirmative action programs to increase employment of minorities and women. In addition, employers initiated programs that provided minorities and women the opportunities for promotion to positions of more responsibility and higher pay. By the end of the 1970s, affirmative action had become standard policy procedure for most large employers in the United States.

An important aspect of affirmative action programs is to ensure that minorities and women are provided fair opportunities in the competition for employment positions. Thus, affirmative action regulations establish specific procedures for conducting searches, hiring, and promotion. Employers are prohibited from using irrelevant personal characteristics that may be biased against women and minorities. Such policies are useful in preventing statistical discrimination.

To appreciate the logic of affirmative action programs, it helps to consider the basic philosophy that led to the adoption of such a policy. As demonstrated in Chapter 9, discrimination against women and minorities has persisted for a long time and market forces cannot be relied upon to eradicate such practices. Past discrimination experienced by generations of minorities and women in labor markets and in the provision of human capital has placed these groups at a disadvantage that cannot be eliminated by merely outlawing current discrimination. Advocates of affirmative action have argued that, given their disadvantaged position, minorities and women always will be in inferior positions unless some deliberate steps are taken to pull them up in order to be on an equal footing with Whites and males. Thus, the adoption of race neutral or gender neutral policies would still leave those who have benefitted from past discrimination at an advantage. The underlying philosophy of affirmative action is that policies that may be considered race or gender neutral do not necessarily translate into equal opportunities. To achieve equality of opportunities, disadvantaged groups should be provided with greater opportunities to allow them to catch up.[5]

Affirmative action programs have been controversial and the concept has been challenged in the courts.[6] The primary criticism focuses on the idea of setting numerical goals for increasing the employment of minorities and women. The setting of numerical goals often has been viewed as a requirement to set aside quotas for minorities and women. A quota has a negative connotation as it implies employment practices based on mere numbers without regard to ability of the employee or of the firm's needs.

---

5. A common analogy that is given to illustrate the need for affirmative action is that of a caboose on a train. Regardless of how fast the train goes, the caboose will never catch up with the engine unless some arrangements are made to change the position of the caboose.
6. See Ron Raymond Taylor, *Affirmative Action at Work: Law Politics, and Ethics* (Pittsburgh, Penn.: University of Pittsburgh Press, 1991).

Quotas are specifically precluded from the intention of the executive orders that established affirmative action programs. Evidence shows that even though employers stipulate numerical goals, these goals are almost never met. Claims of widespread use of quotas in hiring is largely misplaced. These claims tend to be motivated by the falling economic position of younger, less-educated White males, although this has nothing to do with affirmative action. Nonetheless, politicians and the public find quotas an easy target on which to lay the blame.

Affirmative action programs also have been criticized as constituting reverse discrimination. In other words, by trying to help minorities and women, those programs result in preferential treatment of those groups at the expense of White males. Critics argue that in their attempts to increase minority and female representation, employers have to lower the standards so that members of the protected groups can be hired. In the process, given the limited number of positions available, some White males with better qualifications are not hired. Thus, not only does affirmative action result in abuse of the merit principle, it also constitutes reverse discrimination.

Concrete evidence of reverse discrimination is lacking. Most of those who claim that affirmative action results in reverse discrimination (such as Senator Helms of North Carolina) do so to elicit fears among Whites (often for political purposes). According to some of the well-known critics of affirmative action (such as Thomas Sowell), claims of reverse discrimination do not hold up. Using the example of affirmative action in academia, Sowell has argued that because only few jobs are available in academia, many aspiring academics would have had their career goals disappointed, regardless of affirmative action. According to Sowell:

> Now, when a hundred White male applicants are rejected, they can all blame it on one or two minority or female academics who were hired-even though 90 percent of the White males could not have been hired anyway, and there are probably 10 or 20 other White males hired for the one or two affirmative action professors. But administrators can, of course, tell rejected applicants that they lost out because of affirmative action, whether it is true or not, because that may be easier than telling them the real reason.[7]

In regard to merit, because employers are concerned about possible repercussions of firing or not promoting minorities and women once hired, employers tend to hire minorities and women who are overqualified as a precaution against having to take negative personnel actions in the future. Thus, the argument that affirmative action results in the hiring of minorities and women with lower qualifications lacks credibility. Note that an increasing number of blacks have argued against affirmative action

---

7. Thomas Sowell, "Affirmative Action Reconsidered," *Public Interest* 42 (Winter 1976): 58.

because they resent having their success attributed to preferences based on affirmative action rather than individual merit.[8]

Another criticism of affirmative action is that such a policy may not necessarily help the most disadvantaged members. Some researchers have suggested that affirmative action helps those with more education and the majority of those who are poor (such as minorities in the inner cities) do not benefit from such programs. Similarly, it often is stated that the burden of affirmative action falls on marginal White groups with low education and who come from families with low incomes. Affirmative action does not affect upper-class White males. In fact it is most likely that those who have been beneficiaries of past discrimination do not bear any of the burden. Likewise, prejudiced Whites may not be the ones who face a penalty but unprejudiced people could be hurt by affirmative action. Thus, even if it were possible to justify affirmative action as an effective policy to help those who have been subjected to past discrimination, the redistributional effects of such a policy may not be desirable.

Again, most of these criticisms are speculative as little concrete evidence is provided to support them. Although it is true that minorities and women with education are in a better position to take advantage of affirmative action programs, it also is true that low income minorities benefit when contractors are required to hire a certain proportion of minority workers. After all, affirmative action was not designed to create jobs but rather to remove barriers that hindered equal opportunities. As discussed previously, in regard to reverse discrimination, there is little evidence that White males have been seriously harmed by affirmative action programs. If some White males have been harmed, the number affected is quite low.

Despite his strong personal opposition to affirmative action, President Reagan did not eliminate the Office of Federal Contract Compliance Programs (OFCCP) even though he could have done so unilaterally through an executive order. Reagan took no action because of the strong support for the program from big business as represented by groups such as the National Association of Manufacturers and the Business Roundtable. This suggests that the negative effects of affirmative action that are often mentioned (such as higher recruiting costs) are more than outweighed by the benefits of the program to those businesses.

Comparable Worth Policy

As observed, the Equal Pay Act of 1963 does not necessarily guarantee equality of opportunities between men and women. Even after its enact-

---

8. See, for example, Stephen L. Carter, *Reflections of an Affirmative Action Baby* (New York: Basic Books, 1991). Thomas Sowell is probably the most well-known Black critic of affirmative action.

ment, women have continued to earn lower wages than men. On average, women earn 60 percent of what men earn. The continued sexual disparity in earnings suggests that unequal pay for equal work may not be the primary factor that explains the male–female wage differences. A primary factor that has been attributed to the persistent male–female wage gap is that of job and occupational segregation. The argument is that wages in female-dominated jobs are lower than wages in male-dominated jobs even when those jobs are of comparable value to a firm or government agency. In other words, women receive lower wages than men even though they perform work of comparable value. As such, some people (particularly those in the women's rights movement) have argued that a policy of pay equity or comparable worth is necessary for men and women doing different jobs, but with comparable value to eliminate the persistent male–female wage gap.[9]

The comparable worth doctrine keys on the idea that men and women who perform work that is of comparable value to the employer should receive equal pay. Two jobs are said to comprise equal value to an employer if they require equal amounts of knowledge, skill, working conditions, and responsibilities. To make the comparable worth doctrine operational, it is necessary that different jobs be evaluated to determine their worth and the wages that should be assigned to those jobs. Women and men in different jobs, but who are determined to be of equal worth, should then be paid equal wages.

Critics of comparable worth policy argue that the entire idea is flawed and impractical. For example, work conditions in male- and female-dominated occupation vary substantially and, as such, wages would be expected to vary across those occupations. How such working conditions are evaluated and assigned points in terms of worth must be quite subjective and arbitrary.[10] In addition, it is very difficult to evaluate the intrinsic worth of different job requirements or characteristics.[11]

Even if comparable worth policy were enacted, it is not guaranteed that women will benefit. For example, if employers are required to increase the pay in female dominated jobs, they may respond by hiring fewer females, thus hurting females by reducing their employment

---

9. For more in-depth discussion of comparable worth, see Michael E. Gold, *A Dialogue on Comparable Worth* (Ithaca, N.Y.: ILR Press, 1983); Henry J. Aaron and Cameran M. Lougy, *The Comparable Worth Controversy* (Washington, D.C.: Brookings Institute, 1986); Mark Aldrich and Robert Buchele, *The Economics of Comparable Worth* (Cambridge, Mass.: Ballinger Publishing Company, 1986); Frances C. Hutner, *Equal Pay for Comparable Worth* (New York: Praeger, 1986); and Mark R. Killingsworth, *The Economics of Comparable Worth* (Kalamazoo, Mich.: W. E. Upjohn Institute for Employment Research, 1990).
10. See Donald J. Treiman and Heidi L. Hartmann, eds., *Women, Work, and Wages: Equal Pay for Jobs of Equal Value* (Washington, D.C.: National Academy Press, 1981).
11. Essentially, comparable worth policies focus on inputs, not outputs.

opportunities.[12] It also is possible that a policy that increases the wages of females in female-dominated occupations would attract more females to those occupations. This would increase segregation resulting in occupational crowding, which may tend to depress female wages.

Nevertheless, several states have conducted, or are planning to conduct, job evaluations to see if female dominated occupations are paid less relative to male-dominated jobs of comparable value. Some states have started implementing comparable worth salary schemes.[13]

EQUAL OPPORTUNITY IN EDUCATION

It has been observed that racial minorities do not have equal opportunities in education. Most Black and Hispanic children attend schools that are isolated from the mainstream society, often in poor ghetto neighborhoods. As those schools are poorly funded, the quality of education often is much lower than that offered to White students in the suburbs. Thus, minorities end up performing much more poorly on standardized tests and consequently are not able to compete for admission to good colleges. In other words, differences are exacerbated as the children grow older. The effect is that by the time they enter the labor market, minorities are seriously disadvantaged.

Equal education opportunity policies have focused primarily on reducing racial isolation and fiscal disparities between poor and rich school districts. Other policies have focused on providing compensatory education and the establishment of college admission procedures that are favorable to disadvantaged groups. These policies are discussed next.

Desegregation

Similar to many other public services and facilities, schools in the South and in many other parts of the country were racially segregated for many years. Attempts to desegregate schools and other public facilities started during the late 1890s when various lawsuits were initiated. Among the most famous of these cases is the 1896 *Plessy v. Ferguson*. In this case, the Court upheld a Louisiana statute requiring "separate but equal accommodation for the white and colored race" in passenger trains. Although *Plessy* was not a school case, it was used to justify school segregation under state constitutions. In the 1908 *Berea College v. Kentucky* decision, the Court

---

12. Ehrenberg and Smith (1987) find that the effects of female employment resulting from comparable worth adjustments in state and local governments are likely to be small. See Ronald G. Ehrenberg and Robert S. Smith, "Comparable Worth Wage Adjustments and Female Employment in the State and Local Sector," *Journal of Labor Economics* 5 (1) (January 1987): 43–62.
13. See Ronald G. Ehrenberg and Robert S. Smith, "Comparable Worth in the Public Sector," in David Wise, ed., *Public Compensation* (Chicago: University of Chicago Press, 1987).

upheld a state statute requiring segregation even by private schools. The statute also made it unlawful to attend an integrated school. Private schools could maintain separate branches for each race as long as the branches were not less than 25 miles apart. In various other cases during the first half of the twentieth century, the Court concentrated on the issue of whether the alternatives offered to non-Whites actually were equal, but not on the legality of segregation.

It was not until *Brown v. Board of Education of Topeka* (1954) that the Court declared "separate and equal" as unconstitutional. In *Brown*, the Court agreed with arguments presented that segregation had a negative impact on non-White students especially in the development of their self image and personality. Therefore, segregation deprived minority children of equality of opportunity. The Court therefore ruled that the laws of 21 states requiring (or permitting) racial segregation in public schools were in violation of the equal protection clause guaranteed by the Fourteenth Amendment. In particular, the Court ruled that "separate educational facilities are inherently unequal." The Court recommended admission to public schools on a racially nondiscriminatory basis. The Court did not require desegregation to be instituted at once but as soon as was practicable, and "with deliberate speed."

The *Brown* decision set in motion a process of school desegregation all over the United States. Until the late 1960s, however, the pace of desegregation was slow and many Black students continued to attend racially segregated schools. At the end of 1961, 775 out of 2,837 biracial school districts in 17 southern states were desegregated to some extent. In the next two years, 31 other districts had voluntarily initiated desegregation plans, and 13 had done so under court order. The pace of segregation was accelerated after the 1969 Supreme Court ruling in a case involving desegregation in certain Mississippi school districts. The Court changed the requirement to end segregation with "deliberate speed" to "terminate at once."

To a large extent, the *Brown* decision marked the end of de jure segregation in the United States. However, even after *Brown*, de facto segregation remained and continues even to the present time. A number of policies have been enacted to reduce de facto segregation in schools. Most important among these are busing and rezoning. The courts also have prohibited some of the practices (such as transfer programs and freedom of choice options) that increase segregation or hinder the process of desegregation.

Even though de jure segregation has been outlawed, segregated housing patterns have largely resulted in de facto segregated school systems. Thus, the goal of reducing racial isolation has been illusive. One policy that has been used to increase racial integration in schools while leaving the residential neighborhoods largely segregated is busing. Busing involves transporting children to schools with a different racial composition than that of their residential neighborhood. The use of busing as a means of promoting equal opportunity in education was declared legal by the Supreme

Court in the 1971 *Swann v. Charlotte-Mecklenburg Board of Education* decision when it ordered the transportation of underprivileged Black children to schools with 70 percent or more White students. Busing was ordered in various parts of the country through the 1970s. Cross-busing, which involves the transportation of White students to predominantly Black schools and Black students to predominantly White schools, has been adopted in many communities across the country.[14]

Busing as a policy to provide equal education opportunity has been controversial since the *Swann* decision. Surveys on attitudes toward busing show that a large number of Blacks and Whites oppose busing plans. Some surveys show that close to 75 percent of the population is opposed to busing. Some of the reasons provided for opposing busing, include the following:

1. White parents in the suburbs have argued that busing inner-city Black children to the suburbs increases crime, creates racial conflicts in schools, and enormously increases discipline problems in schools.

2. Busing is seen as eroding the autonomy of neighborhood schools, resulting in a loss in social, racial, and community identity.

3. Some opponents of busing have argued that some children have tendencies toward mental disorders if they are removed from a stable environment. Thus, busing children from their neighborhood is psychologically harmful.

4. Often it is feared that integration by busing students across neighborhoods causes the quality of education to decline.

5. Busing is expensive; it takes money away from other educational activities.

6. A powerful argument against busing is that it encourages white flight to private schools and therefore can never actually result in the desired integration. Thus, forced integration by busing is viewed as self defeating.

The other approach to desegregation has been changing the school attendance zones. Where school districts have been drawn for the purpose of avoiding integration, courts have ordered rezoning of the attendance areas in order to create racial balance. In some areas, this has involved the consolidation of school districts. Similarly, in various cases, the courts have invalidated the choice of new school sites when it has been shown that those plans would increase segregation or hinder speedy integration.

---

14. For recent developments and cases concerning busing, see Rosemary C. Salomone, *Equal Education Under the Law: Legal Rights and Federal Policy in the Post-Brown Era* (New York: St. Martin's Press, 1986).

Upon the requirement to desegregate, a number of school districts established some practices that had the effect of reducing integration efforts. One such practice was the establishment of a special transfer program, which allowed students to select the school that they wanted to attend, thereby making it possible for those in predominantly Black schools to avoid them. In one such case, *Goss v. Board of Education* (1963), two Tennessee school districts (Knoxville and Davidson County) had designed desegregation plans that involved redrawing of the attendance zones without regard to race. However, the desegregation plans also included a transfer program. That policy allowed students who were assigned to a school where the majority of the student body was a different race to transfer to a school where his or her race was in the majority. The U.S. Supreme Court invalidated the transfer program and declared that it violated the equal protection clause of the Fourteenth Amendment.

"Freedom of choice" plans are a related practice that has hindered desegregation in some areas. Freedom of choice plans were widely used in the South in the 1960s. Under these plans, children are reassigned if the parents expressed a preference for them to attend a school other than the one to which they would be assigned. The effect of freedom of choice plans was that in many communities the racially separate school systems were maintained. White children who were assigned to predominantly Black schools requested to be reassigned to predominantly White schools. In a number of cases (both in the North and South), courts have ruled against the use of such plans if it is shown that they slow or hinder integration.

The school choice idea is now being used as way of providing inner-city residents an opportunity to choose better schools out of their neighborhoods. Although this idea has not been adopted in many places, it is being seriously considered in many states. Such a program has already been started in Milwaukee, Wisconsin.

Fiscal Equalization

Inequality of educational opportunity also arises because of differences in resources available to various school districts. Because schools rely heavily on local property taxes as sources of funding, poor districts often are unable to offer quality education, thereby creating inequality in educational opportunities between rich and poor districts. Some state courts (including California, Michigan, and New Jersey) have held that inequality in financing of education due to differences in resources is discriminatory. In *Serrano v. Priest*, the California Supreme Court held that the state's system (which relied on local property taxes to finance public schools and therefore caused substantial disparities in the expenditures per pupil across various school districts) discriminates against the poor and therefore was in violation of the equal protection provisions of the federal and state constitutions. Although the U.S. Supreme

Court and most states have not taken such a strong position in regard to school financing, the federal government has enacted various programs to equalize funding across states and school districts.

The first major effort by the federal government to aid poor students was the Elementary and Secondary Education Act (ESEA) of 1965. Title I of ESEA authorized direct federal support of elementary and secondary schools. Allocation of funds to the states is based on the number of children from families that fall below specified income levels. The Higher Education Act of 1965 provided loans and scholarships for undergraduates. A large percentage of those covered under the Higher Education Act of 1965 are from families with low incomes. There also have been various deliberate efforts to help disadvantaged groups finance college education. These have included special loan and financial aid packages that target minorities and women.[15]

Compensatory Education

Children brought up in poor families face various problems that hinder them from achieving their full academic potential. Often most poor children lack basic nutritional and social services that are necessary for proper child development. Therefore, by the time they start school, those children lack many essential skills that should be possessed by children before they enter school. Because of such deficiencies, those children often are unable to catch up with their counterparts from well-off families, and thus, inequalities in educational achievement may persist, and even widen. One policy that has been used to deal with this problem is provision of compensatory education. The most compensatory program is Head Start which was established in 1965 to help disadvantaged preschoolers. Head Start is supposed to help disadvantaged children get an equal start by providing educational, health, nutritional, and social services.

Preferential Admission

We have observed that minorities face various barriers in their attempt to acquire education. Such disadvantages may be because of family background or the quality of the public schools that they attend. As such, in many instances, minorities are less prepared for college than Whites of otherwise equal ability. Thus, because of disadvantages experienced at lower grades, minorities are less likely to meet the normal college admission standards. If minorities and Whites are subjected to similar college entrance standards, a lower proportion of minorities would succeed in

---

15. During the late 1980s, the Bush administration was engaged in efforts to declare minority financial aid discriminatory.

securing places in colleges. Therefore, it has been suggested that a way to provide equal education opportunities is to adopt admission policies that are favorable to members of those disadvantaged groups. In essence, such a policy involves preferential admission; minorities with lower scores than normally required for Whites are admitted.

A famous case challenging preferential admission policies on the basis that those policies seek to establish quotas is the *Regents of University of California v. Bakke.* The University of California had set aside 16 places in its medical school for Black students. Bakke, a White applicant, was denied admission into the medical school although he scored higher than some of the Blacks who were admitted. In a 5–4 decision, the Supreme Court ruled against the university and stated that its practices constituted an impermissible quota. Nevertheless, the Court held that it was appropriate to use race as a criteria for university admission.[16]

Although they remain controversial, virtually all colleges in the United States provide some form of preferential treatment to minorities in the form of admission policies and special funding programs. A popular program is the Minority Summer Workshops offered by colleges. Those workshops help high school students who may have not have all the requirements for admission to a particular college meet those requirements during the summer.

EVALUATION OF EQUAL OPPORTUNITY POLICIES

As a final note on equal opportunity policies, it is necessary to review the effectiveness of those policies in improving the economic status of minorities and females. In particular, as antipoverty measures those policies should be evaluated in terms of their effectiveness in reducing poverty of the targeted groups.

There appears to be clear evidence that the various antidiscrimination policies and special programs have played an important role in helping minorities acquire more and better education and jobs. Nevertheless, continued racial isolation casts doubts on the ability (or the necessity) of government to legislate integration.

Empirical evidence on the effect of equal employment policies is mixed and therefore no consensus exists as to the effectiveness of these policies in achieving the intended goals. One problem is that it is difficult to isolate the impact of antidiscrimination policies from that of other policies and factors. An influential study by Freeman (1973) showed that federal antidiscrimination efforts were important in reducing Black–White

---

16. For a discussion of preferential admission policies, see Iredell Jenkins, *Social Order and Limits of Law: A Theoretical Essay* (Princeton, N. J.: Princeton University Press, 1980).

income differentials.[17] A number of other studies that investigated the
effects of affirmative action in its formative years found that, although
there was only weak enforcement, affirmative action nevertheless had a
positive and significant effect on the employment of minorities.[18] The
studies find that affirmative action increased Black employment among
federal contractors. However, affirmative action did not increase the share
of Blacks employed in skilled occupations. This implies that, in absence of
strict enforcement, employers could have met the employment obligations by hiring minorities into relatively low skill occupations and not
promoting them into more skilled positions.

In a more recent study, Jonathan Leonard (1984) investigated the
growth of minority and female employment at federal contractor establishments and in noncontractor establishments that face no affirmative action
obligations.[19] Comparisons were made using data on employment demo-
graphics reported by 68,690 establishments in 1974 and 1980. The results
showed that between 1974 and 1980, employment of minorities and
females increased faster in contractor establishments than in noncontractor
establishments. In analyzing the effect of affirmative action on the occupational advancement of Blacks, Leonard finds that Black males' share of
employment increased faster in contract than in noncontract establishments in most occupational categories.[20]

In evaluating equal opportunity programs, it also is important to note
that several criticisms are directed at those programs. The equal opportunity policies in place today have at some time faced a form of opposition
from the courts, politicians, and the public. Controversies still surround the
validity of affirmative action programs in employment and also the preferential admission and financing programs that favor minorities and
women. A particularly sensitive issue that continues to generate considerable opposition is legally enforced racial integration in schools. To say the
least, race- and sex-based policies have been extremely divisive. The addition of comparable worth policy to the existing policies can be expected to
increase the controversies.

---

17. Richard B. Freeman, "Changes in the Labor Market for Black Americans, 1948–1972,"
    Brookings Papers on Economic Activity 4 (1), 1973: 67–120.
18. See Orley Ashenfelter and James Heckman, "Measuring the Effect of an Antidiscrimination
    Program," in Orley Ashenfelter and James Blum, eds., *Evaluating the Labor Market Effects of
    Social Programs* (Princeton, N.J.: Princeton University Press, 1976); Morris Goldstein and
    Robert S. Smith, "The Estimated Impact of the Anti-Discrimination Program Aimed at
    Federal Contractors," *Industrial and Labor Relations Review* 29 (July 1976): 523–43; and James
    J. Heckman and Kenneth I. Wolpin, "Does the Contract Compliance Program Work? An
    Analysis of Chicago Data," *Industrial and Labor Relations Review* 29 (July 1976): 544–64.
19. Jonathan S. Leonard, "The Impact of Affirmative Action on Employment," *Journal of Labor
    Economics* 2 (4) (October 1984): 439–63.
20. Jonathan S. Leonard, "Employment and Occupational Advance Under Affirmative
    Action," *Review of Economics and Statistics* 66 (August 1984): 377–85.

SUMMARY

It has been argued that one cause of poverty among minorities and women arises from barriers that these groups face in labor markets and in acquiring education.Thus, antipoverty policy that seeks to improve the economic status of those groups should seek to establish equality of opportunity.

Over the last three decades, the federal government has taken an active role in attempting to eradicate discriminatory practices in both education and labor markets. Although the main focus of these policies has been to ensure equality of opportunity, some policies have been designed purposely to offer preferences to minorities and women. Although the policies may have helped in improving the status of the targeted groups, the evidence is mixed. However, one clear result is that those policies have generated numerous controversies, criticisms, and opposition.

Although this text has emphasized the importance of desegregation and fiscal measures as means of achieving equality of educational opportunities, it would be illogical to assume that equality will be achieved by having minority children attend the same schools with White children. Actually, the poor quality of schools in ghetto neighborhoods is due to many factors, including the low average educational background of parents; families that provide students with too little encouragement, emotional support and discipline; drug use; and extremely low teacher morale (even when pay is adequate). Without appreciable change in these factors, integration or increasing funding cannot be expected to lead to better schools. Much more is needed to transform the lifestyles of the poor in inner cities. This and other issues related to ghetto poverty are discussed in Chapter 11.

STUDY AND DISCUSSION QUESTIONS

1. Evaluate the various policies that are used to create equality of opportunities for women in terms of how well those policies have achieved the desired goals.

2. Evaluate the various policies that have been used to create equality of opportunities for racial minorities in terms of how well those policies have achieved the desired goals.

3. What do you understand by affirmative action policy?

4. Clearly discuss what you understand by comparable worth policy.

5. What is the meaning of reverse discrimination? Does the Civil Rights Act, Equal Pay Act, or affirmative action constitute reverse discrimination?

6. Do you think that we should be concerned in attempting to correct inequalities that are due to past discrimination? Why or why not?

7. An ongoing debate concerns whether, in discrimination complaints, the burden of proof should be on the employer or on the person who is discriminated. Does it matter who has the burden of proof in terms of reducing discrimination? Provide a critical analysis of the issues.

8. Rebecca and Mary, both White, were born the same day and are of equal intelligence. Rebecca's parents live in the exclusive suburbs of Boston while Mary lives in the Boston ghetto with her mother. Both Rebecca and Mary are ambitious students who want to join the Harvard Law School (Rebecca's parents are professors there).

   (a) Suppose both students score equal points in the law school entrance exams. If there is only one slot, which student do you think should be admitted?

   (b) Conversely, suppose that Rebecca scores 10 points higher than Mary. Would your answer to (a) change? Why or why not?

   (c) Would a practice of lowering the admission standard for students from disadvantaged families constitute a preference? Why or why not?

9. Now suppose that Rebecca is White and Mary is Puerto Rican. Discuss parts (a) and (b) of question 8.

10. Suppose now that Rebecca is Black and Mary is White. Discuss parts (a) and (b) of question 8. Carefully compare your answers to questions 3, 5, and 6.

11. Discuss the various policies that have been suggested to deal with racial inequalities in education.

12. You are provided with detailed facts that clearly demonstrate that the poverty of minorities is due to current and past discrimination. You also are told that although most Americans would like some policies to deal with discrimination against minorities, they do not like the current laws. You have been asked by the president to formulate a number of new approaches to deal with current and past discrimination. Write a report that discusses

   (a) why many Americans may not like the current laws,

(b) new approaches to dealing with the problem of discrimination.

13. Current affirmative action policy is based on race or gender, and so forth. What would be the implications of an affirmative action policy that targets low-income people regardless of their race or gender?

14. Compare the use of a *disparate impact* and *disparate treatment* to establish discrimination. Which standard do you think is more appropriate?

15. On average, White students in the Deep South states score lower than White students in the Northeast. In the past, some prestigious schools have admitted White students from the Deep South with lower scores than those of students in the Northeast. Are White students in the Deep South recipients of some type of affirmative action? How can such a policy be justified? How different is such a policy from one that benefits Blacks, Hispanics, and females?

ADDITIONAL READINGS

1.   Bolner, James and Robert Shanley. *Busing: The Political and Judicial Process.* New York: Praeger Publishers, 1974.

2.   Clayton, Susan D. and Faye J. Crosby. *Justice, Gender, and Affirmative Action.* Ann Arbor: The University of Michigan Press, 1992.

3.   Ezorsky, Gertrude. *Racism and Justice: The Case for Affirmative Action.* Ithaca, N. Y.: Cornell University Press, 1991.

4.   Flicker, Barbara, ed. *Justice and School Systems: The Role of the Courts in Education Litigation.* Philadelphia: Temple University Press, 1990.

5.   Fogel, Walter. *The Equal Pay Act: Implications for Comparable Worth.* New York: Praeger Publishers, 1984.

6.   Graglia, Lino A. *Disaster by Decree: The Supreme Court Decisions on Race and the Schools,* Ithaca, N. Y.: Cornell University Press, 1976.

7.   Paul, Ellen Frankel. *Equity and Gender: The Comparable Worth Debate.* New Brunswick, N. J.: Transaction Publishers, 1989.

8.   Willborn, Steven L. *A Comparable Worth Primer.* Lexington, Mass.: Lexington Books, 1986.

11

INNER-CITY POVERTY: THE GHETTO UNDERCLASS

In analyzing poverty in the United States, it is necessary to give special attention to a group of people referred to as the *underclass*. In the United States, the underclass mainly refers to minorities (for example, Blacks, Puerto Ricans) who are concentrated in the poorest parts of major cities.[1] The concentration of poverty in the inner cities has continued to rise even with increased social welfare spending and during periods of economic expansion. The 1991 race riots in Los Angeles highlight the desperation of many residents in major cities and the need for long-term solutions to such poverty.

This chapter considers inner-city poverty, beginning with a brief description of the underclass. The nature of inner-city poverty is then considered, focusing on the characteristics that are typical of the underclass environment. Next, the extent of poverty and the process that concentrated it in the inner cities is discussed. This section shows that inner-city or ghetto poverty is much more complex and, therefore, more difficult to deal with than other types of poverty. Finally, some public policies that have been proposed to deal with ghetto poverty are examined.

UNDERCLASS AND THE CULTURE OF POVERTY

Ken Auletta describes the typical member of the underclass as a person who "generally feels excluded from society, rejects commonly accepted values, suffers from *behavioral* as well as *income* deficiencies. They don't just tend to be poor; to most Americans their behavior seems aberrant."[2]

---

1. Rural whites (mainly in the Appalachian region) and Blacks (in the Deep South) also are considered as members of the underclass. However, the numbers of the rural underclass are relatively low. For a discussion on White and Black rural underclass, see Ken Auletta, *The Underclass* (New York: Random House, 1982), Chapters 12 and 13.
2. Ken Auletta, *The Underclass*, p. xiii. Emphasis in the original.

According to Auletta, the underclass operates outside generally accepted boundaries of society and is set apart, not only because of its poverty, but also because of its deviant behavior and bad habits. Other poverty analysts consider the underclass as having a culture entirely different from that of mainstream society.

Oskar Lewis populized the idea of the *culture of poverty* to describe the lifestyles of the underclass.[3] The culture of poverty argument advances the idea that some people, often concentrated in the inner city, have their own particular ethos, which makes their plight insensitive to various antipoverty measures. The behavioral traits of those with a culture of poverty do not breed success in the mainstream society, but rather frequently lead to undesirable outcomes. Central to the culture of poverty idea is that children raised in families with the culture of poverty acquire, while still young, those traits that hinder success. According to Lewis

> The culture of poverty, however, is not only an adaptation to a set objective conditions of the large society. Once it comes into existence it tends to perpetuate itself from generation to generation because of its effects on children. By the time slum children are age six or seven, they have usually absorbed the basic values and attitudes of their subculture and are not psychologically geared to take advantage of changing conditions or increased opportunities which may occur in their lifetime.[4]

According to Lewis, the culture of poverty emerges as a result of extreme economic deprivation, endemic unemployment, and limited opportunities for mobility that particular groups of poor people face. Subjected to these circumstances, a particular ideology that allows the poor to cope with their desperate economic and social conditions develops. The behavioral patterns that emerge are ones in which the individual places a high value on present time gratification and places low value on family relationships. Among those with a culture of poverty, family ties are weak, have low marriage rates, and high rates of divorce and abandonment.

Children who grow up in families with a culture of poverty are denied a childhood and often engage in sexual activity while still teenagers. Therefore, the culture of poverty is associated with dysfunctional families that provide little support to children to perform well in school or prepare themselves to be productive members of the society. As a result, offspring have a high probability of being poor. Children get trapped into poverty because of the low employment opportunities and the low levels of human capital investment. Young people get trapped into a life of crime and other underground activities. Thus, for those people with a culture of poverty, their value system

---

3. In this chapter, "underclass," "lower class," and "culture of poverty" refer to the same groups of people: those inner-city poor whose behavioral patterns are different from those of mainstream society.
4. Oskar Lewis, *A Study of Slum Culture: Background to LaVida* (New York: Random House) p. 6.

differs from that of mainstream and tends to replicate poverty. After the culture of poverty is established, it becomes an independent cause of poverty itself, perpetuating poverty from generation to generation. Initially, people are not poor because of the culture of poverty; it is poverty that initiates this culture and then the culture perpetuates the poverty.

The problem of the underclass was articulated by Daniel Patrick Moynihan in 1965 (then an assistant secretary of labor). In a report to President Johnson entitled, *The Negro Family: The Case for National Action*, Moynihan elaborated on the idea that high unemployment of Black males and the resulting family instability were resulting in a situation where poverty was transmitted from one generation to the next. Moynihan's main analysis focused on the disintegration of the two-parent family among Blacks and warned that increasing dominance of a Black matriarchy placed Blacks at a distinct disadvantage. Although Moynihan did not use the terms *underclass* or *culture of poverty*, he used language such as "tangle of pathology" that reflect the same ideas that are discussed today in reference to the underclass. The Moynihan report was criticized particularly because it deflected blame from the true sources of poverty to its victims. Scholars suggested that the problems faced by Blacks were due to racism. Nonetheless, some of the important elements of the Moynihan report (such as the relationship between male unemployment and female headship and the consequential intergenerational transmission of poverty) are central to contemporary debate concerning the underclass.[5]

In *The Unheavenly City*, Edward Banfield refers to the inner-city poor as the "lower class culture."[6] Banfield suggests that those with the lower class culture, mainly Blacks, brought dysfunctional behavioral patterns with them from rural areas and now these patterns are passed on from one generation to the next. According to Banfield, ghetto poverty can be eliminated only if the poor alter their bad habits. Note that both Lewis and Banfield suggest that these bad habits are transmitted across generations. However, Banfield attributes poverty to be a result of bad habits and thus fails to take into account how the problems the poor face lead to the emergence of those habits. Essentially, Banfield blames members of the underclass for their problems.

Once again the underclass and the culture of poverty debate has been resurrected both in academia and policy circles. Two influential works that have fueled the debate are by Charles Murray and William Julius Wilson.[7] According to Murray, the underclass has been created by the generous

5. See Lee Rainwater and William L. Yancey, *The Moynihan Report and the Politics of Controversy* (Cambridge, Mass.: MIT Press, 1967).
6. Edward C. Banfield, *The Unheavenly City* (Boston: Little Brown, 1970).
7. Charles Murray, *Losing Ground: American Social Policy, 1950–1980* (New York: Basic Books, 1984); and William Julius Wilson, *The Truly Disadvantaged: The Inner City, the Underclass and Public Policy* (Chicago: University of Chicago Press, 1987).

welfare programs. Social programs have eroded work incentives and have weakened the two-parent family. Welfare benefits reduce the benefits of marriage, causing high rates of marital dissolution and teen pregnancies. Thus, social programs have resulted in a demoralized way of life among minorities that is characterized by female headship, welfare dependency, and crime. Murray, therefore, blames the American social policy for the emergence of the underclass.

Wilson, on the other hand, blames the emergence of the Black underclass on the structural transformation of the inner-city economy. The decline in manufacturing and the outward movement of jobs have created extensive joblessness in the inner cities. Joblessness among males has reduced the pool of marriageable males, which consequently has increased female headship. In addition, the movement of well-off Blacks to the suburbs have left the worst in the inner cities lacking the necessary institutions, resources, and values for success in a post-industrial economy.

Regardless of the different views about the factors that have been responsible for the emergence of the underclass, there is agreement that the underclass does exist and its numbers are increasing. Additionally, there is agreement that the underclass has a different value system that hinders its members from succeeding.

Thus, the inner-city poor face the disadvantage of deprivation of the resources and values that are conducive to success. The lower-class culture generates a concentration of poverty against which traditional antipoverty policies are ineffective. Next, we consider some of the features of inner-city poverty that make it unique.

NATURE OF INNER-CITY POVERTY

Inner-city poverty differs from poverty in other areas not only because of its racial component, but also because of other features. These additional features of ghetto poverty are associated with the underclass or the culture of poverty previously discussed. The uniqueness of ghetto poverty makes it much more difficult to deal with, making it a challenge for policymakers. This section considers some of the factors of inner-city poverty that make it different from poverty in other areas.

Concentration

One troublesome feature of ghetto poverty is the growing concentration of poor people, particularly minorities, in the inner cities. As will be discussed in the next section, the out migration of higher income residents to the suburbs has left the very poor and those with limited skills in the central cities. Table 11-1 shows the percentage of people below the poverty line by type of area for the years 1975, 1980, and 1985. Central-city poverty

Table 11-1   Number and percentage of persons below poverty level by type of area

	1975		1980		1985	
	No.		No.		No.	
Residence	(Thousands)	%	(Thousands)	%	(Thousands)	%
Central cities	9,090	15.0	10,644	17.2	14,177	19.0
Central-city poverty areas	4,446	34.9	4,284	38.1	7,837	37.5
Suburbs	6,259	7.6	7,377	8.2	9,097	8.4
Nonmetropolitan areas	10,529	15.4	11,251	15.4	9,789	18.3

Source: Bureau of the Census, *Characteristics of Population Below Poverty Level*, 1982, Current Population Reports, Series P–60, No. 144 (Washington, D.C.: U.S. Department of Commerce, 1984); and Bureau of the Census, *Characteristics of Population Below Poverty Level*, 1983, Current Population Reports, Series P–60, No. 147 (Washington, D.C.: U.S. Department of Commerce, 1985).

rates were 15 percent in 1975, 17.2 percent in 1980, and 19.0 percent in 1985, more than double the poverty rates in the suburbs. Note, however, that poverty is concentrated in particular areas of central cities. In 1985, 7.8 million of the nearly 14.2 million city poor lived in areas that the Bureau of the Census classifies as poverty areas, which are census tracts where 20 percent or more of the residents are below poverty level. Poverty rate in poor central city areas increased from 34.9 percent in 1975 to 37.5 percent in 1985.

Unlike poor Blacks, poor Whites do not live in areas where the majority of the residents are poor. Table 11-2 shows the distribution of poor Whites and poor Blacks in the 50 largest central cities. The data show that in 1980, 66 percent of poor Whites lived in cities where the poverty rate was less than 20 percent, and only about 8 percent were in neighborhoods where the poverty rates exceeded 40 percent. Poor Blacks, on the other hand, lived in areas of high concentration of poverty. In 1980, only 16 percent of poor Blacks lived in areas where poverty was under 20 percent. On the other hand, 36 percent of poor Blacks lived in neighborhoods where the poverty rates exceeded 40 percent.

Table 11-3 shows the much higher concentration of poor Blacks as compared to other Americans. In 1989, for example, 40 percent of poor Whites were concentrated in poverty neighborhoods. In the same year, 71 percent of poor Blacks were concentrated in poor neighborhoods. Although the concentration of poverty declines in suburbs, the difference in concentration of poverty between Whites and Blacks is even wider. In 1989, poor Blacks in suburbs were three times as likely as poor Whites to be concentrated in

Table 11-2   Distribution of poor Whites and poor Blacks in the 50 largest central cities, by poverty rate in the census tract of residence

Percentage in Poverty in the Census Tract	Poor Whites % 1970	Poor Whites % 1980	Poor Blacks % 1970	Poor Blacks % 1980
Under 20	64	66	20	16
20–29	18	17	26	21
30–39	10	9	27	27
40 and over	8	8	27	36

Sources: U.S. Bureau of the Census, *Poverty Areas in Large Cities*, in *1980 Census of the Population*, Vol. 2 (Washington, D.C.: U.S. Government Printing Office), and U.S. Bureau of the Census, *Low Income Areas in Large Cities, 1970 Census of the Population* (Washington, D.C.: U.S. Government Printing Office).

Table 11-3   Percentage of poor people concentrated in poverty areas by race.

	1975 White	1975 Black	1980 White	1980 Black	1985 White	1985 Black	1989 White	1989 Black
Central city	32.1	70.1	25.4	58.8	42.8	74.9	40.0	71.0
Suburbs	10.2	39.3	13.3	44.1	14.1	45.4	13.0	40.1

Source: U.S. Bureau of the Census, *Current Population Survey, Money Income and Poverty Status in the United States*, Series P–60, various years.

poverty neighborhoods in the suburbs. This result illustrates that even when Blacks move out of the city, most of them go to areas that are merely an extension of the ghetto.

The data presented in Table 11-2 documents that the concentration of poverty for Blacks is on the rise. Estimates show that the concentration of poverty in the inner cities among Blacks and Hispanics continued to increase during the early 1990s. Thus, not only are minorities and Blacks much poorer than Whites, they also are surrounded by more poverty.

Isolation

Although the inner cities are populated predominantly by minorities, most well-off minorities have moved to the suburbs, thanks to federal legislation outlawing discriminatory practices in housing. Thus, poor minorities are left in the inner cities, isolated from the mainstream of society. William Julius Wilson argues that one reason for the continued deterioration of the inner-city poor is isolation from the mainstream, which has been accelerated by the movement of well-off minorities to the suburbs. When discrimination and housing segregation forced Blacks to live together, both the poor and the relatively well-off Blacks lived in close proximity. A sense of community existed and the more advantaged Blacks contributed in positive ways to help the poor. Today, well-off blacks have left their unsuccessful counterparts. The largest fraction of those left behind have low labor market potential, are drug dealers and addicts, have poor work habits, are thieves, and so forth. As a result, positive role models for youngsters are few and far between. As stated by Wilson

> Indeed, in the 1930s, 1940s, and 1950s such communities featured a vertical integration of different segments of the urban Black population. Lower class, working class, and middle class Black families all lived in more or less the same communities (albeit in different neighborhoods), sent their children to the same schools, availed themselves of the same recreational facilities, and shopped at the same stores. . . . The Black middle and working classes were confined by restrictive covenants to communities also inhabited by the lower class, and their very presence provided stability to inner-city neighborhoods and reinforced and perpetuated mainstream patterns of behavior.
>
> Today's ghetto neighborhoods are populated almost exclusively by the most disadvantaged segments of the Black urban community, that heterogeneous grouping of families and individuals who are outside the mainstream of the American occupational system. Included in this group are individuals who lack training or skills and either experience long-term unemployment or are not part of the labor force, individuals engaged in street criminal activity and other forms of aberrant behavior, and families who experience long-term spells of poverty and/or welfare dependency.[8]

Isolation of the poor is particularly harmful as it develops hostile and deviant subcultures. People feel little attachment to the community or family and generally resent authority. Once such subcultures take hold, they propagate poverty as individuals engage in activities that further remove

---

8. William Julius Wilson, "Cycles of Deprivation and the Underclass Debate," *Social Service Review* 59 (4) (December 1985): 545–46.

them from the mainstream. For example, the isolated poor lose the motivation to succeed and expect failure. Some form of learned helplessness emerges among the ghetto poor because they interact for the most part with failures. The expectation of failure is one common feature of the inner-city poor.

Poor Labor Market Prospects

As already mentioned, employment opportunities continue to deteriorate in the ghettos so that unemployment rates in these areas are extremely high. Table 11-4 presents data for unemployment rates in selected central cities by race and sex for 1976, 1980, and 1985. In general, unemployment rates in the central cities are high across all racial groups, but much higher for minorities. The high unemployment rates result from the collapsing labor market opportunities in those areas. In particular, a large number of blue collar and low-skill jobs have left the inner cities. Industries that provided much employment to Blacks, particularly manufacturing, have shrunk the most. Thus, ghetto residents face poor labor market prospects.

John Kasarda describes how changes in the economy have caused an out migration of jobs from the inner cities.[9] According to Kasarda, current inner-city labor market conditions emerged from a long process of industrial restructuring, beginning in the 1950s. During the 1950s and 1960s, cities converted from manufacturing to service economies. Since the 1970s, the cities changed from service economies to information and administration centers. The transformation from centers of goods production to information processing has been accompanied by the movement of manufacturing activities to the suburbs and to nonmetropolitan areas. Even warehousing activities have moved to more easily accessible locations along beltways and interstate highways. Furthermore, retail trade and various other service activities (such as gas stations) have followed wealthy customers to the suburbs. The out migration of more wealthy persons has been accompanied by the loss of various blue collar jobs that used to provide employment to inner-city residents.

Although some sections of the cities continue to experience accelerated growth with high-rise office buildings, this growth has not benefited the poorest residents. In fact, according to Kasarda, such developments reduce the employment opportunities of the poor. The new construction in the central cities drives the rental prices in the central business districts to such high levels that other businesses have a difficult time competing. Thus, department stores and other businesses that occupy large floor space have closed with the expansion of high-rise office buildings. Unfortunately,

9. John D. Kasarda, "Jobs, Migration, and Emerging Urban Mismatches," in Michael G. H. McGeary and Laurence E. Lynn, Jr., eds., *Urban Change and Poverty* (Washington, D.C.: National Academy Press, 1988), pp. 148–98.

Table 11-4   Unemployment rates in selected major northern central cities by race and sex

City and Sex	Whites %			Blacks and Other %		
	1976	1980	1985	1976	1980	1985
New York						
Total	10.7	7.7	7.2	12.8	10.8	10.1
Men	10.9	7.5	7.4	14.4	12.6	11.2
Women	10.3	7.9	6.9	11.0	8.9	8.8
Philadelphia						
Total	7.9	7.7	6.5	19.2	20.4	12.0
Men	8.5	7.8	6.1	24.9	21.8	13.4
Women	7.0	7.6	7.0	11.7	18.9	11.4
Chicago						
Total	5.9	9.0	8.0	14.6	15.4	24.6
Men	6.6	9.8	8.8	16.7	17.7	25.8
Women	5.0	7.8	7.0	12.3	12.8	23.0
Detroit						
Total	11.3	16.2	13.3	15.0	26.2	30.3
Men	11.3	18.9	15.9	12.5	13.6	29.7
Women	11.3	12.4	9.5	18.2	22.2	30.9

Source: Adapted from John D. Kasarda, "Jobs, Migration, and Emerging Urban Mismatches," in Michael G. H. McGeary and Laurence E. Lynn, Jr., eds., *Urban Change and Poverty* (Washington, D.C.: National Academy Press, 1988), Table 14, p. 183.

these businesses offer employment to inner-city residents with low skills and limited education. As Table 11-5 demonstrates, many major cities have lost those jobs that require lower levels of education and gained jobs that require more than a high school education. Although some cities have had gains in the number of jobs that require less than a high school education, such increases have been small. Because most inner-city residents have low levels of education, the loss of jobs that require low skills translates directly to high unemployment rates.

The labor market conditions described herein are frequently summarized by the spatial mismatch hypothesis. The basic element of this hypothesis is that with the expansion of industrial cities, higher income families have moved out of inner cities and low income jobs have also followed the movement of these families. Manufacturing and retail industry also has been drawn outward due to factors such as cheaper land, better transportation networks, better environment (such as less crime and drugs), and the presence of wealthier customers. The result is that inner cities have

Table 11-5   Central-city jobs in industries by mean education of employees

City and Education Mean Industry	Number of Jobs (Thousands)			Change (Thousands)	
	1959	1970	1985	1959-70	1970-85
New York					
Less than high school	1,561	1,525	1,048	-9	-504
Some higher education	682	1,002	1,270	320	268
Philadelphia					
Less than high school	466	430	243	-36	-187
Some higher education	135	205	256	70	51
Boston					
Less than high school	180	189	137	-1	-52
Some higher education	117	185	261	68	76
Baltimore					
Less than high school	236	207	132	-29	-75
Some higher education	59	90	124	31	34
St. Louis					
Less than high school	221	210	117	-11	-93
Some higher education	61	98	97	37	-1
Atlanta					
Less than high school	130	179	189	49	3
Some higher education	42	92	143	50	51
Houston					
Less than high school	192	348	567	156	219
Some higher education	59	144	368	85	224
Denver					
Less than high school	92	120	130	28	10
Some higher education	42	72	132	30	60
San Francisco					
Less than high school	143	155	174	12	19
Some higher education	82	138	218	56	80

Source: Kasarda, Table 11, p. 177.

been left with high-skilled white collar jobs and low-skilled blue color workers who are primarily minorities. Thus, the most disadvantaged groups are trapped away from places where jobs are available.[10]

Poor employment opportunities imply that many of the ghetto residents have never worked and are not searching for work. These are the discouraged workers discussed in Chapter 6. Even those with some work experience have weak attachments to the labor market as their jobs are in the secondary sector where employment is unstable.

Poor Education

A declining income base adversely affects the local community in many ways, especially through the deterioration of public schools. The performance of inner-city students is extremely poor and continues to deteriorate. Gordon Berlin and Andrew Sum report that, based on National Assessment of Education Programs, the average Black 17-year-old reads at the same level as the average White 13-year-old. In addition, Black high school graduates score lower than White high school dropouts on the Armed Forces Qualification Test.[11] The poor state of inner-city education is reflected by the high school dropout rates. It is not uncommon to see Black inner-city high schools with a dropout rate that exceeds 40 percent. Several forces weaken student performance in the inner cities. First, students go to schools that have fewer resources, such as computers, books, and quality teachers. Second, most parents have low education attainment and do not encourage their children. In addition, many children grow up in homes that are not conducive to learning. Third, the school environment does not encourage learning. The values are so distorted that students become more popular by joining a gang than doing well in school. The frequent shootings in inner-city high schools highlight the poor environment. To the extent that human capital investment helps the poor escape poverty, the conditions in the ghetto schools hold little promise that these children can escape poverty.

Female Headship and Welfare Dependency

One reason that inner-city families are poor is their family structure. As mentioned previously, one of the most important features of a culture of poverty is the early initiation to sex, the result of which is a large number

---

10. See Harry J. Holzer and Wayne Vroman, "Mismatches and the Urban Labor Market," in George E. Peterson and Wayne Vroman, eds., *Urban Labor Markets and Job Opportunities* (Washington, D.C.: Urban Institute Press, 1992), pp. 81–112.
11. Gordon Berlin and Andrew Sum, "Toward a More Perfect Union: Basic Skills, Poor Families and Our Economic Future," Occasional Paper 3 (New York: The Ford Foundation, 1988).

of teenage pregnancies. Kevin Hopkins states that "girls who grow up in family and cultural environment that accept, fail to discourage, or even encourage early out-of-wedlock sex, are themselves more likely to begin intercourse at a young age and have sex more frequently as a teenager."[12] Hopkins suggests that lower class girls assign significantly higher benefit/cost ratio to pregnancy than do other girls.

The family structure—whether two-parent or single-parent— affects the probability of a family being poor. Female-headed households have a much higher incidence of poverty than male-headed households. During the 1980s, poverty rates for central-city households headed by women were about 50 percent. Table 11-6 provides data on female-headed households in central cities for 1983. In that year, 35.5 percent of Whites and 59.1 percent of Black families headed by women were poor. The increased female headship in the ghetto almost guarantees the continuation of poverty in those areas. A large number of ghetto children from female-headed households are in poverty. For example, in 1983, 53.6 percent of related children under 18 in White households and 70.1 percent of the same in Black households were poor.[13]

Table 11-6   Characteristics of female-headed central-city households (numbers in thousands), 1983

	All Persons (Thousands)	Related Children under 18 years old (Thousands)
White		
Total	5,912	2,289
Below Poverty (numbers)	2,096	1,228
Percentage	35.5	53.6
Black		
Total	6,090	2,878
Below Poverty (numbers)	3,601	2,071
Percentage	59.1	70.1

Source: Bureau of the Census, *Characteristics of Population Below Poverty Level, 1983,* Current Population Reports, Series P–60, No. 147 (Washington, D.C.: U.S. Department of Commerce, 1985).

---

12. Kevin R. Hopkins, "A Behavioral Theory of Dependency," in K. R. Hopkins, ed., *Welfare Dependency: Behavior, Culture, and Public Policy* (Alexandria, Va.: Hudson Institute, 1987), pp. 10–82.
13. The relationship between poverty and family structure is discussed in Chapter 12. The focus is on the feminization of poverty in the United States.

With collapsing labor market opportunities, low incomes, and increased female headship, one of the main sources of income in the ghetto is public assistance. A significant number of ghetto residents (especially females who head families) are heavily dependent on welfare. One important negative effect of welfare dependency is that it discourages work. The children of welfare recipients become dependent on welfare themselves so that intergenerational transmission of welfare dependency occurs as predicted by the culture of poverty hypothesis.[14]

Crime and Drugs

Finally, ghetto poverty closely associates with criminal activity. With limited labor market opportunities, ghetto residents turn to drug dealing, a lucrative but illegal economic activity. The proliferation of drug activity has caused a rapid increase in serious crimes. The main victims of this trend have been young Black males who are killed in large numbers by other Blacks. Today, many young Black males are incarcerated due to their criminal activity. A national study of the Sentencing Project estimated that in 1989, approximately 23 percent of Black males between 20 and 29 years old were in serious trouble with the criminal justice system; 8 percent were incarcerated, 12 percent were on probation, and 3 percent were on parole.[15] Other underground activities include prostitution and theft.

Life in the ghetto then is one in which residents suffer economic deprivation, and whose values differ significantly from those of other members of society. The next section studies the various factors that have been responsible for urbanization of poverty in the United States.

URBANIZATION OF POVERTY

The concentration of poverty in the inner cities of the United States is a fairly recent phenomenon. Before 1959, most poor lived in rural areas. Since then, however, the number of poor people living in metropolitan areas has increased. The concentration of poverty in major metropolitan areas is traced to the settlement patterns over the last four decades.

Mechanization of agriculture dramatically reduced the demand for labor in rural areas. The migration of displaced labor from rural areas to the cities emerged. Most displaced poor had limited skills (in other words, limited human capital) and were ill-equipped for urban life. Migration

---

14. The problem of welfare dependency and its consequences is discussed in more detail later in this book as one of the special topics.
15. See John Bound and Richard B. Freeman, "What Went Wrong? The Erosion of the Relative Earnings and Employment of Young Black Men in the 1980s," National Bureau of Economic Research, Working Paper, 1990.

proceeded from Appalachia, the South, Puerto Rico, and so on, to the metropolitan areas where a significant number of the immigrants were non-White. This migration shifted the concentration of poverty to the cities and slowed the progress of poverty reduction in the cities. Although major migration to the cities has ceased, the concentration of inner-city poverty continues to intensify.

Probably the most significant trend that explains the current composition of American ghettos was the migration of Blacks to northern metropolitan areas. The majority of American Blacks are descendants of slaves freed at the end of the Civil War. Until the end of World War II, most American Blacks lived in southern rural areas. They resided in the least prosperous part of the nation and were subjected to Jim Crow policies and practices that made economic success extremely difficult.[16] They had low incomes and most had limited educational training or skills. Massive migration of Blacks to the cities occurred in the 1940s and continued through the 1960s. Thus, while 73 percent of Blacks lived in rural areas in 1910, 73 percent of Blacks were in urban areas by 1960. By 1970, 81 percent of Blacks lived in areas classified by the Census Bureau as urban.

Of concern is not just the fact that poverty is very high in metropolitan areas, but also that poverty is highly concentrated in the inner cities of many such areas and also among racial minorities (particularly Blacks and Puerto Ricans). In most metropolitan areas, the number of the poor falls dramatically as one moves from the inner city to the suburbs and the racial composition changes, becoming predominantly White. Generally, the more affluent groups live in the suburbs while the poor live in the central cities.[17] This outcome (the urbanization of poverty) results from various factors, including the process of economic development, racial prejudice, and various public policies that encourage out migration of middle and upper income families. This section discusses the most important factors that are responsible for the concentration of poverty in the inner cities.

Traditionally, inner cities have been centers of employment for the poor. The concentration of low-skill jobs attracted poor to the inner cities as they could easily go to work without incurring high transportation costs. Mobility within the inner city is facilitated by public transportation that often connects the close residential areas to the employment centers. In addition, the older, less expensive houses, are located in the inner cities. These two factors, concentration of low-skill jobs and of inexpensive housing in the inner cities, naturally lead to a concentration of poor in these areas.

---

16. Jim Crow era practices included de jure segregationist policies, prohibition of Blacks from participating in some trades or holding some jobs, and other such explicit discriminatory policies.
17. See Sara McLanahan, Irwin Garfinkel, and Dorothy Watson, "Family Structure, Poverty and the Underclass," in Michael G. H. McGeary and Laurence E. Lynn, Jr., eds., *Urban Change and Poverty* (Washington, D.C.: National Academic Press, 1988), pp. 102–47.

Economic growth that raises personal incomes makes it possible for middle- and upper-income families to buy newer and bigger homes in the suburbs. Furthermore, various inducements, such as home financing arrangements and income tax policies, encourage the wealthy to buy houses in the suburbs.[18] In addition, highways connecting the suburbs to the cities have made it easier to commute to work. These incentives to buy houses in the suburbs do not affect the choices made by the poor who cannot afford to buy. The movement to the suburbs makes it more attractive for the poor to settle in the inner cities because the rents decrease for the houses vacated by the higher-income families, thus making it more affordable for lower income families.[19] Suburbanization of mainly White well-off families has resulted in a high proportion of Blacks in the inner cities.

Although initial settlement patterns were largely influenced by economic factors, racial prejudice became increasingly important. As more Blacks moved into the inner cities, racial tensions increased and this tension accelerated the exodus of Whites to the suburbs. The out migration in response to the movement of Blacks has been explained by the *tipping point*, an upper limit to the racial mix in neighborhood housing beyond which most Whites flee.

Oscar Cohen states that, "Although the movement of Whites out of the area may proceed at varying rates of speed, a tipping-point is soon reached which sets off a wholesale flight of Whites."[20] Similarly, Morton Grodzins suggests that when "the proportion of non-Whites exceeds the limits of the neighborhood's tolerance for interracial living" the tipping point is reached.[21] Other researchers have used a scare point hypothesis to refer to the proportion of non-Whites that frighten Whites so much that they move out in mass numbers.[22] Based on evidence, the tipping point occurs when the non-White population exceeds 30 percent.[23] As the tipping point was

---

18. Tax policies (such as the deduction of mortgage interest payments) increases the opportunity cost of renting for middle- and upper-income families as opposed to buying.
19. This is the filtering process. As middle- and upper-income families move into new housing, the vacated housing becomes available to others who currently occupy less desirable housing units. Those who move to the newly vacated houses vacate other houses and others who have even poorer accommodations move into those houses. However, for these adjustments to take place, rent must be lowered as lower-income people move to housing that was for higher-income people. A series of rent reductions occurs so that even the poorest are able to move into better housing. The poorest leave the worst houses that may remain vacant or are demolished.
20. Oscar Cohen, "The Case for Benign Quotas in Housing," *Phylon* 21 (1) (Spring 1960): 21.
21. Morton Grodzins, *The Metropolitan Area As a Racial Problem* (Pittsburgh: University of Pittsburgh Press, 1958), p. 6.
22. See Eunice Grier and George Grier, *Privately Developed Interracial Housing: An Analysis of Experience* (Berkeley: University of California Press, 1960).
23. See, for example, Martin Meyerson and Edward C. Banfield, *Politics, Planning and the Public Interest* (Glencoe, Ill.: The Free Press, 1955); and Hans Spiegel, "Tenants' Intergroup Attitudes in a Public Housing Project with Declining White Population," *Phylon* 21 (1) (Spring 1960): 30–9.

reached in many cities, a rapid out migration of well-off Whites resulted in wealthy White suburbs, and poor, predominantly Black inner cities.

The exodus of Whites to suburbs is consistent to a model proposed by Thomas Schelling.[24] According to Schelling, even small differences in racial tolerances between races can result in a high degree of residential segregation. Even though Whites may accept some members of minority groups, they may not want a large number of minorities. According to the observed behavioral patterns, Whites generally prefer lower proportions of Blacks in their neighborhoods. Conversely, a racially integrated neighborhood is more attractive to Blacks. Thus, because Whites prefer lower proportions of minorities than do Blacks, after a Black family moves into a predominantly White neighborhood, a certain White family's tolerance threshold is reached and that family moves out of the neighborhood.[25] However, such a move causes the proportion of Blacks in the neighborhood to increase. As more Blacks move in, and thus the proportion of Blacks increase, the tolerance thresholds of more White families are exceeded and those families move out. This process continues to the point where a once all-White neighborhood changes to an all-minority neighborhood. Thus, although one may observe neighborhoods that have a few Blacks, that is not to say that Whites in those neighborhoods are tolerant to Blacks but rather it is just that their tolerance thresholds are not reached. If more Blacks move into such neighborhoods, there often is a rapid transformation of the racial mix as Whites exit to neighborhoods with lower proportions of minorities.

Several other factors contributed to the residential segregation during the 1950s and 1960s, which resulted in the concentration of Blacks in poor residential areas. Blacks who had incomes that permitted them to buy houses in the suburbs were prohibited from moving there by the system of segregation.[26] For example, racial covenants explicitly forbade an owner from selling to Blacks in White neighborhoods.[27] In other cases, racial zoning legally prevented Blacks from buying houses in White areas.

Although these were extreme cases, several other practices were quite effective in enforcing housing segregation. Deliberate efforts were made to

---

24. Thomas C. Schelling, "Dynamic Models of Segregation," *Journal of Mathematical Sociology* 1 (1971): 143–86; and *Micromotives and Macrobehavior* (New York: Norton, 1978).
25. It is important to note that tolerance is a comparative measure. Thus, according to Schelling, Whites who appear to be less tolerant in one location of Blacks than other Whites may be merely more tolerant of the alternative locations. See *Micromotives and Macrobehavior*, p. 155.
26. For example, in 1965 52 percent of nonpoor non-White families lived in poverty areas while only 10 percent of nonpoor Whites lived in such areas. See *Poor in America*, Report of the National Commission on Urban Problems to the Congress and to the President of the United States (Washington. D.C.: U.S. Government Printing Office, 1965).
27. Restrictive racial covenants also were aimed at preventing other groups such as Mexicans, Orientals, Native Americans, and Jews from buying houses in particular White neighborhoods.

discourage Blacks from buying or renting in some White neighborhoods. Various forms of intimidation and threats of violence such as throwing garbage on lawns, making threatening phone calls, and burning crosses in yards were common means of keeping Blacks away. Preemptive purchases also were used to prevent Blacks from buying property in White neighborhoods. Implicit and even explicit collusion by realtors, bankers, and mortgage companies effectively prevented Blacks from moving into White neighborhoods.[28]

The federal government contributed to increased racial segregation of neighborhoods. For example, the Federal Housing Administration (FHA) intentionally prevented integrated housing, arguing that financial stability of neighborhoods required that they be occupied by the same race and social group. In fact, the FHA advised appraisers to lower their valuation of properties in mixed neighborhoods. This policy served to abet the segregation process. The FHA actually drove some developers out of business when they insisted upon open housing policies.[29]

More importantly, the federal government accelerated housing segregation through the housing policies used by some of its agencies. Favorable financing programs that were extended by the FHA's mortgage insurance program and the Veterans Administration's (VA) loan guarantee program made home ownership more accessible to a wide group of families. These programs extended benefits to young families by requiring low down payments and lenient credit terms. The beneficiaries had to demonstrate good credit histories and good prospects for future income. Generally, the families who qualified were relatively well-off. Other families (older ones, those with low earnings, or with erratic work histories) did not qualify for these programs. These families were left in the cities, as the beneficiaries, predominantly young Whites, moved to the suburbs. The majority of those left in the inner cities were poor Black, a few Whites, the old, and the physically and mentally handicapped. In other words, FHA- and VA-subsidized loans to people who would qualify for conventional mortgages. Thus, the VA and FHA programs indirectly enhanced housing segregation, concentrating poverty in the inner city.

Another federal program that increased housing segregation and concentrated poverty in the inner cities was the subsidized low-income housing that was administered by the Public Housing Administration. Federal low-income housing involved the construction of public projects composed

28. See, for example, Amos H. Hawley and Vincent P. Rock, eds., *Segregation in Residential Areas* (Washington, D.C.: National Academy of Sciences, 1973); and Robert E. Forman, *Black Ghettos, White Ghettos, and Slums* (Englewood Cliffs, N.J.: Prentice Hall, 1971).
29. After 1948 when restrictive racial covenants were held unconstitutional, the FHA stopped insuring properties where such covenants were in effect. Nevertheless, it continued to provide insurance where builders and mortgage companies would not lend, and owners would not rent, to Blacks. Thus, the FHA continued to support segregation policies. See William Tabb, *The Political Economy of the Black Ghetto* (New York: Norton, 1970).

of numerous low-income dwellings. To qualify for those subsidized low-income housing units, applicants were subjected to a maximum, rather than minimum, income level. Under this criteria, few Whites qualified because most had incomes higher than the set standard. Thus, the program attracted mainly Blacks.

Other factors have magnified the concentration of inner-city poverty. An important factor has been the out migration of manufacturing and blue-collar jobs. There is clear evidence that white flight from central cities was followed closely by the suburbanization of economic activity. The out migration of jobs to the suburbs has made the poverty of inner-city residents more severe. Inner-city residents face higher commuting costs, and therefore find it more difficult to search for and hold jobs in the suburbs. Furthermore, the information about suburban job openings may not be available. The employment prospects of inner-city residents is compounded by racial discrimination by employers in the suburbs.[30]

Another factor that has concentrated poor in the inner cities is the availability of public services. Cities often provide services such as public hospitals and public transportation that may not be available in the suburbs. These services attract poor people. At the same time, public transit makes it difficult for inner-city residents to reverse commute to jobs in the suburbs.

Although most of the explicit segregationist policies that were used in the past are not used today, integration of Black and White communities has not occurred. As the evidence shows, segregation continues to be the norm. Most people believe that barriers to racial integration that were erected by prejudiced Whites are no longer existent and that the current patterns of residential segregation reflect income differences. The fact that middle-income Blacks have moved into predominantly White neighborhoods without harassment is used as evidence that the Whites' aversion to Blacks is no longer important. It is now commonly stated that *class* not *race* is more important in explaining residential patterns.

In a 1993 study, Douglas Massey and Nancy Denton demonstrate that the only way that primarily White neighborhoods have been maintained is because of the existence of mechanisms that effectively keep Blacks out.[31] Successful White flight can occur only if Blacks are not likely to follow. Massey and Denton document various contemporary examples of practices that limit Black entry into particular neighborhoods. One common strategy is the practice of realtors to keep Blacks from some areas.

> The absence of overt discrimination does not mean that exclusionary practices have ended, however; rather, the character of discrimination has changed. Black homeseekers now face a more subtle process of exclusion.

---

30. See the papers in George M. von Furstenberg, Bennet Harrison, and Ann R. Horowitz, *Patterns of Racial Discrimination* (Lexington, Mass.: D.C. Heath and Co., 1974).
31. Douglas S. Massey and Nancy A. Denton, *American Apartheid: Segregation and the Making of the Underclass* (Cambridge, Mass.: Harvard University Press, 1993).

Rather than encountering "White only" signs, they face a covert series of barriers. Instead of being greeted with derisive rejection, "no niggers allowed," they are met by a realtor with a smiling face who, through a series of ruses, lies, and deceptions, makes it hard for them to learn about, inspect, rent, or purchase homes in White neighborhoods.[32]

A common practice that has received much publicity recently is *steering*. Steering involves a situation where realtors in a given metropolitan area steer would-be minority home buyers to predominantly minority neighborhoods and White buyers are directed to primarily White neighborhoods. Such a practice reduces the probability of integration and further magnifies racial segregation.

Blacks and other minorities also face problems in securing financing. Biases by mortgage companies implies that many may not be able to secure the necessary financing to buy houses in suburbs and are only able to buy low quality houses. Furthermore, improving the quality of housing in low-income areas inhabited by minorities is hindered by the continued discriminatory practices of conventional lenders. Generally, these lenders finance housing in predominantly White communities. A common practice is *redlining*, which is the process by which lenders discriminate by denying commercial and residential credit to certain neighborhoods, often the poor minority neighborhoods. Redlining continues to be a problem all over the country and makes it difficult for minorities to improve their own communities.

In many parts of the country, the ability of low-income minorities to move out of the inner cities is hindered by several local ordinances. Exclusionary and restrictive zoning make it difficult for the inner-city residents to find low-income housing in suburbs. Regulations that stipulate minimum lot sizes for houses are one barrier that makes it difficult for low-income people to buy houses in the suburbs. In many parts of the country, it is not uncommon to find local ordinances that require lot sizes of at least two acres or so for every house. Such requirements inflate the prices of housing and thus effectively exclude low-income populations. Another important practice that limits the ability of poor to move out of the inner cities is the Not In My Back Yard (NIMBY) syndrome. The NIMBY syndrome occurs when local communities block any attempt to build low-income houses in their neighborhoods.

PUBLIC POLICY

The current situation of urban America clearly demonstrates the difficulty of dealing with ghetto poverty. Attempts to deal with ghetto poverty face obstacles associated with the underclass that are not conducive to the

---

32. Douglas S. Massey and Nancy Denton, *American Apartheid*, p. 97.

elimination of poverty. In addition, the poor-quality, inner-city educational system does not give residents the necessary job skills, even if employment opportunities are available. Furthermore, many businesses do not locate in inner cities because of the various transaction costs that they face. Problems areas such as crime, drugs, and so forth, impose heavy penalties on businesses that locate in the inner cities. The current situation in the ghettos does not imply that policymakers have neglected the poor. In fact, attempts have been made to deal specifically with inner-city poverty, but most have been unsuccessful in reducing poverty. In some cases, antipoverty policies have been counterproductive, increasing rather than reducing poverty.

Some policies that deal with ghetto poverty are similar to those that deal with the general problem of poverty. For example, both cash and in-kind transfers are used to alleviate inner-city poverty. Although such transfers do provide some basic needs such as food (food stamps), housing (subsidized housing and housing subsidies), medical benefits, and cash assistance to families with children (Aid to Families with Dependent Children (AFDC)), these benefits have not reduced poverty rates significantly. As mentioned previously, some analysts argue that public assistance has created dependent groups of recipients, making their exit from poverty much more difficult. Although it is not clear what the best policy may be, clear evidence exists that welfare policies must be reformed to minimize the undesirable effects while promoting independence.[33] Other strategies to deal with ghetto poverty focus on direct job creation and on employability improvement (as discussed in Chapter 8).

Because cities do not provide a climate that is conducive to investment, one policy that has been suggested and implemented in various parts of the United States to attract investors has been the establishment of *enterprise zones*. Enterprise zones are designated areas in which investors are given tax breaks and other benefits as an incentive to invest in otherwise unattractive areas. Evidence about the effect of enterprise zones in improving poor inner-city residents is mixed. Although jobs are created, often such jobs are high skill and rarely benefit the poor inner-city residents. Most of the people who get those jobs are the already well-off who live in the suburbs. Since the beneficiaries do not live in the inner cities, their incomes are spent in the suburbs. Thus, enterprise zones actually could benefit the suburbs more than the inner cities they are meant to help. It is not clear that the tax revenue lost as a result of tax breaks outweighs the benefits.

It is improbable that investment incentives such as tax breaks, or the creation of enterprise zones will attract enough firms to the inner cities to solve

---

33. The effects of public transfers are discussed in Chapters 14 and 16.

the current ghetto job problem, given the transaction costs that businesses face. Rather than only attempting to move jobs to the inner cities, a better short-run strategy may be to make it easier for inner-city residents to find jobs in the suburbs. Several problems confront city residents in finding and keeping suburb jobs, including transportation costs and poor information about job openings. Improving the public transportation system from the inner cities to the suburbs should be given priority. Mechanisms to spread information about jobs in the inner cities would help the unemployed and discouraged city residents in their job search.

The important issues that need to be given priority are those that affect the participation in the labor markets. Although public assistance may affect labor market choices, for the poor the more important factors are those that increase the opportunity cost of working. Vital elements are child care costs and medical benefits. A major problem with the current medical care system is that it helps the poorest, but penalizes those who attempt to earn market incomes. For most poor, there is a high cost of working since their medical benefits may be lost while the jobs available to them pay low wages and do not provide medical protection.

Mothers of young children may not participate in the labor market because of the high cost of child care. Additionally, many single mothers do not receive child support from absent fathers. Thus, a policy that would go a long way toward helping the inner-city poor is a system that provides for child care and reforms the current child support system to make absent fathers more responsible.

It is strange that today's liberal scholars and politicians advocate policies that deal with inner-city poverty, but not necessarily policies that would help the poor leave the city and integrate with other members of society. As demonstrated by Douglas Massey and Nancy Denton in their classic book, *American Apartheid*, although segregation has been central to the inner-city problems, there is little effort to integrate minorities and Whites. It seems that a shift in policy is necessary if any major reductions in inner-city poverty are to be achieved. Such policy initiatives should involve strategies that will make it possible for minorities to buy or rent houses in the suburbs. Integrating residential neighborhoods will alter the value system of poor inner-city residents, provide them with better educational opportunities, and solve the spatial mismatch labor market problem that exists.

Finally, inner-city residents must control their neighborhoods and assume more responsible for their destiny. This probably is the only solution to inner-city problems. It is unlikely that ghetto residents will take control unless they also own the resources in those neighborhoods. Private home ownership by the poor may be the only way that people will start investing in their neighborhoods, and pushing out the drug dealers, thieves, and others who make the inner cities unattractive places to invest.

SUMMARY

Ghetto poverty is much more difficult to deal with than other types of poverty. This chapter traced the evolution of the present-day ghetto with its high concentration of poor, mainly minorities. Inner-city poverty is complicated by factors such as its high concentration, isolation of the poor from the mainstream, deteriorating school systems, female-headed families, welfare dependency, and criminal activities. The flight of businesses from the inner cities has left behind a large population that has never worked, or is unemployed.

Several policies to deal with ghetto poverty have been suggested, including job creation, employment policies, and child care and health care policies. Nevertheless, the ultimate solution to ghetto poverty may require inner-city residents to take control and adopt responsible values that are conducive to success.

STUDY AND DISCUSSION QUESTIONS

1. Focusing on a particular city in the United States, attempt to describe the racial composition in various sections of the city. Would you consider that city to be racially segregated?

2. Carefully discuss the various factors that explain the current residential patterns in major metropolitan areas.

3. Compare the ghetto poor and the rural poor. Carefully outline why it may be easier to deal with rural poor as compared to the ghetto poor.

4. The concept of "underclass" implies a group of people who are different from the mainstream. Do you think this term is appropriate? Are people in the ghetto really different from everyone else or do they face different circumstances? Explain.

5. Outline various policies that can be used to deal with inner-city poverty.

6. It appears that some degree of racial residential integration will be necessary to reduce inner-city poverty. Discuss policies that can be used to increase racial integration in residential neighborhoods.

7. In South Africa, the system of apartheid effectively maintained segregated neighborhoods for many years. What policies do you think could be used to integrate residential neighborhoods in that country? Would you recommend such policies for the United States? Explain carefully. You should discuss the emergence of segregated neighborhoods in the United States.

8. What is your opinion on residential segregation? Do you think that it should be the goal of the United States to achieve more racial integration?

9. Suppose that communities exercise their freedom of choice and exclude Blacks from a particular neighborhood. Should the government interfere? What if the communities exclude Jews or the Irish?

10. Many people now talk about "empowering the ghetto poor." What exactly does empowerment imply? Is this possible? That is, can people be empowered or do they have to empower themselves?

11. It has been suggested that some people in the inner city commit crimes so that they can go to in prison because life in the ghetto is much worse. Using newspaper and television news accounts, compile a list of events in one city (that is near your school) over a period of one week which demonstrates how life is in the ghetto.

ADDITIONAL READINGS

1. Bluestone, Barry and Bennett Harrison. *The Deindustrialization of America*. New York: Basic Books, 1982.

2. Ellwood, Davis T. *Poor Support: Poverty in the American Family*. New York: Basic Books, 1988.

3. Franklin, Raymond S. *Shadows of Race and Class*. Minneapolis: University of Minnesota Press, 1991.

4. Goldsmith, William W. and Edward J. Blakely. *Separate Societies: Poverty and Inequality in U.S. Cities*. Philadelphia: Temple University Press, 1992.

5. Heilbrun, James. *Urban Economics and Public Policy*. New York: St. Martin's Press, 1981.

6. Levy, John M. *Urban and Metropolitan Economics*. New York: McGraw-Hill Book Company, 1985.

7. McGeary, Michael G. H. and Laurence E. Lynn, Jr., eds. *Urban Change and Poverty*. Washington, D.C.: National Academy Press, 1988.

8. Sackrey, Charles. *The Political Economy of Urban Poverty*. New York: W. W. Norton and Company, 1973.

12

FAMILY STRUCTURE AND POVERTY: THE FEMINIZATION OF POVERTY

It is now common knowledge that a strong relationship exists between family structure and the incidence of poverty. Specifically, female-headed households are at a much higher risk of falling into poverty than male-headed households.[1] The general public and the media frequently associate female-headship with poverty and welfare use. Race, sex, and marital status of the head of a household are the most important determinants of a family's poverty status in the United States. Female-headed households have the highest poverty rates of all poor groups (such as the aged and the disabled). Furthermore, the differences have been increasing between the poverty rates of female-headed households and of other poor groups. Although poverty rates among other groups have been declining, poverty among female-headed households has been increasing. The dramatic increase in the proportion of families headed by females over the last three decades and the high poverty rates among these households has attracted interest from both researchers and policymakers. Liberal and conservative policymakers and academics agree that one of the important factors leading to contemporary poverty has been the change in family structure. The high poverty rates of female-headed households has led to the term *feminization of poverty*.[2]

This chapter discusses the transformation of the American family in relation to poverty and public policy. It starts with a brief look at the changes in family structure and the feminization of poverty. It then examines some of

---

1. Family size also affects poverty. Households with more members have a higher probability of experiencing poverty than those with fewer members. It also is the case, however, that poverty can influence the household size. Specifically, poor households tend to have more children. See James Cramer, "Births, Expected Family Size, and Poverty," in James N. Morgan, ed., *Five Thousand American Families: Patterns of Economic Progress* (Ann Arbor, Mich.: Institute for Social Research, University of Michigan, 1974).

2. This term was first used by Diana Pearce in 1978 after observing that in 1976, almost two-thirds of poor persons over 16 years of age were women and almost half of the poor families were headed by females. See Diana Pearce, "The Feminization of Poverty: Women, Work and Welfare," *Urban and Social Change Review*, special issue on women and work, 2 (1–2) (1978): 28–36.

the factors that have been responsible for changing family structure. Later, the chapter focuses on the causes and consequences of poverty in female-headed households and public policies that could be used to alleviate poverty of single-parent households.

FEMALE HEADSHIP AND THE FEMINIZATION OF POVERTY

Trends in Female Headship

There are several routes to female headship, including marital breakdown (divorce and separation), death of a spouse, and out-of-wedlock births. Both marital instability and out-of-wedlock births have increased rapidly since the 1960s, and they have been largely responsible for the increase in female-headed households. The combination of these factors has resulted in radical transformation of the American family.

Figure 12-1 depicts the growth of female-headed families over the period 1954–1991. In 1954, there were just about four million families headed by a female with no husband present. In 1991, there were close to 12 million such families, a fourfold increase. During the same period, families composed of married couples increased from just over 32 million to 52.5 million families. The fastest growth of female headship occurred during the 1960s and 1970s. Thus, by 1990, close to 22 percent of all families in the United States were headed by females, more than double the proportion of the late 1940s.

As noted, the growth of female headship has been primarily due to marital instability and out-of-wedlock births. Figure 12-2 plots annual divorce rates for 1950 to 1990 per 1,000 population. The divorce rate per 1,000 population was about 2.5 in 1950 and 2.2 in 1960. By 1979, the divorce rate had increased to 5.2 per 1,000 population. The increase in divorce rate is more clearly demonstrated by expressing the rate per 1,000 married couples. Divorce rates per 1,000 married couples increased from about 9.2 in 1960 to 22.6 in 1980. Although the rates fell somewhat during the 1980's, they remained more than double what they were in 1960.

Probably the most significant contributor to female headship has been out-of-wedlock births. Figure 12-3 depicts out-of-wedlock births per 1000 live births for White and non-White women from 1952 to 1988. In 1952, there were only 17.5 out-of-wedlock births for every 1000 births to White women. This number had increased by 1980 to 110.4 per 1000 births and over 177 per 1000 births by 1988. For non-Whites, the number of out-of-wedlock births was 179.6 per 1000 live births in 1952, 485.5 per 1000 live births in 1980, and 539 per 1000 live births in 1988. Thus, although it is true that out-of-wedlock births continue to be much higher for non-Whites, the rate of increase has been more significant for Whites.

In discussing issues pertaining to family structure, one must be particularly concerned with those families with children. Table 12-1 shows the dramatic change in family structure of families with children present by race for

Figure 12-1   Growth in the number of female-headed households, 1954–1991

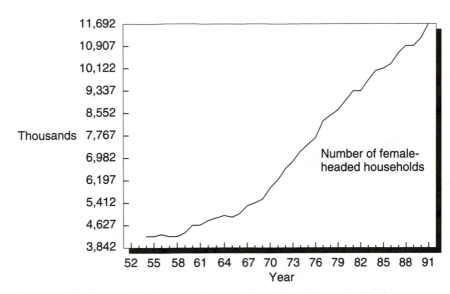

Source: U.S. Bureau of the Census, "Household and Family Characteristics," *Current Population Reports*, 1992.

Figure 12-2   Divorce rates, 1952–1990

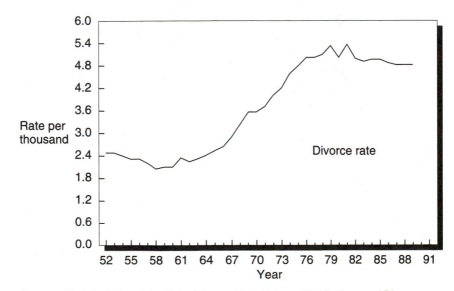

Source: Vital Statistics of the United States 1987, Volume III: Marriage and Divorce. *Statistical Abstract of the United States*, 1991.

Figure 12-3   Out-of-wedlock births by race, 1952–1988

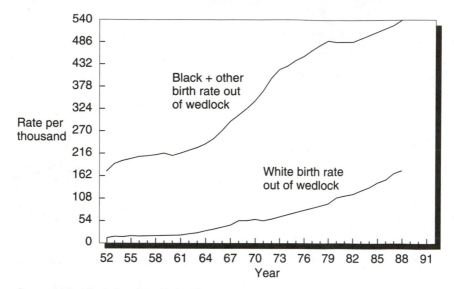

Source: Vital Statistics of the United States, Volume I: *Natality*; various editions.

selected years between 1970 and 1991. In 1970, two-parent families comprised 87.1 percent of all families with children, in 1985, 73.7 percent, and in 1991, 71.1 percent. Note that the absolute number of two-parent families also decreased over this period. Families with a female head accounted for 11.5 percent of all families in 1970, 23.2 percent in 1985, and 25 percent in 1991. Over this period, the proportion of White families headed by females more than doubled from 8.9 percent in 1970 to 17.8 percent in 1985 and to 19.3 percent in 1991. The proportion of Black families headed by females, increased from 33 percent in 1970 to 56.7 percent in 1985 and to 58 percent in 1991.

Table 12-2 shows the various components of change in the family structure. In 1970, 6.5 percent of all female family heads, 2.8 percent of White female heads, and 15.1 percent of Black female heads had never been married. In 1986, these numbers were 14.8 percent White and 49.2 percent Black female heads. In 1991, the never married female-headed households were 19.4 percent White and 54.2 percent Black. Once again, this shows that female headship among Black families is dominated by those in the never married category. Conversely, female headship in White families is primarily a result of marital instability. In 1970, 35.3 percent of White female heads were divorced. In 1986, this number had increased to 44.9 percent; it fell to 39.2 percent in 1991.

A few observations can be drawn from these data. First, although there are some single-parent households headed by males, most single-parent households are headed by females. For example, in 1991, 83.7 percent of all White and 92.6 percent of all Black one-parent families were headed by

Table 12-1   Family groups with children under 18 years old by race: 1970–1991

	1970		1980		1985		1991	
	No. (Thousands)	*%*	*No. (Thousands)*	*%*	*No. (Thousands)*	*%*	*No. (Thousands)*	*%*
All Races								
Total families	29,631	100.0	32,150	100.0	33,353	100.0	34,973	100.0
Two-parent	25,823	87.1	25,231	78.5	24,573	73.7	24,863	71.1
One-parent	3,808	12.9	6,920	21.5	8,779	26.3	10,110	28.9
Mother	3,415	11.5	6,230	19.4	7,737	23.2	8,745	25.0
Father	393	1.3	690	2.1	1,042	3.1	1,365	3.9
White								
Total families	26,115	100.0	27,294	100.0	27,629	100.0	28,443	100.0
Two-parent	23,477	89.9	22,628	82.9	21,873	79.2	21,893	77.0
One-parent	2,638	10.1	4,664	17.1	5,757	20.8	6,550	23.0
Mother	2,330	8.9	4,122	15.1	4,912	17.8	5,482	19.3
Father	307	1.2	542	2.0	844	3.1	1,068	3.8
Black								
Total families	3,219	100.0	4,074	100.0	4,659	100.0	5,173	100.0
Two-parent	2,071	64.3	1,961	48.1	1,856	39.8	1,933	37.4
One-Parent	1,148	35.7	2,114	51.9	2,802	60.1	3,240	62.6
Mother	1,063	33.0	1,984	48.7	2,802	56.7	3,000	58.0
Father	85	2.6	129	3.2	160	3.4	239	4.6

Source: U.S. Bureau of the Census, "Household and Family Characteristics: March 1985," *Current Population Reports,* Series P–20, No. 411 (Washington, D.C.: U.S. Government Printing Office, 1986), and U.S. Bureau of the Census, "Household and Family Characteristics: March 1991," *Current Population Reports,* Series P–20, No. 458 (Washington, D.C.: U.S. Government Printing Office, 1992).

Table 12-2   Marital status of one-parent families, by race: 1970–1991

	1970		1986		1991	
	No. *(Thousands)*	*%*	*No.* *(Thousands)*	*%*	*No.* *(Thousands)*	*%*
All Races						
All Families	3,808	100.0	8,930	100.0	10,110	100.0
Maintained						
by mother	3,415	89.7	7,842	87.6	8,745	86.5
Never married	248	6.5	2,276	25.5	3,100	30.7
Spouse absent	1,377	36.2	1,724	19.3	1,921	19.0
Separated	962	25.3	1,506	16.9	1,569	15.5
Divorced	1,109	29.1	3,294	36.9	3,225	31.9
Widowed	682	17.9	546	6.1	498	4.9
Maintained						
by father	393	10.3	1,088	12.2	1,365	13.5
Never married	22	0.6	205	2.3	380	3.8
Spouse absent*	247	6.5	218	2.4	285	2.8
Divorced	na	na	571	6.4	630	6.2
Widowed	124	3.3	94	1.1	70	0.7
White						
All Families	2,638	100.0	5,964	100.0	6,550	100.0
Maintained						
by mother	2,330	88.3	5,070	85.0	5,482	83.7
Never married	73	2.8	885	14.8	1,271	19.4
Spouse absent	796	30.2	1,129	18.9	1,301	19.9
Separated	477	18.1	972	16.3	1,062	16.2
Divorced	930	35.3	2,676	44.9	2,565	39.2
Widowed	531	20.1	380	6.4	345	5.3
Maintained						
by father	307	11.6	894	15.0	1,068	16.3
Never married	18	0.7	135	2.3	255	3.9
Spouse absent*	196	7.4	168	2.8	223	3.4
Divorced	na	na	513	8.6	531	8.1
Widowed	93	3.5	78	1.3	59	0.9

Table 12-2   (Continued)

	1970		1986		1991	
	No. (Thousands)	%	No. (Thousands)	%	No. (Thousands)	%
Black						
All Families	1,148	100.0	2,752	100.0	3,240	100.0
Maintained by mother	1,063	92.6	2,597	94.4	3,000	92.6
Never married	173	15.1	1,355	49.2	1,755	54.2
Spouse absent	570	49.7	546	19.8	567	17.5
Separated	479	41.7	510	18.5	472	14.6
Divorced	172	15.0	561	20.4	551	17.0
Widowed	148	12.9	133	4.8	128	4.0
Maintained by father	85	7.4	155	5.6	239	7.4
Never married	4	0.3	60	2.2	99	3.1
Spouse absent*	50	4.4	40	1.5	50	1.5
Divorced	na	na	47	1.7	79	2.4
Widowed	30	2.6	7	0.3	11	0.3

*Data for 1970 includes divorced fathers.
na: Not Available

Source: U.S. Bureau of the Census, "Household and Family Characteristics: March 1986," *Current Population Reports,* Series P–20, No. 419 (Washington, D.C.: U.S. Government Printing Office, 1987) and U.S. Bureau of the Census, "Household and Family Characteristics: March 1991," *Current Population Reports,* Series P–20, No. 458 (Washington, D.C.: U.S. Government Printing Office, 1992).

females. Second, for Whites, female headship has been primarily due to an increase in the proportion of formerly married mothers as a result of divorce and also due to lower remarriage rates. For Blacks, however, female headship is primarily due to out-of-wedlock births.

Poverty in Female-Headed Households

The interest in the changing family structure is not because a two-parent household should be the norm, but because of a concern with the poverty status associated with female headship; particularly because of the problems faced by children who grow up in mother-only households. It has been observed that female-headed households face the highest risk of falling into poverty as compared to other family types. This is illustrated by

Figure 12-4 which shows the poverty rates of female-headed households and of all other families for the period 1972 to 1991. For most years, the poverty rates of female-headed households have been about three times as high as the poverty rates in all families—32.5 percent as compared to 10.1 percent in 1972, and 35.6 percent as compared to 11.5 percent in 1991.

Figure 12-5 plots child poverty rates in male- and female-headed households for the period 1961 to 1989. Although child poverty rates fell considerably for both male- and female-headed households, the rates in female-headed households have remained nearly five times as high as in families with a male head. For example, the child poverty rate in households with married couples was 22.4 percent in 1961 and 10.4 percent in 1989. The child poverty rate in female-headed households was 72.2 percent in 1961 and 51.1 percent in 1989. Thus, children raised in female-headed households are much more likely to be disadvantaged in their formative years.

This data reveals that female-headed households experience much higher poverty rates than other family types. Although such evidence can be used to show the idea of feminization of poverty, it also could be misleading. The idea of feminization of poverty implies that the probability that a family will be poor increases due to the change in family structure, say from a two-parent family to a mother-only family. If a two-parent family was poor initially and then the wife and the husband divorce leading to a poor mother-only household, one should not attribute the poverty of that unit to the fact that it is headed by a female. Similarly, just because female headship is much more prevalent among Blacks does not imply that the higher poverty rates of Black families as compared to White families is due to difference in family structure. Many of the poor households headed by Black females would be poor regardless of the family structure.

Mary Jo Bane (1986) investigated the effect that family structure has had on the overall poverty rates.[3] Bane calculated the extent to which poverty rates in the United States would have been different in 1979 and 1983 if the poverty rates within household composition categories had changed as they did since 1959, but if age and household composition had remained at the 1959 levels. Table 12-3 shows the poverty rates reported by Bane. The first row of each of the panels reports the actual poverty rate and the second row reports the effects in 1969, 1979, and 1983 of holding household composition at the 1959 level. The table also shows the effects in 1983 of holding household composition at the 1979 level. The lower panels report the poverty for Whites and for Blacks, respectively.

In 1979, for example, the poverty rates for all races was 11.6 percent. However, if household composition had remained at the 1959 level, the poverty rate would have been 9.7 percent, or 16 percent lower. The poverty rate in 1979 would have been 9.5 percent if family composition and age

---

3. Mary Jo Bane, "Household Composition and Poverty," in Sheldon Danziger and Daniel Weinberg, eds., *Fighting Poverty: What Works and What Doesn't* (Cambridge: Harvard University Press, 1986).

Figure 12-4   Family poverty rates, 1972–1991

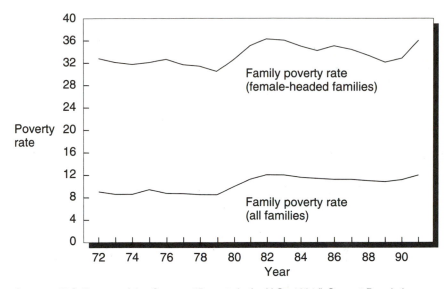

Source: U.S. Bureau of the Census, "Poverty in the U.S.: 1991," *Current Population Reports*, P–60 Series.

Figure 12-5   Child poverty rates and family composition, 1961–1989

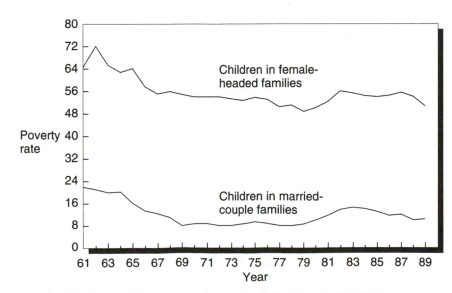

Source: U.S. Bureau of the Census, *Current Population Reports*, P–60 Series, various issues.

Table 12-3   Effects of household composition on overall poverty rate, by race, 1959–1983

	1959	1969	1979	1983
All Races				
Actual poverty rate	22.4	12.1	11.6	15.0
If 1959 composition	–	11.4	9.7	13.0
with age adjustment	–	11.4	9.5	12.4
If 1979 composition	–	–	–	14.8
Whites				
Actual poverty rate	18.1	9.5	9.1	12.0
If 1959 composition	–	9.0	7.8	10.8
If 1979 composition	–	–	–	11.9
Blacks				
Actual poverty rate	55.1	32.2	30.9	35.5
If 1959 composition	–	29.7	24.2	28.5
If 1979 composition	–	–	–	35.3
If White composition	51.8	25.2	20.6	25.1

Source: See Bane (1986), Table 9.2.

were held constant at 1959 levels. If family structure is held constant at the 1979 level, the data reveals that changes in family structure between 1979 and 1983 account for only 0.2 percentage points of the actual increase between 1979 and 1983. Thus, while it is true that changes in the family structure contributed to a sizable portion of the increase in the poverty rate between 1959 and 1979, family composition contributed almost nothing to the increase in poverty rates between 1979 and 1983.

The effect of family structure on poverty, however, is more important among Blacks. In 1979, the poverty rate for Whites was 9.1, and would have been 7.8 percent if family composition were held constant at the 1959 levels. For Blacks, the poverty rate was 30.9 percent in 1979 and would have been 24.2 percent if family composition were held constant at the 1959 levels. The actual poverty rates of Blacks in 1983 was 35.5 percent. If the family composition in 1979 were held constant, the poverty rate for Blacks would have been 35.3 percent in 1983. Thus, again family composition contributed almost nothing to the increase in poverty rates of Blacks between 1979 and 1983. A similar result holds for Whites.

An interesting result reported by Bane concerns what the poverty rates for Blacks would have been if their household composition had been the same as that of Whites. This comparison shows that, in 1983, while the actual poverty rate of Blacks was 35.5 percent, the rate would have been 25.1 percent if the family composition of Blacks was similar to that of

Whites. This evidence therefore shows that some of the racial differences in poverty rates can be attributed to family structure.

The high rates of poverty among female-headed households prompts one to ask not only why such high rates of poverty exist but also why there has been such a rapid increase in female-headed households. It is agreed that the family structure has been changing rapidly, and that poverty rates among female-headed households are much higher than in other families. However, there is no agreement as to the primary factors underlying those changes, or what policies, if any, should be used to deal with female headship. A discussion of the factors underlaying the observed changes in family structure follows.

CAUSES OF GROWTH OF FEMALE-HEADED HOUSEHOLDS

Many factors are suggested as contributing to the increased proportion of American families headed by females. A common explanation is the increased financial independence of females. The most important factor leading to financial independence involves changes in the labor markets, such as the increased labor force participation rates by females and the worsening labor market position of males. Another important factor is the availability of transfer payments that provide incentives for females to establish their own households. The economic position of Black males and the small number of marriageable males relative to the number of females is now considered to be one of the main causes for the increase in female headship in Black families. It also is true that societal attitudes have changed so that female headship and premarital sex are more acceptable (or at least tolerated). A discussion follows on each of these factors as they relate to female headship.

Increased Labor Force Participation by Females

Probably one of the more significant factors that has contributed to the dramatic increase in female-headed households is the rapid increase in the number of females working outside the home. The changes in female labor force participation are depicted in Figure 12-6. In 1950, the labor force participation rate for all females was just under 30 percent. By 1990, it was 57.5 percent.[4] For females between the ages of 20 and 24, the labor force participation rates increased from 46.1 in 1960 to 71.6 in 1990. For women

---

4. Several factors have been responsible for the increased female labor force participation rates. Some of the more important factors include declining fertility, which has reduced the time a mother spends at home taking care of children; increased employment and educational opportunities due to legislation outlawing discrimination; increased social acceptance of women working outside the home; and finally, economic conditions that have made it increasingly difficult for a family to manage with only one income earner.

Figure 12-6   Labor force participation rates of females, 1952–1991

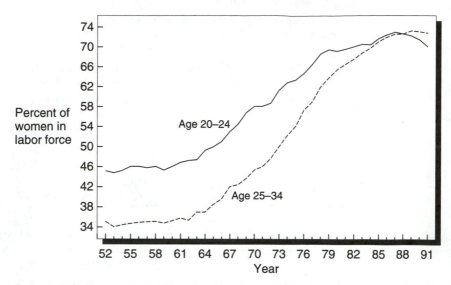

Source: U.S. Bureau of Labor Statistics: *Handbook of Labor Statistics*, various editions.

between the ages of 25 to 34, the increase was even more dramatic: from 36.1 percent in 1960 to 73.6 percent in 1990.

Working outside the home has reduced female dependence on males' earnings, making marriage less attractive financially. The theory of marriage formulated by Becker suggests that the decision to marry (and to remain married) is primarily influenced by the expected gains from such a union.[5] Specifically, Becker argues that the gains from marriage originate from the complementarity between males and females. For example, if a man has a comparative advantage in earning income and a woman has a comparative advantage in taking care of children and the home, then marriage is mutually beneficial.[6] As in the theory of exchange, each should specialize in the production of goods and services in which they enjoy a

---

5. Gary S. Becker, "A Theory of Marriage: Part I," *Journal of Political Economy* 81 (4) (1973): 813–46; Gary S. Becker, "A Theory of Marriage: Part II," *Journal of Political Economy* 82 (2), (1974): 511–26. See also Gary S. Becker, Elizabeth N. Landes, and Robert T. Michael, "An Economic Analysis of Marital Instability," *Journal of Political Economy* 85 (1977): 1149–87.

6. Suppose in one day person A produces 20 units of X and 8 units of Y, and person B produces 10 units of X and 2 units of Y. A is better in producing both X and Y than B. In this case, A is said to have an absolute advantage in producing both goods. However, whereas A is two times as productive in X, he or she is four times as productive as B in the production of Y. In this case, A has a comparative advantage in producing Y. B has an absolute disadvantage in producing both X and Y. However, the disadvantage is less in producing X. Thus, B has a comparative advantage in the production of X.

comparative advantage. As long as both partners derive benefits from the union, marital stability exists.

Less than four decades ago, most females worked at home and had a comparative advantage over males in the production of home services, taking care of children, and so forth. Men, on the other hand, had a comparative advantage in earning market incomes. Thus, marriages were stable as both men and women benefitted from marriage. Increased labor force participation by females provides them with earnings, thereby reducing men's relative advantage in earning market income. Thus, marriage is now less attractive to females because they are more financially independent.[7]

The rise in female labor force participation has been cited as one of the primary causes of divorce in America. Divorce and female labor force participation rates show a clear positive correlation. This relationship supports the idea that increased independence is associated with female headship. In addition, a number of empirical studies confirm that the probability of divorce and separation increase as a wife's earnings increase relative to her husband's. Other evidence shows that divorce rates are higher in those regions of the country where more employment opportunities exist for females.[8]

Other explanations for the positive association between female labor force participation rates and marital instability consider conflicts that arise in marriages that increase the probability of divorce. Marital conflict may arise because in traditional families (where the male is the provider), a working wife may undermine the man's position as the head of the household. Thus, a working wife could cause the man to feel inadequate as a provider. The perception of failure increases the probability of conflict in the home. Marital conflict also may arise because earnings by both wife and husband alter the power relationships in the marriage. Finally, when both husband and wife work outside the home, marital conflict arises in the allocation of duties at home. All these sources of conflict increase tension in the house and frequently translate into separation and divorce.[9]

---

7. Financial independence does not necessarily imply that females are better off financially alone as opposed to being married. Rather, earning market income makes divorce and separation more affordable. Thus, women are less likely to remain in unhappy marriages if they earn income. As will be seen, participation in the labor force by females also may cause conflicts that translate into divorce.

8. For empirical evidence on the role of female labor market participation in promoting marital instability, see Samuel H. Preston and Alan T. Richards, "The Influence of Women's Work Opportunities on Marriage Rates," *Demography* 12 (2) (May 1975): 209–22; Heather Ross and Isabel Sawhill, *Time of Transition: The Growth of Families Headed by Women* (Washington, D.C.: Urban Institute, 1975).

9. For evidence of the incidence of marital conflict as a result of female participation in labor markets, see Alan Booth, et al., "Women, Outside Employment, and Marital Instability," *American Journal of Sociology* 90 (3) (November 1984): 567–83; and Catherine Ross, John Mirowsky, and Joan Huber, "Dividing Work, Sharing Work, and in Between: Marriage Patterns and Depression," *American Sociological Review* 48 (6) (December 1983): 809–23.

Declining Wages and Rising Unemployment of Men

Another factor that has reduced the benefits of marriage to females is the diminished earnings of males. Just as the number of females in the labor force was increasing, the labor market prospects of males, especially young males, was deteriorating. This has been the case particularly for Black males, whose labor market prospects have continued to deteriorate.[10]

Figure 12-7 shows the median income of full-year, full-time male workers for the period from 1967 to 1991 expressed in 1991 dollars. The median earnings of male workers increased steadily throughout the 1960s and early 1970s, reaching a peak of $28,421 in 1973. Since then, earnings have been declining. In 1991, for example, the median earnings for full-year, full-time male workers was $25,527.

The declining labor market fortunes of male workers also is reflected in the rising unemployment rates. Unemployment problems have been particularly severe for young male workers—especially non-White males. Unemployment rates fell for most of the 1960s. Since the late 1960s, unemployment rates have increased dramatically. For minority male workers aged 20 to 24 years, the unemployment rate increased from about 13 percent in 1960 to 31 percent in 1982. Even though unemployment rates declined for most of the 1980s, they remained around 20 percent.

As noted in Chapter 11, the fact that dismal labor market position for males has detrimental effects on the formation and stability of families was recognized several decades ago by Daniel Patrick Moynihan.[11] Moynihan hypothesized that the lack of employment opportunities for Black males was a primary cause of marital instability in Black families. Since the 1960s, the unemployment rates of Black males has continued to rise, and so has female headship in Black families. Likewise, the increased unemployment rates of White males and declining median incomes have been associated with instability of White families.

Ample empirical evidence exists to support the idea that the declining labor market prospects of males have been partly responsible for the formation of female-headed households. For example, increases in unemployment rates during the post World War II period has been shown to have had a strong effect on divorce rates.[12] Saul Hoffman and John Holmes also report evidence that the probability of marital disruption is significantly greater if the husband has experienced unemployment.[13]

---

10. The problems facing minorities in the labor market were discussed in more detail in Chapter 11.
11. Daniel Patrick Moynihan, *The Negro Family: The Case for National Action* (Washington, D.C.: U.S. Department of Labor, Office of Policy Planning and Research, 1965).
12. See Scott J. South, "Economic Conditions and the Divorce Rate: A Time Series Analysis of the Postwar United States," *Journal of Marriage and the Family* 47 (1985): 31–42.
13. See Saul Hoffman and John Holmes, "Husbands, Wives and Divorce," in G. J. Duncan and J. Morgan, eds. *Five Thousand American Families* 4 (Ann Arbor, Mich.: University of Michigan, Institute for Social Research, 1976).

Figure 12-7   Median earnings of full-time male workers, 1967–1991

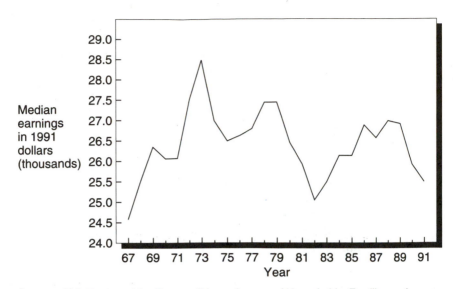

Source: U.S. Bureau of the Census, "Money Income of Households, Families and Persons," *Current Population Reports*, P–60 Series.

Welfare Benefits

Transfer payments, particularly those made to participants in the AFDC program, often are blamed for contributing to increased marital instability and out-of-wedlock births. On purely theoretical grounds, there are various reasons why the availability of transfer payments leads to an increase in the number of female-headed households. Transfer payments reduce the cost borne by a mother in rearing a child. Thus, those women who would have otherwise delayed having children because of their inability to take care of them are less financially constrained due to the availability of welfare benefits. Availability of welfare benefits reduces the incentive to have an abortion or to surrender children for adoption.[14] Furthermore, some welfare programs require a family unit to be headed by a female (or single parent) and to have a dependent child. In absence of any other source of income, having a child out of wedlock satisfies the eligibility requirements for such welfare payments. This has been one of the primary criticisms of the AFDC program.

The fact that welfare could result in female headship also is consistent with Becker's model of the family. The availability of welfare benefits to a

---

14. See Kristin A. Moore and Steven Caldwell, "The Effect of Government Policies on Out-of-Wedlock Sex and Pregnancy," *Family Planning Perspectives* 9 (4) (July-August 1977): 164–68.

female, be it cash or in-kind transfers, reduces the gains from living in a male-headed household. This is particularly the case if the male's income is low. Thus, according to Becker's model of marriage, we expect increasing welfare benefits to lead to marital instability, and consequently to an increase in the number of households headed by females.

Some empirical studies on the effect of welfare use on marital dissolution and out-of-wedlock births support the theoretical proposition just suggested. For example, Marjorie Honing reports results showing that AFDC cash benefits had a positive effect on female headship in 1960 and 1970. Although her findings show the same effect on Whites and non-Whites, among Whites the results were only statistically significant for 1960. In her conclusion, Honing states that by limiting assistance to female-headed families, the AFDC assistance program can be expected to influence female-headship rates. Furthermore, Honing suggests that increases in the level of support provided for AFDC families relative to the earnings of low-income families can be expected to lead to increases in the number of families headed by females.[15]

Charles Murray's influential book, *Losing Ground* (which analyzes the effects of social policies in the United States over the period 1950 to 1980) attributes increased Black poverty to the effect of welfare benefits on the family.[16] A similar conclusion is reached by Lowell Gallaway and Richard Vedder, who provide cross-sectional and time-series support for the proposition that welfare benefits have led to a breakdown in traditional family arrangements.[17] Gallaway and Vedder suggest that because of its effect on the family, welfare may have created more poverty than it eliminated. Phillips Cutright and Patrick Madaras find a positive relationship between AFDC and female headship.[18] Specifically, they find that AFDC recipiency encourages unmarried mothers to establish their own living units. Likewise, Barbara Janowitz provides empirical evidence suggesting that the welfare system affects illegitimacy, especially among young women.[19]

---

15. Marjorie Honing, "AFDC Income, Recipient Rates, and Family Dissolution," *Journal of Human Resources* 9 (3) (Summer 1973): 303–22. See also Ross and Sawhill, *Time of Transition;* and Sheldon Danziger, George Jakubson, Saul Schwartz, and Eugene Smolensky, "Work and Welfare as Determinants of Female Poverty and Household Headship," *Quarterly Journal of Economics* 97 (3) (August 1982): 519–34.
16. Charles Murray, *Losing Ground: American Social Policy, 1950–1980* (New York: Basic Books, 1984).
17. Lowell Gallaway and Richard Vedder, *Poverty, Income Distribution, the Family, and Public Policy.* A study prepared for the use of the Subcommittee on Trade, Productivity, and Economic Growth of the Joint Economic Committee, Congress of the United States (Washington, D.C.: U.S. Government Printing Office, December 19, 1986). The potential effects of transfers on poverty are discussed in Chapter 13.
18. Phillips Cutright and Patrick Madaras, "AFDC and the Marital and Family Status of Ever Married Women Aged 15–44: United States, 1950–1970," *Sociology and Social Research* 60 (3) (April 1976): 314–27.
19. See Barbara Janowitz, "The Impact of AFDC on Illegitimate Birth Rates," *Journal of Marriage and the Family* 38 (August 1976): 485–94.

Research using data from National Longitudinal Surveys of Labor Market Experience shows that women on welfare as compared to women without assistance, have significantly higher rates of separation and divorce.[20] The effect of welfare benefits on family structure depends on the attractiveness of benefits. For example, some evidence supports the proposition that low-income families are more likely to split up if they live in high benefit areas.[21] In addition, high benefits seem to discourage remarriage.[22] In summary, public assistance contributes to marital dissolution by either directly encouraging divorce or indirectly providing alternate means of support for women who are in unsatisfactory marriages.

A number of studies question the welfare-female headship causality. For example, Mark Rank argues that although welfare populations have higher divorce, separation, and nonmarriage rates, such outcomes are not a result of welfare recipiency.[23] Because poverty is associated with stress and tension, these problems lead to separation and divorce and (for unmarried women) they act as a constraint to finding a spouse. Rank concludes that marital instability is not due to welfare availability, but a result of poverty.

Other researchers have presented evidence suggesting that the role of welfare in explaining marital dissolution has been minimal. For example, David Ellwood and Mary Jo Bane, using cross-section and time-series data, find that welfare has had only small effects on out-of-wedlock birth rates and divorce and separation patterns among families with children.[24] Their results, however, do show that AFDC has a large effect on the probability that young, unmarried mothers will live independently rather than with their parents.

Generally, some of the more recent papers on the effects of welfare on female headship suggest that more weight than is probably warranted has been placed on the welfare-female headship relationship. David Ellwood and Jonathan Crane (1990) demonstrate that the claim that generosity of welfare benefits is primarily responsible for the transformation of the Black family is misleading.[25] The authors use data reported in Table 12-4 on the welfare benefit levels and the proportion of Black children not living with two parents and the proportion of all children in families that received AFDC. The data reveals that real benefits increased from $7,652 (1988 dollars) in

20. See Stephen J. Bahr, "The Effects of Welfare on Marital Stability and Remarriage," *Journal of Marriage and the Family* 41 (3) (August 1979): 553–60.
21. See Hoffman and Holmes, "Husbands, Wives and Divorce."
22. See Robert M. Hutchens, "Welfare Remarriage and Marital Search," *American Economic Review* 69 (3) (1979): 369–79.
23. See Mark Rank, "The Formation and Dissolution of Marriages in the Welfare Population," *Journal of Marriage and the Family* 49 (1) (1987): 15–20.
24. David Ellwood and Mary Jo Bane, "The Impact of AFDC on Family Structure and Living Arrangements," Report to U.S. Department of Health and Human Services, 1984.
25. David T. Ellwood and Jonathan Crane, "Family Change Among Black Americans: What Do We Know?" *The Journal of Economic Perspectives* 4 (4) (Fall 1990): 47–84.

Table 12-4   Welfare benefit levels, percent of Black children not with two parents, and percent of Black children in families collecting AFDC, 1960, 1970, 1980, 1988

	1960	*1970*	*1980*	*1988*
AFDC and food stamp payment level (family of four with no income, 1988 dollars)	$7,324	$9,900	$8,325	$7,741
Percent of Black children not living with two parents	33.0	41.5	57.8	61.4
Estimated percent of Black children in families collecting AFDC	10.4	33.6	34.9	30.1

Source: Ellwood and Crane, Table 3, p. 73.

1960 to $9,900 (in 1988 dollars) in 1970. Benefits declined through the 1970s such that by 1988, real benefits had declined to $7,741 (1988 dollars).[26] This means that real benefits to mother-only households fell considerably. Thus, if benefits are that important in explaining female headship, we should have observed a decline in the number of female-headed households. This did not happen.

The data reported in Table 12-4 also reveals that the proportion of children not living with two parents rose steadily through the period between 1960 and 1988 with the largest increase occurring between 1970 and 1980. This was the period when benefits were declining. The third row shows that the proportion of children living in families that were receiving AFDC also increased rapidly between 1960 and 1970 and actually declined between 1970 and 1988. Thus, between 1970 and 1988, although more children were not living with two parents, fewer children were in families that were receiving AFDC. The data suggests that the role of welfare benefits in causing female headship probably is exaggerated.

It is easy to blame welfare for the transformation of the American family. Nevertheless, there is a lot of doubt concerning the validity of the claimed welfare-female headship causality. Thus, although many believe that welfare causes female headship, it is important to note that this issue is not resolved and unqualified statements to the effect that welfare leads to female headship may be irresponsible.

---

26. The benefits reached the highest level in 1972 and have declined since then.

Marriage Markets: The Supply of Marriageable Males

Although female headship has increased across all racial groups, this phenomenon is much more pronounced among black families. As mentioned earlier, Charles Murray attributes the increase in female headship among Black families almost entirely to welfare benefits.[27] Other researchers, however, believe that female headship among Black families is primarily due to unfavorable marriage markets. According to William Darity, Jr. and Samuel Myers, female headship among Blacks reflects a scarcity of suitable male marriage partners.[28] Many potential Black male partners are in jail, are drug addicts, or have been killed by other Blacks in the inner cities. Basically, Darity and Myers suggest that institutional factors have led to the plight of the Black male (both economically and socially). Consequently, Black females are left with only a few men to compete for, making probability of getting married low. As such, many women make a rational decision to have children out of wedlock. Because of their low labor market potential, many of these women end up on welfare. In other words, while one may observe many single Black women with children on welfare, it is not the availability of welfare that causes such female headship. Rather, it is female headship (which arises due to shortage of males) that leads to welfare use.[29]

Changes in Social Norms and Attitudes

A final factor that may have contributed to increased female headship is a change in how society views mother-only households. Although some decades ago divorce and premarital sex were considered unacceptable, this is not true today. The stigma associated with out-of-wedlock births has disappeared and mother-only households have become an acceptable alternative to two-parent households in many communities. It is not clear, however, whether changes in attitudes have contributed to female headship or

---

27. Charles Murray, *Losing Ground.*
28. William Darity, Jr. and Samuel L. Myers, "Changes in Black Family Structure: Implications for Welfare Dependency," American Economic Association, *Papers and Proceedings* (May 1983): 59-64. This point also is made by William Julius Wilson and Katherine M. Neckerman. Wilson and Neckerman consider marriageable men as those who have jobs. See Wilson and Neckerman, "Poverty and Family Structure: The Widening Gap Between Evidence and Public Policy Issues," in Sheldon Danziger and Daniel Weinberg, eds., *Fighting Poverty: What Works and What Doesn't* (Cambridge, Mass.: Harvard University Press, 1986), pp. 232–59.
29. The direction of causality has important implications concerning the appropriate public policy. If welfare is the culprit as Murray contends, then the solution to reducing poverty in Black families may key on reducing welfare benefits or reforming eligibility requirements. Such policies would keep many families intact and thus reduce their probability of being poor. Conversely, if the supply of males is the main cause of female headship, then policies should aim to improve the economic status of Black males.

whether attitudes have changed following the changes in family structure. Nevertheless, a woman who decides to have a child outside the traditional two-parent household will find society more accommodating today than it was in the past.

CAUSES AND CONSEQUENCES OF POVERTY OF MOTHER-ONLY HOUSEHOLDS

Causes of Poverty

Having discussed the poverty among female-headed households and also the various factors that have been responsible for the rapid increase in female headship, let us now consider the causes of poverty in mother-only households. Data show that single-parent households headed by males, although few, do not experience the problems of poverty that face single-mother households. Thus, it is not just because a household has a single parent that determines its poverty status, but whether the single parent head of household is male or female. It is important to understand why female-headed households are so susceptible to poverty.

The poverty of female-headed households is caused by the various factors that generally cause poverty. However, some factors specifically affect female-headed households more severely than other groups: low earnings capacity, inadequate child support from the noncustodial parent, and low welfare benefits.

1. *Low earnings capacity*–Female heads of households face extremely poor labor market prospects—both in terms of employment opportunities and pay. Unemployment and low-wage employment are more prevalent among females who are heads of households than among other groups. Generally speaking, women earn less than men, and therefore have a more difficult time supporting a family. Many single mothers have children while still young and thereby limit their opportunities to acquire human capital through formal education and on-the-job training. Moreover, women tend to enter the labor market much later in life than men and have less seniority. They are not as well protected from layoffs and may not qualify for unemployment compensation after experiencing a job loss. In addition, because they have to care for children (thus spending time out of the labor force) their labor market experience is limited. These problems are compounded by labor market discrimination. Even for those female heads of households who work full-time, the largest percentage earn wages that are too low to lift their family out of poverty.

Particular problems that confront low-income single mothers with young children are welfare policies and the availability of affordable child care. Children seriously affect the labor market prospects of single mothers. A single mother must arrange for day care and have the resources to pay for these services. Given the low wages earned by single mothers, child care itself may take a big portion of the earnings. Child care reduces the benefits of work considerably. Many mothers find it better to withdraw from the labor force or to work part-time. Of course, single mothers with low incomes are eligible for welfare benefits, but those who enter the labor market find that their welfare benefits are reduced considerably. Thus, working does not supplement earnings but rather substitutes for welfare benefits.[30]

2. *Inadequate or nonexistent child support*–Female heads of households shoulder the burden of two parents. After a divorce or separation, the income of the noncustodial parent may not be adversely affected, but that of the custodial parent is. The economic hardship of the custodial parent (often the mother) arises because alimony or child support payments from the absent parent are either nonexistent or inadequate. For never-married single mothers, child support rarely is paid.[31] Thus, little or no support from fathers is one of the main causes of poverty in female-headed households.

Irwin Garfinkel and Sara McLanahan estimate that only about 40 percent of White fathers and 19 percent of Black fathers pay any child support.[32] Even for those who pay, the amounts are low and account only for a small proportion of the female-headed households' total income (approximately 10 percent of White single mothers' income and 3.5 percent of single Black mothers' income). Sheila Kamerman and Alfred Kahn report that of all women eligible to receive child support, only 61.3 received such support in 1985.[33] For those mothers who received payment, less than half received the full amount. Nonpayment of child support is more chronic among Black families, never-married mothers, and the poor, the same groups that most need such support.

3. *Low welfare benefits*–Poverty rates among mother-only households would have been much lower if public transfers were more generous. Generally, benefits to single-parent households are quite low as compared to the income gap. For example, compared to widows, the poverty of single women who head families is much higher. Widows, although they may not work, receive benefits through the Survivors Insurance program

---

30. The incentive effects of the welfare system are discussed in Chapter 14. Chapter 15 discusses some of the same issues in relation to reforming the welfare system.
31. This is due partly to the fact that the mother must first prove paternity before child support payments can be ordered by a judge. A more detailed discussion of child support policies is discussed in Chapter 13.
32. Irwin Garfinkel and Sara S. McLanahan, *Single Mothers and Their Children: A New American Dilemma* (Washington, D.C.: The Urban Institute Press, 1986).
33. Sheila B. Kamerman and Alfred J. Kahn, *Mothers Alone: Strategies for a Time of Change* (Dover, Mass.: Auburn House Publishing Co., 1988).

that is much more generous than the Aid to Families with Children (AFDC) program available to single parents. Thus, those who receive AFDC benefits still remain below the poverty line. As already mentioned, attempts by single mothers to supplement meager public transfer benefits are penalized by the imposition of a high implicit tax on AFDC benefits.

Consequences of Poverty in Female-Headed Households

The current state of poverty among female-headed households adversely affects the welfare of children and their prospects of future success. Similar to other children of poor families, children of poor female heads grow up with limited resources, poor nutrition, inadequate medical services, and often receive limited investment in human capital. These factors deprive children of the opportunity to improve their future earnings potential. The most detrimental consequence of poverty in mother-only households is that such poverty frequently is associated with the intergenerational transmission of poverty.[34]

Evidence shows that being in a one-parent family has a negative effect on IQ scores. Other measures of academic performance show significant differences between children in single- and two-parent families. For example, children from single-parent households have much lower grade point averages and have more behavioral problems in school than those from two-parent families. Other indicators of school performance reveal that children from mother-only households grade lower; have lower probabilities of finishing and graduating from high school; and have higher dropout rates than children from two-parent families.

Likewise, measures of occupational status reveal that children from mother-only households have lower occupational status scores and command much lower earnings than their counterparts who grow up in two-parent families. This evidence implies that female headship initiates a cycle of poverty that children find difficult to escape.[35]

Evidence also suggests that children who grow up in mother-only households tend to have less satisfying interpersonal relationships. For example, daughters of single parents marry at younger ages, have higher divorce rates,

---

34. See Marybeth Shinn, "Father Absence and Children's Cognitive Development," *Psychological Bulletin* 85 (1978): 295–324; Elizabeth Herzog and Cecilia Sudia, "Children in Fatherless Families," in B. Caldwell and H. Ricciuti, eds., *Review of Child Development Research* 3 (Chicago: University of Chicago Press, 1973); and E. Mavis Hetherington, "Children and Divorce," in R. Henderson, ed., *Parent-Child Interaction: Theory, Research and Prospect* (New York: Academic Press, 1981).
35. See Otis Dudley Duncan, David Featherman, and Beverly Duncan, *Socioeconomic Background and Achievement* (New York: Seminar Press, 1972).

and have a higher probability of having children out-of-wedlock.[36] Thus, female headship is transmitted from one generation to another.[37]

As noted earlier, many low-income female-headed households rely on welfare transfers as one of their primary sources of income. An increasing body of literature suggests that welfare dependency is transmitted from mother to daughter. Presumably, daughters in female-headed households become socialized into using welfare and accepting welfare use as just another source of income. Thus, children from families that rely on welfare become heavily dependent on welfare themselves.[38]

The intergenerational consequences of female headship arise not only because of economic deprivation, but also because of too little parental interaction. For example, children who grow up in mother-only households spend less time under the care of a parent and this deprives them of the parental nurture and supervision that other children receive. On the one hand, the father is absent most of the time. On the other hand, the mother has to work most of the time and hence has limited time with the children.

FEMALE HEADSHIP AND PUBLIC POLICY

Two broad issues should guide the formulation of public policies to alleviate the poverty of female-headed households. First, policy should address those factors that lead to female headship. To the extent that female headship is associated with poverty, public policy could focus on manipulating those causal factors in a way that discourages female headship. Nevertheless, there will still be poor families headed by females. Second, policy should address those factors that cause poverty in female-headed households. Although there are limitations to the use of these approaches, a combination of policies could improve the economic well-being of mother-only families.

The evidence suggests that general economic conditions are particularly important in influencing marital stability and marriage rates. One can expect female headship to continue rising if the economic position of males continues to worsen. The economic position of non-White males merits special attention and policies to improve their employability and to increase their employment opportunities must be central to reducing female headship in non-White families.

---

36. See Larry L. Bumpass and James A. Sweet, "Differentials in Marital Instability: 1970," *American Sociological Review* 37 (6) (December 1972): 754–66.
37. The issue of the intergenerational transmission of female headship was alluded to in Chapter 11 in the discussion of the culture of poverty.
38. Intergenerational transmission of welfare dependency is covered in more detail in Chapter 16.

Female headship also has been influenced by the rising labor force participation of females and by the changing attitudes about mother-only households. Although the government could influence behavior by offering counseling and guidance about sexual behavior, little can be done to influence societal attitudes. Likewise, the trend in labor force participation is likely to continue and it is not desirable for the government to alter these trends. Because these changes in society affect female headship (given the association between female headship and poverty) government should deal with the causes of poverty discussed earlier.

Similar policies should address the labor market problems of single mothers. For example, the lack of affordable child care acts as a significant hinderance to earning labor market incomes. A policy that provides affordable child care would increase the labor force participation rates of single mothers. Single mothers frequently have low labor market skills and thus, even when they get jobs, they earn low wages. Programs for skill and job development (as discussed in Chapter 6) should be targeted on single mothers.

Any serious effort to alleviate the hardships experienced by mother-only families must start by reforming child support policies that are in place today. There is no question that child support in the United States is inadequate and urgently needs reform. Although many states have increased their efforts in assuring that absent parents pay child support, much more needs to be done not only in making sure that payments are made but that the level of payments is substantially higher. A more detailed discussion on possible directions of reforming the child support policies is provided in Chapter 13.

Finally, even if full child support is paid, many single mothers would still remain below the poverty line. The income gap could be filled by welfare payments. This would require policies that make welfare benefits much more generous than they are today. However, it has been shown that more attractive benefits have adverse effects on the family. Furthermore, as will be seen in Chapter 14, welfare benefits adversely affect the supply of labor. Thus, welfare policies need to be designed in a manner that takes the welfare of single-mother households into consideration and balances the negative effects of those policies that exacerbate poverty. These issues are detailed in Chapter 15.

SUMMARY

Female headship is increasingly becoming a major cause of poverty in the United States. This chapter has considered the changing trends in family structure and the increasing incidence of poverty among female-headed households. Most of the discussion has focused on explaining the causes of female headship and poverty in those households. It has been noted that poverty of female-headed households is of particular concern not only because of its short-term effect on children, but also because of the negative aspects that are transmitted from one generation to another.

Several public policies to deal with family structure and poverty in female-headed households have been suggested. Although public policies may not significantly alter the trends in family structure, it is necessary that those policies that increase female headship be reevaluated. Generally, it appears that the most fruitful route is to directly confront the causes of poverty in female-headed households. Some policies that are likely to slow the disintegration of the two-parent family and to improve the well-being of female-headed households include improving the economic position of males, enhancing the employability of single mothers, and reforming child support and welfare policies.

STUDY AND DISCUSSION QUESTIONS

1. Discuss the various factors that have been responsible for the transformation of the American Family.

2. Critically evaluate the common view that welfare benefits have been primarily responsible for the increase in female headship.

3. Discuss the main causes of poverty among female-headed households.

4. One concern about the poverty of mother-only households is that it is transmitted from one generation to the next. Explain how such transmission of poverty occurs.

5. What policies can the government adopt to strengthen two-parent households?

6. To some extent, the increased female headship concerns the economic position of the males. Discuss this issue in relation to divorce, separation, and out-of-wedlock births.

7. Suppose there was convincing evidence to the effect that female headship itself causes poverty. Would that provide justification for limited support to those types of families? In other words, should children in mother-only households be considered *deserving* poor.

8. Do you consider the argument that many Black females choose to have children out-of-wedlock because of unfavorable marriage markets credible? Discuss factors that could have been responsible for the low supply of marriageable Black males.

9. Compare data of births to unmarried women in different developed countries. Try to provide explanations for the observed patterns.

10. Discuss some of the policies that could be used to deal with the poverty of mother-only households.

ADDITIONAL READINGS

1. Auletta, Kenneth. *The Underclass.* New York: Random House, 1982.

2. Baldwin, Wendy H. "Adolescent Pregnancy and Child Bearing—Growing Concerns for Americans," *Population Bulletin* 31 (2) (September 1976): 3–34.

3. Bauman, Karl E., and J. Richard Udry. "The Differences in Unwanted Births Between Blacks and Whites," *Demography* 10 (3) (August 1973): 315–28.

4. Bowerman, C. E., D. P. Irish, and H. Pope. *Unwed Motherhood—Personal and Social Consequences.* Chapel Hill, N.C.: Institute for Research in the Social Sciences, 1986.

5. Cherlin, Andrew J. *Marriage, Divorce, Remarriage.* Cambridge: Harvard University Press, 1986.

6. McAnarney, E. R. and G. Stickle, eds. *Pregnancy and Childbearing During Adolescence: Research Priorities for the 1980s.* New York: Alan R. Liss, 1981.

7. Pope, H. and C. W. Mueller. "The Intergenerational Transmission of Marital Instability: Comparisons by Race and Sex," *Journal of Social Issues* 32 (1) (1976): 49–66.

13

CHILD SUPPORT

Chapter 12 studied the issue of female headship in the United States. It was demonstrated that female headship has become an important feature of the American family. Divorce, separation, and out-of-wedlock births have become fairly common, consequently a large number of children now spend part or all their life in a mother-only household. Between 1970 and 1990, female-headed households with children under 18 years of age increased by 146 percent and the number of such two-parent households declined by 3 percent. Between this period, the number of children with a divorced parent more than doubled and the number of children with a never-married parent grew nearly ninefold. Thus, in 1990, 15.9 million children under the age of 18 lived with one parent, 94 percent more than in 1970. Of the 15.9 million children under 18 who lived with only one parent, 87 percent lived with their mothers and 13 percent lived with their fathers. In 1990, over half of all Black children lived in a home in which no father was present.[1]

The numbers presented suggest that there is a need to be concerned about the welfare of children who grow up in one-parent households. Of particular concern are the high poverty rates that many children in female-headed households experience. For example, in 1990, nearly 45 percent of the 7.7 million families maintained solely by the mother with children under 18 had incomes below the poverty threshold. In addition, just over 8 percent of the mothers of these poor children worked full-time full year. The poverty experienced by mother-only households has much to do with the excessive burden placed on them. Generally, single parents play a dual role; not only are they responsible for the regular child-rearing responsibilities but they also are expected to provide for the family. In a two-parent

---

1. United States Congress, Committee on Ways and Means, *Background Material and Data on Programs Within the Jurisdiction of the Committee on Ways and Means* (Washington, D.C.: U.S. Government Printing Office, 1992).

setting, the responsibilities are shared. In most cases one parent bears most of the child-rearing burden while the other is responsible for providing for the family. Thus, married women with young children rarely work full-time full year. For example, during the early 1990s, approximately 30 percent of married women with children worked full-time full year. It is clearly unreasonable to expect single mothers to work full-time full year while still providing nurture to children. Given that mother-only households have become prevalent, there is need to formulate policies that extend sufficient support to those households. One of the policy issues that has become increasingly important in dealing with poverty of single-parent households focuses on child support. Poverty among children in mother-only households could be reduced significantly if a better child support system were in place.

Essentially, there are two types of child support systems in the United States: public and private. Public child support is provided as welfare benefits to families with children. Programs such as Aid to Families with Dependent Children (AFDC) and programs that extend medical and food benefits to children are part of the public support system. Private child support involves financial contribution by the nonresident parent to the resident parent to offset some of the costs of bringing up the children.[2] As observed in Chapter 12, one cause of the very high child poverty rates in mother-only households (as compared to the child poverty rates in households with a male head) is the failure of the absent parent to provide child support.[3] In many cases, nonresident parents do not pay any child support. Even when child support is paid, the amounts frequently are very low.

The public child support system is an important policy for fighting poverty in mother-only households. A number of means-tested programs play an important role in improving the well-being of children in poor households. Public child support policies and other income maintenance programs are examined in Chapter 14. This chapter focuses on the private child support system in the United States. First, some of the elements of the U.S child support system are discussed. As will be shown, one major problem relating to child support concerns the determination of the appropriate award. Some of the suggested approaches to determining how much a nonresident parent should contribute toward raising the children will be studied. Finally, there is a discussion of an innovative child support approach (the Child Support Assurance System) suggested by researchers at the University of Wisconsin.

---

2. The terms *absent* and *noncustodial* parent are frequently used to refer to nonresident parents. The use of the terms *resident* and *nonresident* parent is more inclusive in discussing the various situations in which parents with children do not live together. This chapter uses resident parent to refer to the parent who resides with the child (or children) and nonresident parent as one who does not reside with the child (or children). As has been noted previously, the resident parent often is the mother.

3. The phrase "deadbeat dads" is now used to refer to fathers who fail to meet their child support obligations. Cases of "deadbeat moms" also are increasing.

THE U.S. PRIVATE CHILD SUPPORT SYSTEM

For some time now, Congress has made efforts to increase child support payments made by nonresident parents. The first federal legislation to deal with the problem of child support was in 1950 when Section 402(a)(11) was added to the Social Security Act. Section 402 required that state welfare agencies notify law enforcement officials when AFDC was provided to deserted or abandoned children. The notification procedure had little impact in increasing child support payments. Social Security amendments in 1962 included a provision for federal aid for locating absent parents. Similar legislation in 1965 provided that state and local welfare agencies could obtain information about the place and address of employment of an absent parent from the Secretary of Health, Education, and Welfare for enforcement of parental obligations. Changes in the Social Security Act adopted in 1967 encouraged states to obtain contributions from parents who were financially able and also provided various means through which absent parents could be located and be required to make contributions. States were required to make efforts in the enforcement of child support obligations and to establish paternity. Nevertheless, these efforts met limited success, particularly because of weak enforcement. As the number of children living in one-parent households increased accompanied by increased welfare recipient rates, it became clear that there was a need to adopt serious reforms in the child support system.

The urgency to reform the private child support system was accelerated by findings of a 1971 Rand study.[4] This study, which was presented to the Senate, showed that many poor families, particularly those on welfare, could not afford the costly legal process necessary to initiate child support payments. As a result, many parents did not take action against the nonresident parents. In addition, the report found that the court systems, judges, and lawyers were not receptive to child support cases and many found them boring. Also, state welfare agencies were not interested in enforcing child support obligations after a court order had been issued.

In 1975, Congress established the Child Support Enforcement program (CSE) as Title IV-D of the Social Security Act. CSE was the first significant legislation toward strict enforcement of child support obligations. The CSE program provided federal funding for a public bureaucracy to enforce child support payments. CSE established the Federal Office of Child Support Enforcement with the responsibility for locating absent parents, establishing paternity, and obtaining child and spousal support. Title IV-D required all states to establish a corresponding agency. In addition, states were required to seek to establish paternity of all children receiving AFDC

---

4. See W. Winston and T. Forsher, *Nonsupport of Legitimate Children by Affluent Fathers As a Cause of Poverty and Welfare Dependence*, report by the Rand Corporation presented to the U.S. Senate, 1971.

and also provide such services to non-AFDC mothers if they requested the services. Although most of the enforcement responsibility was left to the states, CSE reimbursed up to 75 percent of the enforcement costs incurred by the states.

The U.S. child support system involves four steps: (1) *identification,* and (2) *location of the nonresident parent,* (3) *determination of the amount of award,* and (4) *actual payment of the award by the nonresident parent to the resident parent.*

Identification

Identification of the nonresident parent is straightforward in divorce and separation cases. If the court awards custody to one parent, the other parent automatically is considered the nonresident parent and the one who is expected to make child support payments to the resident (custodial) parent.[5]

The story is different for unwed mothers. For this group of resident parents, paternity must be established before child support obligation is imposed. Although it is true that most mothers know the fathers of their children, in some cases there could be several possibilities and the mother might not actually know who the father of the child is. In other cases, some mothers may not want to disclose the child's father. This could be because of the feeling that disclosure could jeopardize the relationship with the man. In some cases, it could be that the mother has been threatened by the father. Frequently, however, many women do name the fathers. Men who are named as the fathers can contest the allegation. The Family Support Act of 1988 includes provisions to strengthen the establishment of paternity. States are required to increase the number of cases in which they establish paternity, either by establishing paternity in 50 percent of AFDC out-of-wedlock cases or increasing the proportion of such cases in which they establish paternity by 3 percentage points each year. States also are required to obtain social security numbers of both parents at the time of application for a birth certificate. Additionally, the act requires that all parties in a contested paternity case take a genetic blood test upon the request of any party. The federal government pays 90 percent of the costs of those tests.

Before modern genetic techniques for establishing paternity were in common use, a respondent in a paternity suit could escape child support liability by obtaining the testimony of other men to the effect that they had sexual access with the mother of the child. Such a strategy limited the number of paternity cases filed because there was no clear way of identifying the father. Modern genetic testing has now solved such problems, as paternity can be established with almost 100 percent certainty.

---

5. This is not strictly correct. Sometimes someone else could be the father of the children as is common in cases where the mother was married before or had a child out of wedlock.

In 1989, there were 1,094,169 out-of-wedlock births in the United States. Of these births, paternity under Title IV-D was established for 31 percent of the cases. The number of out-of-wedlock births for which paternity is established varies widely across the states. In 1989, there were 20,708 out-of-wedlock births in the state of Arizona. Paternity under Title IV-D was established in 6.4 percent of the cases. In the same year, there were 21,123 out-of-wedlock births in the state of Missouri and paternity was established for 52.8 percent of these cases.

Locating Nonresident Parent

After identification, the nonresident must be located. This can be, and frequently is, a problem. Before child support obligations can be enforced, the alleged parent must be informed of his right to contest the allegation. If the location of the nonresident parent is not known, the notification process could take time and be costly. Even though it is possible to meet the notification requirements by demonstrating that good faith efforts have been made to contact the alleged parent, it would still be impossible to enforce child support obligations until the nonresident parent is located. To deal with the problem of locating parents, State Parent Locator Services (SPLS) have been established with state CSE offices. SPLS attempts to locate parents by contacting other state agencies such as motor vehicle divisions, department of taxation, the employment commission, and military branches. To facilitate out-of-state searches, SPLS refers cases to the Federal Parent Locator Service (FPLS). FPLS is a computer network run by the federal government for the purpose of locating absent parents who are responsible, and have failed to provide financial support, to minor dependents.

Determination of Child Support Award

The next step involves the determination of the award. Generally, there are two approaches that could be used to establish the appropriate amount of child support award.[6] The first is the *resource sharing approach*. The premise of the resource sharing approach is that children are entitled to share in the resource of both parents proportionately. Thus, children should not suffer a decline in the standard of living in the event of their parents' divorce. In the case of out-of-wedlock births, the resource sharing approach implies that children are entitled to benefit from the resources of both parents even though the parents never got married.

---

6. For a detailed discussion on this subject, see Barbara Bergman, "Setting Appropriate Levels of Child Support Payments," in Judith Cassetty, ed., *The Parental Child-Support Obligation* (Lexington, Mass.: Lexington Books, 1983), Chapter 8.

The second approach is the *cost sharing approach*. According to this method, parents should share in the cost of raising children. The use of the cost approach raises several problems. It is well known that the cost of raising children will depend on the resources available. Thus, if the children live with a poor mother, their standard of living, and therefore the cost will be low. If child support obligations are then based on the cost, the absent parent will be responsible only for low benefits even if he or she has a high income. However, if the resident parent has high income, costs incurred could be quite high and the nonresident parent may be required to make unusually high payments. Because single mothers with children generally have lower incomes than their former husbands, nonresident fathers could end up paying much lower child support than is adequate to maintain the standard of living that children had before divorce if the cost-sharing approach is used.

One particular problem that has plagued child support policies in the United States has been the lack of uniform standards for establishing the appropriate amount of award owed by the absent parent. Thus, the amount of child support traditionally has been determined by courts on a case-by-case basis. The result has been a child support system that treats fathers in similar circumstances unequally and one that places a higher burden on low-income nonresident parents and a relatively low burden on nonresident parents who have higher incomes. Research by Irwin Garfinkel and others shows wide variation in the amount of child support set by courts.[7] The variations across states are particularly large. Furthermore, the child support award seems to favor the absent father as compared to the resident mother and her children. The reason for the lack of uniformity was that in the past, state guidelines were not explicit and were merely advisory. As such, child support awards depended upon disparate state guidelines and the discretion of judges.

In 1984, Congress took steps to reduce variation among state guidelines and instructed the Department of Health and Human Services to establish a uniform approach to setting such guidelines. The Department of Health and Human Services commissioned a study to investigate a way of setting uniform child support payments. The result was what is called the Williams Report.[8] The report proposed the use of the "cost of children" in setting the child support award. Additional pressure was placed on states to establish and enforce child support payments in 1988 when Congress required that by 1989 each state should have in place a set of mandatory judicial guidelines for determining child support payments.

---

7. See, for example, Irwin Garfinkel, "The Evolution of Child Support Policy," Focus 11 (1) (Spring 1988): 11–16.
8. Robert G. Williams, *Development of Guidelines for Establishing and Updating Child Support Orders: Interim Report* (Williamsburg, Va.: National Center for State Courts, 1985).

After a state decides on a cost-based child support payments system, it must establish a scheme to estimate the cost of children. Establishing the cost of children is not easy. Of course, one could use a straightforward approach by adding up all explicit and implicit costs attributable to raising children. However, such a method is bound to result in large errors. For example, it may be difficult to establish which member of the household consumed particular items (or fractions thereof). Furthermore, because many goods and services are consumed jointly, such as heating and electricity, it is difficult to impute the cost to individual family members. A straightforward approach of establishing cost is complicated by economies of scale in household consumption.

Even after deciding on how to calculate the cost of children, a formula must be established that would be used to distribute the cost between the resident and nonresident parents. A number of formulae have been proposed and some are used in various states. Only brief discussion of the main elements of these formulae are covered here. The reader should note that each formula results in a different outcome in terms of the amount paid by the absent parent.[9]

Maintenance Support Formula–This formula starts from the premise that children should not face economic deprivation because of their parents' divorce. In other words, the adverse financial circumstances that result from divorce should not be borne by the children. Thus, the nonresident parent should be obligated to pay the resident parent child support amounts that maintain the child's economic well-being at the predivorce level. This formula places the burden of lost economies of scale on the nonresident parent.

Rawlsian Child Support Formula–The Rawlsian formula is based on the normative theory of optimal distribution formulated by Rawls as was discussed in Chapter 2. The Rawlsian formula seeks to maximize the minimum welfare achieved by both the resident and nonresident parent's household. This formula equalizes the well-being of the two households. Thus, all the available income is divided between the two households according to the number of adults. Based on this formula, the cost of lost economies of scale is shared by both parents.

Utilitarian Formula–As outlined in Chapter 2, the utilitarian theory of optimal distribution seeks an allocation of income such that social welfare is maximized. This requires that a dollar be transferred to the person who derives most utility from it. In the case of child support, dollars should be transferred to the custodian household for so long as the gain in utility to the custodian household is greater than the loss in utility experienced by

---

9. For a comparison of the various formulae, see David Betson, Eirik Evenhouse, Siobhan Reilly, and Eugene Smolensky, "Trade-Offs Implicit in Child-Support Guidelines," *Journal of Policy Analysis and Management* 11 (1) (1992): 1–20.

the noncustodial parent. Thus, according to this formula, the child support award will be at the level where the loss of utility to nonresident from the transfer of an additional dollar exactly equals the resident household's gain in utility as a result of that additional dollar. Such an outcome would lead to maximum welfare for the two households. Increasing the child support obligation above that level would imply that utility loss to nonresident parent exceeds the utility gain by resident household and thus total utility would decline.

A slight modification of the utilitarian formula is what is called the *Equal Living Standards* formula proposed by Judith Cassetty. The Cassetty formula aims at protecting the children's well-being subject to the condition that their welfare is not higher than that of the nonresident parent who provides the support. A key element of this formula is that it expresses well-being as the ratio of household income to the relevant official poverty line.

Income Shares Formula–The basic premise of the income shares formula is that children are entitled to the same share of income as they had in the intact household. The amount which was spent on children is based on the measure of "cost of children" and the cost is assumed to have been shared by parents in proportion to the income of each. In computing the child support using this formula, the income of the absent parent is divided by the combined incomes of both parents, thus yielding the fraction of absent parent's income to total. This is the fraction of the child costs that the non-resident parent is expected to bear. The fraction is then multiplied by the estimated cost of children to arrive at the child support owed by the absent parent.

The Melson Formula–The premise of the Melson Formula is that although the needs of the parents are important, those of the children should come first. Therefore, until the needs of the children are met, a parent is not entitled to retain any income beyond the minimum necessary to keep him or her in the workforce. After the basic needs of children are met, the children are entitled to a fixed share of the income left over.

The Maintenance Support, Rawlsian, Utilitarian, and Equal Living Standards formulae are based on normative theories of distributive justice and are not used in any of the states. The Income Shares Formula (or variants of this formula) has been adopted in most states and a few others have adopted the Melson Formula. Although the other formulae are not used, they are important in that they can be used as benchmarks to evaluate how the other formulae perform in terms of the desired goals.

Note that the various formulae are oversimplified. The formulae are discussed in the context of divorce and where one parent has sole custody. Each formulae would require modification in case of joint custody. Presence of other children, natural or stepchildren as a result of remarriage complicates the allocation of resources and also raises important questions about fairness. For example, would it be fair to require a father to pay the same amount to children of a previous marriage when he has a new family? In other words, is it fair to deprive children from a new marriage's resources because their father had children from another marriage? On the other hand, if allowances are made for new families, there is a concern that fathers may not be able to support all the children, thus defeating the goals of child support policy.

Compliance

After identification and location of the nonresident parent, and after the amount of the award has been established, the issue of payment must be settled. Since 1975, child support payments collected on behalf of children on welfare have been made to the state welfare departments. Before 1984, all child support payments collected on behalf of children on welfare went directly to offset AFDC benefits. Thus, if child support payments were less or equal to the AFDC grant, the custodial parent did not get any benefit from the child support collections. Amendments adopted in 1984 allows custodial parent to retain the first $50 of child support payments. Thus, child support payments do not supplement the incomes of poor children, but are a substitute for AFDC benefits.

Before 1975, resident nonwelfare parents were responsible for collecting overdue child support payments from nonresident parents. This involved seeking a court order requiring the nonresident parent to make the child support payments. After the order was issued, it was then the responsibility of the resident parent to follow up in getting the payments. If payments were not made as stipulated in the court order, the resident parent could then initiate legal action. Since 1975, even nonwelfare cases are enforced by the child support enforcement agencies. If a nonresident parent fails to pay the required obligations, the court has a number of options, including wage garnishment and jail terms. Under Public Law 98-378 enacted in 1983, liens can be imposed against real property for the amount of overdue support owed by a nonresident parent. Such a lien for delinquent child support provides the resident parent with nonpossessory interest in property belonging to the nonresident parent. Thus, the nonresident parent cannot transfer ownership and may find it difficult to use the property to secure credit. As an additional procedure for enforcing child support payments, states are required to report to consumer reporting agencies (credit bureaus) if child support obligations exceed $1000. Still, there are wide variations in the way that these punitive measures are enforced across the states, and from one person to the other.

Amendments passed in 1984 and in 1988 as part of the Family Support Act significantly strengthened the child support enforcement program. States are required to thoroughly seek to establish paternity and adopt procedures obtaining support orders. A key provision of the 1984 amendments required states to withhold child support obligations from wages and all other income sources of nonresident parents who become one-month delinquent in child support payments. This was a major step in the enforcement of child support. The 1988 Family Support Act requires that beginning in 1994, states should implement automatic wage withholding in all new child support cases.

For the most part, the U.S. child support system has been a failure. Data shows that even where child support awards have been ordered, compliance is low. Of all women living with children eligible for child support in 1979, only 13.7 percent of Black, 42.6 percent of White, and 24 percent of Spanish origin, received any child support. Never-married women have the lowest child support recipiency rates. Although 51 percent of divorced women received some child support in 1979, only 6.3 percent of never-married women received such support in the same year.[10] More recent data reveals that little has changed in terms of child support payments. In 1985, only 54 percent of divorced, 28 percent of separated, and 11 percent of never-married women eligible for child support award received any.[11] The issue of child support is of particular concern because those parents who need support most also are the ones least likely to receive any such support. For example, for women who were on welfare (AFDC) in 1977 who had children eligible for child support, only 5.4 percent Black, 15.3 percent White, and 8.2 percent of Spanish origin, received any child support.[12]

Recent trends in child support payments are more promising, but still remain low. As shown in Table 13-1, in 1989, of the nearly 10 million women who had children present under the age of 21 from a noncustodial father, 42 percent were never awarded child support rights, nor did they have an agreement to receive child support payments. Thus, women depend on income sources other than the father. The number of poor mothers without child support award was 57 percent. Even then, however, of the poor mothers who were supposed to receive child support in 1989, 32 percent did not receive that support.

The level of payments also is of serious concern. Table 13-1 shows that in 1989, the mean child support received was $2995 which was only about 19 percent of the average total income. In 1978, the mean child support payment was $1800 and accounted for about 20 percent of the women's income. Thus, although there have been efforts to increase the proportion

10. See Current Population Reports, *Divorce, Child Custody, and Child Support,* Special Studies Series, No. 84 (Bureau of the Census, U.S. Department of Commerce, 1979), and Current Population Reports, *Child Support and Alimony,* Special Studies Series, No. 106 (Bureau of the Census, U.S. Department of Commerce, 1980).

11. U.S. Bureau of the Census, *Current Population Reports,* Series P–23, No. 152. *Child Support and Alimony, 1985* (Washington, D.C.: Government Printing Office, 1987).

12. See Current Population Reports, *Divorce, Child Custody, and Child Support,* Special Studies Series, No. 84 (Bureau of the Census, U.S. Department of Commerce, 1979), and Current Population Reports, *Child Support and Alimony,* Special Studies Series, No. 106 (Bureau of the Census, U.S. Department of Commerce, 1980).

of nonresident parents who pay child support, the amount paid still remains low. The low levels of child support payments suggest that an obvious starting point in dealing with the poverty of children is to reform the current system of private child support such that more child support award payments are made and also that the amounts set are higher. Making nonresident parents meet their responsibility in rearing children is one important strategy for fighting poverty.

It is not clear why fathers don't pay child support although a number of explanations are provided. One possible explanation could be that fathers simply cannot afford to pay; therefore noncompliance reflects lack of resources. However, as reported by Lenore Weitzman (1985), this excuse is not valid.[13] Evidence shows that in most cases, fathers have the resources and actually could pay higher than the required award. David Chambers (1979) found that 80 percent of the Michigan fathers he studied could maintain themselves quite comfortably even after paying full child support award.[14] Furthermore, some evidence shows that noncompliance is not related to income; men with low incomes are just as likely to avoid child support obligations as men with higher incomes. Irwin Garfinkel and Donald Oellerich (1989) arrived at the same conclusion that ability to pay is not the reason for noncompliance.[15] Thus, although it is true that there are some fathers who are not able to pay because of financial hardships, a large number could pay but refuse to comply.

Another possible explanation is that fathers do not consider the laws as fair or reasonable. However, no concrete evidence supports this view that men consider the laws to be unjust, although there are cases when men feel cheated, especially when they do not consider the payments as being used to support the children but rather as a supplement to the resident parent's luxurious consumption. Given the low incomes of many single mothers and the high cost of rearing children, the diversion of child support payments to luxuries is probably not that widespread.

Another common explanation for noncompliance is that the fathers' refusal to pay is in retaliation for visitation problems. Again, there is little evidence to support the validity of this claim. Most mothers who complain of noncompliance also complain about the nonresident parent's failure to visit children. Seltzer and her colleagues (1989) found that nonresident parents who visit their children frequently pay more child support.[16] Thus,

13. Lenore J. Weitzman, *The Divorce Revolution: The Unexpected Social and Economic Consequences for Women and Children in America* (New York: The Free Press, 1985).
14. David Chambers, *Making Fathers Pay: The Enforcement of Child Support* (Chicago: University of Chicago Press, 1979).
15. Irwin Garfinkel and Donald T. Oellerich, "Noncustodial Fathers' Ability to Pay Child Support," *Demography* 26 (May): 219–33.
16. Judith A. Seltzer, Nora Cate Schaeffer, and Hong-wen Chang, "Family Ties After Divorce: The Relationship Between Visiting and Paying Child Support," *Journal of Marriage and the Family*, 51 (4) (November 1989): 1013–31.

Table 13-1 Child support payments awarded and received in 1989—women with children present, by selected characteristics (women with own children under 21 years of age present from an absent father as of spring 1990)

Characteristic of Women	Total (Thousands)	Percent Awarded Child Support[1]	Supposed to Receive Child Support in 1989	Actually Received Support in 1989		
			Total (Thousands)	Percent	Mean Child Support	Mean Income
All Women						
Total	9,955	57.7	4,953	75.2	$2,995	$16,171
Current Marital Status						
Married[2]	2,531	79.0	1,685	72.1	2,931	14,469
Divorced	3,056	76.8	2,123	77.0	3,322	19,456
Separated	1,352	47.9	527	79.7	3,060	14,891
Widowed[3]	65	–	34	–	–	–
Never married	2,950	23.9	583	73.2	1,888	9,495
Race and Spanish Origin						
White	6,905	67.5	4,048	76.5	3,132	16,632
Black	2,770	34.5	791	69.7	2,263	13,898
Spanish origin[4]	1,112	40.6	364	69.8	2,965	14,758

Table 13-1   (Continued)

Characteristic of Women	Total (Thousands)	Percent Awarded Child Support[1]	Supposed to Receive Child Support in 1989	Actually Received Support in 1989		
			Total (Thousands)	Percent	Mean Child Support	Mean Income
Women Below Poverty						
Total	3,206	43.3	1,190	68.3	1,889	5,047
Current Marital Status						
Married[2]	176	72.2	106	67.0	2,275	4,351
Divorced	820	70.4	525	66.3	2,112	5,581
Separated	612	47.1	221	74.2	1,717	4,917
Widowed[3]	8	—	34	—	—	—
Never married	1,590	24.5	334	68.6	1,553	4,543
Race and Spanish Origin						
White	1,763	54.6	827	67.8	1,972	5,010
Black	1,314	29.2	325	69.8	1,674	5,174
Spanish origin[4]	536	33.0	148	63.5	1.824	4,958

Notes:
[1] Award status as of spring 1986
[2] Remarried women whose previous marriage ended in divorce
[3] Widowed women whose previous marriage ended in divorce
[4] Persons of Spanish origin may be of any race

Source: U.S. Bureau of the Census, Current Population Reports, Series P–60, No. 173, *Child Support and Alimony, 1989.*

where there are limited contacts between a nonresident parent and child, either because of visitation problems or the nonresident parent's neglect, noncompliance is higher. This still does not explain why many fathers neglect their children.

Several other factors have been observed to be important in explaining noncompliance.[17] One important consideration that explains noncompliance is the psychological stability of the nonresident parent. Parents who have alcohol or drug abuse problems are much less likely to meet their child support obligations than those who do not have such problems. Noncompliance also is higher if women are successful after divorce. However, the reverse does not always hold. Economic hardships experienced by mothers after divorce does not necessarily motivate absent fathers to meet the child support obligation. Another important factor that is related to noncompliance is if the father's remarriage results in stepchildren or if there are natural children in the father's remarriage. This probably is because of the new demands placed on the nonresident parent.

These reasons do not provide an explanation of why a large number of men neglect their procreation responsibilities. For example, why do many men father children and then not want their identity revealed? Why do men abandon women with children? The observed behavior seems to reflect the fact that males and females have different reproductive strategies. According to sociobiologists, men have a smaller investment in an individual child than mothers do, and are therefore more interested in starting new families.[18] Whether or not this is the real reason for the high rates of noncompliance in meeting child support obligations and for the tendency for males to abandon women with children, there is clearly a need for more effective enforcement of child support obligations.

PROPOSED REFORMS: THE CHILD SUPPORT ASSURANCE SYSTEM

There is no doubt that important steps have been taken toward assuring that nonresident parents meet their share of the burden in raising children. As mentioned, The Family Support Act of 1988 includes various provisions that seek to increase the number of cases in which child support payments are made. Even with the various provisions of this act, many parents still do not meet their obligations, and the system still favors absent fathers. Because of the wide variations in the responsibilities imposed on nonresi-

---

17. See Judith S. Wallerstein and Dorothy S. Huntington, "Bread and Roses: Nonfinancial Issues Related to Fathers' Economic Support of Their Children Following Divorce," in Judith Cassetty, ed., *The Parental Child-Support Obligation*, pp. 135–55.

18. See, for example, Richard Dawkins, *The Selfish Gene* (New York: Oxford University Press, 1976).

dent parents, many consider the entire system as unfair. As a result, the children who should be benefitting from such a system are shortchanged by failed and irregular payments.

The failure of absent parents to meet their child support obligation is one of the causes of poverty among mother-only households. As shown in Table 13-1, in 1989, the average child support payment was $2995. If the full amount of child support were paid, the average amount would have been $3292. Thus, even with full compliance, child support payments are extremely low and the current child support system is ineffective in lowering poverty rates. In 1989, 1.2 million of the 3.2 million women raising children alone with incomes below the poverty level were supposed to receive child support payments. Even if full payments had been made to these 1.2 million women, only 140,000 of them would have received enough income from child support to remove them from poverty. This number is only 4.4 percent of the 3.2 million poor women rasing children alone and 11.8 percent of the 1.2 million who had child support awards in place. A study by Donald Oellerich and Irwin Garfinkel found that the antipoverty effect of the current child support system is extremely low: only 2 percentage points reduction in the poverty rate over the rate in the absence of a child support system.[19] Although child support enforcement has considerable appeal as an antipoverty device, increasing collection rates is not likely to have any appreciable effects on poverty under the current child support system.[20] Nonetheless, it should be noted that child support payments could help reduce the severity of poverty experienced by many children even if they still remained in poverty. Still, there is no question that the current child support system is grossly inadequate.

The issue of child support obligation is closely tied to the entire welfare system and the issue of welfare dependency. Low-income mothers who receive no or low child support payments resort to welfare. However, the welfare system penalizes work resulting in welfare dependency. Also, as noted, one barrier to labor force participation by a single mother is the high cost of child care. Child support payments would obviously help mothers meet child care costs and increase their labor force participation rates. Such participation would increase transitions from welfare. Thus, reforming the child support system should be part and parcel of the larger welfare reform policies. In particular, for child support to be an effective antipoverty device, there is need to increase the proportion of cases with

19. Donald T. Oellerich and Irwin Garfinkel, "Alternative Child Support Regimes: Distributional Impacts and a Crude Benefit-Cost Analysis," in Sheldon H. Danzinger and Kent E. Portney, eds., *The Distributional Impacts of Public Policies* (New York: St. Martin's Press, 1988), pp. 67–86.
20. See Donald T. Oellerich and Irwin Garfinkel, "Distributional Impacts of Existing and Alternative Child Support Systems," *Policy Studies Journal* 12 (September 1983): 119–30; and Philip K. Robins, "Child Support, Welfare Dependency, and Poverty," *American Economic Review* 76 (September 1986): 768–88.

awards and also increase the award amounts. Additionally, increased child support also should accompany increased earnings.

Irwin Garfinkel has proposed a new system of child support that promises to repair the main shortcomings of the current system. Although the proposed system has not been widely tested, it seems promising and may offer hope in reforming the child support system. The proposed system, referred to as the Child Support Assurance System (CSAS) seeks to establish a uniform and enforceable child support system. The basic premise of CSAS "is that parents are responsible for sharing income with children and government is responsible for assuring that children who live apart from the parents receive the share to which they are entitled."[21]

The CSAS has three basic elements: establishment of a child support standard, a policy of routine withholding of income, and an assured child support benefit provided by the government.

Central to a fair child system is the establishment of a uniform child support standard. Garfinkel proposes the use of a percentage-of-income standard that is based on the gross income of the nonresident parent and the number of children to be supported. He proposes child support of 17 percent of the gross income of the nonresident parent for one child. The percentage of income devoted to child support increases as the number of children supported increases: 25 percent, 29 percent, 31 percent, and 34 percent, for two, three, four, and five children, respectively.

The establishment of the standard as proposed by Garfinkel would eliminate arbitrary and unjustifiable variations in the child support award. A fixed percentage of income child support award would reduce the costs involved in litigation to establish an award. In addition, a percentage of income formula allows for automatic indexing of income: when income rises, the amount of award increases even though the percentage remains the same. Thus, there is no need for the resident parent to seek a court order for an increase in the award when income of the nonresident parent increases. The uniform standard also is fair to the nonresident parent. If income declines due to illness or unemployment, then the amount of child support obligation drops automatically.

The next element of the CSAS is routine income withholding. As observed, many of the absent parents do not pay the full amount of child support that they are obligated to pay. To increase the amount of child support payments, the CSAS proposal requires that once an award is determined, the amount should be withheld from the paycheck and subsequently sent to the resident parent. Withholding would ensure that payments are made in a regular, timely manner. Withholding also prevents the accumulation of unpaid child support that otherwise may never be paid.

---

21. Irwin Garfinkel, *Assuring Child Support: An Extension of Social Security* (New York: Russell Sage Foundation, 1992), p. 45.

The last, and probably most controversial, aspect of the proposed system is the Assured Child Support Award. This involves the establishment of government subsidy, the assured benefit, that should go toward the support of children. If the nonresident parent pays less than the assured child support benefit, the government pays the resident parent the difference in the form of an assured child support benefit. The proposed assured child support benefit would be universal and would not be means-tested. Such assured benefit would be available to children until they turn 19 years old. Garfinkel recommends an assured benefit of between $2000 and $2500 per year for one child. The benefit would be increased by $1000, $1000, $500, $500, and $500 for the second, third, fourth, fifth, and sixth child, respectively. An assured child support subsidy would reduce insecurity faced by many children. More important, such a program would be effective in reducing poverty.

To increase the incentives to exit from AFDC, Garfinkel proposes that AFDC benefits be reduced by $1 for every $1 of assured benefit received. But the assured benefit award would not be reduced if the resident parent earns labor market incomes. Thus, the only way that resident parents benefit from the assured benefit program is by exiting from AFDC and earning market incomes. Consequently, a primary benefit of the proposed child support system is the reduction of welfare dependency.

Finally, the proposed system is expected to change one of the weakest aspects of the current child support system—the establishment of paternity. Because eligibility for the assured child support benefit is conditional on entitlement to private child support (which, in turn, requires the establishment of paternity) the proposed program can be expected to increase the incentive for unwed mothers and welfare agencies to establish paternity.

The child support system proposed by Garfinkel appears promising. Unfortunately, there is no evidence as to the effects of such a system because it is not in use in any state. Although the state of Wisconsin adopted recommendations of the Institute for Research on Poverty to adopt the proposed reforms, the reforms were not adopted fully. The percentage-of-income standard was made an option for the court to use in 1983 and became the presumptive child support obligation as of July 1987. The Wisconsin state law now requires courts to establish child support obligations using the fixed percentage of noncustodial parent income. The percentage varies with family size: 17 percent for one child, 25 percent for two children, 29 percent for three children, 31 percent for four children and 34 percent for five or more children. Also, immediate withholding was piloted in 10 counties starting in 1984 and became operational statewide in 1987.

The central element of the proposed system is the assured benefit. An advisory commission appointed to help in the development of the child support assurance system recommended the guaranteed child support amount to be set at $3000 for one child and the benefit to be increased with family size in the same manner as AFDC benefit levels. The assured benefit component of the new system was to be field-tested beginning in January 1990. Unfortunately, the minimum child support benefit was never implemented. The issue has now become politicized and it is unlikely that the child support assurance system will be implemented in the near future.[22]

A number of studies that simulate the effect of the proposed system show that such a program would perform much better than the current system in terms of reducing poverty, in reducing welfare recipiency, and that the system would decrease public spending on welfare.[23] However, the studies are conducted by the same proponents of the system and thus could be biased. Until some states implement the entire proposal, it will be difficult to provide a conclusive statement concerning the benefits of the proposed system.

SUMMARY

The large number of children growing up in one-parent households and the prevalence of poverty in those households suggests that issues of child support will increase in importance in the design of antipoverty policy. We have briefly sketched the main elements of the American system of private child support and some of its weaknesses. An innovative child support system proposed by Irwin Garfinkel has been outlined. This system has several benefits and offers hope for increasing child support payments. Specifically, adoption of the program would result in a reduction in poverty and insecurity experienced by many American children and is expected to reduce welfare dependency and increase the number of cases for which paternity is established. Unfortunately, until such a program is implemented fully, it is not possible to tell whether it would result in the claimed benefits.

The basic message of this chapter is that traditional approach of reforming welfare may no longer be adequate. The responsibility of nonresident parents in raising children should be part of the entire welfare reform debate. Even if the system suggested is not adopted in its entirety as outlined, experimentation with variants of this system would be worthwhile.

---

22. There is hope that the new system will be adopted by some states. The state of New York has commenced a demonstration of an assured child support benefit similar to one proposed by Garfinkel.
23. See Irwin Garfinkel, Philip K. Robins, Pat Wong, and Daniel R. Meyer, "The Wisconsin Child Support Assurance System: Estimated Effects on Poverty, Labor Supply, Caseloads, and Costs," *Journal of Human Resources* 25 (1) (Winter 1990): 1–31; and Donald T. Oellerich and Irwin Garfinkel, "Alternative Child Support Regimes: Distributional Impacts and a Crude Benefit-Cost Analysis," in Sheldon H. Danzinger and Kent E. Portney, eds., *The Distributional Impacts of Public Policies* (New York: St. Martin's Press, 1988), pp. 67–86.

STUDY AND DISCUSSION QUESTIONS

1. Discuss the current child support policy in the United States. What do you consider to be causes of the system's failure?

2. Compare the various formulae for establishing the child support obligation. Explain the advantages and disadvantages of each formula.

3. Attempt to provide reasons as to why many people fail to provide support to their children.

4. Discuss the Child Support Assurance System proposed by Garfinkel. Evaluate this proposal in terms of its potential for dealing with the poverty of children in one-parent households. What are some of the shortcomings of this proposal?

5. Explain what you think would be the best way to reform the child support system.

ADDITIONAL READINGS

1. Cassetty, Judith. *The Parental Child-Support Obligation.* Lexington, Mass.: Lexington Books, 1983.

2. Garfinkel, I. "The Role of Child Support Insurance in Antipoverty Policy," *The Annals of the American Academy of Political and Social Science* 479, 1985: 119–131.

3. Garfinkel, I. and M. Melli. *Child Support: Weakness of the Old and Features of a Proposed New System.* Madison, Wisc.: Institute for Research on Poverty, 1982.

4. Garfinkel, I. and Sara S. McLanahan. *Single Mothers and Their Children: A New American Dilemma.* Washington, D.C.: Urban Institute Press, 1986.

5. Kahn, Alfred J. and Sheila B. Kamerman. *Child Support: From Debt Collection to Social Policy.* Newbury Park, Calif.: Sage Publications, 1988.

14

FIGHTING POVERTY: ECONOMICS OF TRANSFERS

High unemployment rates during the Great Depression motivated the federal government to enact a number of income security programs as part of the New Deal. Most New Deal policies provided income security to formerly working persons and their families. Although a few programs targeted the poor, expenditures on those programs were relatively low and the programs themselves offered limited coverage. Thus, before the early 1960s, fighting poverty directly was never a central policy objective of the federal government. Similarly, no serious efforts dealt with the high poverty and unemployment rates of minorities.

Accelerated efforts to fight poverty in the United States commenced in the 1960s following President Lyndon Johnson's declaration of the War on Poverty. Concern over racial income inequalities and the state of poverty began attracting attention in the late 1950s. As observed earlier, the United States Supreme Court declared racial segregation unconstitutional in 1954. This ruling noted the inherent inequalities that existed in education and in other areas. On the intellectual front, the orthodox view that full employment solved poverty was challenged in two influential books, *The Affluent Society* by John Kenneth Galbraith and *The Other America* by Michael Harrington.[1] Both authors challenged the view that full employment eliminated poverty. The books discuss the "forgotten Americans" and the "invisible poor." In particular, Harrington's book described the state of the poor in America and received wide attention and raised public awareness of the problem of poverty faced by millions of Americans.[2]

In a memorandum to President Kennedy, Walter Heller, then Chairman of the Council of Economic Advisers, presented an analysis showing that the number of poor families had increased between 1956 and

---

1. *The Affluent Society* (Boston: Houghton Mifflin, 1958); and *The Other America: Poverty in the United States* (New York: Macmillan, 1962). See also Dwight MacDonald, "Our Invisible Poor," *New Yorker* (January 19, 1963): 82–132.
2. President Kennedy reportedly read the book and said that it made a deep impression on him.

1960. Furthermore, the analysis demonstrated that even if the economy reached full employment, a large number of people still would be poor. President Kennedy reacted to this report by instructing various agencies including the Council of Economic Advisers, the Bureau of the Budget, and the Departments of Labor, and of Health, Education, and Welfare to make a case for concentrated efforts to attack poverty problems. The urgency of poverty problems (particularly the issues of Black unemployment and other economic problems facing minorities) were highlighted by the civil rights march in Washington in August 1963. As a result of these events and of increasing public concern over the problem of poverty, the president asked his economic team to include antipoverty programs as part of the administration's 1964 legislative program.

After the assassination of President Kennedy, President Johnson continued Kennedy's antipoverty efforts declaring a War on Poverty in his first message on the State of the Union in 1964. The seriousness with which the federal government had taken the issue of poverty was evidenced by the detailed discussion of the problem of poverty in America included in the 1964 *Economic Report of the President*. The report contained detailed analysis of the causes, composition and extent of poverty and it also outlined various proposals for attacking poverty.[3]

In the years that followed, government efforts to deal with the problems of the low-income population focused primarily on the formulation and implementation of various antipoverty programs that comprised the agenda of the Great Society.[4] A large number of those policies involved the implementation of employment and training programs discussed in Chapter 8. The main purpose of employment and training programs is to improve the labor market prospects of low-wage and unemployed workers by providing training and removing employment barriers such as discrimination. Employment and training programs can be viewed as long-term strategies to deal with poverty by raising the future earnings of enrollees. To a large extent, the War on Poverty as outlined by President Johnson was to be fought by helping the poor help themselves.

The other approach for dealing with poverty redistributes income to the poor. These programs deal with poverty directly by providing resources

---

3. The proposals that were suggested then are to a large extent similar to policies that are used to deal with poverty today. They included establishing labor market policies to maintain high employment, economic growth and improving labor market information; fighting racial discrimination; establishing programs targeted to depressed rural and urban communities; expanding educational and training opportunities; assisting the aged and disabled; and improving the nation's health care system. See *Economic Report of the President, 1964*, Chapter 2.
4. Although related, the goals of the Great Society as described in the 1965 *Economic Report of the President* are much broader than those of the War on Poverty. In particular, policies of the Great Society included reducing poverty; ensuring equality of opportunities; and dealing with the problems of urbanization, education, and health care. A key element of the Great Society was the elimination of discrimination.

to the poor. In enacting policies to transfer income, policymakers hoped that the poor would rely on public support temporarily during which times they would prepare to enter the labor market and eventually be self-supporting.[5] During the late 1960s and early 1970s, existing income maintenance programs were expanded and new ones started. President Nixon generally was more supportive of giving cash and food stamps directly to help the poor, as had been favored by Johnson. The result was an explosion in government expenditures devoted to income maintenance.[6]

Although there is a tendency among the public and politicians to blame the increases in transfers on the Democrats, this is not accurate. Democrats were responsible for the War on Poverty, but were not primarily responsible for the rapid increase in transfers, except for the health programs, Medicare and Medicaid. The welfare spending patterns were shaped primarily by the Nixon administration and although President Reagan blamed Democrats for the explosion in welfare spending, it was the Republicans who were responsible for the increased welfare spending.[7]

Today, however, because the number of individuals officially defined as poor remains large (see Chapter 5), the debate has shifted to the effectiveness of welfare programs in eliminating poverty. Specifically, the debate now focuses on why welfare programs have not been more effective in fighting poverty. There are some claims that welfare programs may themselves contribute to increases in pretransfer poverty. Welfare programs also are blamed for adversely affecting work incentives and (as discussed in Chapter 12) welfare programs may have been responsible for the accelerated disintegration of the traditional American family. In addition, the welfare system has produced a category of recipients who rely on public support for prolonged periods, contrary to the stated goals. There also is increasing concern that the cost of supporting the poor has reached unsustainable levels. Because all levels of government are facing severe revenue constraints, the system of poor support needs control, not only to curtail government spending on social welfare programs, but also to minimize the negative outcomes associated with welfare use. In fact, talk of reforming the welfare system has become common when discussing domestic policy formulation.

This chapter considers income maintenance programs that are used to fight poverty in the United States. The first step is an examination of the

---

5. The elderly and permanently disabled are not expected to enter the labor market and thus are expected to receive transfers for long periods—probably throughout their entire life.

6. For a discussion of the various antipoverty programs, see Joseph Kershaw, *Government Against Poverty* (Washington, D.C.: Brookings Institute, 1970); and James T. Patterson, *America's Struggle Against Poverty: 1900–1985* (Cambridge: Harvard University Press, 1986).

7. See Wallace C. Peterson, *Transfer Spending, Taxes, and the American Welfare State* (Boston, Mass.: Kluwer Academic Publishers, 1991).

various programs, the growth of welfare expenditures, and the antipoverty effects of those programs. Next, there is discussion of some of the criticisms that have been directed at income maintenance programs. Some suggestions for reforming the welfare system follow in Chapter 15. Long-term welfare use is discussed in Chapter 16 as one of the special topics.

INCOME MAINTENANCE PROGRAMS

The term *income maintenance* is too broad and frequently results in confusion. Terms such as *welfare, public assistance,* and *income assistance* often are used interchangeably, although they may imply different things. This chapter is concerned with those government transfer programs that provide income or services to groups of people who meet some specific eligibility criteria. These programs can be divided further into two broad groups—programs that extend benefits to citizens on the basis of previous service or contribution *(social insurance programs)* and programs that extend benefits on the basis of need *(means-tested programs)*.

Means-tested programs redistribute resources to the poor and near poor. These programs often are referred to as public assistance or welfare. In addition to a resource test, some of the programs place additional eligibility requirements such as age, disability, or single mothers and their children. This chapter's primary focus is on means-tested programs. Although the largest fraction of the beneficiaries of social insurance programs are not poor, it also is true, however, that social insurance programs aid the needy and prevent many from falling into poverty. Thus, a brief discussion of social insurance programs is included.

Social insurance and means-tested benefits are provided either in the form of *cash* or *in-kind*.[8] Unlike cash transfers whose use is not restricted, in-kind benefits are restricted to particular goods or services. Recent trends in the composition of benefits to the poor has been to increase in-kind benefits relative to cash transfers. Arguments for in-kind benefits include reducing work disincentives and concern that the poor will use cash transfers on luxuries as opposed to spending the resources on necessities such as food and medical care. Thus, although in-kind transfers accounted for only 6.3 percent of all transfers in 1960, they comprised 40.1 percent of all transfers in 1980.[9] If one considers all goods and services that the government provides to the poor, such as education (for example, compensatory education), training programs, supportive services, and so on, the share of in-kind

---

8. In-kind benefits also are referred to as earmarked benefits.
9. See Robert X. Browning, "Priorities, Programs, and Presidents: Assessing Patterns of Growth in U.S. Social Welfare Programs 1950–1985," in Sheldon H. Danziger and Kent E. Portney, eds., *The Distributional Impacts of Public Policies* (New York: St. Martin's Press, 1988), pp. 13–32.

assistance to total assistance was 53 percent in 1968 and nearly 73 percent in 1987.[10]

The most important cash programs under social insurance include the Old Age Survivor's and Disability Insurance (OASDI) and the Unemployment Insurance (UI) programs. Means-tested cash programs include Aid to Families with Dependent Children (AFDC), Supplemental Security Income (SSI), and General Assistance (GA) programs. In-kind benefits under social insurance programs include medical care (Medicare). The most important in-kind means-tested programs include Medicaid, housing (public housing and subsidized private housing), and food stamps. A brief discussion of these programs is included.[11]

Social Insurance Programs

Social Security OSADI and UI were established by the Social Security Act of 1935.[12] Social Security Disability Insurance and Medicare were added to the social insurance programs in 1956 and 1965, respectively. OASDI is the primary source of income to a large and increasing aged population. About 95 percent of those who reach age 65 are eligible for some Social Security benefits.[13]

To be eligible for Social Security benefits, individuals must enroll to receive benefits and must contribute payroll taxes for at least 40 quarters (10 years). Benefits to retired workers and to the permanently disabled are determined by the individual's age of retirement and level of earnings while employed. Benefits of deceased insured workers are paid to surviving children under 18 years of age, dependent parents, and dependent widows or widowers. It is important to note that Social Security is not a true insurance fund, but operates as a pay-as-you-go spending program.

To be eligible for disability benefits, workers should have worked at least 20 of the 40 qualified quarters before becoming disabled. If under age 30, they must have worked half of the quarters since turning 21, but not fewer than six quarters. Medical proof of disability is required. In addition, a five-month waiting period exists before benefits are paid.

Unemployment Insurance (UI) provides workers with benefits during spells of involuntary unemployment. The benefits, in addition to aid the

10. Sar A. Levitan, *Programs in Aid of the Poor* (Baltimore: The Johns Hopkins University Press, 1990), pp. 78–79.
11. Some benefits that go to specific groups such as veterans also are important in dealing with poverty, but are not discussed here.
12. See Edwin Emil Witte, *The Development of the Social Security Act* (Madison, Wisc.: University of Wisconsin Press, 1962), and Arthur J. Altmeyer, *The Formative Years of Social Security*, (Madison, Wisc.: University of Wisconsin Press, 1966).
13. The retirement age is determined by the government, not by the individual. The retirement age has been raised in the past and is likely to continue to be raised to keep the program solvent.

unemployed, help to stabilize the economy during recessions. Unemployment Insurance benefits are based on earnings and work experience, not on need. The benefits are financed by a special payroll tax levied on employers and funds are managed by the federal government. However, the program is operated from state and local employment security agencies and wide variations exist in the level of UI benefits across states. Generally, the benefits range from 50 to 70 percent of a recipient's earnings prior to unemployment.

Eligibility for UI benefits requires a person to have lost a job through no fault of his or her own. In addition, the worker should be willing to accept replacement jobs that are offered. The maximum duration of recipiency is 26 weeks. During recessions, Congress has extended the maximum duration of UI beyond 26 weeks.

Medicare covers most hospital and medical costs for persons 65 years or older and for disabled Social Security beneficiaries. The program helps all elderly persons, regardless of income. Under this program, eligible individuals receive basic hospital insurance that pays most of the major hospital costs, extended care, and home care services. Those eligible for Medicare also can participate in a supplementary medical insurance program which helps cover physicians' fees, diagnostic tests, medical supplies, and prescription drugs. Those enrolled for the supplemental program pay an annually adjusted monthly premium that is matched by the federal government.

The social insurance programs, especially the retirement provisions of Social Security, have been very popular politically. Almost everyone expects to benefit some time in the future. Benefits are related to payroll taxes paid by the individual and are not financed out of general revenue. Still, there is considerable redistribution involved in Social Security. From an antipoverty perspective, those with low earnings can expect to get benefits greater than the taxes they (and their employers) pay. The reverse is true for high earners. Such redistribution, together with the immense size of the program, has made Social Security an extremely effective antipoverty program. It appears that the social insurance approach of the Franklin D. Roosevelt administration has proved to be more effective politically and probably economically as compared to other antipoverty approaches.

Means-Tested Programs

AFDC is the most important means-tested program and is the program that most people refer to when they talk about welfare. It also is the most controversial program that serves the poor. Controversies surrounding AFDC stem from its cost, the growth of the numbers of recipients enrolled in the program, and from a variety of other unintended consequences discussed later in this chapter. The AFDC program was created by the Social Security Act of 1935 to provide assistance to families where the father is absent or disabled. Thus, AFDC has extended benefits to mother-only households with limited income for a long period. Congress permitted, but did not require, states to extend AFDC benefits to two-parent families with a jobless, but employable parent in 1961. The unemployed parent component now exists in slightly over one half of the states.

Participation in the AFDC program increased rapidly after the Supreme Court ruling struck down the man-in-the-house rule in 1968. Previously states considered a man in the house as responsible for supporting the children, even if he was not legally liable for providing such support. This strategy had been used to deny mothers AFDC benefits. In 1969, the Court also invalidated residency requirements used by states to restrict eligibility. These changes, in addition to increased benefit levels, translated into a rapid increase in the number of AFDC cases.

The Supplemental Security Income (SSI) program is the other important means-tested cash program. SSI assists poor people who are 65 years or older, blind, or disabled. Before 1972, states placed strict eligibility requirements so that only the very poor could benefit from the program. The recipients supposedly exhausted their assets before becoming eligible, a condition that was demeaning to the needy. In amendments to the Social Security Act enacted in 1972, these restrictions were replaced by less stringent requirements. SSI requirements now allow recipients to have a house, an automobile of market value of up to $4500, other property for self-support, and life insurance of up to $1500. However, recipients cannot own assets that exceed $2000 in value for an individual or $3000 for a couple. In 1990, the federal SSI benefit for an individual was $386 per month and $579 per month for a couple. Most states supplement the federal SSI benefits, thus there is a wide variation in generosity of benefits across states. In 1990, for example, the maximum SSI benefit for an aged couple living independently was $1167 per month in California and was only $579 in Mississippi. SSI benefits are much more generous than are AFDC benefits.[14] Recipients of SSI are considered as more deserving because they are less capable of supporting themselves.

A less important means-tested program is the General Assistance (GA) program that exists in a majority of states. The program provides assistance to the needy who may not qualify for federally provided support. General assistance frequently is in the form of cash, although there are some cases where the assistance is limited to medical care and burial benefits.

Medicaid, which offers medical assistance to recipients of public assistance programs, was added to the Social Security Act in 1965. Under this plan, the federal government provides grants to states to finance health care for low-income persons. The grants range from 50 percent to slightly

---

14. For example, in 1990, the maximum AFDC benefit for a two-person family was $560 per month in California and $96 in Mississippi.

over 80 percent of the total Medicaid expenses, depending on the states' income. Most individuals who receive Medicaid are poor. For example, recipients of AFDC are automatically eligible to receive medical benefits under Medicaid. A large number of poor, however, are not covered by this program. Recent legislative changes have expanded access to Medicaid to various groups not previously eligible.

Another in-kind program extends food benefits to the poor. Recipients receive coupons (food stamps) that are used to buy food. The value of food stamps received depends on family income and size. The coupons are accepted by grocery stores as legal tender for the purchase of food. The stores receive the face value of the coupons from local banks, who in turn, redeem the coupons at face value from the government. All recipients of public assistance can participate in the food stamp program. Other low income households, that otherwise may not qualify for other programs, are eligible for food stamps.

Another important in-kind program helps the poor obtain adequate housing. Since 1930 the federal government, through the Department of Housing and Urban Development (HUD) has established several programs to alleviate the housing problem of the poor, including subsidies for construction, rental, leasing, purchase, and operation of apartments and houses. The oldest housing assistance program is public housing that is available to families with low incomes (i.e., not exceeding 80 percent of the median income in the local area). In some cases, public housing is restricted to people with lower incomes. In 1990, public housing served about 1.4 million households. Fifty percent of those occupying public houses are minorities (40 percent Black and 10 percent Hispanic).

The Reagan and Bush administrations were less committed to public housing as compared to previous administrations. As a result, spending on public housing was sharply curtailed during the 1980s and the number of public housing units added to the existing stock declined considerably. Thus, while 36,727 public housing units were added in 1980, only 6,947 units were added in 1989.

Most public houses were built as high-rise buildings often in the inner cities. As noted in Chapter 11, this approach to fighting poverty may have been self-defeating because it concentrated the poor, particularly poor minorities, in the same areas. Also, crime and drug use in public projects has made the life of the poor difficult in those homes.

The other important program that helps the poor obtain housing has been through the provision of subsidized housing. Section 8 of the Housing and Community Development Act established a rent supplement program to help low-income families. Under Section 8, local communities are allowed flexibility in the use of block grants to meet local housing needs. Local housing authorities can either lease private units that are then made available to low-income families at reasonable rents or the low-income renters receive direct rent supplements. Section 8 housing increased rapidly during the 1970s, but declined during the 1980s. In 1989, 2.3 million families were in Section 8 housing.

A primary goal of subsidized housing is to provide poor people more options of where they can live. Instead of public housing that has the effect of concentrating poor people in some areas, subsidized housing was viewed as a viable method of reducing such concentration of poverty. Unfortunately, residents in many affluent areas opposed plans to build low-income rental housing in their neighborhoods.[15] Thus, the program also continues to concentrate poor in some areas, although not to the same degree as public housing.

Social Welfare Spending

Although the rate of increase in government spending on social welfare has varied over time, there has been a general real increase in the amount of resources that are devoted to those programs. Table 14-1 shows data of social welfare expenditures under public programs for 1960, 1980, and 1990. In 1960, total social welfare expenditures amounted to $211.4 billion (constant 1990 dollars). Between 1960 and 1980, there was almost a four-fold increase in real expenditures devoted to social welfare. Social welfare expenditures reached $1,045.3 billion in 1990. Figure 14-1 depicts the trend in social welfare expenditures for the period between 1960 and 1990. Note that the largest share of social welfare expenditures is accounted for by social insurance programs, primarily Social Security and Medicare. Of the social insurance programs, expenditures on Medicare have increased at the highest rate. Although expenditures in public aid (means-tested programs) have increased over the entire period, the increase has been much slower as compared to the increase in expenditures devoted to social insurance programs.

ANTIPOVERTY EFFECTS

The ultimate goal of income transfers is to alleviate economic distress experienced by those with low or no income. Thus, the success or failure of those programs should be judged primarily in terms of their antipoverty effects. There are two approaches for assessing the antipoverty effects of government transfers. The first approach compares pretransfer poverty rates with posttransfer poverty rates. Such a comparison provides information as to what the poverty rate would be in the absence of transfers. The monetary value of the transfers made to recipients under various programs is added to obtain the total recipient income (transfers plus earned

---

15. This is the NIMBY (Not In My Back Yard) syndrome discussed in Chapter 11.

Table 14-1   Social welfare expenditures under public programs
1960–1990 [in millions] (1990 constant dollars)

Item	1960	Year 1980	1990
Social Insurance	78,069.0	333,157.7	510,615.7
OASDHI	44,610.4	220,569.2	352,261.8
Medicare	–	50,739.7	106,806.3
Railroad retirement	3,779.5	6,914.9	7,229.2
Public employee retirement	10,391.7	57,263.1	90,364.7
Unemployment insurance and unemployment service	11,441.8	26,574.3	19,971.3
Railroad unemployment insurance	870.1	225.3	64.6
Railroad temporary disability insurance	276.9	99.7	40.3
State temporary disability insurance	1,406.7	1,997.7	3,224.2
Workers' compensation	5,291.0	19,513.7	37,358.9
Public aid	16,583.3	104,368.7	145,641.9
Public assistance[1]	16,343.1	65,345.9	103,923.4
Supplemental security income	–	11,928.9	17,230.4
Food stamps	–	13,171.3	16,254.4
Other	240.19	13,922.4	8,233.6
Health and Medical Programs	18,049.9	39,532.9	62,428.0
Veterans Programs	22,155.8	31,126.2	30,916.2
Education	71,273.7	175,528.3	258,384.6
Housing	714.9	9,974.9	19,468.5
Other Social Welfare	4,607.3	19,719.5	17,917.6
TOTAL	211,454.4	713,409.3	1,045,372.5

[1]Includes Aid to Families with Children, General Assistance, Medicaid, and other means-tested programs under the Social Security act.

Source: *Social Security Bulletin, Annual Statistical Supplement,* 1992, Table 3.A3.

Figure 14-1   Social welfare spending, 1960–1990 (constant 1990 dollars)

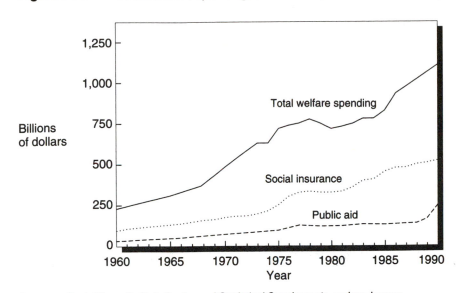

Source: *Social Security Bulletin, Annual Statistical Supplements,* various issues.

income). The other approach of assessing the antipoverty effects of transfers is to estimate the degree to which those transfers reduce the gap
between a poor family's income and the poverty threshold. This is known
as the *poverty gap* or the *poverty income deficit* approach. This approach is
important because although a transfer program that targets the poor may
not remove people from poverty, the transfer reduces the poverty gap and
thus reduces the severity of poverty. Although both methods are straightforward when considering cash transfers, complications arise in valuing
in-kind transfers. As mentioned in Chapter 5, recipients place a lower
value on in-kind transfers than the market value of those benefits.

Probably the most noticeable antipoverty effect of income transfers
was during the 1960s and 1970s when there was a rapid growth in expenditures dedicated to those programs. Between 1965 and the mid-1970s, real
transfers per recipient increased faster than the increase in per capita real
household income. This resulted in rapid decline in posttransfer poverty.
Table 14-2 reports the poverty rate under different income measures for
the period between 1965 and 1980. The data show that in 1965, transfers
reduced poverty from 21.3 to 13.4 percent. Between 1965 and 1980, while
the percentage of pretransfer poor actually increased by 2.8 percent, the
posttransfer (after including cash and in-kind transfers) poverty fell by as

Table 14-2   Percentage of persons in poverty under different income measures, 1965–1980

Year	Pretransfer Poor	Poor after Cash Transfers	Poor After Cash and In-Kind Transfers
1965	21.3	17.3	13.4
1968	18.2	12.8	9.9
1970	18.8	12.6	9.3
1972	19.2	11.9	6.2
1974	20.3	11.6	7.2
1976	21.0	11.8	6.7
1978	20.2	11.4	n.a.
1979	20.5	11.7	6.1
1980	21.9	13.0	n.a.
Percentage changes			
1965–1980	+2.8	−24.9	−54.5*

n.a. = not available.
*Change between 1965 and 1979.

Source: Adapted from Sheldon H. Danzinger and Daniel H. Weinberg, *Fighting Poverty: What Works and What Doesn't* (Cambridge: Harvard University Press, 1986), p. 54. See this source for explanations.

much as 54.5 percent between 1965 and 1979. The data suggest that income transfer programs have had desired antipoverty effects.[16]

More detailed data on the effectiveness of transfers in fighting poverty are provided in Tables 14-3 and 14-4. The data reported in these tables show the magnitude by which different government transfers affect the poverty rate and also the effects of transfers in narrowing the poverty gap. As would be expected, any income transfers should reduce the poverty rate and the poverty gap. On the other hand, taxes reduce disposable income and thus increase the poverty rate and the poverty gap.

Data reported in Table 14-3 show that the number of poor individuals increased between 1979 and 1988, reaching a peak of 52 million in 1983. As expected the number of poor declines as a result of the various government

---

16. For recent discussion of the antipoverty effects of transfers, see Sheldon H. Danziger, "Recent Trends in Poverty and the Antipoverty Effectiveness of Income Transfers," in Sheldon H. Danziger and Kent E. Portney, eds., *The Distributional Impacts of Public Policies*, pp. 33–46.

transfers. For example, in 1988, there were about 49 million poor people (row 1). After social insurance transfers including Social Security, about 33.8 million people still remained poor (row 3). When means-tested cash transfers are included, 31.7 million people remained poor (row 4), and when food and housing benefits are taken into account, the number of people who remained poor was 28.3 million (row 5). When federal taxes are included, the number of people who remained poor was 29.2 million (row 6). Social insurance programs removed 15.2 million people from poverty (row 8) while means-tested programs removed 5.4 million people from poverty (row 9). Thus, in 1988, social insurance programs removed 31 percent of the pretransfer poor from poverty (row 11), and means-tested programs removed 9.4 percent of the pretransfer poor from poverty (row 12).

In 1988, the poverty gap was $121,956 million (1987 constant dollars) (row 13). After all transfers and taxes, the poverty gap was $39,772 million (1987 constant dollars) (row 18). The social insurance programs reduced the poverty gap by 45 percent (row 19) while means-tested programs reduced the gap by 22.3 percent (row 20). Thus, in 1988, the pretransfer poverty was 20.2 percent (row 21) and the posttransfer poverty rate after all transfers and taxes was 12.0 percent (row 26).

Table 14-4 reports the antipoverty effects of various government transfers by family type and presence of children. The data in column A are for all individuals in families with related children less than 18 years old. Data in column B are for all individuals in families with unmarried head and related children less than 18 years old, and column C reports the data for individuals in units with all members 65 years or older. The most important feature to note is the fact that a large proportion of the elderly (73.6 percent) are removed from poverty by social insurance programs (row 11). Although not all elderly are removed from poverty, social insurance programs reduces the poverty gap by 86.6 percent (row 19). For families with children, means-tested programs are more important. This is especially the case for families with an unmarried head. In 1988, means-tested programs reduced the poverty gap of such families by 50.9 percent.

The data presented herein are important in that they show that social welfare expenditures (social insurance and mean-tested programs) are effective in fighting poverty. Millions of Americans are removed from poverty by such programs. Because many of the programs discussed target the poor, they have been effective in achieving the desired goals. Although many people remain poor after the transfers, that should not be used as evidence that the programs are not effective. The poverty gap approach illustrates that social insurance and means-tested programs are effective in reducing the poverty gap. Thus, although a family that receives Medicaid benefits, for example, may remain poor after all transfers, the well-being of members in that family is improved considerably by the availability of government-provided health and other benefits.

Table 14-3   Antipoverty effectiveness of cash and noncash transfers (including federal income and payroll taxes) for all individuals in families or living alone

	1979	1980	1981
Number of poor individuals (thousands)			
1. Cash income before transfers	41,695	46,273	49,184
2. Plus social insurance (other than Social Security)	39,835	44,016	46,974
3. Plus Social Security	27,846	31,638	33,909
4. Plus means-tested cash transfers[1]	25,201	29,114	31,567
5. Plus food and housing benefits	20,931	24,882	27,703
6. Less federal taxes	21,606	26,030	29,983
Number of individuals removed from poverty due to (thousands)			
7. Social insurance (other than Social Security)	1,860	2,257	2,210
8. Plus Social Security (including Social Security)	13,849	14,635	15,275
9. Means-tested cash transfers, food, and housing benefits	6,915	6,756	6,206
10. Federal taxes	–675	–1,148	–2,280
Percent of individuals removed from poverty due to			
11. Social insurance (including Social Security)	33.2	31.6	31.1
12. Means-tested cash transfers, food, and housing benefits, and federal taxes	15.0	12.1	8.0
Poverty gap (millions of 1987 dollars)			
13. Cash income before transfers	100,276	111,613	118,235
14. Plus social insurance (other than Social Security)	93,481	103,424	110,471
15. Plus Social Security	51,881	58,398	63,763
16. Plus means-tested cash transfers	35,981	41,415	46,782
17. Plus food and housing benefits	28,176	32,239	37,441
18. Less federal taxes	28,628	32,945	38,734
Percentage reduction in poverty gap due to			
19. Social insurance (including Social Security)	48.3	47.7	46.1
20. Means-tested cash transfers, food, and housing benefits, and federal taxes	23.2	22.8	22.8
Poverty rate (in percent)			
21. Cash income before transfers	19.1	20.6	21.7
22. Plus social insurance (other than Social Security)	18.3	19.6	20.7
23. Plus Social Security	12.8	14.1	14.9
24. Plus means-tested cash transfers	11.6	12.9	13.9
25. Plus food and housing benefits	9.6	11.1	12.2
26. Less federal taxes	9.9	11.6	13.2

Note: [1]Official definition of poverty.

1982	1983	1984	1985	1986	1987	1988
51,942	52,700	50,943	50,462	49,702	49,679	49,145
48,989	49,468	48,690	48,208	47,466	47,731	47,297
36,204	36,928	35,702	35,171	34,534	34,380	33,850
34,200	35,030	33,700	33,064	32,546	31,745	31,745
30,493	31,697	30,103	29,489	28,988	29,004	28,357
32,549	33,923	32,529	31,840	31,249	30,400	29,214
2,953	3,232	2,253	2,254	2,236	1,1948	1,848
15,738	15,772	15,241	15,291	15,168	15,299	15,295
5,711	5,231	5,599	5,682	5,546	5,376	5,493
−2,056	−2,226	−2,426	−2,351	−2,261	−1,396	−857
30.3	29.9	29.9	30.3	30.5	30.8	31.1
7.0	5.7	6.2	6.6	6.6	8.0	9.4
123,562	126,720	122,517	122,327	122,905	124,246	121,956
114,739	116,617	114,939	115,427	116,299	117,820	116,403
68,480	71,431	69,047	68,280	68,678	69,419	67,000
51,287	53,231	50,671	50,480	50,987	51,650	50,184
40,687	42,409	40,021	39,929	40,316	40,434	38,962
42,119	43,988	41,747	41,601	41,948	41,394	39,772
44.6	43.6	44.2	44.2	44.1	44.1	45.1
21.3	21.7	22.3	21.8	21.7	22.6	22.3
22.6	22.8	21.8	21.3	20.8	20.6	20.2
21.4	21.4	20.8	20.4	19.9	19.8	19.4
15.8	15.9	15.3	14.9	14.5	14.3	13.9
14.9	15.1	14.4	14.0	13.6	13.5	13.0
13.3	13.7	12.9	12.5	12.2	12.0	11.6
14.2	14.6	13.9	13.5	13.1	12.6	12.0

Source: U.S. Congress, *Background Material and Data on Programs Within the Jurisdiction of the Committee on Ways and Means, 1990.*

Table 14-4   Antipoverty effectiveness of cash and noncash transfers (including federal income and payroll taxes) (A) for all individuals in families with related children less than 18; (B) for all individuals in units with unmarried head and related children less than 18; and (C) for individuals in units with all members 65 or older. (All data are for 1988.)

	A	B	C
Number of poor individuals (thousands)			
1. Cash income before transfers	25,305	14,149	11,797
2. Plus social insurance (other than Social Security)	24,257	13,928	11,645
3. Plus Social Security	22,504	13,167	3,118
4. Plus means-tested cash transfers*	21,299	12,514	2,828
5. Plus food and housing benefits	18,901	10,947	2,293
6. Less federal taxes	19,352	10,923	2,306
Number of individuals removed from poverty due to (thousands)			
7. Social insurance (other than Social Security)	1,048	221	–
8. Plus Social Security (including Social Security)	2,801	982	8,679
9. Means-tested cash transfers, food, and housing benefits	3,603	2,220	825
10. Federal taxes	–451	24	–13
Percent of individuals removed from poverty due to			
11. Social insurance (including Social Security)	11.1	6.9	73.6
12. Means-tested cash transfers, food, and housing benefits, and federal taxes	12.5	15.9	6.9

CRITICISMS OF WELFARE PROGRAMS

Welfare programs have had the desirable effects of reducing poverty and income inequality. Without these programs, many people would experience serious economic hardships. Conversely, welfare programs also have generated unintended and undesirable outcomes. The following text concerns these negative consequences. Negative effects of welfare are classified into three broad categories: increase in expenditures and recipients; work disincentives and other undesirable side effects; and inequities and inefficiencies.

Table 14-4   (Continued)

	A	B	C
Poverty gap (millions of 1987 dollars)			
13. Cash income before transfers	47,063	32,142	39,242
14. Plus social insurance			
(other than Social Security)	44,945	31,627	38,300
15. Plus Social Security	39,672	28,632	5,273
16. Plus means-tested cash transfers	28,343	19,481	3,725
17. Plus food and housing benefits	19,182	12,401	3,037
18. Less federal taxes	19,109	12,282	3,046
Percentage reduction in poverty gap due to			
19. Social insurance (including Social Security)	15.7	10.9	86.6
20. Means-tested cash transfers, food, and			
housing benefits, and federal taxes	43.7	50.9	5.7
Poverty Rate (in percent)			
21. Cash income before transfers	18.8	49.5	54.9
22. Plus social insurance (other than Social Security)	18.0	48.7	54.2
23. Plus Social Security	16.7	46.0	14.5
24. Plus means-tested cash transfers	15.8	43.7	13.2
25. Plus food and housing benefits	14.0	38.3	10.7
26. Less federal taxes	14.4	38.2	10.7

*See Table 14-3

Increases in Expenditures and Recipients

Growth of the welfare budget–As shown in Table 14-1 and Figure 14-1, government spending on social welfare programs has increased at an unusually high rate especially the spending on social insurance programs. Thus, although transfers have reduced poverty, such poverty reduction has been purchased at a high price. The rapid growth of social welfare programs is clearly demonstrated by the fact that while social welfare expenditures comprised only 38.4 percent of total government outlays in 1960, they accounted for 57 percent of the total government outlays in 1975. In 1960, social welfare expenditures accounted for only 10.3 percent of gross domestic product (GDP). In 1990, this figure was 19.1 percent. The increase was primarily as a result of expansion of social insurance programs, particularly medical benefits. In 1960, expenditures on social insurance programs accounted for 3.8 percent of GDP and in 1990, they accounted for 9.4 percent of GDP. Similarly, expenditures on means-tested programs (public aid) increased rapidly relative to gross national product: from 0.9 percent of GNP in 1960 to 2.7 percent in 1990. Thus, means-tested programs tripled relative to GDP between 1960 and 1990.

Increased spending on social welfare implies that resources have to be withdrawn from the provision of other goods and services. As would be expected, an increasing welfare budget necessarily translates to higher taxes and to increases in the government debt. These outcomes have negative consequences on long-run growth of the economy.

Increase in number of recipients–The growth in welfare spending has been accompanied by the growth in the size of the welfare population. One criticism of the U.S. welfare system is that it induces poor to join and remain on welfare. Martin Anderson suggests that the welfare system creates a dependent class of Americans who do not break out of the system.[17] Edgar Browning observed in 1975 that although the stated goal of welfare is to make recipients self-supporting, the design of the U.S. welfare system has had the opposite effect—the poor become less self-supporting.[18]

One program that is a frequent target of criticism is AFDC. Figure 14-2 shows the growth in the total number of AFDC recipients (including children) for the years between 1960 and 1990. In 1960, there were just slightly over three million recipients. By 1973, the total number of AFDC recipients had increased more than threefold to nearly 11 million recipients. Since the mid-1970s, the number of AFDC recipients increased only modestly and actually

Figure 14-2   AFDC recipients, 1960–1990

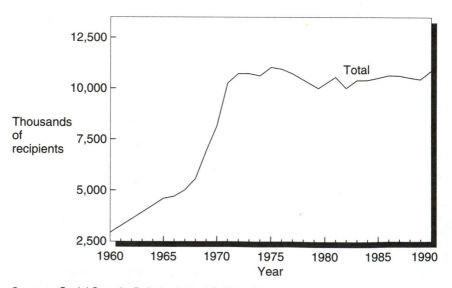

Source: *Social Security Bulletin, Annual Statistical Supplements*, various issues.

17. Martin Anderson, *Welfare: The Political Economy of Welfare Reform in the United States* (Stanford, Calif.: Hoover Institute Press, 1978).
18. Edgar K. Browning, *Redistribution and the Welfare System* (Washington, D.C.: American Enterprise Institute for Public Policy Research, 1975).

declined during the early 1980s.[19] In 1990, the number of AFDC recipients was nearly 12 million. The population receiving other means-tested benefits (such as food stamps) has increased dramatically since the 1960s. In 1962, an average of 143,000 persons participated in the food stamps program. In 1992, the average number of persons who participated in the food stamps program was over 25 million.[20]

Work Disincentives and Other Undesirable Side Effects

Work effort–In the review of historical perspective on poverty and poverty policy in Chapter 3, one of the major arguments against public support for the poor in the early days was that such support discouraged work effort. Today, reduction in work effort is considered to be the most important adverse effect of welfare programs. The effect of welfare income on an individual's labor supply is demonstrated by the simple labor-leisure choice model shown in Figure 14-3. An individual has a choice of either consuming leisure or earning market income. Both income and leisure are further assumed to provide positive utility. We also assume that the individual can choose to work as many hours as he or she wishes at a given market wage rate. If the individual decides to work 24 hours a day when the wage rate is $5 per hour, then his consumption bundle would include $120 of earned income, but no leisure. On the other hand, if he decides not to work, his consumption bundle contains $0 of income and 24 hours of leisure. Line AB represents this individual's budget constraint which shows the possible combinations of income and leisure available to the individual when the wage rate is equal to $5. The decision as to how many hours to work is determined at the point where the individual's highest indifference curve is tangent to the budget line. The indifference curve shows the various combinations of leisure and income that provide the same level of satisfaction. As shown in Figure 14-3, equilibrium is at point E; the individual works eight hours (24 − 16), receives $40 in earned income and consumes 16 hours of leisure per day.

Suppose that the individual now receives $20 of nonlabor income per day from the government in the form of a cash transfer. Such a transfer shifts the budget constraint upward on the vertical axis and parallel to the previous budget line. This new budget line is labelled A^1B^1. Note that an individual who decides not to work receives $20 per day. The individual can now attain a higher level of satisfaction by working six hours, which represents a higher consumption of leisure, and still have a higher total income

---

19. The decline in the number of recipients during the 1980s was primarily due to more stringent eligibility requirements enacted by the Reagan administration.
20. One reason for the increase of in-kind transfers is that such benefits subsidize doctors and farmers, generating powerful interest groups to protect them.

Figure 14-3   Transfers and labor supply

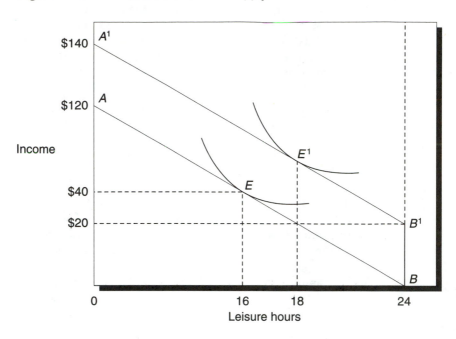

((6 * 5) + 20) than before the cash transfer became available (point E^1). Thus, based on the figure, it is rational for the recipient to reduce the number of hours of work. Although not all recipients behave this way, many recipients do reduce their labor supply when transfers become available.

Some welfare programs may increase the adverse labor supply effects even further. Although the poor face a low income tax rate (often zero) on earned income, the welfare system imposes a high implicit tax rate on earned income. Specifically, because benefits are means-tested, they fall by a certain percentage when a recipient earns income. Lower welfare payments mean that the benefit of working is reduced although earned income is not directly taxed.

Consider the extreme case where for every dollar of earned income, welfare benefits fall by $1. This is equivalent to a 100 percent marginal tax rate on earned income. Figure 14-4 reproduces the budget constraint shown in Figure 14-3. Before welfare, the budget constraint is AB and equilibrium is at point E. The transfer is equal to $20 for a person who does not have any earned income (one who consumes 24 hours of leisure). However, the transfer is reduced by $1 for every $1 of earned income. The implicit tax modifies the budget line to AXB^1B. For labor earnings of $20 or more, the transfer falls to zero. Notice that because of the implicit tax, the recipient is better off by choosing point B^1 where labor supply falls to zero.

In essence, economic theory predicts that transfers to the poor reduce labor supply. The higher the benefit levels and the higher the implicit mar-

Figure 14-4   Implicit tax and labor supply

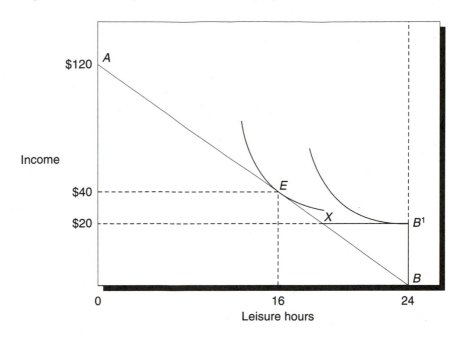

ginal tax, the larger the reduction in labor supply. A large number of studies have attempted to measure the role of transfers in discouraging work effort. The more informative studies on this subjective are based on various income maintenance experiments conducted during the 1960s and 1970s.[21] The experiments investigated individual responses to different levels of benefits and tax rates. Although estimates of the magnitude of the effects of benefits on labor supply differ, the general finding is that welfare benefits reduce work effort.[22]

The work incentive structure of welfare programs remains quite weak. Estimates by the House Means and Ways Committee show that a typical welfare recipient expects only limited benefits from entering the

21. The experiments were conducted in New Jersey and Pennsylvania (1968–1972); Iowa and North Carolina (1969–1973); Gary, Indiana (1971–1974); Seattle; and Denver (1971–1982). The experiment also considered other effects of transfers such as marital instability. For a discussion of the experiments, see Alicia H. Munnell, ed., *Lessons from the Income Maintenance Experiments* (Boston: Federal Reserve Bank of Boston and Brookings Institute, 1987).

22. For a review of various studies on the effect of transfers on labor supply, see Robert Moffitt, "Incentive Effects of the U.S. Welfare System: A Review," *Journal of Economic Literature* 30 (March 1992): 1–61. See also Gary Burtless, "The Work Response to a Guaranteed Income: A Survey of Experimental Evidence," in Alicia Munnell, ed., *Lessons from Income Maintenance Experiments* (Boston: Federal Reserve Bank of Boston and Brookings Institute, 1987), pp. 22–52; and Robert Moffitt, "Work Incentives in the AFDC System: An Analysis of the 1981 Reforms," *American Economic Review* 76 (2) (May 1986): 219–23.

labor market.[23] For example, a single mother with two children in the state of Pennsylvania could receive $6600 in AFDC and food stamps if she did not work at all. Such a recipient would also be eligible for medical benefits under the Medicaid program worth up to $2000 per year. If she entered the labor market and earned $7000 before taxes, her disposable income would be just slightly over $7000, a net gain of only about $400 above a recipient who does not work at all. If she were to earn $8000, the recipient risks the loss of up to $2000 in Medicaid benefits, essentially making her worse off than a person who does not work at all.

Labor supply and savings—social insurance programs–Social insurance programs also may have some undesirable effects. For example, Social Security reduces labor supply by encouraging early retirements. Because of an earnings test, those who earn additional income are subjected to a high implicit tax. This reduces the incentive to work after reaching the age of eligibility. In addition, guaranteed retirement income depresses saving.[24] Unemployment insurance benefits cause the unemployed to remain unemployed for longer durations.[25]

Family–A common criticism of income support programs is that they have contributed to the breakdown of the traditional American family. As discussed in Chapter 13, increased female headship has accompanied increased poverty. As was observed, there is increasing concern that welfare benefits may have been responsible for the increase in female-headed households by increasing marital dissolution and out-of-wedlock births. This is obviously an undesirable outcome of the income support system.[26]

Poverty–The most devastating criticism of public assistance is that transfers actually may increase poverty. This could occur because of the combined effects of welfare on family structure and work effort. One recent proponent of the hypothesis that welfare payments can increase poverty has been Charles Murray.[27] Murray's main argument is that availability of transfers has led some people to voluntarily select combinations of money income and leisure that make them eligible to be included in the poverty population.

---

23. Committee on Ways and Means, U.S. House of Representatives, *Background Material and Data on Programs Within the Jurisdiction of the Committee on Ways and Means* (Washington, D.C.: U.S. Government Printing Office, 1989).

24. See Martin S. Feldstein, "Social Security, Induced Retirement and Aggregate Capital Accumulation," *Journal of Political Economy* 82 (5) (October 1974): 905–26; Martin S. Feldstein and Anthony Pellechio, "Social Security and Household Wealth Accumulation: New Micro Econometric Evidence," *Review of Economics and Statistics* 61 (3) (August 1979): 361–68; and Robert J. Barro, *The Impact of Social Security on Private Saving: Evidence from the U.S. Time Series* (Washington, D.C.: American Enterprise Institute for Public Policy Research, 1978).

25. See Sheldon Danziger, Robert Haveman, and Robert Plotnick, "How Income Transfer Programs Affect Work, Savings, and the Income Distribution: A Critical Review," *Journal of Economic Literature* 19 (3) (September 1981): 975–1028.

26. For evidence on the effect of welfare on female headship, see studies cited in Chapter 12.

27. Charles Murray, *Losing Ground: American Social Policy, 1950–1980* (New York: Basic Books, Inc., 1984).

Lowell Gallaway and Richard Vedder have empirically tested the validity of Murray's hypothesis and find evidence of a positive relationship between welfare expenditures and the poverty rate.[28] Using a poverty-welfare curve that shows the relationship between the level of public aid and poverty (see Figure 14-5), the authors contend that for low levels of spending and when the poverty rate is high (as was the case during the 1960s), increases in aid reduce the poverty rate. As the level of transfers increase, however, transfers no longer reduce poverty but produce more of it. That is, increases in benefits associate with increases in poverty. In other words, although transfers do reduce poverty, it is possible that when benefits are relatively high some people who otherwise would not be poor chose to be poor in order to receive the attractive benefits. This outcome is referred to as "paying people to be poor."[29]

Although the poverty-welfare curve appears convincing and was used during the 1980s to convince policymakers of the adverse effects of a generous welfare system, it is misleading. Better estimation techniques show that the welfare-poverty relationship presented by Gallaway and Vedder does not hold when appropriate factors that cause poverty are taken into account.[30] The idea of poverty-welfare tradeoff as depicted by Gallaway and Vedder loses meaning when one compares levels of expenditures and

Figure 14-5   Poverty-welfare curve

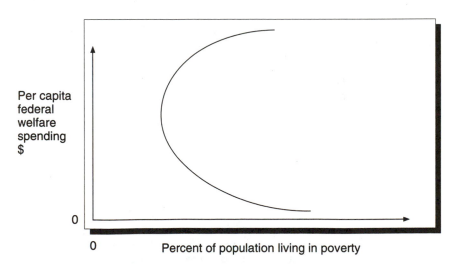

28. Lowell Gallaway and Richard Vedder, *Poverty, Income Distribution, the Family, and Public Policy,* A Study for the Joint Economic Committee, U.S. Congress (Washington, D.C.: U.S. Government Printing Office, December 19, 1986).
29. Lowell Gallaway and Richard Vedder, "Paying People to Be Poor," National Center for Policy Analysis, Policy Report No. 121, 1986.
30. Mwangi S. Kimenyi, "The In-Existence of a Poverty Welfare Curve," working paper (The University of Connecticut, Department of Economics, 1993).

poverty rates in other countries such as Sweden and Germany. Thus, although it is conceivable that some people choose to be poor to be eligible for benefits, it is not the case that the aggregate poverty rate in the United States has increased because of the generosity of benefits.

Inequities and Inefficiencies

Undesirable migration patterns–A good transfer system should seek to achieve horizontal equity so that families that are in similar circumstances are treated equally. One of the noticeable characteristics of the American welfare system is that there are wide variations in the generosity of benefits across states, resulting in significant horizontal inequity. In 1990, for example, the maximum AFDC benefit for a three-person family was $120 in Mississippi and $649 in Connecticut.[31] Similar variations are observed for other means-tested benefits such as SSI (discussed previously). The differences in generosity of the benefits remain even after controlling for differences in the cost of living. One result of the horizontal inequity is the migration of low income persons from low- to high-benefit areas.[32] This is undesirable especially because it concentrates low-income people in particular areas (such as the inner cities).

Inefficiency of in-kind benefits–Another important criticism of the U.S. welfare system is its reliance on in-kind benefits such as food, housing, and medical care. Although there are good reasons for extending benefits in kind rather than in cash, in-kind benefits deny the recipients consumer sovereignty. Because recipients are not free to select the best combination of goods for a given amount of resources (as they are in the case of a cash transfer), paying benefits in-kind results in inefficient consumption choices. Specifically, in-kind benefits place consumers on a lower level of satisfaction as compared to the level they would attain if they received a cash transfer.[33] To the extent that recipients are not free to make their choices, they place a lower value on in-kind benefits than on cash benefits. For this reason, some recipients of food stamps trade the coupons for cash at less than face value.[34]

---

31. U.S. Congress, *Background Material and Data on Programs Within the Jurisdiction of the Committee on Ways and Means, 1990*, p. 561.
32. See Rebecca Blank, "The Effects of Welfare and Wage Levels on the Location Decisions of Female-Headed Households," *Journal of Urban Economics* 24 (2) (September 1988): 186–211; and Paul Peterson and Mark Rom, "American Federalism, Welfare Policy, and Residential Choices," *American Political Science Review* 83 (3) (September 1989): 711–28.
33. See Appendix 1 for a discussion of the effects of an in-kind transfer.
34. A television news program suggested that in New York City the rate of exchange was $1 in food stamps to 50 cents in cash during the late 1980s.

SUMMARY

This chapter has discussed some of the cash and in-kind transfers that are used to fight poverty in the United States. The text illustrates that transfers have had an important impact on reducing poverty. Even when transfers do not lift recipients out of poverty, they do provide much-needed goods and services to the needy and improve their quality of life. Thus, in terms of accomplishing the primary goal of reducing poverty, transfers have achieved that goal with reasonable success.

Unfortunately, transfer programs have undesirable effects, too. For example, it was shown that social welfare spending has contributed to the rapid increase in the size of government. Although income maintenance programs have reduced poverty, the price tag has been extremely high. Other negative aspects of transfers include rapid growth of the welfare population, reduction in work effort, undesirable migration patterns, and disintegration of the family. These negative effects have motivated policy-makers to suggest and implement various welfare reform measures (some of which are discussed Chapter 15).

It is true that welfare benefits have had some undesirable effects. However, there is an unfortunate tendency for critics to exaggerate these negative effects. Conversely, some proponents for welfare programs take the position that the system is fine and what is needed is more government spending on those programs. Both of these extreme positions are incorrect and do not do justice to the poor as they hinder the design of workable policies to help the poor.

STUDY AND DISCUSSION QUESTIONS

1. Discuss the main social insurance programs in the United States. Focus on the goals, eligibility, and size of the programs.

2. Discuss the main income maintenance programs in the United States. Focus on the goals, eligibility, and size of the programs.

3. Provide arguments for and against in-kind transfers.

4. Outline how you would go about evaluating the effectiveness of social insurance and income maintenance programs in improving the well-being of the poor.

5. Demonstrate how income transfers affect labor supply.

6. Critically evaluate the suggestion that transfers could cause poverty.

7. Analyze the various shortcomings of the U.S. transfer system.

ADDITIONAL READINGS

1. Haveman, Robert H., ed., *A Decade of Federal Antipoverty Programs: Achievements, Failures, and Lessons.* New York: Academic Press, 1977.

2. Haveman, Robert H. *Poverty Policy and Poverty Research: The Great Society and Social Sciences.* Madison, Wis.: University of Wisconsin Press, 1987.

3. Morris, Michael and John B. Williamson. *Poverty and Public Policy: An Analysis of Federal Intervention Efforts.* New York: Greenwood Press, 1986.

4. Plotnick, Robert D. and Felicity Skidmore. *Progress Against Poverty: A Review of the 1964-1974 Decade.* New York: Academic Press, 1975.

5. Zarefsky, David. *President Johnson's War on Poverty: Rhetoric and History.* Tuscaloosa, Ala.: The University of Alabama Press, 1986.

15

WELFARE REFORM

Chapter 2 examined theories of optimal income distribution that are based on normative analysis. It was demonstrated that when value judgments are used to formulate the ideal state of income distribution, social choices may not reflect efficiency. It also was noted that normative considerations alone are not a sufficient guide in formulating public policy. Policymakers must take into account the consequences of particular policies. Thus, although there are strong normative arguments for enacting transfer policies to fight poverty and to reduce income inequality, it is necessary to evaluate the costs and benefits of those policies.

Since the mid-1970s, it has been evident that the American system of income redistribution has many faults. As such, efforts have been made to repair the system—what is normally referred to as welfare reform—so as to minimize its unintended consequences. In fact, all presidents since Richard Nixon have presented welfare reform proposals to Congress. However, despite the fact that there is widespread agreement on the necessity for reform, most of those proposals have failed to win congressional support, pointing to the difficulty of reforming the system once it is in place.

This chapter is about welfare reform. First, it will examine the basic economic problem facing policymakers: balancing costs and benefits of a redistributive system. Next, there is a review of some welfare reform policies that have been implemented or suggested to deal with the unintended consequences of transfer programs.

REDISTRIBUTION AND INEFFICIENCY

Discussion in previous chapters alluded to several shortcomings of the American system of poor support. In Chapter 14, some criticisms of welfare programs were discussed, including work disincentives, marital instability, incentives to reduce savings and to migrate to higher benefit states, growth of the welfare budget, and an increase in the number of those dependent on public support. In Chapter 8, it was noted that the current system of support discriminates against low-wage workers by denying them benefits, especially health benefits. It also is true that the current system discriminates against single persons and childless couples who, in most cases, are not eligible for many of the programs that are available to those with children.

Similarly, in the discussion of the feminization of poverty, it was pointed out that one cause of poverty among those households is the inadequacy of welfare benefits. Also, the current system of income redistribution is criticized for being too diverse with many overlapping programs that are administered by different bureaus. The result of this complex system is that a large portion of the social welfare budget goes to cover administrative costs rather than going to help the poor.[1] Furthermore, recipients consider the procedures and rules for eligibility to be dehumanizing and an invasion of privacy. Thus, the current system is criticized not only by taxpayers and academics, but also by the recipients themselves. It is difficult to find someone who does not have something bad to say about welfare.

Most reform efforts have focused on undesirable changes in the behavior of recipients induced by transfers, which result in inefficient resource allocation. There is concern that the current redistributive system has resulted in a misallocation of resources. Although redistribution has some gains, such policies also involve inefficiencies that retard economic growth. In a market economy, optimal growth of the economy arises when market signals (prices, profits, interest rates) direct the allocation of resources. Increased redistribution of income, although achieving desired goals of reducing income inequality, necessarily distort these market signals, the result of which is the loss of production efficiency.

Reduction in work effort due to transfers directly translates into a lower level of output. Furthermore, reduced savings translate into a lower level of investment and thus a slower rate of economic growth. A rising welfare budget necessarily requires increases in the marginal tax rates. One consequence of high marginal tax rates is the diversion of market activities from the formal sector to the informal, yet another source of resource misallocation. So, in redistributing income, a nation must make a tradeoff between equality and efficiency. This position is clearly stated by Arthur Okun.

> The contrasts among American families in living standards and in material wealth reflect a system of reward and penalties that is intended to encourage effort and channel it into socially productive activity. To the extent

---

1. For example, in 1971, administrative costs accounted for 9.6 percent of AFDC benefits. In 1989, administrative costs were estimated to be about 13.8 percent of the benefits. See Department of Health and Human Services, Office of Financial Management, Family Support Administration, "Characteristics of State Plans for AFDC," 1989.

that the system succeeds, it generates an efficient economy. But the pursuit of efficiency necessarily creates inequalities. And hence society faces a trade-off between equality and efficiency.[2]

If both equality and efficiency are valued, and neither takes absolute priority over the other, then, in places where they conflict, compromises ought to be struck. In such cases, some equality will be sacrificed for the sake of efficiency and some efficiency for the sake of equality. But any sacrifice of either has to be justified as a necessary means of obtaining more of the other (or possibly of some other valued social end). In particular, social decisions that permit economic inequality must be justified as promoting economic efficiency.[3]

Okun describes the redistributive system as a "leaky bucket." As government transfers income from those who have earned it to those who have not, losses occur due to administrative costs, reduced work effort, and decreases in saving and investment. Thus, any form of redistribution entails losses. This tradeoff suggests that reducing the size of the transfer system would increase economic efficiency and economic growth. The leaky bucket argument has been used to blame welfare policies for contributing to a slowdown in economic growth in the United States.

Unlike Okun's leaky bucket, Robert Haveman suggests that it is possible to achieve more equality without sacrificing efficiency.[4] This is because redistribution has several benefits that increase efficiency. While acknowledging that the redistribution system entails costs, Haveman suggests that it is possible to choose a redistributive system for which the gains exceed the losses. There are several gains from redistribution that directly or indirectly contribute to economic growth. For example, income redistribution helps low-income families acquire human capital which contributes to higher productivity, and, thus, to an increase in the rate of economic growth in the future. Similarly, transfers increase the well-being of the poor and reduce their economic insecurity, both valued social goals. In addition, transfers sustain demand during recessions and therefore play an important function of stabilizing the economy. By reducing inequality, income redistribution can increase social cohesion and thus the well-being of the society as a whole. Although there are losses associated with the transfer system, there also are clear gains from such a system and the goal should be to design a system that maximizes the net gains.

Haveman suggests that as the size of the income redistribution system increases, the gains from redistribution also increase, but at a decreasing rate, reflecting the usual diminishing marginal returns principle. On the

---

2. Arthur M. Okun, *Equality and Efficiency: The Big Tradeoff* (Washington, D.C.: The Brookings Institute, 1975), p. 1.
3. Ibid, p. 88.
4. See Robert Haveman, *Starting Even: An Equal Opportunity Program to Combat the Nation's New Poverty* (New York: Simon and Schuster, 1988).

other hand, the costs of redistribution increase at an increasing rate. The change in the gains and losses with respect to the size of the redistribution system are depicted in Figure 15-1. The vertical axis measures the total costs *(TL)* and total gains *(TG)* of redistribution and the horizontal axis shows the size of the redistribution system measured as a percentage of gross national product. For small sizes of the redistributive system, the gains are greater than losses. At larger sizes, the losses exceed the gains.

If the redistributive system is too large so that the losses are greater than the gains (point *V*), then reducing the size of the system to the level where gains are greater than losses would be necessary. If the only choice is either to maintain the status quo or to eliminate the system, then the latter choice would be preferred. On the other hand, if the system is so small that expanding the system results in larger gains than losses, then that would be the appropriate policy. For example, net gains increase if the redistribution system is expanded from *Z* to *Y*. But even when gains exceed losses, it is possible to increase the net gains from redistribution by scaling back the size of the system. For example, reducing the size of the redistribution system from *X* to *Y* in Figure 15-1 would result in higher net gains. Therefore, one way of maximizing the gains from redistribution is to change the size of the system. Reducing or increasing the size of the redistributive system in order to maximize net gains requires that policymakers know the effects of those adjustments. That is, they should have information regarding the position of the *TG* (total gains) curve relative to the *TL* (total loss) curve.

Adjusting the size of the system is one way of maximizing net gains. It is unlikely that expansion of the redistribution system would find political support given the various problems associated with the current system. In fact, available evidence suggests that the system is too large and probably should be scaled back. Edgar Browning and William Johnson estimate that for every $100 transferred to the poor, taxpayers sacrifice $350.[5] This implies that there is a net loss of $250 in transferring $100; an extremely high deadweight loss. Moderate estimates indicate that although the losses from transfers may be much lower than suggested by Browning and Johnson, they are still substantial.[6] Expanding the transfer system would therefore result in adding more losses than gains. As Haveman observes:

> [W]e have about exhausted the poverty-inequality-insecurity reduction potential of the taxation-income transfer strategy—a conclusion reached by assessing practical matters and empirical relationships. At this point, additional gains in economic security, welfare, and equality appear too

---

5. See Edgar Browning and William Johnson, "The Trade-off Between Equality and Efficiency," *Journal of Political Economy* 92 (2) (1984): 175–203.
6. See Gary Burtless and Robert Haveman, "Taxes and Transfers: How Much Economic Loss," *Challenge* 30 (1) (March/April 1987): 45–51.

Figure 15-1   Economic gains and losses from the redistribution system

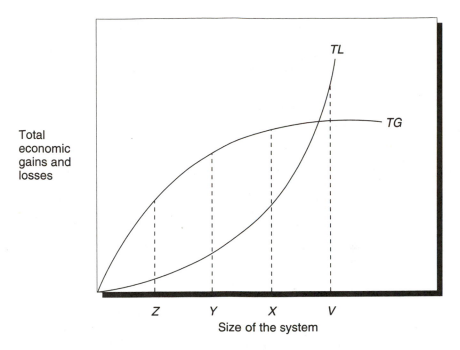

costly in terms of economic efficiency to warrant continued expansion—
at the margin the losses may well exceed the gains.[7]

This observation suggests that the way to deal with problems associated
with welfare is not to increase the size of the redistributive system. Because
there are many benefits from redistribution, the goal should not be to eliminate the entire system, but rather to restructure welfare policies so as to
reduce the costs associated with the system. On the one hand, there is the
need to continue a transfer system that helps the truly needy. On the other
hand, such a system must balance the gains achieved with the negative
effects of transfers. Thus, while an ideal transfer system should provide adequate benefits to the poor, it must take into account the unintended effects.
Welfare reform policies seek to minimize the costs of redistribution and to
increase the gains from redistribution.

7. Robert Haveman, *Starting Even: An Equal Opportunity Program to Combat the Nation's New
   Poverty,* p. 145.

WELFARE REFORM POLICIES

In discussing welfare reform policies, it helps to start by considering the proper objectives of an effective income transfer system. During the early 1970s, researchers became increasingly concerned that the U.S. welfare system was not consistent to principles of efficiency and equity. As a result, attempts were made to outline a statement of objectives that could guide in reforming the system. One such statement was outlined in the mid-1970s by Michael Barth and his colleagues.[8] The authors identified nine objectives that an effective transfer system should meet. These objectives are relevant even today and are important in the design of welfare reform policies. These objectives are

1. *Adequacy*–A means-tested transfer system should be designed in tandem with employment and social insurance systems so that people who can work and people who cannot work have access to a nominally adequate income level.

2. *Target efficiency*–Benefits should be targeted to those most in need. Thus tradeoffs between possible increases in expenditures on social welfare programs should be evaluated in this regard.

3. *Administrative efficiency*–The welfare system should be designed in a manner such that objectives are achieved at minimum cost. Therefore, if multiple programs are required, there should be a high degree of coordination and integration of programs that serve the same populations.

4. *Horizontal equity*–People in similar circumstances should be treated equally. This requires reducing administrative discretion and interstate benefit differentials. In addition, horizontal equity requires uniformity of eligibility rules so that families and individuals with generally similar characteristics are eligible for comparable benefits.[9]

5. *Vertical equity*–People and families who earn more should receive more total income. Those with greater need should receive more assistance.

---

8. Michael C. Barth, George J. Carcagno, and John L. Palmer, *Toward an Effective Income Support System: Problems, Prospects, and Choices* (Madison, Wisc.: Institute for Research on Poverty, University of Wisconsin, 1974).

9. There are instances where programs result in horizontal inequities because they cause some families to surpass or leap over other families in the income ranking. This is referred to as *leapfrogging* and is an indication of inequity in the transfer system. See Robert D. Plotnick and Felicity Skidmore, *Progress Against Poverty: A Review of the 1964–74 Decade* (New York: Academic Press, 1975).

6. *Work incentives*–A welfare system should be designed in a manner such that it should be in the interest of people who are able to work to do so. Those who work and earn more should end up with more incomes than those who do not work. As much as is possible, welfare recipients who work should not be penalized.

7. *Family stability incentives*–The welfare system should be designed in a manner that minimizes incentives for family breakup.

8. *Independence*–The welfare system should be designed in a manner that does not promote dependence. That is, the system should encourage families and individuals to be self-sufficient so that they no longer require assistance.

9. *Coherency and Control*–The welfare system as a whole should be understandable in its operation and effects, it should have the effects intended and be subject to policy and fiscal control.

These nine objectives are key to the formulation of welfare reform policies. A good welfare reform proposal should seek to meet as many of these objectives as possible. The following reviews some of the important welfare reform proposals.

Some suggestions for reforming the welfare system already have been discussed in previous chapters. In Chapter 8, it was noted that there is need to expand medical coverage to low-wage workers, including two-parent households. In addition, provision of child care would go a long way in helping low-wage workers who have young children. Most of these families have to make difficult decisions concerning whether to work and pay for child care or withdraw from the labor market all together. As has been illustrated, expanding the transfer system may be too costly. Thus, extending child care benefits to those groups should be done by restructuring the entire system in a manner that avoids overall expansion of the redistribution system. Provision of child care benefits would have the effect of encouraging labor force participation and increase work effort, both of which have a positive effect on the economy. Another proposal that was suggested to help the working poor concerns the earned income credit. To the extent that such a policy prevents some low-income families from falling below the poverty threshold, it has the effect of reducing the population that relies on welfare. Providing guaranteed jobs to the poor (as discussed previously) is another way of reforming welfare. Providing jobs facilitates those who would otherwise rely on welfare to be self-supporting.

An important welfare reform measure concerns the child-support system. This issue was discussed in detail in Chapter 13. Although the topic was discussed separately, it must be part of the entire welfare reform strategy. In fact, given the problem of mother-only households and the prevalence of such households, reforming the child support system probably is the most important and urgent welfare reform policy of the 1990s.

The other important reform policies are those that seek to reduce work disincentives and long-term welfare dependency. Some of these policies include a negative income tax and mandatory work or training as a condition for receiving welfare benefits. It should be noted that most states have implemented, or have suggested, various strategies to reform the welfare system. Thus, the policies discussed here are by no means comprehensive.

Negative Income Tax

The idea of a negative income tax (NIT) was first proposed by George Stigler years before the War on Poverty.[10] Stigler was concerned that the use of minimum wage laws to fight poverty would have undesirable effects. Stigler also felt that minimum wages would not be consistent with the fundamental principle of fighting poverty, namely that those who are equally in need should be treated equally. He proposed the use of a system that grants assistance to the poor with regard only to need as established by the family composition. Stigler's proposal called for extending the personal income tax to the lowest income brackets with negative rates in these brackets. Stigler indicated that a properly designed negative rates structure would retain some measure of incentives for families to increase their incomes. The idea of NIT was later populized by Milton Friedman and James Tobin.[11] The NIT proposal by Stigler and Friedman was intended to simplify the transfer system by integrating welfare into the tax system. Thus NIT was meant to offer universal benefits as opposed to categorical payments. In addition, all payments under the NIT scheme were to be made in cash and not in-kind. Presently, the NIT is viewed by economists as one way of reducing work disincentives associated with welfare. In a previous discussion, it was found that a guaranteed income accompanied by a 100 percent implicit tax on earned income has the effect of eliminating work incentives. One goal of a negative income tax is to restructure the benefit reduction rate in order to minimize work disincentives.

Figure 15-2 depicts the case where earned income is subject to 100 percent implicit tax as discussed in Chapter 14. The vertical axis shows the net income received after taxes and transfers. The horizontal axis shows leisure hours. In absence of a transfer, the optimal point for this individual is at point E where the indifference curve is tangent to the budget line TN. Thus, the individual works AT hours and earns an income equal to Y_2.

10. George J. Stigler, "The Economics of Minimum Wage Legislation," *American Economic Review* 36 (3) (June 1946): 358–65.
11. Milton Friedman, *Capitalism and Freedom* (Chicago: University of Chicago Press, 1962); and James Tobin, "The Case for an Income Guarantee," *The Public Interest* 4 (1966): 31–41.

Figure 15-2   Work–net income budget constraint under public assistance (100% implicit tax)

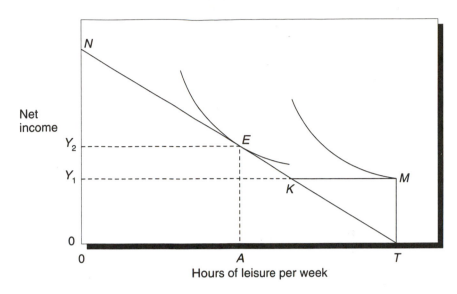

Assume that the individual does not pay taxes at this level of income so that earned income equals net income. Suppose that a minimum guaranteed income equal to *TM* is made available and assume also that the benefit is subject to a 100 percent implicit tax. Thus, for every dollar of earned income, the transfer is reduced by a dollar. For labor market earnings less than *TM*, the individual's net income remains at Y_1 ($Y_1 = TM$). The relevant budget constraint in presence of the transfer is therefore *TMKN*. The individual in question is better off not working at all thereby receiving an income equal to the guaranteed income (Y_1) although it is less than previous earnings (Y_2). In this case, the individual in question chooses point *M*.

In Figure 15-3, the amount of transfer also is reduced as earnings increase. However, the benefits are reduced less rapidly. Unlike Figure 15-2 where benefits are only extended to those with earnings less than Y_1 (which is equal to the amount of transfer), in Figure 15-3 the benefits are extended up to a level of income equal to Y_4 (point *B*). The amount of transfers decline with higher earnings as shown by the shaded area between *TB* and *MB*. Under this scheme, individuals who do not work receive a basic transfer equal to *TM*, the minimum guaranteed income. Those who enter the labor market have their benefits reduced only by some fraction of their earnings rather than being reduced by their entire amount of earnings. Those who choose to work any number of hours less than *DT* hours receive a transfer equal to the shaded area. Note that the transfer is equal to zero at point *B* (*DT* hours of work).

Figure 15-3   Work–net income budget constraint under public assistance (negative income tax scheme)

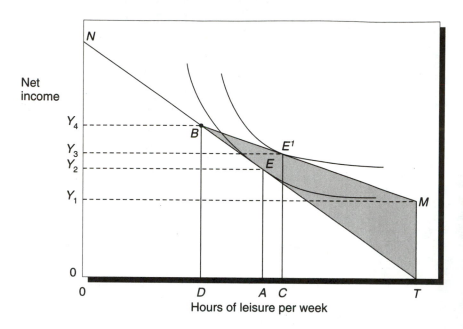

Under the lower implicit tax, the individual works CT hours (point E_1
on the new budget line MB) and receives Y_3 in total income. Thus,
although the individual is working less than before the transfer was made
available, he or she works more hours than under the case of a 100 percent
implicit tax. Of course, the decision as to how many hours an individual
works depends on the shapes of one's indifference curves. Table 15-1 presents some data of the effect of the different implicit taxes assuming a $100
minimum weekly guaranteed income. Although most of those earning less
than $100 per week under a 100 percent implicit tax are likely to choose not
to work, the lower implicit rate provides incentives for work because the
benefits are reduced by only a small amount of earnings.

The lower implicit tax is an example of an NIT scheme. It is referred to
as an NIT because recipients receive income transfers from the government
instead of paying taxes and, as their earnings increase, the amount of transfer income is reduced up to a level of earned income at which the subsidy
falls to zero. As earnings increase further, earned income is subject to a
positive income tax, meaning that individuals pay taxes to the government. Thus, the basis of an NIT is to extend the positive tax structure
beyond the zero tax bracket to a negative range where the government
makes payments to persons with low or no incomes.

From a theoretical standpoint, NIT provides more attractive incentives
for work. Furthermore, by making the program universal, NIT would not

Table 15-1   Transfers subject to different implicit tax rates

Guaranteed income	100	100	100	100	100	100
Earnings	0	10	50	100	150	200
Benefit Reduction						
100% implicit tax	0	10	50	100	100	100
50% implicit tax	0	5	25	50	75	100
Net Transfer						
100% implicit tax	100	90	50	0	0	0
50% implicit tax	100	95	75	50	25	0
Net Income						
100% implicit tax	100	100	100	100	150	200
50% implicit tax	100	105	125	150	175	200

have adverse effects on marital stability because families in similar circumstances would be treated equally. Furthermore, an NIT scheme can be expected to lower the administration costs that are currently incurred in administering numerous cash and in-kind programs. Also, by offering benefits in cash, an NIT scheme would eliminate inefficiencies associated with in-kind programs by restoring consumer sovereignty.

Several variants of the NIT have been proposed.[12] The basic elements of an NIT scheme include (1) a basic minimum guarantee, G; (2) a benefit reduction schedule, t; and (3) a break-even level of income at which transfers fall to zero, BE. If the benefit reduction rate (R) is constant, then the breakeven level of income $BE = G/R$.[13] The key is to adopt an NIT scheme that reduces work disincentives. Of course, the lower the implicit tax rate, the more effective the scheme will be in encouraging work. One particular problem, however, is that such a plan is likely to entail large expenditures and policymakers may be forced to lower the guaranteed level of income, a strategy that, although effective in reducing work disincentives, results in a situation where some genuinely needy members of the population receive benefits that are not adequate to meet basic necessities. Thus, an NIT scheme that has good work incentives may not provide adequate support to the genuinely needy, particularly those who are not able to work.

Before 1967, participants in the AFDC program faced a 100 percent implicit tax on earned income. The effective rate was actually lower

---

12. See Richard A. Musgrave and Peggy B. Musgrave, *Public Finance in Theory and Practice* (New York: McGraw-Hill Book Company, 1984).
13. For example, in Table 15-1, the minimum guaranteed income is 100. For a benefit reduction rate equal to 50 percent, the breakeven point is $100/.5 = 200$.

because some allowances were provided before the tax was applied. Costs that were deemed necessary for work (for example transportation and child care expenses) were deducted from the amount against benefits. Therefore, although the nominal implicit tax was 100 percent, the effective rate was lower. After 1967, the nominal implicit tax on earned income was reduced to 67 cents to the dollar. However, the effective tax rate increased in 1981 as a result of several changes in the procedures and reduction in the allowed expenses.[14]

Some important evidence on how recipients respond to different levels of guaranteed income and different levels of benefit reduction schemes comes from studies based on Income Maintenance Experiments.[15] Participants in the experiments were assigned to one of several NIT benefit plans or to a control group. Members of the control group received the regular benefits for which they were eligible. The behavior of the recipients in the experimental group was then compared to the behavior of those in the control group. In analyzing the change in behavior induced by transfers, various individual and family characteristics were taken into account. The results of these experiments suggest that recipients reduce labor supply when guaranteed income is increased and the implicit marginal tax rate is high. However, the labor supply reduction turned out to be much smaller than critics expected and probably more than what the proponents of NIT had hoped. For example, estimates from experiments imply that a basic benefit increase that raised the income of poor family heads by 10 percent would reduce their average labor supply by .7 percent to 1.7 percent.[16] These estimates are lower than those obtained from nonexperimental data. These estimates of the labor supply effects suggest that implementing some NIT scheme may be worthwhile.[17]

Serious attempts to implement the NIT scheme were made during the Nixon and Carter administrations. President Nixon proposed an NIT under the Family Assistance Plan (FAP). Nixon's plan, which was

14. Effective rates were probably less than 50 percent before 1967 and lower than 25 percent by 1971. As a result of the 1981 reforms, the effective rates increased to about 70 percent by 1982. See James Fraker, Robert A. Moffitt, and Douglas A. Wolf, "Effective Tax Rates and Guarantees in the AFDC Program, 1967–82," *The Journal of Human Resources* 20 (2) (Spring 1985): 251–63.

15. See Alicia H. Munnell, ed., *Lessons from the Income Maintenance Experiments* (Boston: Federal Reserve Bank of Boston and The Brookings Institute, 1987).

16. Gary Burtless, "The Economist's Lament: Public Assistance In America," *Journal of Economic Perspectives* 4 (1) (Winter 1990): 57-78.

17. We caution that, although social experimentation has added to our understanding of how individuals behave subject to different constraints, it is not quite clear how useful these experiments have been. There are so many sources of error and the results have been inconsistent. Thus, much less is known about the effects of NIT than was originally hoped when experiments were started. It is therefore not clear whether welfare reform policies should be based on the results from those experiments.

unveiled in a television speech in August 1969, contained a guaranteed income to both poor families with one parent and those with two parents or intact families. The NIT plan under FAP also included work requirements and a national minimum benefit for poor who are aged and disabled. The NIT elements of the FAP, which included a comprehensive national minimum benefit for welfare families, was rejected by Congress mainly because of concerns over its effect on labor supply. The other components of the FAP—the work requirements and national minimum benefit for poor aged and disabled persons—were enacted into law.

President Carter proposed the Program for Better Jobs and Income (PBJI) with an NIT as the main element. Carter's proposal emphasized differential treatment for those who could work and those who could not work. For those who could work, PBJI offered lower income support benefits along with guaranteed public service jobs for those who did not secure jobs in the private sector. Like Nixon's NIT proposal, Carter's proposal also failed to win congressional support.

It is ironic that while NIT has been recommended by economists as an effective way of simplifying the transfer system and reducing the work disincentives, the proposal has received the least political support. A possible reason for this is that, although most people want to reform welfare, the goals of various reformers are inconsistent. Some emphasize generosity to those in need. Usually they want a high guaranteed income and sometimes a low benefit reduction rate. Others emphasize work incentives. In this case, a low guarantee is recommended together with a low benefit reduction rate. A low benefit reduction rate helps those on welfare, but increases the breakeven level of income. The third major objective is to reduce program costs. In this case, a low guaranteed income is needed. If the work incentive effects are modest, then a high benefit reduction rate also should be adopted to reduce eligibility. Thus, because of the various objectives that require choice of different guaranteed income, benefit reduction rate, and the breakeven point, reformers have not formulated an NIT scheme that could be considered optimal. Political opposition for NIT proposals is primarily due to the uncertainty about labor supply effects and the concern over the potential cost of such a program.

Although most comprehensive proposals of a negative income tax have not been adopted, the food stamp program does contain some elements of the NIT. The food stamp program provides benefits that are similar to those that would be available under a low guarantee—low benefit reduction rate—negative income tax plan as suggested by Friedman and Tobin. The program is designed such that food stamp allotment is adequate to offer a family adequate diet. Thus, the food stamp program has what may be considered a minimum guarantee benefit. Nonetheless, the food stamp program differs from NIT proposals as suggested by Friedman and Tobin in that the benefits are in-kind and the program did not replace any existing program.

Mandatory Work for Benefits

Since the mid-1960s, the growth in the number of AFDC recipients combined with concern over the effects benefits have on work effort have motivated the design of a variety of reform policies that will maintain adequate
support, yet encourage labor force participation by recipients.[18] Until
recently, most mothers did not work outside the home, but remained at
home and took care of the children while the husband went to work. When
Aid to Families with Dependent Children was started in 1935, the goal was
to help single mothers (mainly widows) remain home to provide a reasonable quality of life for the children. It was not reasonable to expect widows
to work when the norm was that other mothers remained at home.
However, several things have changed since then. More females have
entered the labor force, including mothers in two-parent households. Thus,
there is no longer a justification that single mothers should not work like
other mothers. In addition, there is no evidence that a working mother hurts
a child's well-being. Another change has been the composition of the recipients. Although the program was aimed primarily at widows, today most of
the recipients are either never-married or divorced. This change in the composition of recipients has led to an argument that AFDC may be responsible
for marital instability. Because of these changes, it is now common to expect
more from the recipients. In particular, there have been a number of
attempts to mandate some form of work as a condition of recipiency.

Mandating work as a condition for recipiency is not new. The Speenhamland system of 1619 discussed in Chapter 3 required that able-bodied
poor work in exchange for support. A more recent example of a program
that has required some form of work obligation as a condition for welfare
recipiency is the Work Incentive program (WIN). WIN, which was started
as a discretionary program in 1967 and became mandatory in 1971, requires
that adults who do not have preschool children or another problem that
prohibits them from working, should make themselves available to participate in the labor market as a condition for receiving AFDC benefits. The
recipients are required to register with the state employment service and
participate in job training or other activities, and to accept employment
offers. WIN therefore imposed some work obligation. However, the program was never implemented fully.[19]

---

18. For a review of various work related programs pertaining to AFDC, see Demtra Smith
    Nightgale, "Workfare and Work Requirement Alternatives for AFDC Recipients," in
    National Conference on Social Welfare, *The Social Welfare Forum* (1982/1983): 73–85.
19. Several problems hinder work requirements. Inadequate funding frequently is a problem.
    A major problem has to do with the difficulty of enforcing the requirement when jobs are
    scarce. Also, it is not difficult for someone to avoid obtaining a job if that is the person's
    goal. Thus, such programs may call for providing jobs that welfare recipients may be
    required to take.

The common term that is now used to refer to work requirements for welfare recipients is *workfare*. This term came to be in common usage after President Nixon used it in his 1969 television speech:

> In the final analysis, we cannot talk our way out of poverty; we cannot legislate our way out of poverty, but this nation can work its way out of poverty. What America needs is not more welfare, but more "workfare."[20]

Under the workfare plan, no benefits are provided for working above the welfare check except for expenses related to work. The primary goal of workfare is to force able-bodied people to work in return for the welfare checks.[21] Nevertheless, workfare programs also are supposed to accomplish a number of other goals including:

1. *Strengthen work incentives*–Because welfare benefits are conditioned on work, the program helps develop the work ethic of recipients. Thus, requiring work for welfare brings the values of the recipients in line with those of the mainstream.

2. *Improve employability of recipients*–When recipients are assigned work responsibilities, they gain a sense of responsibility, change work habits, and develop useful skills. It is hoped that those experiences help them become more productive members of society.

3. *Social benefits*–When welfare recipients do no work, they do not contribute anything to the nation. By requiring that recipients participate in the labor market, it is hoped that they perform useful work that benefits society.

4. *Reduce the welfare rolls*–An important goal of requiring work is to reduce welfare rolls and thus reduce dependence on welfare. With work requirements, welfare use is not as attractive as when no work is required. Some people who would otherwise have participated in those programs are likely not to do so. Some of the recipients are expected to exit from welfare more quickly, thus reducing long-term dependency. Also, because of the job skills acquired by participating in the mandatory work programs, it is hoped that some recipients will exit from welfare to jobs that pay reasonably well.

---

20. Richard P. Nathan, *Turning Promises into Performance: The Management Challenge of Implementing Workfare* (New York: Columbia University Press, 1993), p. 14.
21. Originally the term workfare meant working off one's grant in unpaid government jobs. Today, the term has a broader meaning, including private job search, education, training, and government employment. We focus on the unpaid work element that remains the central feature of workfare.

5. *Dignity of recipients*–Finally, when recipients work for the benefits, they acquire self confidence and dignity. That is, as opposed to receiving benefits with no contribution to society, work requirements make recipients feel that they are doing something worthwhile. Thus, workfare generates psychic benefits.

Although it is true that work requirements may have several benefits, there could be some drawbacks. For example, although such requirements may improve employability of some recipients, the reverse could also be true. In some cases, employers believe that those in subsidized employment learn poor work habits and are worse employment risks than those that have not had such experience. Also, although workfare generates psychic benefits, if it is harshly administered, it could be demeaning to the recipient.

To investigate the effectiveness of work-related reforms, the Omnibus Reconciliation Act of 1981 offered states a number of options to experiment with work-for-welfare initiatives on a demonstration basis. Evaluations of the effectiveness of workfare programs indicate that the results are largely positive.[22] Specifically, work-related reforms appear to increase employment and earnings of the participants, not only while they participate in the program, but also in the post-program period. Such increases in post-program earnings lead to cost savings due to a reduction in welfare expenditures. On average, such savings appear to exceed the costs of the program. However, the effectiveness of the programs vary from state to state, and by program design. In some cases, the work programs have not shown any positive effect. For example, in West Virginia, the programs did not increase earnings or the employment of participants. This suggests that the programs may not be particularly effective in areas with very high unemployment rates.

The work-for-welfare strategy now in place in most of the states has been criticized on a number of grounds. One criticism is that recipients who participate in workfare programs do not have the rights that are extended to other workers. For example, they cannot join a union, do not receive employer-provided health insurance or Social Security, and are not entitled to Worker's Compensation or sick leave. Workfare also is criticized for displacing workers and depressing wages. There have been cases where workers have lost jobs only to find themselves doing the same jobs as workfare participants.

Although there are clearly positive effects of mandating work for welfare, the evidence available from the demonstration experiments suggests

---

22. See Judith M. Gueron, "Work and Welfare: Lessons on Employment Programs," *The Journal of Economic Perspectives* 4 (1) (Winter 1990): 79–98.

that gains are moderate. Many of the participants remain dependent on welfare and even those who exit welfare tend to remain poor. Thus, although workfare could be an important component of the reform policies, it is not a solution by itself.

SUMMARY

Although income support policies have various benefits, they also are associated with undesirable outcomes. Evidence suggests that expanding the U.S. welfare system is likely to result in losses that exceed gains. This realization has therefore motivated suggestions for reforming the system in a manner that reduces the unintended outcomes. This chapter, has focused on reforms that seek to minimize work disincentives and dependency. Specifically, it has analyzed the theoretical aspects of a negative income tax and also discussed workfare proposals. Although it is possible that these types of programs could help solve some of the dilemmas associated with supporting the poor, limited experimentation on the proposals prevent making conclusive generalizations.

The main message of this chapter is that there are compelling reasons for reforming the U.S. welfare system. It is not likely that any one single policy will solve the current problems of the welfare system. Rather, a combination of various policies may need to be enacted. The fact that the proposals discussed here have shown some success offers hope that it may be possible to restructure the welfare system.

STUDY AND DISCUSSION QUESTIONS

1. Compare and contrast Okun and Haveman's views of the redistributive system. Which position do you think is more realistic?

2. Discuss the objectives of an effective transfer system.

3. Discuss the negative income tax proposal. Why have policymakers not adopted a negative income tax scheme although economists seem to think it is the most appropriate way of reforming the welfare system?

4. Discuss the rationale for placing work obligations on recipients on welfare. What are the potential benefits for mandatory work programs?

5. Discuss other approaches to reforming the welfare system.

ADDITIONAL READINGS

1. Aaron, Henry J. *Why Is Welfare So Hard to Reform?* Washington, D.C.: The Brookings Institute, 1973.

2. Gueron, Judith M. *Reforming Welfare with Work,* New York: Ford Foundation, 1987.

3. ———. "State Welfare Employment Initiatives: Lessons From the 1980s." *Focus* 11 (1) (1988): 17–24.

4. Sanger, Mary Bryna. "The Inherent Contradiction of Welfare Reform," *Policy Studies Journal* 18 (3) (Spring 1990): 663–80.

16

WELFARE DEPENDENCY

Chapter 14 considered various income maintenance programs in the United States. Although Great Society programs have had some success in reducing poverty, they also have produced some undesirable outcomes. As demonstrated, transfer benefits have adverse effects on labor supply. There also is a growing concern over the effectiveness of welfare programs in eliminating poverty. Although income transfers reduce pretransfer poverty, those reductions are a result of a large amount of resources devoted to fighting poverty. As observed in Chapter 12, welfare benefits also are blamed for contributing to the breakdown of the traditional American family, an outcome that has far-reaching negative consequences on poverty. Another serious problem associated with transfer programs and a major criticism of Great Society programs is welfare dependency.

Welfare dependency has several meanings. In its simplest usage, welfare-dependent individuals rely on income transfers or other forms of public assistance for basic necessities such as food, medical care, housing, and so forth. In this context, welfare dependency merely refers to participation in welfare programs. Another definition relates to the share of an individual's total income that comes from government transfers. While some people receive a significant amount of income from government transfers, those transfers only comprise a small share of total household income. To others, however, transfer income represents a large share of their total income; some others rely entirely on transfers. When transfer payments are large relative to earned income, then recipients of those benefits are considered to be dependent on welfare.[1]

Welfare dependency also refers to an individual who could be self-supporting but relies on government support. This dependency implies

---

1. Note that based on this definition, a recipient who receives only a small amount in transfers and has low or no earnings is considered more dependent than one who receives more transfers but also has income from other sources.

that the recipient fails to exit the system even when such opportunities present themselves. This definition of welfare dependency blames the recipients. It is this type of dependency that John Gillin refers to as abnormal dependency, which is "that condition in which a person prefers to depend for his sustenance, in whole or in part, upon someone other than his natural supporter rather than to earn his own living."[2]

Finally, welfare dependency refers to long-term reliance on welfare. Although this definition does not specifically blame recipients, it does imply that there is a duration of recipiency beyond which individuals become dependent on welfare. This definition reflects the goals of the welfare programs as short-term not long-term solutions to poverty.

All these definitions are important. This chapter primarily focuses on welfare dependency as defined by duration of recipiency.[3] Even so, the duration-of-recipiency definition incorporates other types of dependency.

Long-term reliance on welfare is a serious problem not only because such dependency indicates persistent poverty, but because long-term welfare use indicates a failed public policy. In inaugurating the Great Society, President Lyndon Johnson declared that welfare relief was only a short-term strategy to help the poor.

> We are not content to accept endless growth of relief or welfare rolls. We want to offer the forgotten fifth of our population opportunity and not doles—the days of the dole in our country are numbered.

The proponents of the Great Society programs expected the poor to be self-supporting after short periods of welfare use. President Johnson was too optimistic. The data presented in Chapter 14 reveals that expenditures on welfare programs have continued to rise. Additionally, a significant proportion of recipients rely on welfare for extended periods.

The long-term reliance on welfare is now a major national concern and one that requires urgent attention. In order to design and formulate appropriate public policies, it is necessary to have a good understanding of the process that leads to the long-term reliance on welfare. This chapter begins with a brief look at some of the information concerning the length of time that individuals spend on welfare. Next, there is a review of some theories of welfare dependence and evidence on the determinants of long-term welfare use. Finally, there is a discussion of some suggestions for policy to deal with long-term welfare use. Emphasis is on the need to adopt policies that attempt to get people off welfare as early as possible because using welfare at one time increases the probability of future use.

---

2. John Lewis Gillin, *Poverty and Dependency* (New York: D. Appleton-Century Company, 1937), p. 21. This type of dependency is equivalent to the case discussed in Chapter 14 where a recipient prefers not to work in order to receive welfare benefits.
3. It is common to refer to the previous three definitions as static measures of dependency and to the duration on welfare as a *dynamic* measure of welfare dependency.

DURATIONS OF WELFARE RECIPIENCY

Although the main national data sets do not contain complete information on recipiency (particularly in regard to the time spent on welfare) they do reveal that some recipients remain on welfare for long periods.[4] For example, studies, using data from the Panel Study of Income Dynamics (PSID), reveal that between 40 and 60 percent of AFDC recipients have welfare careers that last for more than five years; over 25 percent of the recipients have welfare careers of more than nine years. Since this information is based on incomplete histories of recipiency, it is fair to conclude that durations of recipiency are much longer than reported.[5]

Greg Duncan and his colleagues find that 30 percent of AFDC recipients in PSID remain on welfare for one to two years, 40 percent receive welfare for three to seven years, and 30 percent receive welfare for eight or more years.[6] Charles Murray and Deborah Laren, using data from a sample of women under 40 who entered the AFDC rolls between 1968 and 1973, find that over 51 percent of the recipients remain on welfare for five or more years.[7] Utilizing a sample from Tennessee that has complete AFDC recipiency history, Mwangi Kimenyi finds the mean duration of recipiency to be about five years with approximately 21 percent of recipients having welfare careers of eight or more years.[8]

Table 16-1 reports data on the length of time that various subgroups in the population spend on welfare. The data are from a study by David Ellwood that used PSID data and also takes into account multiple spells of recipiency.[9] The data show that, whereas the observed duration of recipiency at any one time ranges between 4.37 and 9.33 years, many recipients will remain on welfare for much longer durations. For example, 39.3 percent of

---

4. Common data sets used to estimate time on welfare are based on longitudinal surveys that interview program participants at different time intervals. The most important data sets are the National Longitudinal Survey (NLS) of Young Women and the Panel Study of Income Dynamics (PSID). For a brief discussion of the shortcomings of these and other data sets in evaluating welfare durations, see Mwangi S. Kimenyi, "Rational Choice, Culture of Poverty, and the Intergenerational Transmission of Welfare Dependency," *Southern Economic Journal* 57 (4) (April 1991): 947–60.
5. It is important to distinguish between duration of welfare spells and the duration of welfare careers. A spell of welfare refers to a single continuous episode of welfare use. Welfare careers, however, refer to the cumulative duration of recipiency. Since most recipients have multiple episodes of recipiency, it is important to consider welfare careers in investigating the extent of welfare dependency.
6. Greg J. Duncan, Martha S. Hill, and Saul D. Hoffman, "Welfare Dependence Within and Across Generations," *Science* 239 (January 1988): 467–71.
7. Charles Murray and Deborah Laren, "According to Age: Longitudinal Profiles of AFDC Recipients and the Poor by Age Group," Report Prepared for the Working Seminar on the Family and American Welfare Policy, September 1984.
8. See Mwangi S. Kimenyi, "Rational Choice, Culture of Poverty, and the Intergenerational Transmission of Welfare Dependency."
9. David T. Ellwood, "Targeting Would-Be Long-Term Recipients of AFDC: Who Should Be Served?" Princeton, N.J.: Mathematica Policy Research (January 1986).

Table 16-1   Percentage of AFDC recipients with various characteristics and total durations of AFDC receipt

Recipient Characteristics at Time of First Spell Beginning	Percent of All First-Time Recipients (New Beginnings)	Percent of Recipients at Any Point in Time	Average Number of Years of AFDC Receipt	Percent Who Will Have AFDC Spells of 10 or More Years
Age				
Under 22	30.0	35.9	8.23	32.8
22 to 30	40.7	41.9	7.08	25.8
31 to 40	11.8	8.8	5.15	15.0
Over 40	17.6	13.4	5.23	15.8
Race/ethnicity				
White	55.2	47.7	5.95	19.6
Black	40.1	47.4	8.14	32.0
Other	4.8	4.8	6.94	25.5
Years of Education				
Under 9	9.7	9.6	6.81	24.5
9 to 11	37.6	41.9	7.65	29.2
Over 11	52.7	48.5	6.33	21.8
Marital Status				
Single	29.5	40.0	9.33	39.3
Divorced	28.1	20.2	4.94	13.7
Separated	32.3	31.9	6.80	24.4
Widowed	8.4	5.3	4.37	10.2

Table 16-1   (Continued)

Recipient Characteristics at Time of First Spell Beginning	Percent of All First-Time Recipients (New Beginnings)	Percent of Recipients at Any Point in Time	Average Number of Years of AFDC Receipt	Percent Who Will Have AFDC Spells of 10 or More Years
Number of Children				
0 to 1	43.4	48.7	7.71	29.7
2 to 3	42.8	37.3	6.04	20.1
Over 3	13.8	13.7	6.83	24.5
Age of Youngest Child				
Under 3	51.3	60.4	8.09	31.9
3 to 5	22.5	22.3	6.79	24.2
6 to 10	19.7	12.9	4.51	11.3
Over 10	6.5	4.4	4.71	12.4
Work Experience				
Worked in the last two years	65.8	59.6	6.53	23.0
Did not work in the last two years	34.2	39.8	8.00	31.2
Disability Status				
No disability	81.6	81.4	6.85	24.8
Disability limits work	18.4	18.6	6.97	25.0

Source: David T. Ellwood, "Targeting Would-Be Long-Term Recipients of AFDC," Table IV.1.

never-married women can be expected to spend 10 or more years on welfare. The data also reveals that duration of welfare receipt varies considerably across subgroups.

Clearly, long-term reliance on welfare is of major concern. Long-term welfare users are responsible for the largest proportion of social welfare expenditures. In addition, recipients in this group are the ones often associated with various other problems of welfare use. Thus, long-term reliance on welfare poses a serious challenge to the American system of welfare. Even those who support the spirit of the Great Society concede that the primary goal of the War on Poverty, to make people self sufficient, has not been achieved. Instead, both welfare use and dependency have increased among some segments of the American population. The concern over welfare dependency was the underlying motivation for the adoption of the Family Support Act of 1988. As stated, the intent of the legislation is "to encourage and assist needy children and parents under the new program to obtain the education, training, and employment needed to avoid long-term welfare dependence...."[10] President Clinton has indicated that he wants to restructure the welfare system to reduce the long-term reliance on welfare.

THEORIES OF WELFARE DEPENDENCY

The task of analyzing welfare dependency should start with a theoretical framework that relates individual characteristics, behavior, environment, incentives, and constraints to long-term welfare dependency. Long-term welfare use necessarily associates with long-term poverty. Thus, the development of a theory of welfare dependency requires an investigation of those factors and behavioral patterns that lead to persistent poverty among some segments of the population. In other words, it is necessary to investigate why some people use welfare for only a short time while other, seemingly identical, people remain on welfare for extended periods. This observation suggests that long-term welfare use may be a result of the interaction of various factors, both economic and cultural. This text considers three theories that offer credible explanations for long-term welfare use: cultural, expectancy, and rational choice models. A discussion follows of how each of these theories explain long-term welfare use.

Culture of Poverty and Dependency

Sociologists and anthropologists have long recognized that when several generations grow up and remain in poverty, a way of life evolves within

---

10. Congress of the United States, *Public Law 100-485,* 100th Congress, October 13, 1988.

these groups that is different from that in society's mainstream and that this way of life hinders the exit from poverty. Oscar Lewis[11] referred to this way of life as the Culture of Poverty. As noted in Chapter 11, the culture of poverty hypothesis posits that individuals who exhibit this culture are not only different from the rest of the society economically, but they also manifest patterns of behavior and values differing significantly from those of the mainstream society. When they emulate those patterns of behavior, the result is that they remain in poverty; many remain trapped in a state of welfare dependency.

For the culture of poverty to emerge, poverty must exist in a particular area, region, or slum for an extended length of time. For this reason, the culture of poverty is used to explain behavioral patterns of poor Blacks and Puerto Ricans in major metropolitan areas of the United States. Figure 16-1 comprises a flowchart of how poverty could manifest itself across generations and thereby lead to long-term welfare use. It starts with a family that is poor and on welfare and lives in an area with a high concentration of poverty. Extensive poverty breeds crime and delinquency. Additionally, schools in these areas provide low-quality education, and, given the low socioeconomic status of the parents, children from these neighborhoods are not encouraged to do well in school. Many students drop out of high school. The children receive a poor education that translates into dismal labor market prospects. If the parents receive welfare, then the children easily accept welfare use as a normal way of life. The cycle of poverty and welfare use repeats itself in the next generation. Therefore, those who exhibit a culture of poverty are likely to be dependent on welfare for extended lengths of time, and possibly, permanently.

Most people consider welfare to be degrading and to be evidence of personal failure. If one feels inadequate because of receiving welfare, pressure will build to be self-sufficient. Such views are consistent with mainstream values in American society. To imply that reliance on welfare is easily accepted as a normal way of life by those with a culture of poverty suggests that the members of this group of poor have a different value system than the middle class, or even other poor who have not emulated the culture of poverty.

Chapter 12 showed the relationship between family structure and poverty. Female headship is positively related to poverty and thus to welfare use. Daughters of mother-only households have a higher probability of having children out of wedlock and also of experiencing marital instability than those from two-parent households. The intergenerational transmission of family structure leads to welfare use and dependency. As was observed

---

11. See Oscar Lewis, *Five Families: Mexican Case Studies in the Culture of Poverty* (New York: Basic Books, 1959); and *La Vida: A Puerto Rican Family in the Culture of Poverty—San Juan and New York* (New York: Random House, 1965).

Figure 16-1   Intergenerational transmission of poverty

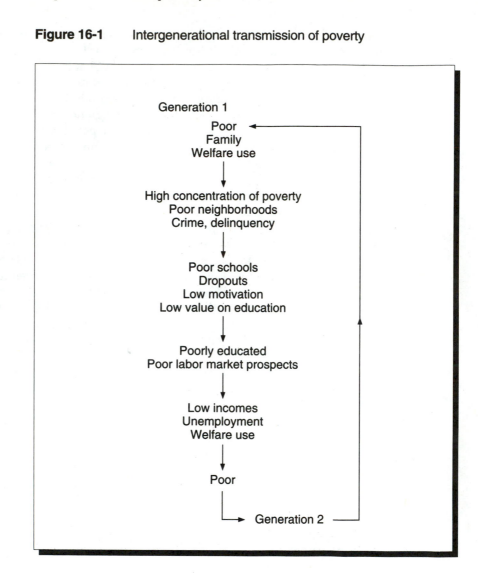

in Chapter 11, girls from families that exhibit lower-class culture have a higher probability of having children while still teenagers and are therefore likely to experience long-term poverty themselves. Figure 16-2 depicts the intergenerational transmission of family structure and welfare dependency that is consistent with the predictions of the culture-of-poverty hypothesis.

Thus, the culture-of-poverty hypothesis provides a plausible explanation for long-term welfare use. A critical extension of this hypothesis suggests that values and attitudes about welfare are transmitted from one generation to the next. Therefore, those who possess a culture of poverty are likely to be chronically dependent on welfare.

Figure 16-2   Family structure and the intergenerational transmission of welfare dependency

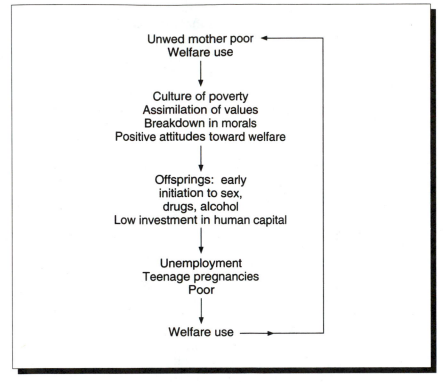

Expectancy Model of Dependency

The expectancy model of welfare dependency extends psychological theories of motivation that focus on success and failure. The expectancy model assumes that an individual's behavior in attempting (or not attempting) to overcome a task is primarily determined by the probability of success that the individual expects. Expectations are formed based on past experiences. If an individual has had success in a particular task in the past, the expectation of future success is high, and such an individual will be motivated to try. On the other hand, past failures lead the individual to expect future failures, which may deteriorate to a state where the individual does not try at all.

Poverty is obviously not a preferred state, and those living in poverty have failed to exit from that state. Such failure is not only determined by personal endowments (abilities, opportunities, resources, and so forth), but also by the degree to which individuals are motivated to achieve success or to avoid failure. The theory of motivation suggests that the tendency to approach success depends on the interaction between the degree of an individual's motivation, the expectancy or probability of success, and the incentive value of success at a particular activity.[12] Although the degree of motivation is fairly general, the expectancy and incentive value of success depend crucially upon the individual's past experiences. The stronger the expectation of success and the incentive value associated with such success, the higher the motivation to achieve, and consequently the stronger the tendency toward success.

If an individual who is poor attempts various activities (job search, business ownership) but fails, he or she develops an expectation that any subsequent attempts also will be met with failure. Under those circumstances, the motivation to approach success is weakened with each failed attempt. When an individual's attempt to overcome a particular hurdle is met with consistent failure, the individual develops an attitude that the situation is out of his or her control. In other words, the task exceeds the individual's possible limits of action. According to the psychological theory of reactance, when an individual perceives a situation as uncontrollable, the initial reaction is to vigorously attempt to regain control.[13] But such attempts depend to a great extent on the expectations of regaining control. If repeated reactance leads to failure, then the degree of reactance diminishes, and may eventually lead to complete inactivity. The loss of control persists and the individual comes to accept the situation as uncontrollable—and consequently does nothing about it. This outcome is referred to as *learned helplessness.*

Both the motivational theory and the theory of reactance are based on expectations. Expectations result from past experiences. Learned helplessness matches the motive to avoid failure—that is, an individual who stops trying has learned helplessness. Learned helplessness interferes with an individual's ability to seek and recognize opportunities for exercising control. Thus, the permanently poor who do not attempt to improve themselves, even when opportunities for doing so arise, may be considered as having reached the stage of learned helplessness. A prediction of the psychological theories is that those people are likely to remain poor because they have come to accept their position as unavoidable and uncontrollable. As such, when they enter the welfare system, they view welfare use as the only alternative open to them. Learned helplessness leads to long-term poverty and consequently to long-term welfare use.

With the psychological theories, it is not clear how the cycle of poverty begins. The cycle must at least start with repeated failure. Such failure may originate from personal deficiencies such as lack of good educational training and inability to perform well in jobs that do not necessarily require particular

---

12. See John William Atkinson, *An Introduction to Motivation* (Princeton, N.J.: Van Nostrand Company, 1964).
13. See Jack W. Brehm, *A Theory of Psychological Reactance* (New York: Academic Press, 1966).

skills. Alternatively, consistent failure could be a result of labor market imperfections such as racial discrimination. Repeated failure to obtain employment due to the above factors could lead to a state of learned helplessness, long-term poverty, and long-term welfare dependency.

Rational Choice Model of Dependency

The economic model of decision making assumes that individuals are rational and that they seek to maximize some subjectively valued utility given a set of alternatives and constraints. The choices made by an individual are subject to change as available alternatives and the constraints that confront the individual change. From this perspective, welfare dependency is not a cultural adaptation or a psychological phenomenon, but rather the result of a rational choice process based on the alternatives available and the constraints confronting the individual at any given time.

The labor-leisure tradeoff model demonstrates that under some circumstances, individuals who receive welfare benefits voluntarily withdraw from the labor market. If welfare allows the individual to achieve a higher level of satisfaction than he or she would earning a market income, then it is rational to choose to remain on welfare. Based on the rational-choice model, long-term reliance on welfare simply arises because the recipient consistently feels better off on welfare than off welfare. For a given level of welfare benefits, one can expect those with lower market-earnings potentials to rely on welfare for longer durations. In addition, increasing welfare benefits relative to market earnings should increase durations of recipiency.

The labor-leisure choice model considered the wage rate as the only relevant constraint. In evaluating long-term welfare recipiency, however, it is necessary to take into account various other constraints that recipients face and that may influence how long they rely on welfare. For example, the presence of young children in the recipient household may present a significant obstacle to exiting from welfare due to the cost of child care. As would be expected, recipients would make rational calculations as to whether to join the labor market and to pay for child care or to remain at home and receive welfare.

DETERMINANTS OF LONG-TERM WELFARE USE

One way to understand the dynamics of welfare recipiency is to investigate the events that are associated with beginnings and endings of recipiency spells. In particular, understanding the exit routes from welfare provides information as to why some individuals may remain on welfare for extended periods. Table 16-2 reports such data. The data reveal that the most important events that lead to a spell of AFDC recipiency is marital disruption and

Table 16-2   Events associated with the beginnings and endings of AFDC spells

Beginnings	Percent	Endings	Percent
Divorce/separation	45	Marriage	35
Childless, unmarried woman becomes a female head with children	30	Children leave parental home	11
Earnings of female head fell	12	Earning of female head increased	21
Earnings of others in family fell	3	Earnings of others in family increased	5
Other income fell	1	Transfer income increased	14
Other (including unidentified)	9	Other (including unidentified)	14
All	100	All	100

Sources: Data for beginnings are from Mary Jo Bane and David T. Ellwood,"The Dynamics of Dependence: The Routes to Self-Sufficiency," p. 18. Data for endings are from David T. Ellwood,"Targeting Would-Be Long-Term Recipients of AFDC," p. 46.

the out-of-wedlock birth. On the other hand, the most important factors that lead to exit from recipiency are marriage and increases in earnings. The data then suggests that family events and labor market conditions are important in explaining why some people remain on welfare for long periods while others exit after short periods.

Although analysis of the events that lead to spells of recipiency end provide information on why some people remain longer on welfare than others, there are many more factors that affect how long recipients remain on welfare. The key to understanding long-term welfare use is to investigate empirically how various factors affect the time spent on welfare. For example, because earnings affect the time a recipient remains on welfare, this suggests that it is necessary to investigate how various factors affect earnings and thus durations of recipiency. Studies of the determinants of the time that recipients remain on welfare are few; most of them have been conducted since the mid-1980s. Although these studies do not test the appropriateness of the various theories of welfare dependency discussed previously, the proxies used in estimating the models provide some evidence in support of some of the theories.

Most studies investigate the determinants of welfare durations using various data sets of AFDC recipients.[14] Generally, the studies estimate the determinants of duration of recipiency by considering various recipiency and program characteristics. The general idea in modeling welfare dependency is to assume that the behavior of recipients is consistent with utility maximization such that an individual recipient remains on welfare if the utility on welfare is greater than the utility off welfare. Any factor that increases the utility of being on welfare increases the duration of recipiency. Alternatively, factors that increase (reduce) the cost of being on welfare increase (lower) the probability of a spell of recipiency terminating. Factors that reduce (increase) the probability of exit then increase (reduce) duration of recipiency. Some of the factors that have important effects on duration of recipiency include benefit levels, labor market potential of recipients, the state of the economy, family background, number and age of children in recipient household, and race of recipients. Marital status and age of first receipt also have been found to be important in influencing welfare durations.[15]

Benefit Levels

An important determinant of welfare dependency is the attractiveness of public aid benefits relative to potential labor market earnings. As noted in Chapter 14, significant variations exist across states in terms of the generosity of welfare benefits. Moreover, the total package of benefits vary across individuals in the same jurisdiction depending on their circumstances. Exiting from welfare implies that even individuals who earn similar wages will experience losses of differing magnitudes. The decision to exit welfare involves taking into consideration the expected loss. Those with a higher expected loss are expected to have lower exit probabilities and thus longer durations on welfare. Virtually all studies find that duration of welfare recipiency is positively related to benefit levels.

Labor Market Potential

As mentioned, the decision to exit from welfare involves a comparison of the value of benefits with the expected labor market earnings. If a recipient has a low earnings potential, then the expected gain from exiting from welfare is

---

14. As noted previously, the AFDC program has attracted attention because of the explosion in the growth of expenditures and because of the negative consequences associated with the program.
15. See Rebecca Blank, "Analyzing the Length of Welfare Spells," *Journal of Public Economics* 39 (3) (August 1989): 245–73; John Fitzgerald, "Welfare Durations and the Marriage Market: Evidence from the Survey of Income and Program Participation," *Journal of Human Resources* 26 (3) (Summer 1991): 545–61; Robert Hutchens, "Entry and Exit Transitions in a Government Transfer Program: The Case of Aid to Families with Dependent Children," *Journal of Human Resources* 16 (2) (Spring 1981): 217–37; and Mwangi S. Kimenyi, "Rational Choice, Culture of Poverty, and the Intergenerational Transmission of Welfare Dependency."

low and thus those recipients can be expected to remain on welfare for longer durations. Proxies (such as having a high school diploma or having undergone job-related training) are used to measure labor market potential of recipients. The evidence from the studies confirm that those with higher potential market wages have shorter durations than those with lower expected wages. In particular, there is clear evidence that recipients with a high school diploma remain on welfare for considerably shorter periods compared to those who do not possess a high school diploma.

Unemployment

Duration of recipiency probably is influenced by the business cycle. For many individuals, welfare recipiency begins with an unemployment spell due to a downturn in the economy. Because there are wide regional variations in the unemployment rate, durations of recipients vary depending on the unemployment conditions in a recipient's area of residence. For example, some states have higher unemployment rates for several years. In Chapter 11, it was observed that inner cities have much higher unemployment rates than suburbs. Generally, exit rates from welfare are lower for recipients in areas where unemployment rates are higher. There are two reasons for this outcome. High unemployment rates imply a low probability of finding a job. High unemployment also imply downward pressure on market wage rates, which raises the expected loss from exiting from welfare. Consistently higher rates of unemployment in a region implies long-term reliance on welfare. This helps explain why inner-city residents have longer welfare careers than welfare recipients in other areas.

Family Background

The culture-of-poverty hypothesis suggests that there is intergenerational transmission of family types. Daughters from mother-only families have a high probability of becoming single mothers themselves. Also, recipients who are raised in families that use welfare are expected to view welfare more favorably (experience less disutility from welfare use) than other recipients, thus lowering the probability of exit from welfare. Individuals who grow up in families who use welfare are more likely to be more dependent on welfare. Morley Glicken states that a "disturbing trend has become apparent in America's welfare rolls. In the case of one of the most rapidly expanding programs, Aid for Families With Dependent Children (AFDC), the single group most likely to end up receiving welfare has proved to be people whose parents were recipients—people who have been socialized into the welfare system as children."[16]

---

16. See Morley D. Glicken, "Transgenerational Welfare Dependency," *Journal of Contemporary Studies* (Summer 1981): 31–41, 31.

Not many studies have empirically investigated intergenerational transmission of welfare dependence. Greg Duncan and colleagues have provided data for AFDC intergenerational patterns showing that 20 percent of daughters who grew up in highly dependent families were themselves dependent on welfare. Although the authors do not consider the intergenerational transmission of welfare dependency to be pervasive, they find that "the fraction of daughters from highly dependent homes who themselves become highly dependent (20 percent) is much greater than the fraction of daughters from nonrecipient families who become highly dependent (only 3 percent)."[17] Kimenyi finds that, all other things remaining equal, AFDC recipients whose parents were on welfare have longer durations than other recipients.[18] These results suggest that welfare dependency is transmitted from one generation to the next.

Children

Children constrain exiting from welfare recipiency. Children imply that a recipient must incur considerable child care costs upon exiting the welfare rolls and entering the labor market. The presence of children also implies that parents leave work more frequently to provide child services (such as, periods of sickness). This could reduce the probability of finding employment as employers may avoid hiring those employees who are likely to take off many days from work. All studies find that the number of children (particularly preschool children) is positively related to expected duration on welfare.

Race

Various studies find that non-Whites have longer welfare careers than do Whites. It is documented that, other factors being equal, non-Whites face more unfavorable labor market prospects than Whites because of labor market discrimination. Consequently, non-White recipients may remain on welfare for longer periods than White recipients. Race also could influence durations of recipiency if there are systematic racial differences in attitudes toward using welfare.

A more plausible explanation for racial differences in welfare careers keys on the marriage markets. One important exit route from welfare is through marriage. If Black women face more unfavorable marriage markets than White women, then one could expect Blacks to have longer welfare careers. There is increasing evidence supporting the idea that marriage

---

17. Greg J. Duncan, Martha S. Hill, and Saul D. Hoffman, "Welfare Dependence Within and Across Generations," p. 469.
18. Mwangi S. Kimenyi, "Rational Choice, Culture of Poverty, and the Intergenerational Transmission of Welfare Dependency."

markets are important in explaining both static and dynamic welfare dependency.[19]

Marital Status and Age of First Receipt

Some studies investigate the effect of marital status and the age at which recipients started receiving welfare. Generally, women who have never been married remain on welfare for considerably longer periods than those who have been married. While married, they may not have been eligible for benefits or may not have needed transfers. Alternatively, never-married women may receive child support that may help them exit from welfare, thus reducing the duration of recipiency.

A good predictor of welfare duration is the age at which recipients first enter the welfare rolls. Specifically, those who begin receiving welfare while teenagers remain on welfare for considerably longer durations than those at later ages. By having children while still teenagers, those recipients necessarily forgo investing in human capital and lack work experience. Having children while still teenagers also reflects the effects of the culture of poverty previously discussed. That is, most girls who have children while teenagers often come from mother-only households and live in areas of high concentration of poverty. In addition, many are from welfare families and have a less negative attitude toward using welfare.

PUBLIC POLICY

One reason why the issue of long-term reliance on welfare demands serious policies is because using welfare at any one time affects the probability of future use. This phenomenon is known as *duration dependence*. Duration dependence means that the probability of exiting from welfare is influenced by the length of time that a recipient has been on welfare. If welfare use is characterized by positive duration dependence, then the probability of exit increases the longer a recipient remains on welfare. Conversely, negative duration dependence implies that the probability of exit declines the longer a recipient remains on welfare. By and large, most of the studies find that welfare use is characterized by negative duration dependence.[20]

---

19. See William A. Darity Jr., and Samuel L. Myers, Jr., "Does Welfare Dependency Cause Female Headship? The Case of the Black Family," *Journal of Marriage and the Family* 46 (4) (November 1984): 765–80, and Mwangi S. Kimenyi, "Rational Choice, Culture of Poverty, and Intergenerational Transmission of Welfare Dependency."

20. See, for example, Rebecca Blank, "Analyzing the Length of Welfare Spells"; John Fitzgerald, "Welfare Durations and the Marriage Market: Evidence from the Survey of Income and Program Participation"; Robert Hutchens, "Entry and Exit Transitions in a Government Transfer Program"; Robert D. Plotnick, "Turnover in the AFDC Population: An Event History Analysis," *Journal of Human Resources* 18 (1) (Winter 1983): 65-81; and David Ellwood, "Targeting 'Would-Be' Long-Term Recipients of AFDC," Princeton, N.J.: Mathematica Policy Research, 1986. Some of the studies find weak negative duration dependence.

Welfare use today could increase the probability of its future use by worsening the labor market prospects of recipients. If current receipt reduces labor supply, those who use welfare have less work experience, which subsequently reduces their employment prospects. Less work experience implies an increased probability of welfare use in the future.

Another avenue through which current participation may affect future use is through family structure. As mentioned, welfare use has increased the number of single-parent households and average family size. Both effects increase the probability of welfare use in the future.

Finally, there is disutility associated with welfare use. The longer a participant remains on welfare, the more likely that he or she will accept welfare as a genuine source of livelihood. Thus, the disutility associated with welfare use declines over time as a recipient remains on welfare. Welfare use at one time increases the probability of future recipiency. This implies that it is necessary to identify potential long-term welfare users and help them terminate reliance on public support as early as possible.

The theories and evidence discussed herein suggest a number of public policies to deal with the long-term reliance on welfare. Based on the available evidence, it is possible to identify potentially long-term users by considering the various factors that lead to long-term dependency. Policy makers can then target specific polices on those individuals who are likely to remain on welfare for extended durations. Such policies could include training or subsidies to employers to induce them to hire these potential long-term users. Although such programs may be costly, they could be justified on the grounds that the same individuals will otherwise end up costing taxpayers much more in the form of income transfers.

Human capital investment (for example, graduating from high school) is an important way of reducing dependency. The most chronically dependent recipients do not possess a high school diploma. Thus, more emphasis on public education (specifically focusing on reducing high school dropouts) is essential. The inner-city situation needs special attention. Since long-term welfare use is crucially influenced by family background, targeted antipoverty efforts are needed in those areas where poverty is concentrated.

Racial differences exist in welfare dependence. Results suggest that welfare reform policies should identify those factors that increase the probability of dependence among Blacks. Such an approach may imply race-specific policies, which, although controversial, may be beneficial in the long run. As suggested by Kimenyi (1991), an active policy to deal with the economic status of Black males may be the key to solving the welfare dependency of Black females. Such programs could increase employability and job creation. Blacks may remain on welfare for longer durations because they have a lower probability of obtaining employment due in part to racial discrimination in employment. This suggests that the government should continue to enforce equal employment laws as discussed in Chapter 10.

Some welfare recipients remain on welfare because benefits are attractive and conditions for recipiency may not be stringent enough. Although it is necessary to help the poor, the benefit structure should discourage dependency. This issue is central to welfare reform as discussed in Chapter 15.

To a large extent, long-term welfare use is due to various constraints that recipients face. It is unreasonable to expect single mothers to exit from welfare if they cannot afford child care. Also, if the recipients lack skills that would help them obtain employment, it is difficult for them to exit from welfare. Thus, policies to provide child care, and stricter enforcement of child support should be central to solving the long-term welfare use problem.

Probably the most important policies that would reduce long-term welfare use are those that make work more attractive. Policies such as health care and earned income tax credit should be emphasized.

Policies that demand more from welfare recipients may be important in reducing welfare dependence. Workfare programs discussed in Chapter 15 could be expected to reduce the time spent on welfare. However, as noted previously, not much is known about the effectiveness of those programs. If the programs serve a punitive role, they are not likely to solve the dependence problem. Any work obligations should be designed in a manner that promises skill development that would make recipients exit from welfare.

Other policies also could be used to reduce duration of recipiency. For example, it is possible to place a limit on the length of time that recipients are eligible for benefits. Alternatively, benefits could be reduced the longer a recipient remains on welfare. Other strategies could be to reduce benefits when a recipient has more children. These types of policies may be effective. However, the largest burden of those policies are likely to be borne by the children. For the society to shift such a burden to the children is obviously not consistent with principles of fairness that are expected in civilized nations. This suggests that probably the best policies to reduce welfare dependence are those that help recipients enter and remain in the labor market.

SUMMARY

This chapter has examined the long-term reliance on welfare. Prolonged welfare use signals failure of public policy and the persistence of poverty. The chapter also presented theories that explain long-term welfare use. Some of the important determinants of welfare dependency were considered. The evidence suggests that welfare dependency is the result of both rational choice and cultural adaptation. Finally, it has been suggested that welfare use is characterized by negative duration dependence.

Various public policies to deal with welfare dependence have been proposed. It is suggested that the key to solving the problem of long-term welfare use is to identify potential long-term users and target these recipients with specific policies. Since welfare use probably exhibits negative duration dependence, the most cost-effective method of dealing with long-term use is to get recipients off welfare as early as possible. The longer a recipient remains on welfare, the more difficult it will be to terminate welfare use. Although many policies could effectively reduce durations of recipiency, punitive measures may not be appropriate.

STUDY AND DISCUSSION QUESTIONS

1. Evaluate the theories of welfare dependency. Which theory do you think best explains why some recipients remain on welfare for extended periods?

2. Outline how you would investigate the factors that determine long-term welfare use.

3. Focusing on the various factors that are associated with long-term welfare use, discuss the policies that you would propose to deal with the problem of welfare dependency.

4. If one believes that culture influences welfare dependency, what policies do you think would be appropriate?

ADDITIONAL READINGS

1. Auletta, Ken. *The Underclass*. New York: Random House, 1982.

2. Barr, Nicholas and Robert Hall. "The Probability of Dependence on Public Assistance," *Economica* 48 (190) (May 1981): 109–23.

3. Corcoran, Mary, Greg Duncan, Gerald Gurin, and Patricia Gurin. "Myth and Reality: The Causes and Persistence of Poverty," *Journal of Policy Analysis and Management* 4 (4) (Summer 1985): 516–36.

4. Goodwin, Leonard. *Causes and Cures of Welfare: New Evidence on the Social Psychology of the Poor*. Lexington, Mass.: Lexington Books, 1983.

5. Kane, Thomas. "Giving Back Control: Long-Term Poverty and Motivation," *Social Service Review* 61 (3) (September 1987): 405–19.

6. Taylor, Shelley E. "Hospital Patient Behavior: Reactance, Helplessness or Control?" *Journal of Social Issues* 35 (1979): 156–84.

17

HOMELESSNESS

Official poverty estimates are based on periodic surveys of household incomes. As such, homeless people are not included in the poverty statistic. The omission of the homeless in the poverty count underestimates the number of poor—especially the extremely poor. Although much is known about the general poor population (including their numbers, income levels and sources, and family types), much less is known about the homeless. Thus, while progress has been made in dealing with the poverty of the general poor population, little has been accomplished in dealing with the homeless.

Three main issues have hindered the formulation of appropriate homelessness policies. A primary obstacle in the formulation of a national homelessness policy has been the lack of a consensus on the extent of this problem. There is agreement that there are a large number of people who are homeless across the United States, but there is no consensus as to the size of this population, the primary causes of homelessness, or what should be done about the problem. In addition to the lack of a consensus as to the size of the homeless population, public policy to deal with homelessness has been hindered by the general view that the homeless population is primarily comprised of the undeserving poor. A large number of homeless have alcohol and drug problems. Therefore, it has been common to blame the homeless for their problems. Until recently, the public and policymakers used derogatory terms to describe the homeless. The homeless were viewed as dirty, lazy, and drunk bums. Even today, many people still consider the homeless as social misfits who have brought their problems upon themselves and thus do not deserve help from the society. When a group of people is considered as undeserving poor, there frequently are no serious public policies that are enacted to deal with their problem. The final dilemma that has hindered the enactment of appropriate public policies to deal with homelessness is that a large number of homeless advocates have failed to articulate the true causes of homelessness. Most advocates view the problem as one of lack of affordable housing. In other words, the advocates stress policies that make housing available to low income populations. Obviously, this is a valid policy approach. However, advocates tend to ignore some of the other factors that could be important causes of homelessness. Failure to acknowledge other primary causes of homelessness (such as alcoholism and drug addiction) results in adoption of policies that do not effectively deal with the root causes.

During the 1980s (as a result of the political activities of homeless advocates, most notably Mitch Snyder and other members of the Community for Creative Non-Violence (CCNV)), the issue of homelessness attracted national attention. Interest in the homeless issues is evidenced by numerous studies conducted during the 1980s that sought to estimate the number of homeless population and also the characteristics of members of that population. Today, many people (including politicians, social workers, and the general public) agree that the problem has reached an extent that demands more focused initiatives.

This chapter examines some aspects of the homeless problem. It begins by looking at the extent of homelessness in the United States as revealed by various estimates. In addition, it briefly discusses the composition and problems experienced by this population. Finally, there is coverage of some of the factors that are responsible for causing homelessness and public policy suggestions.

EXTENT AND COMPOSITION OF THE HOMELESS

Size of the Homeless Population

Like poverty, defining homelessness is crucial to understanding the extent of the problem. In attempting to obtain an accurate count of the homeless population, questions arise as to which people should be included in this group. For example, should a person who doubles up with friends and relatives be considered homeless? Should families housed in welfare hotels be counted as homeless? Are children who run away from their homes and end up in the streets homeless? Or are battered women in shelters for battered women homeless? The homelessness rate will vary depending on which groups are included in the definition of homeless. The Stewart B. McKinney Homeless Assistance Act of 1987 defines homeless as

> (1) An individual who lacks a fixed, regular, and adequate nighttime residence; and (2) an individual who has a primary nighttime residence that is (a) a supervised publicly or privately operated shelter designed to provide temporary living accommodations (including welfare hotels, congregate shelters, and transitional housing for the mentally ill), (b) an institution that provides a temporary residence for individuals intended to be

institutionalized, or (c) a public or private place not designated for, or ordinarily used as, a regular sleeping accommodation for human beings.[1]

In Chapter 5, it was noted that obtaining an accurate number of the poor is quite difficult. Counting the homeless is even more difficult. As defined herein, the state of homelessness is fairly broad and a measure of the extent of the problem should include those who sleep in streets, shelters, abandoned buildings, cars, subway systems, and other transportation depots. Even when there is agreement on how to define the homeless, attempts to obtain a comprehensive count of homeless people is complicated by a number of factors. The first is that homeless people are extremely mobile. A homeless person may be at several street corners, shelters, transportation depots, all in the same day. The mobility of the homeless increases the likelihood of overnumeration. Furthermore, some homeless people may be in places that are not known to enumerators (the people who conduct the surveys) and as such will be excluded from the count. A significant proportion of homeless persons have an interest in concealing where they live to avoid being harassed by the general public and by law enforcement authorities. Another problem is that it is not always easy to distinguish homeless people from other members of the population. Some homeless people do not differ to any significant degree in appearance or behavior from that of other members of the population.[2] Finally, interviewing the homeless to gather information on their characteristics and service needs meets serious problems because many of them may not provide accurate information.

The common method of enumerating the homeless include street counts, counting those who sleep in shelters, or obtaining counts based on service usage such as soup kitchens. Each of these methods has its problems. Thus, although there have been several attempts to estimate the number of homeless people in the United States, those counts are at best rough estimates. As already mentioned, it is difficult to obtain an accurate number of homeless people who are not in a fixed place (such as a shelter) for an extended period of time because of the possibility of double counting. On the other hand, although those who use shelters, especially those who use shelters at night, can be conveniently enumerated, such a procedure omits those who sleep outside in the streets, abandoned buildings, in cars, and other such places. Also, the number of homeless people in shelters vary widely depending on the weather. Shelters report much larger numbers of homeless during cold nights. Attempts to count the homeless based on service usage

---

1. *Public Law 100-77*, July 22, 1987. This act was enacted following relentless demonstrations by members of the Community for Creative Non-Violence led by Mitch Snyder.
2. The number of homeless people in this category probably is not large. Most homeless people are easily distinguished from other members of the population.

(such as soup kitchens) can be a problem, too; there are many people who eat in soup kitchens who are not homeless and there is a large number of homeless who do not use any services at all. However, numbers based on street counts do not include many other homeless people.

Although it is difficult to enumerate the homeless, policies to deal with the problem should be based on some credible estimate of the size of this population. Faced with a growing number of homeless and pressure from various advocacy groups to establish policies to deal with the problem, there has been a number of attempts to assess the extent of homelessness in various parts of the country. Although most surveys report only the people who are actually homeless, there have been attempts to estimate the population that is at risk of becoming homeless. If one considers availability of affordable housing to be the main cause of homelessness, then it is necessary to consider the extent of doubling and crowding because these measures indicate problems in finding affordable housing.

The most comprehensive estimates of the national homelessness rates come from studies conducted by the Department of Housing and Urban Development (HUD) and by the Urban Institute.[3] The HUD study primarily gathered information on the number of homeless indirectly by interviewing local persons who are knowledgeable of the homeless situation. Overall, about 500 telephone interviews were held with public and private representatives in 60 metropolitan areas. The information gathered from interviews was complemented with a survey of shelter usage. Interviews were conducted on a random sample of 184 shelters in the metropolitan areas selected. The HUD study estimated national homelessness in January 1984 to be in the range of 200,000 and 600,000. HUD considered the most reliable range to be between 250,000 and 350,000 homeless persons. The study estimated homelessness rates in metropolitan areas with populations of 250,000 and over to be 13 persons per 10,000 population while smaller metropolitan areas (50,000 to 250,000 population) had an average homelessness rate of 6.5 persons per 10,000 population.[4]

All existing studies report higher homelessness rates in cities as compared to rural and small towns. There are a number of reasons for this. More shelters and services are available in larger urban centers, which therefore attracts homeless people to these areas. Migration to cities with the hope of obtaining employment also adds to the number of homeless. Also, urban centers are more conducive to the homeless as they are not as visible as in small towns. Finally, officials in small towns and rural areas have been known to provide homeless people in their areas with bus tickets

---

3. A 1980 Bureau of the Census survey of the homeless was not comprehensive enough and is not seriously used.
4. See Kathleen Peroff, "Who Are the Homeless and How Many Are There?" in Richard D. Bingham, Roy E. Green, and Sammis B. White, eds., *The Homeless in Contemporary Society* (Newbury Park, Calif.: Sage Publications, 1987), pp. 33–45.

to large out-of-state cities. This practice, known as *greyhound therapy*, is comparable to the passing out strategy discussed in Chapter 3.[5]

The Urban Institute study surveyed the urban homeless focusing on 20 statistically representative cities which had 100,000 or more people in 1984. A random sample of 1,704 homeless persons who used soup kitchens or shelters was interviewed.[6] Estimates of the number of homeless based on this survey suggest that in cities with a population of 100,000 and over across the country, there were about 229,000 homeless people who used services in March 1987, a homelessness rate of 37.4 persons per 10,000 population. Because a large number of homeless persons do not use services, the actual number of homeless persons can be expected to be much higher.

Projections of the homeless in United States as a whole based on the Urban Institute study assuming 50 nonservice users for every 100 service users, placed the number of the homeless in 1987 at between 567,000 and 600,000, a homelessness rate of between 23.5 and 24.9 persons per 10,000 population. Burt and Cohen suggest that because the estimated number of homeless was based on people homeless for one night, the number of homeless during the entire year is much higher. The authors state that since the number of homeless in the course of a year is about double the number homeless at any given time, then over 1 million people were homeless at some time in 1987.

Tables 17-1 and 17-2 report homelessness rates across a number of jurisdictions in the United States. Table 17-1 reports data from the Urban Institute study that were obtained by actual counts of the homeless or by estimates of the number of homeless in a particular night. The data show that there are wide variations in the homelessness rates across jurisdictions. Large metropolitan areas such as Boston and the District of Columbia have higher homelessness rates than rural areas. Although the homelessness rate in Washington, D.C., was 41 people per 10,000 population in 1985, the rate in rural Ohio counties was only about 2.4 per 10,000 population in the same year. Table 17-2 reports data on the extent of homelessness in some of the cities included in the HUD survey. The data shows that large cities (such as, San Francisco, Los Angeles, Miami, Chicago, and New York) have the highest homelessness rates. Although homelessness in small towns is much lower, the problem exists. Table 17-2 also includes data on the extent of crowding and doubling up. Even without making a judgment as to whether the number of homeless is large or small, the data presented here does suggest that there is reason to design and implement policies to deal with homelessness.

---

5. There is not much documented evidence that this practice is widespread today.
6. See Martha R. Burt and Barbara E. Cohen, *American Homeless: Numbers, Characteristics, and Programs That Serve Them* (Washington. D.C.: The Urban Institute Press, 1989).

Table 17-1   Homeless rates for different cities (based on estimates from studies with street counts)

Area	Year Data	Estimated Number of Homeless	City Population	Homeless Rate (Number per 10,000) (in thousands)
Boston	1983	2,115	571	37.0
	1986	2,863	574	49.9
Chicago	1985	2,200	2,992	7.4
District of Columbia	1985	2,652	623	41.1
Nashville	1983–1984	791	462	17.1
Phoenix	1982	1,264	824	15.3
Pittsburgh	1983	549	403	13.6
Fairfax County, Virginia	1987	426	670	6.8
Ohio—16 rural counties	1985	261	1,091	2.4
California Alameda	1987	817	1,209	6.8
Orange		764	2,167	3.5
Yolo		71	126	5.6

Source: Martha R. Burt and Barbara E. Cohen, *American Homeless: Numbers, Characteristics, and Programs That Serve Them,* Table 2.1, p. 24.

There are a number of other estimates of the size of the homeless population, but the numbers vary widely and it is difficult to evaluate their credibility. One source of bias is that the groups conducting the estimates frequently have a special interest in overestimating the size of the population either for funding purposes or in order to influence public policy. The more extensive the problem is made to appear influences how seriously the policymakers will consider the problem to be. If the homeless population is large, more resources are likely to be devoted to dealing with the problem. The Committee for Creative Non-Violence (CCNV), a homeless advocacy group, estimated the homeless population to be between two and three million, a homelessness rate of 100 persons per

10,000 population, a much higher number than estimated by HUD and the Urban Institute.[7]

Of particular concern is the fact that a significant proportion of the homeless are children. As such, several surveys have attempted to estimate the number of children who are homeless. Table 17-3 reports estimates of children who are homeless from various surveys. Notice that estimates vary depending on the procedures used in the enumeration and also on who is included in the survey. The data show that advocacy groups report much higher numbers of homeless children than is reported by other groups. Nonetheless, the data reported here suggest that there is need to be concerned about homeless children and their families.

Clearly, it is impossible to pinpoint the actual number of homeless people in the United States. Nevertheless, even though the estimates of the homeless population vary widely, the available data suggest that the homeless problem warrants national and local policy initiatives. Furthermore, most studies show that there is a new group of homeless population that has emerged in the last few decades. This group includes children and women who have traditionally not been part of the homeless population. The presence of children among the homeless demands urgent public policy initiatives. Still, more sophisticated and comprehensive counts of the homeless are necessary.

Even without relying on actual counts, there are some indirect indicators of the extent of homelessness. One such indicator is the demand for services: soup kitchens, shelters, transitional housing, mental health services, and other such social services. The U.S. Conference of Mayors reports that the demand for services increased during the late 1980s. One important indicator of the extent of homelessness based on service demand is the turnaway statistics reported by shelters. This is the number of people seeking shelters, who are not provided one because of lack of space. The U.S. Conference of Mayors reports that in 1988, 19 percent of requests for shelters went unmet.

Another indirect measure of the risk of becoming homeless is the demand for low-income housing. Various communities have reported long waiting lists for public housing and other low-income rental units. This reflects a relatively low supply of affordable housing, which may translate into homelessness.

Finally, eviction rates can be used as a proxy of housing affordability. Large cities such as New York, Chicago, Milwaukee, and others, reported

---

7. See Mary Ellen Hombs and Mitch Snyder, *Homeless in America: A Forced March to Nowhere* (Washington, D.C.: Committee for Creative Non-Violence, 1982). There is good reason to believe that CCNV inflated the number of homeless.

Table 17-2   Extent of homelessness and other measures of poor housing outcomes

City	Homelessness per 100,000 Population	Crowding per 100,000 Population	Doubling-up per 100,000 Population
San Francisco, Calif.	535.1	4,300.6	1,259.9
Los Angeles, Calif.	412.0	10,106.6	1,803.1
Miami, Fla.	348.8	11,491.2	1,978.5
New York, N.Y.	346.2	6,389.6	1,673.9
Chicago, Ill.	323.9	4,639.2	1,792.5
Worcester, Mass.	259.9	1,735.4	938.8
Fort Wayne, Ind.	208.1	2,051.7	1,520.4
Las Vegas, Nev.	205.0	4,383.8	1,688.7
Houston, Tex.	200.7	6,265.5	1,803.5
Seattle, Wash.	187.6	1,833.9	1,011.7
Detroit, Mich.	173.8	3,043.8	1,997.1
Reno, Nev.	147.7	2,901.8	1,165.7
Richmond, Va.	147.6	2,224.4	1,690.5
Portland, Oreg.	136.4	1,862.0	866.5
Hartford, Conn.	112.2	2,556.2	1,455.4
Little Rock, Ark.	103.5	3,744.9	1,892.2
Davenport, Iowa	94.5	1,982.0	1,031.3
Boston, Mass.	86.6	2,429.8	1,159.5
Tampa, Fla.	86.3	2,566.3	1,202.2
Philadelphia, Pa.	75.5	2,499.7	2,287.6
Lincoln, Nebr.	65.3	830.8	451.0
Birmingham, Ala.	64.2	4,195.1	1,733.3
Phoenix, Ariz.	62.7	4,609.0	1,730.6
Cincinnati, Ohio	62.1	3,227.9	1,975.2
Columbia, Mo.	61.3	1,652.5	381.4
Louisville, Ky.	59.7	2,903.2	2,055.2
Danville, Va.	58.5	3,784.6	1,649.7
Syracuse, N.Y.	57.7	1,722.6	1,226.6
Grand Rapids, Mich.	55.9	1,857.9	947.0
Salt Lake City, Utah	52.4	4,388.1	1,105.3
Sioux City, Iowa	46.5	2,323.2	454.6
Monroe, La.	45.6	5,136.1	1,571.5
Minneapolis/ St. Paul, Minn.	45.3	1,623.8	527.7
Raleigh/Durham, N.C.	42.2	2,855.3	1,304.7
Pittsburgh, Pa.	40.8	1,964.8	1,539.2
Pueblo, Colo.	38.0	3,258.1	1,712.6
Jackson, Mich.	32.7	1,769.9	919.0
Baton Rouge, La.	32.5	5,106.5	1,262.2
Dayton, Ohio	31.7	1,770.2	1,442.6
Athens, Ga.	31.1	2,874.0	847.5
Baltimore, Md.	30.7	2,853.2	2,197.8

Table 17-2   (Continued)

City	Homelessness per 100,000 Population	Crowding per 100,000 Population	Doubling-up per 100,000 Population
Tyler, Tex.	29.4	4,410.6	1,731.2
Colorado Springs, Colo.	27.9	2,090.4	939.9
Charlotte, N.C.	26.7	3,625.3	1,858.7
Kansas City, Mo.	25.1	2,092.8	1,446.2
Cleveland, Ohio	22.0	1,791.2	1,483.0
Binghamton, N.Y.	19.9	1,305.8	1,282.1
Charleston, S.C.	17.5	3,937.5	1,778.2
Rochester, N.Y.	13.6	1,255.1	1,116.5
Fall River, Mass.	6.8	3,125.0	1,250.0

Source: The data are for 50 of the 60 metropolitan areas surveyed by HUD and reported in Marjorie Honig and Randall K. Filer, "Causes of Intercity Variation in Homelessness," *American Economic Review* 83 (1) (March 1993): 248–55, Table 1.

increased eviction rates during the 1980s. Most of these evictions were actions against low-income families, many of whom were on public assistance. Obviously, eviction increases the probability that families will be homeless. In some cases, those evicted have no place to go or resources to rent other housing, thus they become homeless once evicted.

Composition of the Homeless

Another important dimension to understanding the extent of homelessness is the composition of the homeless and the problems that this population faces. Although homelessness implies the lack of housing, it frequently is associated with many other problems.[8] Below we discuss the composition and the problems faced by homeless persons.

Age–One notable change in the composition of the homeless population over the last few decades has been in their age. In earlier days, most of the homeless were older men who had participated in the labor market, but for various reasons their relationship with the labor market had been broken. Today, however, the homeless are much younger and most of them have not had a stable relationship with the labor market. A 1963 study by Donald Bogue of homeless people in 41 cities found the mean age

---

8. For a more detailed discussion of the composition of the homeless population and their problems, see Peter H. Rossi, *Down and Out in America: The Origins of Homelessness* (Chicago: University of Chicago Press, 1989).

Table 17-3   Estimates of the number of homeless children

Year and Source	Number	Explanations
1987 Urban Institute	35,000 homeless children	Includes only homeless using shelters over a seven-day period in cities with a population over 100,000. Based on a national representative sample of service-using homeless individuals and providers of food and shelter for the homeless. Data collected in March 1987.
1988 U.S. Department of Housing and Urban Development	40,000 homeless children[1]	Includes only shelter-using population in cities with population over 25,000 on an average night in 1988. Based on a probability sample of 200 shelters.
1987 National Academy of Sciences	100,000 homeless children[2]	Refers to any given night in the United States. Estimate based on total of 735,000 homeless on any given night. Of these, 25 percent are members of intact families of whom 55 percent are children.

Table 17-3   (Continued)

Year and Source	Number	Explanations
1988 U.S. Department of Education	220,000 school-aged homeless children[3]	Based on state-collected data received from 45 states. Combines data of a variety of types, including daily counts, annual estimates, and partial counts from two states. The majority of states (40) reported annual counts. Fourteen states included data on numbers of preschool children, which totalled 33,119.
1984 National Coalition of Homeless	500,000 homeless children	Refers to any given night in United States. Calculated by advocacy groups based on their contacts with service providers and shelter operators nationwide.

[1]HUD reported that the total number of homeless people was 180,000, 30 percent of whom were single parents and their children, and 6 percent of whom were couples with children.
[2]The sources for the numbers used in this estimate are as follows: 735,000 homeless on any given night – National Alliance to End Homelessness, 1987; 25 percent are family members – U.S. Conference of Mayors, 1986; of these, 55 percent are children.
[3]State education agencies encountered difficulties in gathering data, and used different methods and sources. Thus, the quantity and quality of information varied across locations.

Note: Estimates of homeless population take two forms: annual estimates and point-in-time counts. The former attempts to assess the number of people in need of help in a year; the latter provides information on the number of shelter beds that are needed on a given night.

Source: "U.S. Children and Their Families: Current Conditions and Recent Trends, 1989," A Report of the Select Committee on Children, Youth, and Families, September 1989.

of the homeless to be between 45 and 74 years. In a 1964 study of the homeless in Philadelphia, James Rooney found the mean age to be 55 years. This is similar to the mean age reported by Howard Bahr and Ted Caplow in a mid-1960s study of the homeless in New York City.

The change in the age of the homeless population is demonstrated in recent studies. Ellen Bassuk and colleagues found the mean age of the homeless in Boston in 1983 to be 34 years. In a 1985 study of a city in the Northwest, Marilyn Whitney, et al., found the mean age to be 36 years. Clearly, the homeless population is much younger today than was the case just a few decades ago.[9]

Sex–Historically, the homeless have primarily been single men. Today, men still comprise the majority of the homeless population. However, there has been an increase in the number of females. On average, studies of the homeless find that single women account for between 10 and 15 percent of single adult homeless population.

Race–Before the 1960s, the homeless were primarily White males. This has changed dramatically. Although the racial composition of the homeless varies from place to place, nationwide over 50 percent of the homeless are minorities—Blacks and Hispanics.

Health–Information about the homeless gathered from various studies reveal that the homeless often are inflicted with serious health problems and disabilities. A common problem among the homeless is mental health. Various studies of homelessness find between 20 and 60 percent of homeless people have some form of mental disorder.

Alcohol and drug abuse–Alcohol and drug abuse are prevalent amongst the homeless. Alcohol abuse has long been recognized as the most common problem of the homeless. Before 1960, people with drug and alcohol problems accounted for nearly all homeless people. Today, the number of alcoholics is rivaled by those with mental problems. Studies report the incidence of alcoholism among the homeless to be between 40 and 70 percent.

AIDS–There is evidence that increasingly more homeless people are afflicted with AIDS. This problem is closely related to the problem of drug use. Homeless people live in unhealthy environments and because of the lack of resources and information about the risk involved, they frequently share needles. This increases the probability of being infected with AIDS. In addition, those with AIDS are more likely to lose jobs and thus end up homeless. They also may find it difficult to find housing because of discrimination.

Interaction with legal authorities–Homelessness exposes people to law enforcement officials. Many homeless are arrested, sometimes when they

---

9. For sources and citations, see Mark La Gory, Ferris J. Ritchey, Timothy O'Donoghue, and Jeffrey Mullis, "Homeless in Alabama: A Variety of People and Experiences," in Jamshid A. Momeni, *Homelessness in the United States* 1 (New York: Greenwood Press, 1989), p. 9.

have not committed any criminal violations. The economic situation of the homeless also leads them into involvment in petty survival crimes. If arrested, such people are not likely to meet pretrial bail and thus have high probability of incarceration. A study of homeless people in Baltimore, found that over 58 percent had been arrested at least once.

Table 17-4 reports characteristics of the homeless population based on the Urban Institute sample. In addition to the various characteristics discussed herein, the data reports the duration of homelessness, income, and benefit recipiency. For single adults, the mean duration of homeless reported is 41.3 months. Generally, most homeless people do not have any cash income and the average income for single adults is only $146 per month. The data also reveals that only a small proportion of the homeless receive welfare benefits.

Combining the number of homeless and the various characteristics (especially the problems that the homeless population face) demonstrates that the problem is extensive. This suggests that the dilemma of homelessness should not be assumed away. An examination of some of the causes of homelessness follows.

CAUSES OF HOMELESSNESS

The key to solving the problem of homeless people is to understand the causes of this problem. There are several factors that lead to homelessness.[10] The most important include lack of low-income housing, poverty and unemployment, inadequate mental health care, and low welfare benefits. Also some of the problems of the homeless discussed previously could be responsible for their situation. However, it is difficult to isolate characteristics of the homeless from the causes of their homelessness. For example, alcoholism could cause homelessness. As individuals spend more of their resources on alcohol, they may be unable to meet their rent payments, thereby causing their eviction. Conversely, it could be that, once homeless, persons may start to consume drugs and alcohol as methods of escape. Discussion of some of the more important causes of homelessness follow.

Lack of Low-Income Housing

The basic problem of homelessness is the lack of low-cost housing. A good indicator of the availability of low-income housing is the share of income that is spent on rent. If rental prices increase much faster than earnings, low-income earners are left with few options. Some double up with relatives and

---

10. For a recent empirical analysis of the causes of homelessness, see Marta Elliot and Lauren J. Krivo, "Structural Determinants of Homelessness in the United States," *Social Problems*, 38 (1) (February 1991): 113–29.

Table 17-4   Characteristics of homeless adults in cities of populations over 100,000 (In weighted percentages)

	Single	Homeless Adults In Families	Total
Total	77	8	85[1]
Sex			
Male	88	12	81
Female	12	88	19
Race			
Black	39	54	41
Hispanic	9	20	10
White	49	22	46
Other	3	4	3
Age			
18 to 30	–	–	30
31 to 50	–	–	51
51 to 65	–	–	16
66+	–	–	3
Marital Status			
Married	9	23	10
Divorced/separated	30	25	29
Widowed	6	6	5
Never married	56	47	55
Medical History			
Mental hospitalization	20	11	19
Chemical dependency	35	12	33
Criminal History			
Jailed for five or more days	56	18	52
State or federal prison	26	2	24
Number of Months Homeless			
Mean	41.3	14.6	–
Median	12.0	4.5	–
Monthly Cash Income			
Mean	$146	$301	–
Median	$64	$300	–
Receiving Benefits:			
Food stamps	15	50	–
AFDC	1	33	–
General assistance	10	33	–

[1]The remaining 15 percent of homeless individuals are children in homeless families.

Source: All data are from a study done by the Urban Institute on 1704 service-using homeless persons.

friends while the rest end up homeless. A good indicator of affordability of rental housing is the ratio of rent to income. When this ratio increases, the implication is that rent is increasing faster than income (or income is falling), making it increasingly difficult for low income households to afford housing. The rent-to-income ratio increased rapidly during the 1970s and 1980s. For example, between 1970 and 1983, the median monthly rent increased by 192 percent while the income of renters rose by only 97 percent. With such large increases in rental prices, a larger share of income of a low-income household is devoted to housing. Between 1970 and 1988, the gross rent burden increased by an average of 28.7 percent across the country; 40.1 percent in the Northeast, 33.8 percent in the Midwest, 6.5 percent in the South, and 28.6 percent in the West.[11] As expenditures on housing rise relative to income, more and more people are faced with hard choices of paying rent or other essential goods and services. High gross rent burden has been a primary reason for the increase in eviction rates.

Increasing rent-to-income ratio reflects the relatively low supply of low-income rental units. Several factors have contributed to the reduction in the stock of low-cost rental housing units. The most commonly cited factor is the sharp decline in federal support for public housing construction and subsidies. Since the mid-1930s, the federal government has played a major role in increasing the number of low-income houses available.

Federal housing programs for low income households are administered by the Department of Housing and Urban Development (HUD) and the Farmers Home Administration (FmHA). Federal housing assistance falls under three programs. The first type of assistance is in the form of project-based housing units. Such units include newly constructed or substantially rehabilitated units specifically for low-income households. The second form of assistance includes household-based subsidies that allow renters to choose standard housing units in the existing stock of private rental houses. The final form of assistance helps low-income households to purchase their own houses. In this case, the federal government makes a long-term commitment to reduce the mortgage interest so that low income households are able to buy their own houses.

Between 1970 and 1979, the federal government financed the construction and rehabilitation of 1.5 million low-income rental units. This number represented 31 percent of the total growth in the stock of rental housing. Between 1980 and 1989, the government was responsible for 0.9 million new or rehabilitated units, that accounted for only 14 percent of total growth in the stock of rental units. Table 17-5 reports the trend in federal participation in the provision of low-income housing. The data reveals a sharp decline in federal involvement in provisions of housing. Table 17-6 reports the changes in funds appropriated for housing aid from 1977 to

---

11. See Martha R. Burt, *Over the Edge: The Growth of Homelessness in the 1980s* (New York: Russell Sage Foundation, 1992).

Table 17-5   Net new commitments for renters and new commitments for home buyers, 1977–1990

| Fiscal Year | New Commitments for Renters | | | New Commitments for Home Buyers |
	Existing Housing	New Construction	Total	
1977	127,581	247,667	375,248	112,234
1978	126,472	214,503	340,975	112,214
1979	102,669	231,156	333,825	107,871
1980	58,402	155,001	213,403	140,564
1981	83,520	94,914	178,434	74,636
1982	38,372	47,618	85,990	66,711
1983	54,071	23,861	77,932	54,550
1984	78,726	36,719	115,445	44,409
1985	85,741	42,667	128,408	45,387
1986	85,476	34,375	119,851	25,479
1987	72,788	37,247	110,035	24,132
1988	65,295	36,456	101,751	26,200
1989	68,858	30,049	98,907	25,264
1990 (estimate)	70,572	28,901	99,473	25,580

Source: U.S. Congress, Committee on Ways and Means, *Background Material and Data on Programs Within the Jurisdiction of the Committee on Ways and Means, 1990,* p. 1309. See source for additional explanations.

1990. Again, there was a sharp decline in the resources devoted to low-income housing between 1977 and 1990. This shift in the share of rental units financed by the government implies that an increasing number low-income families have to rent from private owners. Rental prices of privately owned units are substantially higher than those of public rental units.

During the 1970s and 1980s, there were increased efforts to revitalize the cities—what is known as urban renewal. In many instances, urban renewal meant the demolition of old residential buildings, particularly low-rent, single-room-occupancy residential accommodations. The low-cost residential units have been replaced by businesses and office buildings. The result has been a reduction of low-cost rental units across the country. Some estimates indicate that between 1970 and 1982, about one million single-room-occupancy units (nearly half the nation's supply of such units) disappeared.[12] New York City lost 30,385 single-room-occupancy rental units between 1975 and 1981. In San Francisco, 5,723 (11.7 percent) of 32,214 single-room-occupancy units disappeared between 1975 and 1979. Seattle lost 15,000 rental units to urban renewal between 1960

---

12. Kim Hopper and Jill Hamberg, *The Making of America's Homeless: From Skid Row to New Poor* (New York: Community Service Society, 1984).

Table 17-6   Net budget authority appropriated for housing aid, administered by HUD, 1977–1990 (in millions of current and 1989
dollars)

Fiscal Year	Net Budget Authority	
	Current Dollars	*1989 Dollars*
1977	28,579	54,043
1978	32,169	56,852
1979	25,123	40,849
1980	27,435	41,012
1981	26,022	35,375
1982	14,766	18,702
1983	10,001	12,162
1984	11,425	13,386
1985	11,071	12,581
1986	10,032	11,100
1987	8,979	9,679
1988	8,592	8,952
1989	8,879	8,879
1990[1]	10,631	10,226

[1]Includes $1,074 million for renewing expiring Section 8 contracts.

Source: U.S. Congress, Committee on Ways and Means, Background Material and Data on
Programs Within the Jurisdiction of the Committee on Ways and Means, 1990, p. 1311. See
source for additional explanations.

and 1981. This story holds true for virtually all major metropolitan areas in
the country.[13]

The decline in the available rental units also has been blamed on government policies that reduce the incentives for investors to build low-income
housing, even in the face of increasing demand. For example, rent control
lowers the expected return to owners of rental units. Therefore, many owners
of such units have chosen to convert rental units to condominiums and business premises. The high incidence of crime and vandalism in the inner cities
makes investing in rental housing in those areas unprofitable.

Poverty and Unemployment

Homelessness increases with levels of poverty and unemployment. When
poverty and unemployment increase, more people are unable to pay rent
and therefore their risk of becoming homeless increases. Although the

13. See Martha R. Burt, *Over the Edge: The Growth of Homelessness in the 1980s* (New York:
Russell Sage Foundation, 1992).

relationship between the economy and homelessness is not perfect, historical evidence shows that the number of homeless people increases during economic downturns. For example, during the Great Depression the number of homeless increased dramatically.

Welfare Benefits and Eligibility

Changes in eligibility and levels of benefits during the early 1980s frequently are cited as causes for the increase in the number of homeless persons. Many people who relied on AFDC and Social Security disability benefits had their benefits reduced or became ineligible for benefits.[14] The Omnibus Reconciliation Act of 1981 (OBRA) radically changed the eligibility and benefit levels for the main means-tested programs including AFDC, Supplemental Security Income, and Food Stamps. For example, as a result of OBRA of 1981, 500,000 families became ineligible for AFDC and about 300,000 families' benefits were reduced. The result was that these families slipped into poverty. One result of the welfare changes was that some of those affected were not able to pay for rental units and thus their probability of becoming homeless increased. Likewise, eligibility requirements for SSI were tightened so that new applicants found it more difficult to qualify for benefits. Studies find that many mentally ill patients who are otherwise eligible for SSI benefits do not receive them.

Deinstitutionalization

One cause of the increased number of homeless people is attributed to changes in the provision of mental health services. In particular, the deinstitutionalization of mental health patients that occurred since the 1960s has contributed significantly to the increase in the homeless population. For example, in 1955 there were 559,000 patients in public mental health hospitals.[15] In 1978, the number was 150,000 patients and the numbers have continued to decline since then. Deinstitutionalization was meant to be a more humane approach of dealing with the mentally ill. Instead of being confined in mental institutions, mentally ill patients were to be provided services in community-based treatment centers. It was hoped that such an approach would help the patients lead a more normal life rather than being isolated from the other members of the society. Unfortunately, this approach resulted in inadequate support for the mentally ill. With fewer federal and state funds devoted to treating mental health patients in institutions, more individuals who cannot function properly in society and

---

14. See Joel Blau, *The Visible Poor: Homeless in the United States* (New York: Oxford University Press, 1992).
15. See Michael Harrington, *The New American Poverty* (New York: Penguin Books, 1984).

who cannot hold jobs or establish families have ended up homeless in the streets.

Discrimination in Housing Markets

The increase in the number of minorities in the homeless population is mainly due to the higher poverty rates among those groups. In addition, minorities continue to face discrimination in the housing markets which increases their risk of becoming homeless. As observed in Chapter 11, the residential segregation evident in the United States today is partially a result of discriminatory practices in the housing markets. Most poor minorities reside in or near inner cities. Such housing frequently is the target of disinvestment, abandonment, or conversion. These factors reduce the pool of available housing to minorities, and given the problems they face in securing housing outside the ghetto, many minorities risk becoming homeless.

Alcoholism and Drug Abuse

Although it is common to consider alcoholism and drug addiction as two of the problems that are common among the homeless, many times it also is true that these are the causes of homelessness. Alcoholism and drug addiction could result in homelessness in various ways. First, people with such problems may become unable to hold a job and thus are not capable of earning labor incomes; therefore they are not able to pay for housing. Second, alcoholism and drug addiction may cause people to spend all their resources on alcohol and drugs so that they are unable to pay for rent or mortgage even if they earn sufficient income to provide housing. Third, alcoholism and drug addiction may cause families to break up, which increases the risk of homelessness. Finally, alcoholism and drug addiction frequently cause mental problems, which make people dysfunctional and thus increase the risk of their becoming homeless.

HOMELESSNESS POLICY

Homeless people face similar problems to other poor. As such, policies discussed to deal with poverty would reduce the problem of homelessness. In particular, policies to create better-paying jobs, reduce unemployment, and increase employability (such as human capital improvement strategies) would be necessary to deal with the homeless. However, for such policies to be implemented, the homeless must be in stable residences. It would not make much sense (nor would it be practical) to extend training to persons who do not have housing that meets some minimal standard. Thus, any policy to deal with the homeless must focus on making housing available.

An obvious starting point would be adoption of policies that increase the availability of low-income housing. This would require more public and private partnership in construction of new and rehabilitation of old structures. It also may be necessary to increase the population that is eligible for housing subsidies and low-income housing. Simultaneously, to the extent that rent control could result in a reduction in the available pool of low-income housing, it is necessary to evaluate such regulations and adopt those policies that make it attractive for investors to add to the stock of available low-income housing.[16]

However, the homeless have specific problems that require specific policies. As already discussed, the problem of homelessness is a combination of poor health, alcoholism and drug addiction, economic conditions, and lack of affordable housing. Thus, policies to deal with homelessness should focus on these special problems.

To the extent that benefit reductions contribute to the homelessness problem, welfare reform policies should consider housing affordability. If reducing benefits disrupts families so severely that they become homeless, then such policies are counterproductive and should be reevaluated.

Most homeless advocates and researchers tend to blame the problem of homelessness primarily on the shortage of low-income housing and reductions in welfare benefits. Thus, the federal government is viewed as the main culprit. Those proponents call for increased government spending both in providing low-income housing and also in welfare expenditures. As observed, this approach would help some of the homeless population. However, the policies may not be effective in reducing the number of people who are homeless.

The main problem lies in the fact that most advocates do not admit that alcohol and drug addiction are primary causes of homelessness. The reason for this is that society has long-refused to acknowledge that alcoholism and drug addiction are health problems. Instead, alcoholism and drug addiction are viewed as personal failures. Thus, because many homeless people suffer from such problems, society considers them as undeserving poor. Until the government and public accepts these problems as health issues, it is unlikely that much will be accomplished by focusing on housing and welfare benefits. Thus, effective policies must include serious drug and alcohol treatment programs.

It is clear that the issue of mental health treatment is central to the homelessness problem. Similarly, policies to deal with the problems of drugs and AIDS require more emphasis. A national health policy that

---

16. Although economic theory predicts that rent control results in a reduction in the supply of low-income housing and thus the presence of rent-control law should be related to homelessness, this is not supported by empirical evidence. See Marjorie Honig and Randall K. Filler, "Causes of Intercity Variation in Homelessness," *American Economic Review* 83 (1) (March 1993): 248–55.

includes these special problems will go a long way in preventing the incidence of homelessness.

SUMMARY

Although there is no consensus as to the size of the homeless population, it is evident that the number is large enough to demand more focused public policies. This chapter has presented various estimates of the homeless population. It also has discussed some of the characteristics of the homeless and the causes of this problem. As the text reveals, the homelessness problem is complicated and arises from a variety of factors. Policy suggestions include tackling the housing problem and other issues such as employment and the general health of the homeless population.

In order to formulate effective policies to deal with homelessness, it will be necessary for the public and policymakers to accept that alcoholism and drug abuse are major problems in society that contribute to homelessness. Unless these problems are considered health problems, it is unlikely that other policies will reduce homelessness significantly.

STUDY AND DISCUSSION QUESTIONS

1. Do you think that homelessness in the United States is a serious problem? Justify your answer.

2. What do you consider to be the main causes of homelessness?

3. The homeless have been considered as undeserving poor. Why do you think this has been the case? In your opinion, are the homeless deserving poor? Explain.

4. Outline several policies that could be used to deal with homelessness in the United States.

5. Some researchers state that the homeless are people like you and me. Is this correct? Discuss the composition of the homeless.

6. Homeless advocates consider homelessness to be primarily a housing problem. Others see homelessness as a result of poverty and unemployment, and yet others see it as a result of government regulations. However, homelessness also appears to be a health problem. Evaluate all these causes.

ADDITIONAL READINGS

1. Breakey, William R. and Pamela J. Fischer. "Homelessness: The Extent of the Problem," *Journal of Social Issues* 46 (4) (1990): 31–47.

2. Burghardt, Steve and Michael Fabricant. *Working Under the Safety Net: Policy and Practice with the New American Poor*. Newbury, Calif.: Sage Publications, 1987.

3. Caton, Carol L. M. *Homeless in America*. New York: Oxford University Press, 1990.

4. Hopper, Kim and Jill Hamberg. *The Making of America's Homeless: From Skid Row to New Poor*. New York: Community Service Society of New York, 1984.

5. Robertson, Marjorie J. and Milton Greenblatt. *Homelessness: A National Perspective*. New York: Plenum Press, 1992.

18

INTERNATIONAL COMPARISONS OF INEQUALITY AND POVERTY

The previous chapters have examined poverty and poverty policy in the United States. The discussion has focused primarily on the causes and composition of poverty and the various policies that are used to deal with this problem. As observed, a large share of the country's resources is devoted to fighting poverty. The current system of poor support has been instrumental in the reduction of the incidence of poverty.

As noted in Chapter 14, the posttransfer poverty rate is considerably lower than the pretransfer poverty rate. Even for those persons who remain poor after receiving public transfers, the severity of their poverty is reduced considerably, as demonstrated by the reduction in poverty gaps. Were it not for the current transfer system, a sizable fraction of Americans would not have resources to meet basic needs such as food, housing, and medical care.

In addition to cash and in-kind transfers, the U.S. redistributive system involves a wide array of programs, including manpower development and job training programs that help raise the future earnings of low-wage workers. Some legislative changes also have been important in reducing the incidence of poverty amongst minorities and women. Specifically, equal opportunity laws discussed in Chapter 10 are credited for reducing poverty within these groups. There is no doubt that the U.S. transfer system has been important in reducing poverty.

Still, proponents of welfare programs assert that the United States could do a much better job of eradicating poverty. It is argued that the country spends too little in fighting poverty. Many compare the status of the poor in the United States with those in other countries and suggest that, although the Unites States is a much wealthier country, its poor are worse off than the poor in other developed countries. For example, it is frequently claimed that the Canadian health care system is superior to that of the United States because the Canadian system extends benefits to all citizens while many in the United States, including low-wage workers, lack even basic medical coverage.

Some people claim that the United States policies toward its children are inadequate when compared to policies in some developing countries. A common example is the fact that infant mortality in the United States is higher than in some countries with much lower incomes. For example, in 1991, the infant mortality rate in the United States was 10.3 per 1000 live births. In the same year, Taiwan had an infant mortality rate equal to 5.9 per 1000 live births. The U.S. system is criticized, especially for failing to deal adequately with poverty of children in mother-only households.

Frequently, critics of the U.S. welfare system cite the condition of inner cities as evidence of ineffective government policies combined with pure neglect of poor minorities. Also, the inequality in the distribution of income is used as evidence of the limited efforts by the government to transfer incomes to the poor. Recent evidence suggesting that the richest groups became richer during the 1980s while the middle class diminished has provided ammunition to critics who believe the system has abandoned the goals of the War on Poverty. In short, some people criticize the U.S. government for spending too little toward fighting and preventing poverty.

Opponents of large government spending argue that the United States' antipoverty policy is too costly and that the transfer system has been responsible for the rapid growth in the size of government. Critics argue that the welfare system is self-defeating: it causes a breakdown of traditional American family, and results in a diminution of work effort. The unintended outcomes of the welfare system result in more poverty. There are suggestions from some politicians that America may be losing its economic competitiveness because of the rapid expansion in social welfare programs. On this side of the political spectrum, the U.S. transfer system is viewed as having grown to the limit, and it is suggested that it should be scaled back.

In Chapter 3, a brief study of historical views on poverty was provided. The purpose of that discussion was to emphasize the point that the debate on poverty and poverty policy is not new. A historical review of poverty and income distribution is important or the student may be misled into thinking that only in recent times has fighting poverty become a public policy issue. Having now discussed contemporary problems of poverty and income distribution in the United States, students may wonder how well the United Stated fairs in comparison with other developed countries. This requires a comparative analysis of poverty and income distribution across countries. Such a comparison would provide an idea as to how successful U.S. welfare policies have been in fighting poverty relative to other countries. Also, by comparing the state of income distribution across other countries, one may be able to uncover whether income distribution in the United States is indeed much more unequal as compared to the distribution of income in other countries.

This chapter briefly explores how the state of income distribution and poverty in the United States compares with that of other nations. It is not the intent to provide an account of the various programs used in other countries as such would require extensive coverage. The primary goal is to present some basic comparative statistics on poverty and income distribution. While attempting to make some comparisons, one must be cautious, particularly in regard to drawing conclusions as to the most effective redistributive policy. Any cross-country comparisons of poverty necessarily requires consideration of the political and economic systems, levels of income, standard of living, and composition of the population, among other factors.

First, let us focus on income distribution in a number of high-income countries. Next, some comparative data on poverty will be presented. The focus is specifically on the effectiveness of antipoverty efforts in a number of developed countries.

COMPARISONS OF INCOME DISTRIBUTION

Table 18-1 reports some of the economic indicators across some high-income countries as classified by the World Bank. Per capita income and some other indicators related to government spending are included. As is evident from the data, even among the richest countries, there is a wide variation in the per capita income. For example, in 1988 the per capita income in oil-rich Saudi Arabia was $6200 as compared to per capita income for Switzerland of $27,500. Clearly, based only on the per capita income, the United States is one of the richest countries.

The GNP per capita recorded can be misleading in making comparisons across countries. The numbers shown are obtained by converting the income in the various countries using the exchange rate. Unfortunately, although such data are more readily available, they do not provide an accurate indicator of real value of goods and services in a particular country. To obtain data that are comparable across countries, it is necessary to use a measure that captures the real differences in the volumes of goods and services in those countries. This is achieved by using the purchasing power parities (PPP). Purchasing power parities show the number of units of currency needed in one country to buy the same amount of goods and services that one unit of currency will buy in the other country. Thus, the data of Gross Domestic Product (GDP) per capita reported in Table 18-1 is better for making country comparisons. Notice that, in 1988, the GDP per capita using PPP was higher in the United States than in Switzerland.

Table 18-1 also shows the allocation of resources toward the provision of a number of services across the countries. Data is included for expenditure shares on education, health, and social welfare services. Size of the governments also is included, which is expressed as government spending as a percentage of gross national product (GNP). The data represent central government expenditures and therefore should be interpreted with caution. For example, the reason for the relatively low share of government spending allocated to education in the United States (1.7 percent) is that most educational expenditures are at low levels of government.

Table 18-1   Income and government expenditures in high-income countries, 1988

Country	GDP per Capita (Based on PPP)[1]	GNP per Capita US $	Percentage of Total Central Government Expenditure Spent on			Total Expenditures as a Percentage of GNP
			Education	Health	Social Welfare	
1. Saudi Arabia	—	6,200	—	—	—	—
2. Spain	10,089	7,740	—	—	—	34.1
3. Ireland	8,568	7,750	11.8	12.4	30.3	58.1
4. Israel	—	8,650	9.6	3.7	21.2	50.6
5. Singapore	—	9,070	14.4	3.6	11.0	35.0
6. Hong Kong	—	9,220	—	—	—	—
7. New Zealand	12,164	10,000	11.1	12.4	29.7	49.1
8. Australia	—	12,340	7.0	9.6	28.6	28.7
9. United Kingdom	14,118	12,810	2.2	13.6	30.9	37.6
10. Italy	14,161	13,330	7.6	10.4	35.4	51.3
11. Kuwait	—	13,400	14.2	7.7	20.1	35.7
12. Belgium	14,206	14,490	12.2	1.8	43.3	52.4
13. Netherlands	13,664	14,520	11.9	10.9	39.6	55.7
14. Austria	14,356	15,470	9.3	12.8	47.5	40.1
15. United Arab Emirates	—	15,770	—	—	—	—

Table 18-1   (Continued)

| Country | GDP per Capita (Based on PPP)[1] | GNP per Capita US $ | Percentage of Total Central Government Expenditure Spent on | | | Total Expenditures as a Percentage of GNP |
			Education	Health	Social Welfare	
16. France	15,319	16,090	–	–	–	43.1
17. Canada	17,648	16,960	3.1	5.9	37.3	23.4
18. Denmark	15,053	18,450	9.0	1.3	41.1	41.2
19. Germany, Fed. Rep.	16,100	18,480	0.6	18.2	49.4	29.9
20. Finland	14,504	18,590	13.9	10.6	36.1	30.2
21. Sweden	15,368	19,300	9.2	1.1	54.2	40.8
22. United States	19,525	19,840	1.7	12.5	31.5	22.9
23. Norway	14,532	19,990	8.2	10.7	36.1	41.5
24. Japan	14,875	21,020	–	–	–	17.0
25. Switzerland	18,641	27,500	–	–	–	–

[1]PPP stands for purchasing power parity. The data for GDP per capita, expressed in terms of purchasing power parity, are from the *U.S. Statistical Abstract*. Other data are from World Bank: *World Development Report 1990*, Table 11.

Social welfare expenditures include housing, amenities, social security, and welfare.

Generally, the data reported provide a good comparison of government expenditures that have direct redistributive consequences. The shares of government expenditures devoted to social welfare services are particularly interesting. While only 11 percent of Singapore's government expenditures are dedicated to those social welfare services, Sweden dedicates 54.2 percent of all expenditures to those services. The United States ranks somewhere in the middle, with 31.5 percent of government expenditures devoted to social welfare services.

Not much can be concluded based on the numbers discussed unless one looks at the overall size of the government. For example, it is possible that a particular government dedicates a high proportion of government expenditures to social welfare services, yet the actual expenditures may be low if the overall size of the government is small. The last column in Table 18-1 reports the size of the governments. Of the countries considered here, Ireland has the largest government, with government expenditures accounting for 58.1 percent of the GNP. The United States' government is relatively small with the central government expenditures accounting for 22.9 percent of the GNP. Again, the overall government expenditures in the United States are much higher because expenditures by lower levels of government are not taken into account.

Table 18-2 reports data on income distribution across the various high-income countries. Note that the data for income distribution are for different years. Nevertheless, because the state of income distribution in a particular country changes slowly, the data are fairly adequate for comparative purposes. The data clearly show that inequality in the distribution of income is the norm in all the high-income countries. However, there are significant differences. In Australia, the poorest 20 percent of the population receive only 4.4 percent of the national income while the poorest 20 percent in Sweden receive 8 percent of national income. There also are wide differences in the share of income received by the richest groups. In Singapore, the richest 20 percent of the population receives 48.9 percent of national income as compared to 36 percent of national income received by the richest 20 percent in Belgium. Again the United States is somewhere in the middle.

As mentioned earlier, a major hindrance to a systematic cross-country comparative analysis of the state of income distribution and poverty has been the lack of data that conforms to common standards. A major breakthrough in this area has been the development of the Luxembourg Income Study (LIS).[1] LIS contains microdata for seven developed countries that can be used to make comparisons on income distribution and poverty. LIS data has been reorganized to conform to common standards, concepts, and

---

1. See Timothy M. Smeeding, Michael O'Higgins, and Lee Rainwater, *Poverty, Inequality and Income Distribution in Comparative Perspective: The Luxembourg Income Study* (LIS) (Washington, D.C.: The Urban Institute, 1990). Most of the discussion that follows is based on this source.

structures. In addition to permitting for consistent comparisons in income distribution, the database is useful for comparing pretransfer and post-transfer poverty, which provides important information of the various governments' effectiveness in fighting poverty.

Table 18-3 reports income distribution and the Gini coefficients for seven countries based on the LIS data. The top panel shows the distribution of family gross income and the lower panel shows distribution based on net income.[2] The data are fairly close to those reported in Table 18-2. The data show that, compared to the poor in other countries, those in the United States receive the lowest share of national income (3.8 percent). Of the countries reported here, the poorest in Sweden receive the highest share of national income (6.6 percent) as compared to the share received by the poorest group in the other countries. The richest 20 percent in West Germany receive 46.9 percent of national income as compared to 32.9 percent of national income received by the richest 20 percent in Sweden. As revealed by the Gini coefficient, the distribution of income is most unequal in the United States, West Germany, and Israel.

The lower panel reports income distribution based on net income. These data are interesting as they provide some information about the effectiveness of the tax system in altering the market-determined state of income distribution. As expected, the share of net income that goes to the poorest groups is higher than the share of gross income received by this group. This is because the poor are net recipients of income transfers. It is nevertheless interesting to note that the decline in the share of income received by the richest group after taxes is quite small. Taxes and transfers reduce the state of income inequality in all countries as reflected by a lower Gini coefficient for the distribution of income based on net income as compared to the Gini coefficient based on the distribution of gross income.

Based on the shares of income received by the poorest groups, the richest groups, and the Gini coefficients, one can conclude that income distribution is most equal in Sweden followed by Norway, United Kingdom, and Canada. On the other hand, income distribution is much more unequal in Israel, the United States, and West Germany.

COMPARISONS OF PRETRANSFER AND POSTTRANSFER POVERTY

Comparisons of income distribution are easier than comparisons of poverty. In making intercountry comparisons of poverty, it is necessary that a comparable definition of income and families be used. More important, a

---

2. The countries included in the study are Canada (CAN), United States (US), United Kingdom (UK), West Germany (WG), Sweden (SWE), Norway (NOR), and Israel (ISR). The data reported are for 1979, except for Canada and West Germany, both of which are for 1981. We refer to West Germany as this was before reunification.

Table 18-2   Income distribution

| Country | Year | Percentage Share of Household Income by Percentile Group of Households | | | | | | |
		Lowest 20%	2nd 20%	3rd 20%	4th 20%	Highest 20%	Highest 10%
1. Saudi Arabia	—	—	—	—	—	—	—
2. Spain	1980–1981	6.9	12.5	17.3	23.2	40.0	24.5
3. Ireland	—	—	—	—	—	—	—
4. Israel	1979	6.0	12.1	17.8	24.5	39.6	23.5
5. Singapore	1982–1983	5.1	9.9	14.6	21.4	48.9	33.5
6. Hong Kong	1980	5.4	10.8	15.2	21.6	47.0	31.3
7. New Zealand	1981–1982	5.1	10.8	16.2	23.2	44.7	28.7
8. Australia	1985	4.4	11.1	17.5	24.8	42.2	25.8
9. United Kingdom	1979	5.8	11.5	18.2	25.0	39.5	23.3
10. Italy	1986	6.8	12.0	16.7	23.5	41.0	25.3
11. Kuwait	—	—	—	—	—	—	—
12. Belgium	1978–1979	7.9	13.7	18.6	23.8	36.0	21.5
13. Netherlands	1983	6.9	13.2	17.9	23.7	38.3	23.0
14. Austria	—	—	—	—	—	—	—
15. United Arab Emirates	—	—	—	—	—	—	—

Table 18-2   (Continued)

Country	Year	Lowest 20%	2nd 20%	3rd 20%	4th 20%	Highest 20%	Highest 10%
						Percentage Share of Household Income by Percentile Group of Households		
16. France	1979	6.3	12.1	17.2	23.5	40.8	25.5
17. Canada	1987	5.7	11.8	17.7	24.6	40.2	24.1
18. Denmark	1981	5.4	12.0	18.4	25.6	38.6	22.3
19. Germany, Fed. Rep.	1984	6.8	12.7	17.8	24.1	38.7	21.7
20. Finland	1981	6.3	12.1	18.4	25.5	37.6	21.7
21. Sweden	1981	8.0	13.2	17.4	24.5	36.9	20.8
22. United States	1985	4.7	11.0	17.4	25.0	41.9	25.0
23. Norway	1979	6.2	12.8	18.9	25.3	36.7	21.2
24. Japan	1979	8.7	13.2	17.5	23.1	37.5	22.4
25. Switzerland	1982	5.2	11.7	16.4	22.1	44.6	29.8

Source: World Bank: *World Development Report 1990*, Table 30.

Table 18-3   The distribution of income (LIS data)

Variable	Quintile Shares (Percent) of Income						
	CAN	*US*	*UK*	*WG*	*SWE*	*NOR*	*ISR*
Distribution of Family Gross Income Among Quintiles of Families							
Lowest quintile	4.6	3.8	4.9	4.4	6.6	4.9	4.5
Second quintile	11.0	9.8	10.9	10.2	12.3	11.4	10.5
Third quintile	17.7	16.6	18.2	15.9	17.2	18.4	16.5
Fourth quintile	25.3	25.3	25.3	22.6	25.0	25.5	24.9
Top quintile	41.4	44.5	40.8	46.9	38.9	39.8	43.6
Gini coefficient	37.4	41.2	36.5	42.9	32.9	35.6	39.5
Revised Gini for West Germany[1]				41.4			
Distribution of Family Net Income Among Quintiles of Families							
Lowest quintile	5.3	4.5	5.8	5.0	8.0	6.3	6.0
Second quintile	11.8	11.2	11.5	11.5	13.2	12.8	12.1
Third quintile	18.1	17.7	18.2	15.9	17.4	18.9	17.9
Fourth quintile	24.6	25.6	25.0	21.8	24.5	25.3	24.5
Top quintile	39.7	41.0	39.5	45.8	36.9	36.7	39.5
Gini coefficient	34.8	37.0	34.3	40.9	29.2	31.1	33.8
Revised Gini for West Germany[1]				38.9			

[1]The revised Gini for West Germany was calculated because the data for that country had a large number of zero and negative incomes. The revised Gini excludes income units with such incomes. See Smeeding et al. for details.

Source: Timothy M. Smeeding, Michael O'Higgins, and Lee Rainwater, eds., *Poverty, Inequality and Income Distribution in Comparative Perspective: The Luxembourg Income Study (LIS)*, Table 2.2, p. 34.

common poverty line must be used, otherwise poverty rates would not be comparable. The data based on LIS are comparable. The definition of poverty used is what is referred to as *economic distance poverty*, which is based on the concept of equivalent disposable income. Equivalent disposable income is obtained by adjusting cash income by the number of equivalent adults in a family in order to construct a measure of economic welfare available to a family. The poverty line is then defined as 50 percent of the median equivalent income. This provides a common standard from which to compare economic welfare of families across countries. The poverty rates obtained by using 50 percent of the median equivalent income are higher than the national poverty rates in some countries (for example, the United States) and lower in others (for example, Sweden).

Table 18-4 reports the pretransfer and posttransfer economic distance poverty rates for persons in the seven countries whose data are included in the LIS database. Data are reported for the elderly and various family types. Based on the definition of income used by LIS, Sweden has the highest pretransfer poverty rate (41 percent). Data of the poverty rates by family types reveals that the pretransfer poverty rates among the elderly are much higher than for all other groups in all countries. Individuals in single-parent families have the second highest pretransfer poverty rates.

The high pretransfer poverty rate for Sweden is attributed to that country's extensive welfare system and the inability to separate occupational from public pensions.[3] Similarly, the high pretransfer poverty rates among the elderly in all the countries reflect the importance of public sector pension transfers. Nevertheless, the reliance on public pensions varies across countries. For example, in the United States occupational pensions play a significant role for only a minority of the elderly, which explains the high pretransfer poverty rate amongst the elderly (72 percent). In other words, because most elderly persons in the United States rely on public pensions, the pretransfer poverty rate of the elderly can be expected to be high. Israel has the lowest pretransfer poverty rate for elderly persons although its public pension system is not large. The main reason for the relatively low pretransfer poverty among the elderly in Israel is attributed to the tendency for the elderly to live with their offspring and/or the prevalence of regular interhousehold transfers between extended families.

More informative data are those for the posttransfer poverty rates. Comparing the overall posttransfer poverty rates shows that Norway has the lowest poverty rate (4.8 percent) followed by Sweden with a posttransfer poverty rate of 5 percent. The United States has the highest posttransfer rate (16.9 percent). Thus, the United States has been less successful in reducing poverty as compared to other developed countries.

Except for Israel, people in single-parent families have the highest posttransfer poverty rates. By and large, persons in two-parent families and other family types have the lowest posttransfer poverty rates except in Sweden where posttransfer poverty among the elderly is virtually nonexistent. The United States does particularly poorly in reducing the poverty of persons in single-parent families.

Many people tend to believe that the reason why it is more difficult to fight poverty in the United States is primarily because of the prevalence of female-headed households, particularly among minorities. The increase in the number of births to unmarried women frequently is cited as the main problem in fighting poverty in the United States. Table 18-5 reports some

---

3. See Smeeding, et al., p. 66.

Table 18-4   Pretransfer and posttransfer economic distance poverty rates for people

		Percentage of People Who Are Poor			
Country Poverty	Total (%)	Elderly Families (%)	Single-Parent Families (%)	Two-Parent Families (%)	Other Families (%)
Sweden					
Pretransfer	41.0	98.4	55.0	21.3	30.5
Posttransfer	5.0	0.1	9.2	5.0	7.0
% Reduction	87.8	99.9	88.3	76.5	77.0
United Kingdom					
Pretransfer	27.9	78.6	56.3	17.6	12.8
Posttransfer	8.8	18.1	29.1	6.5	4.1
% Reduction	68.5	77.0	48.3	63.1	68.0
Israel					
Pretransfer	29.0	56.8	52.6	26.1	14.3
Posttransfer	14.5	23.8	11.8	14.9	5.5
% Reduction	50.0	58.1	77.6	42.9	61.5
United States					
Pretransfer	27.3	72.0	58.5	16.0	15.4
Posttransfer	16.9	20.5	51.7	12.9	9.8
% Reduction	38.1	71.5	11.6	19.4	36.4
Norway					
Pretransfer	24.1	76.9	44.0	7.8	18.7
Posttransfer	4.8	4.6	12.6	3.4	5.7
% Reduction	80.1	94.0	71.4	56.4	69.5
Canada					
Pretransfer	25.6	73.6	48.4	18.5	15.2
Posttransfer	12.1	11.5	37.5	11.0	8.5
% Reduction	52.7	84.4	22.5	40.5	44.1
West Germany					
Pretransfer	28.3	80.3	34.8	12.9	20.1
Posttransfer	6.0	9.3	18.1	3.9	5.4
% Reduction	78.8	88.4	47.1	69.8	73.1

Source: Timothy M. Smeeding, Michael O'Higgins, and Lee Rainwater, eds., *Poverty, Inequality and Income Distribution in Comparative Perspective: The Luxembourg Income Study (LIS)*, Table 3.5, p. 67.

Table 18-5   Births to unmarried women, selected countries, 1960 to 1989

	1960		1990	
Country	Total Live Births (1000)	Percent Born to Unmarried Women	Total Live Births (1000)	Percent Born to Unmarried Women
United States	4,258	5	4,041	27
Canada	479	4	384	23
Denmark	76	8	62	46
France	820	6	766	28
Italy	910	2	567	6
Japan	1,624	1	1,269	1
Netherlands	239	1	189	11
Sweden	102	11	116	52
United Kingdom	918	5	777	27
West Germany	969	6	662	11

Source: *U.S. Statistical Abstract*, 1992, p. 828.

data for births to unmarried women in a number of developed countries. The data shows that since 1960 the proportion of births to unmarried women has increased rapidly in the United States, but this trend also is evident in other countries with the exception of Japan. In fact, if the problem of female headship was the main problem, then posttransfer poverty rates would be much higher in other countries such as Sweden.

The reason that posttransfer poverty rates of single parents are much higher in the United States than in other countries is because of the meager support these family units receive. This probably has much to do with the stigma attached to female headship in the United States. Female headship is viewed by many as an undesirable type of family structure. This is especially the case for female heads in the never-married category who are considered to have made irresponsible choices. Similar to the homeless discussed in Chapter 17, poor female heads are considered undeserving poor. Consequently, the support they receive in the form of transfers is not generous. Even more important, supportive services such as child care that can help those parents to enter labor markets are grossly inadequate or nonexistent in the United States. In other countries (for example, Denmark and Sweden) female headship is accepted and respected. As a result, there are several public policies that are used to help female heads. In particular, mothers are provided with adequate child care so that they are able to return to work after having a child.

As observed in Chapter 14, even if transfer benefits do not remove some people from poverty, they do reduce the severity of poverty. Thus, another measure of the effectiveness of transfer programs is the effects of those programs in reducing the poverty gap. Such data are reported in Table 18-6. Again, the degree to which transfers reduce the poverty gap varies across the countries. The United Kingdom and Israel are most successful in reducing the poverty gap. The United States transfer system has the lowest impact in reducing the poverty gap.

SUMMARY

This chapter has presented data of income distribution and poverty rates across various countries. It has been observed that there are wide differences in both the state of income distribution and poverty. Focusing on Canada, United States, United Kingdom, West Germany, Sweden, Norway, and Israel, we have seen that there are striking differences both in the poverty rates of various family types and the effectiveness of transfers in reducing poverty. Overall, the United States appears to perform rather poorly in reducing poverty, while Sweden is much more successful. Of the various family types, single-parent families have the highest posttransfer poverty rates. It is in dealing with the poverty of persons in single-parent families that the United States performs relatively poorly. This evidence is consistent with discussions in previous chapters and demonstrates why child support recommendations outlined in Chapter 13 should be given some serious consideration.

This is not an attempt to make a normative judgment as to which country has a better redistributive system. The goal of this discussion has been to provide the reader with some basic comparative statistics. Although the comparative analysis is not meant to offer a guide to policy, it is useful in pointing to how countries can improve the design of their transfer policies.

STUDY AND DISCUSSION QUESTIONS

1. Conduct a brief survey of the antipoverty programs in various developed countries. Provide some comparisons of those policies with the policies used in the United States.

2. Based on the information provided in this chapter, what do you think explains the differences in income distribution and pretransfer poverty rates?

3. Sweden has fairly attractive benefits for single mothers. Do you think the United States should increase benefits to single mothers?

Table 18-6   Pretransfer and posttransfer poverty gaps; equivalent income deficit as a percentage of poverty line

| | | Percentage of Poverty Gap Among Persons Living in | | | |
Country Poverty	Total (%)	Elderly Families (%)	Single- Parent Families (%)	Two- Parent Families (%)	Other Families (%)
Sweden					
Pretransfer	80.7	97.8	57.3	39.0	67.4
Posttransfer	40.0	45.2	33.4	28.2	43.2
% Reduction	50.4	53.8	41.7	27.7	35.9
United Kingdom					
Pretransfer	72.6	83.1	67.1	33.0	70.7
Posttransfer	16.0	10.9	17.7	10.8	24.3
% Reduction	78.0	86.9	73.7	67.3	65.6
Israel					
Pretransfer	57.6	72.1	55.5	36.6	58.3
Posttransfer	16.3	13.4	13.7	20.4	13.3
% Reduction	71.7	81.4	75.3	44.3	77.2
United States					
Prettansfer	71.0	81.2	59.3	43.0	67.1
Posttransfer	39.9	29.1	43.0	33.3	50.6
% Reduction	43.8	64.2	27.5	22.6	24.6
Norway					
Pretransfer	79.7	87.4	59.7	37.1	79.5
Posttransfer	40.8	48.3	27.7	29.2	47.6
% Reduction	48.8	44.7	53.6	21.2	40.1
Canada					
Pretransfer	69.8	83.3	72.3	42.0	65.7
Posttransfer	33.9	18.8	37.0	30.5	41.8
% Reduction	51.4	77.4	48.8	27.4	36.3
West Germany					
Pretransfer	86.3	94.1	61.1	36.6	81.4
Posttransfer	30.6	28.5	31.4	23.2	48.4
% Reduction	68.2	69.7	48.6	36.6	40.5

Source: Timothy M. Smeeding, Michael O'Higgins, and Lee Rainwater, eds., *Poverty, Inequality and Income Distribution in Comparative Perspective: The Luxembourg Income Study (LIS),* Table 3-5, p. 68.

4. Evaluate the redistributive system in the United States. Do you think that the United States could do a better job in redistributing income?

ADDITIONAL READINGS

1. Atkinson, A. B. *Poverty in Britain and Reform of Social Security.* London: Cambridge University Press, 1969.

2. Beckerman, W. *Poverty and the Impact of Maintenance Programs in Four Developed Countries.* Geneva: International Labour Organization, 1979.

3. Greenberg, Harold, I. and Samuel Nadler. *Poverty in Israel: Economic Realities and the Promise of Social Justice.* New York: Praeger Publishers, 1977.

4. Mack, Joanna and Stewart Lansley. *Poor Britain.* London: George Allen & Unwin, 1985.

5. Mann, W. E., ed. *Poverty and Social Policy in Canada.* Vancouver: The Copp Clark Publishing Company, 1970.

6. Townsend, P. *Poverty in the United Kingdom.* Harmondsworth: Penguin, 1979.

7. Van Praag, B., A. Hagenaars, and H. van Weeren. "Poverty in Europe," *Review of Income and Wealth* 28 (4) (1982): 345–59.

19

POVERTY IN THE UNITED STATES: CHALLENGES AND PRIORITIES.

The preceding chapters have sought to analyze poverty in the United States. The primary objectives of this book have been to provide the reader with insights as to how economists look at poverty and to provide a detailed account and analysis of the state of low-income population in the United States. These objectives have been met by providing a detailed discussion of the causes of poverty and various antipoverty policies. Although a large amount of resources has been devoted toward the fight against poverty, and much has been accomplished in reducing the income insecurity faced by millions of Americans, many people still remain in poverty. Poverty continues to be an important domestic public policy concern in the United States. This chapter outlines some of the important issues that should be given priority in the fight against poverty. The chapter begins with a brief summary of the main issues discussed in the book and then outlines issues that need special focus in the fight against poverty.

SUMMARY OF ISSUES

Although there is overlap in the issues discussed in the various chapters, the materials covered in this book can be classified into four broad categories: (a) preliminaries in the study of economics of poverty, (b) the causes of poverty, (c) antipoverty policies, and (d) special topics in the economics of poverty and antipoverty policy. A brief summary of the main issues discussed in each of these categories follows.

Preliminaries in the Study of the Economics of Poverty

To appreciate the economic approach to analyzing poverty, some basic economic concepts were introduced. Simple demand and supply analysis was presented to offer the reader basic knowledge of the working of markets.

The simple analysis was extended to demonstrate the effects of government interference with markets. The discussion revealed that government's interference with markets has costs, a dilemma that policymakers have to expect whenever they propose policies that alter the market-determined outcomes. The economic principles were extended to analyze the theory of individual choice, for example, in the labor market and consumption. The concept of utility maximization subject to budgetary constraints was used to demonstrate decision making by individuals. As in the case of supply and demand, the theory of consumer choice demonstrated the effects of government policies. For example, we demonstrated how income transfers could affect labor supply decisions.

The economic concepts were used to explain some of the arguments as to why governments should be involved in the fight against poverty. A number of common theories of optimal distribution were presented. The basic story that emerges from this discussion is that, while markets are efficient in the allocation of resources, such market determined outcomes may not necessarily be consistent to what society deems optimal. In other words, it is frequently the case that society's welfare is enhanced by adopting policies that alter the market determined state of distribution. Nonetheless, while seeking to meet those normative goals, society must also confront the actual consequences of the polices so adopted. Thus, the importance of both normative and positive analysis in fighting poverty and reducing inequality has been emphasized.

In the study of poverty and antipoverty policy, it is necessary to clearly identify cause-and effect relationships. For example, it is important to be able to investigate how the effect of a particular individual characteristic contributes to poverty or the effect of a particular policy in reducing poverty. Thus, this book provides a brief discussion of the statistical analysis of the economic data important in the study of poverty. Frequently, not only do we want to identify the relationship among variables in terms of the cause and effect, but also we want to know how strong those relationships are. Statistical analysis, especially the use of multiple regression, is therefore an important tool in the economics of poverty.

There is much that can be learned from history. Although our goal is to deal with contemporary poverty issues, this book presents a brief discussion of early poor support. The main objective of this discussion is to provide the reader with an appreciation of the fact that poverty and poverty policy are not new and were of concern to policymakers long before the advent of the New Deal policies or the inauguration of the War on Poverty. The discussion also reminds the reader that policies proposed to combat poverty largely depend on what are believed to be the causes of the problem, thus emphasizing the need for researchers and policymakers to carefully analyze and evaluate the causes of poverty before they recommend particular policies.

The final introductory issues concern defining and measuring inequality in the distribution of income and the extent of poverty in the

United States. Some of the measurement issues that are important in discussing both inequality and poverty are presented. These issues are important since the concern that society places on a particular issue largely depends on how serious that problem is seen to be. In addition, good measures of poverty and inequality are essential in our attempts to evaluate the effectiveness of public policies. There is considerable inequality in the distribution of income and such inequality may have increased in recent years. Likewise, this book discussed in detail the problem associated with defining poverty and in drawing the poverty line. It is important for the reader to appreciate the fact that poverty could be defined in various ways and each of these definitions has its advantages and disadvantages. The problem of poverty, however defined, affects millions of Americans.

Causes of Poverty

At the core of the study of economics of poverty is an analysis of the various causes of poverty. The design of appropriate antipoverty policy demands a clear understanding of the various causes of poverty. As such, a large part of this book is devoted to discussing the causes of poverty. There are many causes of poverty, and in many instances, these causes interact in complex ways resulting in the observed poverty status of different individuals and some times of groups of individuals. By and large, this book focused on economywide, institutional, and individual factors that cause poverty. For example, we have looked at the relationship between labor markets and poverty, focusing specifically on unemployment and low-wage employment. The causes and types of unemployment as well as the relationship between unemployment and poverty were also studied. For example, the composition of unemployment was discussed focusing on why minorities frequently experience higher unemployment rates and consequently high poverty rates. Likewise, we looked at various explanations for low-wage employment.

There is no question that poverty affects households headed by minorities and women disproportionately. We have discussed the various explanations as to why poverty is higher among these groups, including arguments such as lack of opportunities, cultural explanations, and discrimination in labor markets and the provision of education. Issues such as de facto and de jure segregation, ghetto poverty, "white flight," the underclass debate, and the spatial mismatch hypothesis were presented with special focus on how they relate to the poverty of minorities.

While there are several factors that explain poverty, family structure appears to have become an increasingly important predictor of poverty status. Specifically, a large proportion of poor families are headed by females. The relationship between family structure and poverty and also the factors that have been responsible for the changing family structure in America were discussed. The feminization of poverty in the United States is tied not only to factors that lead to female headship but also to other aspects of the welfare system and to poor labor market prospects faced by female heads of households. In addition, the weak enforcement of child support obligations was identified as an important cause of poverty among female-headed households.

Antipoverty Policies

Ultimately, the objective of studying economics of poverty is to be able to formulate policies that can be used to deal with that problem. This book attempted to provide an objective analysis of the various polices that are used to deal with poverty in the United States.

Given the importance of labor markets status in explaining poverty, we have devoted considerable time examining public policies that have been suggested to address the problems of unemployment and low-wage employment. Several demand and supply management policies, including monetary policy, tax cuts, tax credits, wage subsidies, training policies, and direct job creation were discussed. An evaluation of these policies, primarily how they affect wages and employment level, as well as the problems associated with these policies, was presented.

Probably no other issue has divided Americans more than policies that focus specifically on race and gender. We have considered the rationale for targeting some policies on minorities and women and the controversies surrounding these policies. In particular, equal employment opportunities and equal education opportunity policies were emphasized. Controversial policies, such as affirmative action and comparable worth, were discussed in detail. Other policies such as mandating desegregation were considered and critically evaluated.

A large part of antipoverty efforts in the United States has taken the form of providing cash and in-kind transfers including food stamps, AFDC, Supplemental Security Income, Medicare, Medicaid, Housing Assistance, and so on. We have looked at the role that these programs play in fighting poverty. These transfers have helped reduce the number of people in poverty and the poverty gap. Nevertheless, these reductions involve large amounts of public expenditures.

A central issue in the economics of poverty is understanding how various policies affect behavior. A matter of concern to policymakers relates to the effects of antipoverty policies on behavior. For example, an analysis of how public transfers to the poor could affect labor supply and contribute to marital instability was presented. These unintended effects of transfers pose a problem to policymakers, because these policies tend to result in higher poverty rates rather than lower.

Because of the various problems associated with income transfers, such as reduced work effort, growth of government, and increased marital instability, it has become clear that the welfare system needs to be reformed. A discussion on suggestions for reforming the American welfare system, for example, introducing work and education programs, the negative income tax, and enforcing child support obligations was presented.

Special Topics

One of the most pressing concerns in the design of antipoverty policy is the problem of welfare dependency—the prolonged reliance on public support. While proponents of Great Society programs hoped that welfare recipients would rely on public support for only short durations, evidence shows that a large segment of welfare users remain on welfare for long durations. The process of welfare dependency is complex and Americans must try to understand it rather than just blame welfare users. Clearly, there is a need to adopt policies that reduce the time recipients can rely on public support.

In most cases, some poor people do not appear in poverty statistics and frequently those groups of poor do not receive public assistance. The most important such group is the homeless. A brief chapter on the homelessness problem in the United States was included. The discussion revealed that homelessness is a complex problem involving the interactions of poverty, mental health, alcoholism, drug use, and housing markets. As the discussion presented reveals, attempts to attribute the problem to only one cause may hinder progress in helping the homeless.

Various developed countries use different approaches in dealing with poverty. Some countries have been more successful in fighting poverty than others. This book presented some basic statistics that help us compare the success of the United States in fighting poverty with that of other developed countries. The goal of these comparisons was not to offer ammunition to critics of U.S. welfare policy, but to help us compare the effectiveness of antipoverty policy across a number of developed countries.

ANTIPOVERTY POLICY: CHALLENGES AND PRIORITIES

The preface of this book noted that the United States is a wealthy nation, yet there are many poor Americans. The discussion presented in the book shows that although poverty has persisted in the United States, there have been many serious efforts to deal with the problem. In particular, a large amount of the nation's resources have been directed to fighting poverty. The resources have gone to fund programs that serve the poor such as job training programs, job creation, employment programs, health, housing, and a multitude of other direct and indirect transfer programs. It is not likely that devoting more resources to fight poverty would necessarily be the answer to eradicating poverty. Nonetheless, much more needs to be done in the fight against poverty. Such efforts may have to be directed to restructuring the welfare system in a manner that yields more benefits for each dollar of expenditure.

While all issues discussed are important, it helps to mention a few that may require urgent focus both in attempts to understand them and in the design of public policies. This discussion is deliberately brief.

Race and Poverty

The persistence of a wide gap between the incidence of poverty among Whites and non-Whites is worrisome and demands new and innovative policy efforts. Given the projected increase in the number of minorities in the labor market, there is need to evaluate the education and labor market opportunities available to minorities. Although it is true that racial discrimination is an important factor in explaining the persistence of the racial income gaps, this is but one cause of the poverty of minorities. As such, public policies must take a broader view. While antidiscrimination laws have had some effects in reducing the racial discrepancies, the adoption of equal opportunity polices that are seen as penalizing Whites are likely to be self-defeating. A primary goal should be to adopt policies that help minorities acquire the necessary human capital that makes them competitive in labor markets. It also appears that the long-run improvement in the relative economic status of minorities will largely depend on the position that these groups will occupy in terms of ownership of businesses and other property. Thus, public policies should focus attention in this direction.

Urban Poverty

The issue of urban poverty needs to be given serious policy reevaluation. Racial segregation continues to be a problem and recent research reveals that this has made poverty in the inner cities more severe. The characteristics of ghetto poverty are worrisome and given the intergenerational transmission of poverty in those areas, it is important to stop the cycles of deprivation. Research in this area concerning effective approaches is still urgently needed. For example, radical policies that seek to disperse the location of the poor over wider geographical areas may need to be given serious consideration. Barriers to desegregation that continue to exist need serious scrutiny.

The continued Black-on-Black violence and the resulting high mortality rates of young men should be seen as an outcome of prolonged deprivation and hopelessness in the inner cities. This problem clearly calls for urgent measures. Solution to this problem will take the cooperation of all levels of government and also the ghetto residents themselves. Ignoring the problem by blaming it on the victims as has been the case to date is by itself irresponsible and demonstrates a poor understanding of the extent and complexity of inner-city problems.

Feminization of Poverty

Female headship is now widely considered as a serious problem. In many instances, poor female heads are blamed for their choices. Whatever the arguments against female headship, female headship is likely to remain an important type of family structure in the United States. Regardless of the process that leads to female headship, the poverty in those types of households require serious public policy efforts. Focus should be on the children, not on the mistakes of their parents.

There is clearly an obligation on the part of the society to help those children who find themselves disadvantaged because of being in a poor household. It is not, however, enough to leave the burden of solving the poverty of female-headed households on the public sector. Both female heads and the fathers of the children should be held to a higher degree of accountability. More should be expected from all parents. As such, the design and strict enforcement of child support policies must be given priority. Likewise, ways need to be designed that help mothers participate fully in the labor market. This calls for innovative approaches for providing child care.

Health Care

The extent to which the United States will be successful in fighting poverty largely depends on what type of health care policy is adopted. We have demonstrated the link between low-wage employment, welfare use, and the availability of health benefits. The current welfare policy penalizes those who try to exit from welfare because not only are their welfare benefits reduced but earning market incomes frequently makes them ineligible to receive medical benefits. Under such a benefit structure, it is rational for many low-income people to remain below the poverty line by avoiding work so that they can be eligible for medical benefits.

It is clear that any viable welfare reform policy must include health care reform. It is also clear that there are no easy choices. Whether the option is to have a universal health insurance under a public program or mandating employers to provide workers with such coverage, the system will be expensive. These issues not withstanding, there are many compelling arguments for reforming the welfare system.

Inequality

For a long time now, economists have held the view that more equality could only be achieved at the expense of growth. Recent experience reveals that although economic growth has slowed, inequality has also increased. It is becoming more evident that growth is not necessarily incompatible with more equality. As a matter of fact, some of the countries that have shown impressive growth in recent years have also had reductions in inequality in the distribution of income.

This is not to suggest that equality is desirable in the market economy. Extreme inequality, however, is also not consistent to economic growth. The fact that inequality in the distribution of income has been on the increase in the United States suggests that policies that have been used in recent years need to be carefully reevaluated.

SUMMARY

This closing chapter has attempted to provide a brief summary of the main issues discussed in the text. The goal was not to describe all the issues in a comprehensive manner, but to highlight key issues. We have then provided discussion of the issues that should be given priority in the fight against poverty. Issues concerning the poverty of minorities, urban poverty, feminization of poverty, health care policy, and the increasing inequality in the distribution of income should be given priority. As a starting point, more comprehensive studies that seek to understand those issues and that seek to evaluate alternative policies are essential.

SUBJECT INDEX

421

Y

INDEX OF NAMES